ESCAPING ALCATRAZ

The Untold Story of the Greatest Prison Break in American History

Michael Esslinger
and **David Widner**

ESCAPING

The Untold Story of the Greatest Prison Break in American History

ALCATRAZ

FOREWORD BY
Richard Tuggle
Screenwriter of the Classic Motion Picture
Escape from Alcatraz

OCEAN VIEW PUBLISHING
SAN FANCISCO, CALIFORNIA

ESCAPING ALCATRAZ

The Untold Story of the
Greatest Prison Break in American History

Michael Esslinger and David Widner

For information contact:

Ocean View Publishing
P.O. Box 2303
Marina, CA 93933-9203
www.AlcatrazHistory.com

ISBN-10: 0-9704614-5-3
ISBN-13: 978-0-9704614-5-2

The principal interviews included in this collection were conducted by Michael Esslinger. The official inmate case files in this collection are held as United States Public Records in the National Archives and Records Administration, United States Library of Congress, and the Bureau of Prisons. Formatting of passages, textual editing, combining of documents and paragraphing changes specific to the interviews and official casefile records have been made to improve readability, but the context has not been altered. Excerpts from interviews with James Bulger are from: *James "Whitey" Bulger, AZ-1428; The Last Interviews and Letters from Alcatraz*, by Michael Esslinger. Select elements from *Alcatraz: A History of the Penitentiary Years and Letters from Alcatraz* were also used by permission. All rights are protected under copyright.

No convicts, past or present, families, friends, associates, and/or any other person named within this work were compensated for interviews, photos, or any historical material included in this collection. No biographies, narratives or individuals featured in photographs have been authorized or endorsed, implied or otherwise by those persons named or associated. Their photograph or likeness shall not imply or represent their endorsement or as a contributor to this work. The views expressed in the interviews, letters, narratives and other commentary are solely those of the individuals providing them, and do not necessarily reflect the opinions of the author, publisher, contributors to this work, or any other affiliates.

Original Book Design and Composition by John Reinhardt Book Design
Original Book Cover Design by James Zach
Editors: Kelly Rabe and Claire Keating

IN LOVING MEMORY

Nicholas Bradley Widner

January 2, 1998 – September 8, 2015

MOVIETONE NEWS

SAN FRANCISCO, CALIF.

ALCATRAZ

ESCAPE!

Contents

Clint Eastwood with Richard Tuggle during the production of Escape from Alcatraz.

Foreword

SO IN 1978, while living in San Francisco, I finish my script *Escape from Alcatraz*, go to LA to sell it. It's the story of the greatest prison escape from the most famous prison in the world...so I figure Hollywood studios will be eagerly waiting with open arms. They weren't. In fact they weren't interested at all. But I call the friend of a friend of a friend, finally get the Paramount story department to read it. They hate it. Thought it was a melodramatic 1930s type prison movie with no women. Naturally, it being Hollywood, Paramount ended up making the movie. But I digress.

In 1975, my pal Sandra takes me on the Alcatraz tour. Today the prison's more crowded than Disneyland, but back then it wasn't prime tourist turf. A guide took us along a cellblock, pointed to three cells and said in 1962 inmates dug out the back of those cells, climbed the utility corridor to the top, drilled through the roof, grabbed life rafts they'd made in the shop, paddled away into the fog... and were never seen again. Wow, I thought, that'd make a great movie. But the closest I got to the movies was the 99 cent film buff theater in North Beach. So I forget about Alcatraz. Sort of...

Two years later I'm editing a health magazine and I get fired. Not knowing what to do with myself, I thought about that escape. So I go down to Fisherman's Wharf, buy a bunch of tourist books on Alcatraz. One book by *San Francisco Chronicle* reporter John Campbell Bruce, told the history of Alcatraz and had excellent information on every escape attempt. What interested me was the chapters on the escape I'd been shown by that guide.

Bruce lived in Berkeley, I go see him, tell him I'm going to write a screenplay about the escape, wanted to use information in his book, and I'd give him some of the profits if I sold it. I didn't know what I was doing, but he was a good guy and he said go ahead. But first call the publishing company because they retained some of the rights. I keep calling them, they never call back. I finally get them on the phone, they say they'll give me the rights if I'll just leave them alone. I ask why they'd give me the rights for free, they say because my chance of selling my script was so small it wasn't worth their time to hassle out a contract.

With that confidence builder, it was time to write, but I had no idea what to do. Unlike today, there were very few screenwriting books. But I found a single copy at a theater bookseller, read it, sat down to write. But wait, I figured I need to know more about the escape, so I go to the Bureau of Prisons office south of San Fran, read their files. I discover the escape is still an open case, and the FBI has material. I read their files. I go back two months later to check facts, there's a new agent, he tells me I can't see their files and I shouldn't have been allowed to see them in the first place. I figured Hollywood would be a breeze compared to these guys, but little did I know.

Once in Hollywood, I slept in a friend's living room, badgered everyone to read my script. When someone would say no, I'd think back to those Alcatraz cells, those cellblocks, that chilly water...the mystery of what happened. I knew the movie should be made.

Don Siegel of Dirty Harry fame finally reads my script, gave it to Clint Eastwood, Paramount gives it a green light. I'd arrived in March, they're shooting the movie in October right on the Rock itself. That's not how most movies are made. But this one was.

So read Michael Esslinger and David Widner's terrific and exciting book *Escaping Alcatraz: The Untold Story of the Greatest Prison Break in American History* and then take your tour of the Rock. Stop in front of those three cells. And think back to the night of June 11, 1962, and four inmates trying to accomplish the impossible. Some think they might have done it...we'll never know. But if they did, one person will be wrong. As the warden says in the movie: "No one has ever escaped from Alcatraz...and no one ever will".

RICHARD TUGGLE
Santa Monica, California
May 2017

Preface

"No prison can hold me; no hand or leg irons or steel locks can shackle me. No ropes or chains can keep me from my freedom."
—HARRY HOUDINI

ALBERT YOUNG was a junior officer assigned the four to midnight shift in the west gun gallery on the night of the legendary 1962 escape. The gun galleries were narrow encased corridors, barred in tool proof steel which offered a high level view of the cellhouse floor and various other sections of the prison. From this post assignment, Young could walk the length of the west end of the cellhouse, with full access into the solitary confinement section known as the treatment unit, as well as having views into the hospital and mess hall.

Armed with a Thompson Machine-Gun, high powered rifle, pistol and direct phone line to the control center, the gun gallery was also considered one of the safest assignments for an officer working inside America's most notorious prison. Despite being under such fortified conditions, Young knew that you always had to keep an eye looking over your shoulder. On Alcatraz, dangers lurked in wait...

From the upper levels, Young could see a dented steel panel on the third tier of C Block, aftermath from a bullet that was fired from the same gallery during a violent thwarted escape in 1946. As one officer would later point out, it was much more than an unrepaired steel access panel; it was a profound reminder to inmates and officers alike. Alcatraz had a wretched history...

Bernard Paul Coy (AZ-415), was a forty-six-year-old Kentucky bank robber serving out the remainder of a twenty-five-year sentence on the Rock. Bernie, as he was known to friends, devised a clever scheme to climb and break entry into the west gun gallery using a crudely fashioned homemade bar-spreader. Once inside, he hid and ambushed the unsuspecting officer; violently choked and bludgeoned him into unconsciousness, then passed down high-powered weapons to fellow conspirators. Their hostile and murderous impulses became a toxic formula when

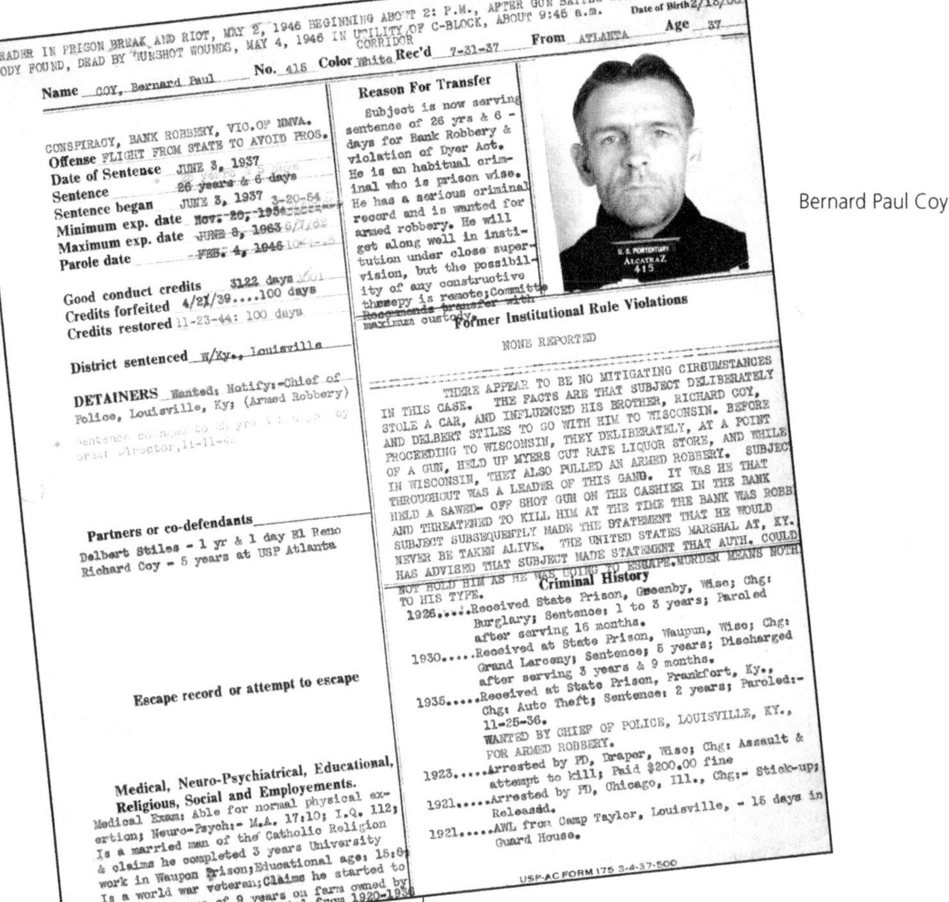
LEADER IN PRISON BREAK AND RIOT, MAY 2, 1946 BEGINNING ABOUT 2: P.M., AFTER GUN BATTLE WITH OFFICERS, BODY FOUND, DEAD BY GUNSHOT WOUNDS, MAY 4, 1946 IN UTILITY OF C-BLOCK, CORRIDOR ABOUT 9:45 a.m.

Date of Birth 2/13/00
Age 37
From ATLANTA
Rec'd 7-31-37

Name COY, Bernard Paul No. 415 Color White

Offense CONSPIRACY, BANK ROBBERY, VIO.OF NMVA. FLIGHT FROM STATE TO AVOID PROS.
Date of Sentence JUNE 3, 1937
Sentence 26 years & 6 days
Sentence began JUNE 3, 1937
Minimum exp. date ~~Nov. 20, 1954~~ 3-20-64
Maximum exp. date ~~JUNE 8, 1963~~ 6/7/62
Parole date ~~FEB. 4, 1946~~

Good conduct credits 3122 days
Credits forfeited 4/21/39....100 days
Credits restored 11-23-44: 100 days

District sentenced W/Ky., Louisville

DETAINERS Wanted; Notify:-Chief of Police, Louisville, Ky; (Armed Robbery)

* Sentence changed to 25 yrs ... by order Director, 11-11-4...

Partners or co-defendants
Delbert Stiles - 1 yr & 1 day El Reno
Richard Coy - 5 years at USP Atlanta

Escape record or attempt to escape

Medical, Neuro-Psychiatrical, Educational, Religious, Social and Employements.
Medical Exam: Able for normal physical exertion; Neuro-Psych:- M.A. 17:10; I.Q. 112; Is a married man of the Catholic Religion & claims he completed 3 years University work in Waupon Prison; Educational age; 15:6; Is a world war veteran; Claims he started to work at the age of 9 years on farm owned by father; Owned & operated hotel from 1920-1936

Reason For Transfer
Subject is now serving sentence of 26 yrs & 6 days for Bank Robbery & violation of Dyer Act. He is an habitual criminal who is prison wise. He has a serious criminal record and is wanted for armed robbery. He will get along well in institution under close supervision, but the possibility of any constructive therapy is remote; Committe ~~Recommends transfer with~~ maximum custody.

Former Institutional Rule Violations
NONE REPORTED

THERE APPEAR TO BE NO MITIGATING CIRCUMSTANCES IN THIS CASE. THE FACTS ARE THAT SUBJECT DELIBERATELY STOLE A CAR, AND INFLUENCED HIS BROTHER, RICHARD COY, AND DELBERT STILES TO GO WITH HIM TO WISCONSIN. BEFORE PROCEEDING TO WISCONSIN, THEY DELIBERATELY, AT A POINT OF A GUN, HELD UP MYERS CUT RATE LIQUOR STORE, AND WHILE IN WISCONSIN, THEY ALSO PULLED AN ARMED ROBBERY. SUBJECT THROUGHOUT WAS A LEADER OF THIS GANG. IT WAS HE THAT HELD A SAWED- OFF SHOT GUN ON THE CASHIER IN THE BANK AND THREATENED TO KILL HIM AT THE TIME THE BANK WAS ROBB... SUBJECT SUBSEQUENTLY MADE THE STATEMENT THAT HE WOULD NEVER BE TAKEN ALIVE. THE UNITED STATES MARSHAL AT, KY. HAS ADVISED THAT SUBJECT MADE STATEMENT THAT AUTH. COULD NOT HOLD HIM AS HE WAS GOING TO ESCAPE. MURDER MEANS NOTH... TO HIS TYPE.

Criminal History
1926.....Received State Prison, Greenby, Wisc; Chg: Burglary; Sentence: 1 to 3 years; Paroled after serving 16 months.
1930.....Received at State Prison, Waupun, Wisc; Chg: Grand Larceny; Sentence; 5 years; Discharged after serving 3 years & 9 months.
1935.....Received at State Prison, Frankfort, Ky., Chg: Auto Theft; Sentence: 2 years; Paroled:- 11-25-36.
WANTED BY CHIEF OF POLICE, LOUISVILLE, KY., FOR ARMED ROBBERY.
1923.....Arrested by PD, Draper, Wisc; Chg: Assault & attempt to kill; Paid $200.00 fine
1921.....Arrested by PD, Chicago, Ill., Chg:- Stick-up; Released.
1921.....AWL from Camp Taylor, Louisville, - 15 days in Guard House.

USP-AC FORM 175 3-4-37-500

Bernard Paul Coy

the prospect of a successful escape faded and the men decided it was better to be buried dead than buried alive; a metaphor for a life set in slow motion on Alcatraz.

Despite their complex and thorough planning, their escape was ultimately foiled by the ingenuity of officers, redundancies in security, and a little bit of fortuitous luck when an officer failed to return a key that the inmates needed to make their escape to the prison yard area. The Battle of Alcatraz ended in the deaths of two officers and three inmates (including Coy), along with the court ordered executions of two others for their role in the violent escape attempt.

Charlie Berta (AZ-132), once considered by officers the toughest inmate on Alcatraz in the 1930s, later opened up about the grim conditions as to why he felt the conspirators reached such a low desperate point. He emphasized that Alcatraz was a "place without hope...a prison of the mind" and offered "The only thing that kept me going was the thought that I could someday get out. I had a home to come to. A lot of these guys have gone through a lot of suffering...They had nothing left...But no matter what kind of time a guys' doing,

A period view of the main prison corridor known as Broadway. An armed officer can be seen in the west gun gallery keeping watch over the cellblock.

it's a counting game. One's counting off the time he's lost and the other is counting down the time until the end..." Behind the mythical steel curtain was a world that had fallen into moral shreds. For many men at Alcatraz, there was little or no hope and escape was their only real chance for freedom.

By 1962, after almost three decades of operation, Alcatraz was becoming the spirit of a different era. Some of the strict security measures that had once been at the heart of Alcatraz's escape-proof reputation had slowly eroded due to a litany of budget cuts and staffing shortages. When it first opened as a federal prison in 1934, the Federal Bureau of Prisons enhanced the U.S. Army's existing fortifications by adding a multitude of additional safeguards including six exterior guard towers and two interior gun galleries. By 1962, four of the six primary towers had been closed and only one was manned twenty-four hours a day. The east gun gallery post had also been eliminated as a cost saving measure. There were some exceptions, but generally it was only staffed when the inmates were brought to the upstairs theatre for movies, religious services, or whenever severe weather hit and the inmates couldn't go to the yard for their weekend recreation. Other roles by the officers had also been combined. Floor officers now handled the mail censoring and even the prison boat deckhand officer had taken on dual roles. After tying up the boat in the late hours, he was expected to patrol the island on foot at night by himself, armed with only a flashlight and whistle.

On the night of June 11, 1962, just after roll call, Young was escorted by a fellow officer to the entrance of the gallery, located on the west side of the prison's exterior. Young, holding a thermos and lunch pail, waited patiently as he'd soon be locked in the caged enclosure for the next eight hours with conditions not much different from those he was guarding. As he waited for the off going

(Above right) A view inside the west gun gallery. Gun galleries were positioned at the east and west ends of the main cellblock, allowing guards to carry weapons while secured behind barriers that were beyond the prisoners' reach. These galleries enabled the armed guards to oversee all prisoner activities and to cover the officers who walked through the cellhouse unarmed.

(Below right) An exterior view of the west gun gallery looking towards the area known and nicknamed by prisoners as Times Square.

Marine Major Albert Arsenault describes for radio listeners a blow by blow account of the Battle of Alcatraz.

officer to emerge, the gusting icy cold wind felt more like winter than summer, and made the wait a little bit more uncomfortable than usual. After a quick greeting and light exchange of conversation, the steel door slammed shut, immediately followed by a sound of a turning key to engage the lock; and then the muffled footsteps of the two departing officers faded off into the distance.

Young had a critical role. He was the lifeline to the unarmed officers working the cellhouse floor and it was important that he maintain a high level of awareness of the subtle gestures and behaviors of not only fellow officers, but of the convicts now locked-down for the night. On the surface, it would seem like a typical shift buried in the stone cold monotonous routine that had been forged over several decades. In a report that he later filed to Alcatraz Captain Thomas Bradley, Young commented that everything seemed "uneventful" and that the only sounds he could hear was the inmates playing music up until 7:00 P.M., when the daily protocol dictated that instruments be put away in their cases. Against the sounds of the convicts practicing their music, the inter-workings of what would become the greatest escape in American history was now set fast in motion. Even legendary fugitive James "Whitey" Bulger, who was serving time on Alcatraz for bank robbery, later recounted that those who were in the know couldn't sleep a wink as their hearts were racing with anticipation. From inside the gallery, all Young could hear after the inmates put away their instruments was the muffled chattering that could be heard until lights out.

Young realized in hindsight that something was amiss... His report written the day following the escape:

> On the night of June 11, 1962, I was assigned as the west gun gallery officer. The watch was uneventful, with only the musical instruments playing until 7:00 P.M., and the usual chattering of the inmates until lights out. And then silence.
>
> Along about 09:00 P.M. the wind began blowing strong; between 10:00 P.M. and 10:30 P.M.. I began hearing a noise that resembled a rumble, such as that if you were to hit the bottom of a steel drum with the heel

Members of a Marine Corps combat contingent monitor the violent events during the Battle of Alcatraz in May of 1946.

of your hand. My immediate thought was the hospital, as the sound was seemingly above me. I went to the top gallery and looked at the area through the glass gun port. I then flashed my flashlight across the top of B and C Block and saw nothing. While investigating on top of the gallery, the noise ceased. The cellhouse officer was at this time investigating the main floor of the cellhouse. When he returned, I went over to the treatment unit side. Just as I went through the door, the rumbling began again. I immediately called the Lieutenant, Mr. Weir. He was in the control center, and started listening over the electrical listening device. I told him I thought it could possibly be the dining room cage door banging. He said "No," it is over in the hospital. I immediately returned to the top gallery and again the noise stopped . . . the noise had ceased and never re-occurred . . .

Young wasn't the only officer who heard odd sounds. Irving "Levy" Levinson, the officer assigned to the hospital ward also reported noises coming from the roof area to the control center. In fact, Levy commented that he spoke with Young through the gun port, and both agreed that the sounds shouldn't be shrugged off, but rather checked to be fully certain.

Little did Young, Levinson and their fellow officers know that the most iconic prison escape in American history was happening right under their watch. That rumble was much more than just the wind…That night, Frank Morris and the Anglin brothers, using lifelike dummy heads escaped their cells; tunneled through cement and then using a homemade raft and floatation devices, paddled off under the cover of night to launch one of the largest manhunts in American history. They were never to be seen or heard from again…

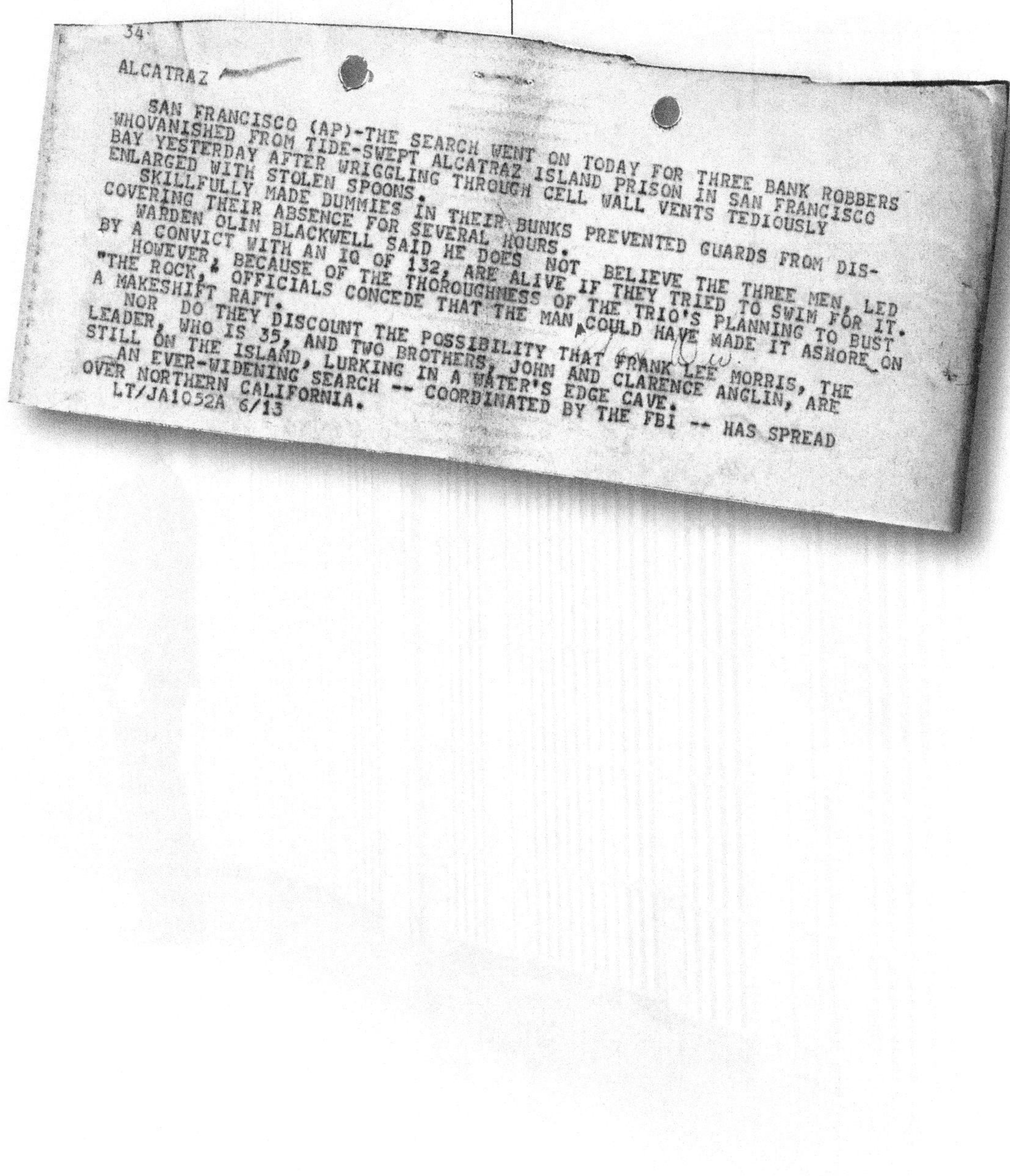

34

ALCATRAZ

SAN FRANCISCO (AP)-THE SEARCH WENT ON TODAY FOR THREE BANK ROBBERS WHOVANISHED FROM TIDE-SWEPT ALCATRAZ ISLAND PRISON IN SAN FRANCISCO BAY YESTERDAY AFTER WRIGGLING THROUGH CELL WALL VENTS TEDIOUSLY ENLARGED WITH STOLEN SPOONS.

SKILLFULLY MADE DUMMIES IN THEIR BUNKS PREVENTED GUARDS FROM DISCOVERING THEIR ABSENCE FOR SEVERAL HOURS.

WARDEN OLIN BLACKWELL SAID HE DOES NOT BELIEVE THE THREE MEN, LED BY A CONVICT WITH AN IQ OF 132, ARE ALIVE IF THEY TRIED TO SWIM FOR IT.

HOWEVER, BECAUSE OF THE THOROUGHNESS OF THE TRIO'S PLANNING TO BUST "THE ROCK," OFFICIALS CONCEDE THAT THE MAN COULD HAVE MADE IT ASHORE ON A MAKESHIFT RAFT.

NOR DO THEY DISCOUNT THE POSSIBILITY THAT FRANK LEE MORRIS, THE LEADER, WHO IS 35, AND TWO BROTHERS, JOHN AND CLARENCE ANGLIN, ARE STILL ON THE ISLAND, LURKING IN A WATER'S EDGE CAVE.

AN EVER-WIDENING SEARCH -- COORDINATED BY THE FBI -- HAS SPREAD OVER NORTHERN CALIFORNIA.

LT/JA1052A 6/13

(Above and right) Alcatraz Federal Penitentiary in 1934.

(Left) Attorney General Homer Cummings and Warden James Johnston inspecting the correctional officer staff during the opening of the prison in 1934.

(Below) Warden Johnston on August 18, 1934, leading a tour for dignitaries only days before the first shipment of prisoners arrive. From left to right are San Francisco Mayor Angelo Rossi; Attorney General Homer Cummings, one of the conceptual founders of the prison; Warden Johnston and San Francisco Police Chief William Quinn.

United States Federal Penitentiary Alcatraz Island

"It's the toughest pen I've ever seen...
The hopelessness of it gets you. Capone feels it.
Everybody does..."
—HENRY AMBROSE

WHEN ALCATRAZ OPENED in August of 1934 as a federal penitentiary, it was intended to turn the colorful and spectacular criminal dispositions of America's most notorious outlaws into a world of black and white. It was the melting pot for the cream of the criminal crop...The Alcatraz regimen demanded more than simple conformity. It was considered America's Devil Island and touted that no one could escape alive. Stern discipline was the foundation countered against cramped cells, an unrelenting routine, and a set of rules and regulations that shaped most every aspect of daily life on the Rock. Strict rules were heavily enforced during Alcatraz's years as a federal penitentiary and the lives of the Anglins' and Frank Morris became an existence that was stripped of the most basic freedoms. This was the Alcatraz trademark and it proved to silence the voices of some of America's most notorious outlaws.

The inmates sent to Alcatraz were considered the worst of the worst, and many were a breed of outlaws that the government had failed to contain. They were comprised of the famous, infamous, unknowns, and were not only bank robbers and murderers, but organized crime figures that orchestrated complex crime syndicates where corruption was boundless and infiltrated even the most sacred levels of law enforcement. Men like Al Capone, Machine Gun Kelly, Roy Gardner, Mickey Cohen, James "Whitey" Bulger and Robert Stroud (the

James A. Johnston, the first appointed federal warden of Alcatraz Island.

Birdman of Alcatraz) helped fuel the air of mystery that shrouded the island.

Alcatraz was born from the concept of housing public enemies who had resisted reform while incarcerated and continued to facilitate corruptive activities from within the federal prison system. These high profile criminals would be housed under a single roof and completely isolated from the public eye. A ticket to Alcatraz was not necessarily based on ones' crimes against free society. Recruitment to Alcatraz was a model with no specific prototype or criteria as to what would initiate a transfer. Generally, space was reserved for inmates who were prone to escape, high profile, difficult, unruly, badly behaved or simply created delinquency challenges for the prison staff in the federal prison of their confinement. Alcatraz was a tough, minimum privilege prison meant to deter the racketeers and those who tried to emulate them. Alcatraz's first warden, James Johnston, remarked on how convicts were selected for placement on the island prison:

> They [the federal prison wardens] send their most troublesome prisoners—habituals, incorrigibles, gangsters whose associations should be disrupted, men with long criminal records, men with long prison records, men wanted by other jurisdictions for additional crimes and escape artists who showed ingenuity in securing weapons and instigating violence in escapes from other institutions.

Warden Johnston personally supervised the design of numerous essential security features that had become trademarks of Alcatraz.

The first groups of inmates transferred from other federal penitentiaries were brought to the island shackled, in train cars that had carried them across the United States. They were considered the nations' most incorrigible criminals and officials took no chances on security. The railcars were loaded directly onto barges and towed across the waters of the San Francisco Bay under heavy guard.

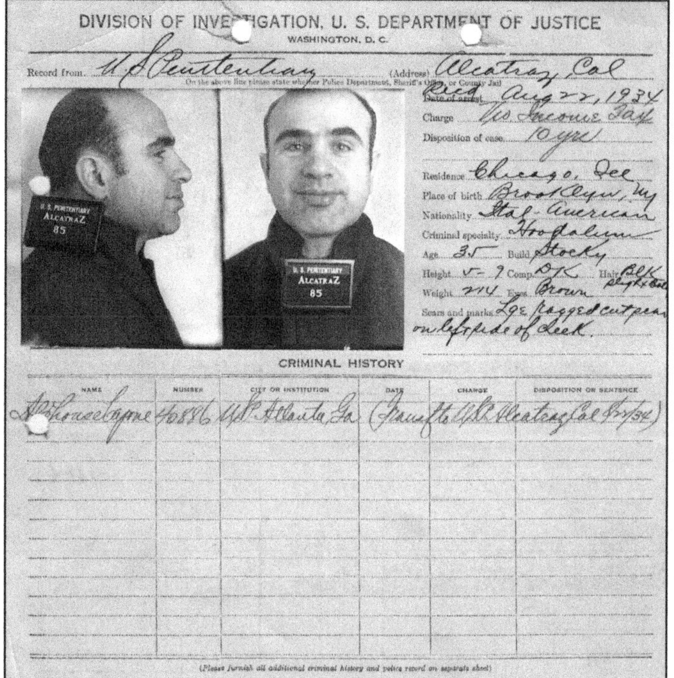

DIVISION OF INVESTIGATION, U. S. DEPARTMENT OF JUSTICE
WASHINGTON, D. C.

Record from U.S. Penitentiary (Address) Alcatraz, Cal

Rec'd Date of arrest Aug 22, 1934

Charge US Income Tax

Disposition of case 10 yrs

Residence Chicago, Ill

Place of birth Brooklyn, NY

Nationality Ital-American

Criminal specialty Hoodlum

Age 35 Build Stocky

Height 5-9 Comp. Dk Hair Blk

Weight 214 Eyes Brown

Scars and marks Lge ragged cut scar on left side of cheek.

U. S. PENITENTIARY ALCATRAZ 85

CRIMINAL HISTORY

NAME	NUMBER	CITY OR INSTITUTION	DATE	CHARGE	DISPOSITION OR SENTENCE
Alphonse Capone	40886	USP Atlanta, Ga	(Transf to USP Alcatraz Cal 8-22/34)		

(Please furnish all additional criminal history and police record on separate sheet)

Al Capone arrived on Alcatraz in August of 1934 with one of the first shipments of federal prisoners.

Former United States Attorney General Homer Cummings reflected on the conception of Alcatraz and defended its strict regimen:

> Shortly after I became Attorney General, I conceived the idea of an institution for the most unmanageable of our federal prisoners. I lived with that idea… I first discussed the matter with President Roosevelt and after obtaining his approval, I made an extensive search for a site. I studied the possibilities of the Aleutian Islands, the islands off the Florida coast and other places. San Francisco Bay was finally decided upon. I selected the warden and the guards, and followed closely each step in the making of the new prison. For five years after that, as Attorney General, I supervised its operation.
>
> In the federal prison system, Alcatraz represents the ultimate in isolation… These men are hourly conscious of the hum of life about them. Life is so near, but liberty so far. In this setting, Uncle Sam has isolated his most dangerous public enemies. On June 19, 1934, the Department of Justice took this island over from the War Department. The Department of Justice has not gone out of its way to give publicity to the individual inmates who are confined there and for good reason. As gangsters and racketeers, many of these men fed on publicity. In Alcatraz, they are completely separated from the public that are often too thrilled at their exploits and fed their ego. The department has also been anxious to keep a morbid and sometimes sadistic interest in the individuals confined there from throwing out of focus the constructive and rehabilitative work it is trying to perform in the other federal institutions.
>
> How did the Department of Justice come to establish Alcatraz? I had long had the idea that we needed in the federal prison system a particular type of institution that would be devoted to those incorrigible and long-term offenders who impair discipline at the other institutions, and who need what the Bureau of Prisons

Historical photographs of Broadway, the main prison corridor.

Silent System Whips Most Bold`and Ruthless Law-Breakers Into Realization That They Will Never Leave 'the Rock.'

now call "super-maximum security." We needed some place where the "end products" of our law-enforcement system could be incarcerated. We needed a place for ingenious "escape artists," and for those who are intractable or break down discipline or seek to maintain contact with the underworld. Half a dozen troublemakers in a large institution can completely disrupt morale. There is always some smart fellow who thinks the way to get chocolate sundaes placed on the prison menu is to start a riot in the mess hall. We needed a place for this type. By the summer of 1933, the kidnapping law that was enacted the year before was bringing into the federal courts a particularly dangerous type of criminal. If convicted, he was destined to serve a life term, or at least a long "stretch." On August 1, 1933, I wrote one of my assistants as follows: The matter was given considerable attention and in the meantime I commenced the search for a site. In the summer of 1933, I learned that the War Department had comparatively little use for the famous little island in San Francisco Bay. It seemed to me to be exactly the spot for our purposes. Several informal conferences were held with the Secretary of War, the Honorable George H. Dern, and shortly thereafter I requested Sanford Bates, director of the Federal Bureau of Prisons, to commence serious negotiations for the acquisition of the island. A good beginning...

We were unable to effect a permanent acquisition; the War Department agreeing only to a five-year revocable permit. This, however, was sufficient for our purposes. It was my feeling that if I could get the prison established, its advantages would be so clearly apparent that the final formalities would follow in due course. In fact, it was not until April 26, 1938, that the permanent transfer of Alcatraz to the Department of Justice was authorized by the Congress and later affected. But in 1933, as suggested, we weren't so much interested in securing title to the property as we were in securing the right to use it, and by the summer of 1934 all arrangements had been made for our actual occupancy and the army evacuated.

The original army prison was erected in 1909 and is situated on the highest part of the island. There were quarters for the officers, barracks for enlisted men and a number of shops built around one side of the island. The cell house contained four cellblocks of six hundred individual cells, measuring nine 9 x 5 feet, and almost 8 feet high. Each cell was equipped with a toilet and lavatory, electric lights, and a bed and shelf for personal effects. In 1933, the entire fronts of the cells were grated. Most of the six hundred soft steel cell fronts were removed and tool proof steel replaced them. But there remained much to be done if it was to be made escape proof. Nature helped out. Swift cold tides raced along the island shores, and only an expert swimmer in good training can negotiate the one and one-half miles to San Francisco, the nearest shore point. Not by any stretch of the imagination can Alcatraz be considered a threat to the safety of the citizens of San Francisco. There is no more formidable barrier to an escaping prisoner than the mile and a half of water that separates the island from the shore. That's a barrier we don't have at any other institution, state or federal. So as far as we know, no escaped inmate has ever reached the mainland. We can be glad the water is there.

There is a popular misconception that a judge can sentence any defendant directly to Alcatraz. It can't be done. There are no direct commitments from the courts. Inmates are sent only by transfer from other federal prisons and upon the orders of the Attorney General. Discipline is rigorous and the routine is strict at Alcatraz, but both are tempered as much as circumstances allow by the humaneness that must characterize a civilized penal system.

> On August 18, 1934, I left my hotel in San Francisco and boarded the launch McDowell, which was to take me across the Bay for the first official inspection. As I made the crossing, I was aware that in the dead of the previous night, the "elect" had been taken from their cells at Atlanta Penitentiary and hurried to a special chartered train. The curtains were drawn tightly and when the travelers awoke they were, although they didn't know it, on the first leg of their journey to the Rock. When I arrived at the island the cellblock was empty-almost. There were still about twenty-five military prisoners left.
>
> As I made my way about the island, the conviction grew with me that here surely was a prison from which no man could escape... We were ready...

Cummings' vision materialized to become America's solution to silencing the most incorrigible menaces of society. It would be the end of the line for the nation's irredeemable and lawless. A place where their statue in crime rings had no value, and escape was thought to be impossible; conditions at Alcatraz changed little over the decades.

As early as the 1860s, Alcatraz Island had become a convenient place to incarcerate insolent soldiers but had also been effectively utilized for civilian purposes. Alcatraz would be used to confine political prisoners during the Civil War years. When news of President Lincoln's assassination in April of 1865 reached San Francisco, altercations broke out between defenders of Lincoln and those who cheered his murder. An order was put out that anyone who publicly cheered Lincoln's killing would be arrested and Alcatraz received nearly forty civilian inmates to be housed which in one article stated "for their own protection." By the turn of the century, Alcatraz was thriving as a penitentiary and its role as a military fortress had faded.

On March 21, 1907, the island received its official designation as United States Pacific Branch Disciplinary Barracks. By 1912, a large cellhouse completed construction on the island's central crest, and by the late 1920's, the three-story structure was nearly at full capacity. Ironically, it was built using an inmate labor force, and the 480 foot cellhouse with 18 inch thick walls became the largest reinforced concrete structure in the world.

The new modern cement structure completely eliminated the looming hazards that had once terrorized the inmates with fear. Alcatraz was to become the U.S. Army's first long-term prison, and it was already beginning to build its reputation as a tough detention facility by exposing inmates to harsh confinement conditions and ironhanded discipline. The erratic currents sweeping around the island made it practically impossible for a prisoner to escape by swimming. Escapes from Alcatraz, even back during the military era, were not uncommon and prisoners were relentless in scheming and plotting breaks.

From 1862 until Alcatraz was turned over to the Federal Bureau of Prisons, escapes from the Rock were familiar headlines. Some of the plots showed careful planning and ingenuity, while others clearly were ill-fated from their

Alcatraz was originally established as a military fortress during the Civil War era. The Rock would serve as both a fortification and military prison until 1934 when it was turned over to the Bureau of Prisons to become a federal penitentiary.

beginnings. In all, news reports showed over thirty-five attempts and numerous plots to escape Alcatraz during its years as a military prison. The headlines always captured public attention and hinted to the dramatic events commonplace on Alcatraz:

> Escaped from Alcatraz... Dangerous Felons Escape the Rock... Alcatraz Prisoner Attempts to Escape Across Bay on Plank... Prisoners put to Sea in a Tub... Alcatraz Prisoners at Sea in a Bread Trough... Army Officials are Mystified... Soldiers Escape from the Island... Bay Foils Alcatraz Break... War Slackers Try to Escape Alcatraz... Death Ends Flight of 4 Prisoners...

The prisoners of that early era faced many of the similar challenges of the federal inmates, but it was the tides and swift currents that created the biggest escape obstacle as more than seventeen military prisoners disappeared and were believed to have drowned. Alcatraz remained a military prison for more than eighty years.

Alcatraz's first warden, James Johnston, was an experienced reformer who had overseen such tough institutions like Folsom and San Quentin prison. Johnston handpicked his correctional officers from the entire federal prison system. He figured that if Alcatraz was designed to hold the cream of the criminal crop, then he would select the finest officers from within the federal system to manage them. He also looked for best practices from within both state and federal prisons to determine the best model for housing America's worst convicts. It was well understood that Alcatraz would eventually be tested by some of the most intelligent criminal minds of the era.

All privileges would be limited, and no inmate, regardless of his public stature, would be allotted special rights or freedoms. As former inmate Jim Quillen (AZ-586) would later comment: "You weren't a name, you were a number..." And that is how men existed... Prisoners would be given restricted access to the prison library, but no newspapers, radios, or other non-approved reading materials would be allowed. Receiving and sending mail would be considered a privilege, and all letters both in-coming and outgoing, were to be screened and typewritten after being censored by prison officials. Work was also seen as a privilege and not a right, and consideration for work assignments would be based on an inmate's conduct record. Prisoners were assigned their own cell, and only the basic minimum life necessities were allotted such as food, water, clothing, medical and dental care. Wardens from the various federal penitentiaries were polled, and they were permitted to send their most incorrigible inmates into secure confinement on the Rock. The prison population at

Associate Warden C. J. Shuttleworth with his staff of correctional officers in June of 1936. The officers were handpicked to guard the nation's most notorious prisoners.

Officers lining up for duty at the main entrance of the prison. On Alcatraz, the original officer to prisoner ratio was one to three, compared to other prisons where the ratio often exceeded one to twelve.

Alcatraz was thus made up of inmates who had histories of unmanageable behavior, escape attempts, or high-profile inmates who had been receiving special privileges because of their public status and notoriety.

There was a ratio of one guard to every three prisoners on Alcatraz, as compared with other prisons, to which the ratio exceeded one guard to every twelve inmates. With the gun galleries at each end of the cellblocks and the frequent inmate counts (twelve official counts per day), the guards were able to keep extremely close track of each and every inmate.

By June of 1962, in the face of eroding security and the physical deterioration of the now half century old aging cement structure, the Rock's escape proof reputation had remained virtually untarnished. Alcatraz still offered a greater measure of security than all of the traditional maximum security prisons across the nation. Additionally, it continued to provide a solution to relieve higher security institutions of the small minority of uncontrollable convicts that compromised civility.

Despite its hallmark role in America's fight against crime and continued support by officials like J. Edgar Hoover, Alcatraz was not without fierce criticism. Critics cited that Alcatraz was nothing more than a dumping ground for celebrity and high profile inmates, and the prison was still plagued by the same challenges that made the military consider a more cost effective approach.

The cost to run and maintain Alcatraz was exceptionally higher than at all of the other penitentiaries, and rising. In an example given by Bureau Director James Bennett in 1960, the daily per capita cost at Alcatraz was $10.10 compared with $3.00 at USP Atlanta. With no natural resources and no connectively to the mainland, Alcatraz proved itself a logistical headache for federal officials. Every aspect of operations came at a considerable cost. Even the most basic necessities had to be brought over by barge. Electricity had to be self-generated, secure ferry services required special staffing and with no source of fresh water, nearly one million gallons of water had to be barged to the island each week. Bennett stated that Alcatraz had also become an "administrative monstrosity" and that "guards and staff don't like to be assigned to the barren island any more than the prisoners like to be sent there." Captain of the Guards, Phil Bergen supported this statement. He indicated that Alcatraz was plagued with recruitment problems throughout his tenure.

Exposure to the elements also took its toll. After a half century, the physical structure was showing its age. The variances in cement quality, a result of unskilled military inmates who were tasked with mixing and pouring the concrete had become a significant security liability. Alcatraz had passed its day when it was once a necessity. Both James Bennett and Thomas C. Clark, the United States Attorney General during the 1940s had spent well over a decade lobbying the chambers of Congress to reexamine the effectiveness of Alcatraz. In February of 1962, just four months before Morris and the Anglins would make their break from Alcatraz, a feature article entitled *The Rock is Crumbling; Alcatraz is Reaching the End of the Line* made clear that Alcatraz was ailing. Bennett urged the prison be abandoned. The cost of repairs were mounting as each year the Bureau spent more than $100,000 just trying to keep pace with the aging structure. These elements paired against the eroding security created a perfect storm for Frank Morris and the Anglin Brothers.

Keys to Freedom

"There was machine guns, grenade rifles, and Springfields. Between every burst of gunfire, I can still remember that white crown sparrow that sang on the roof..."

—JOHN GILES,
AZ-250 (remembering the 1946 Battle of Alcatraz)

DARWIN COON (AZ-1422), a fellow bank robber, arrived at Alcatraz in September of 1958 and like so many of his criminal colleagues, his past was paved with brazen escape attempts.

He was a good fit on the Rock. Looking through the dusty lens of history, facts often become impure with time, but Darwin's memory of life on Alcatraz remained remarkably clear. His mind was filled of haunting and bitter memories of his time on the Rock. He recalled that there were many prisoners who intensely studied every inch of the prison, every procedure, every staff member; their habits, routines, any and every object that could be used as a tool or weapon, and even the most minuscule weaknesses in the redundant security measures that could be used to their advantage. No detail on Alcatraz was considered too trivial...

Coon knew all of the players in the '62 break. All were skilled professionals in the art of escape. This was how most men had earned their place on the

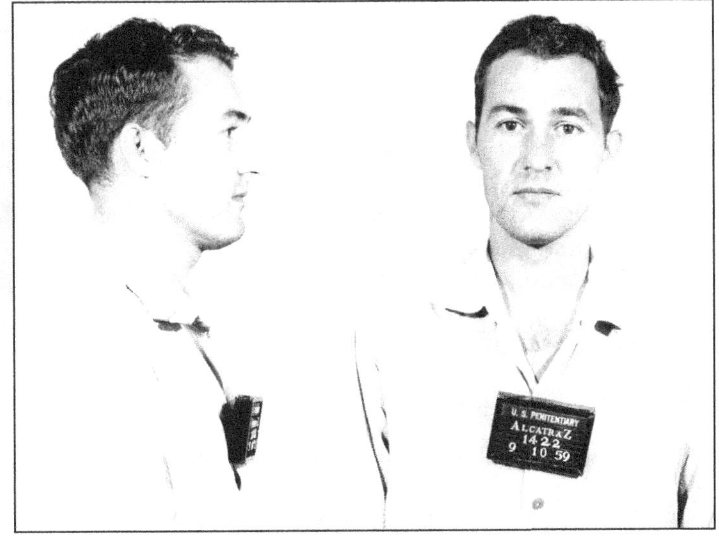

Darwin Everett Coon the day he arrived on Alcatraz in 1959.

Rock. That was the case for the Anglin brothers, Frank Morris and even their co-conspirator Allen West. Their inmate case files were bursting with plots and schemes of prison breaks.

Coon recalled that many of the men at Alcatraz were serious and viciously determined to beat the escape proof reputation of Alcatraz at nearly any cost. Convicts were fed a steady diet of brutal monotony and the sights and smells of the vibrant city were constant reminders of their lost freedom. The topic of escape was constant among the men, and some obsessed over it "to the point of craziness," former inmate Jim Quillen (AZ-586) later commented. Quillen served on Alcatraz from 1942 to 1952. He had also attempted to escape and well understood the state of mind. Cons talked through escape scenarios in exhaustive detail, analyzing every element from past escapes that worked along with factors that contributed to failure. Every element was played against their current conditions on Alcatraz. Quillen explained during a 1994 interview:

James Quillen

> "Hell, these men had nothing to look forward to; it was how they existed; they were in misery with the idea of no future; you know, their young life was now spent; no turning going back in time to make things right. I even found myself in that desperate state of mind, knowing I was never going to get that back. Trust me, some of these guys were very-very serious about getting out, one way or another... Prison life was tough enough, but Alcatraz amplified the grimness... San Francisco was right there in front of you... The sights, the sounds, even the smells were taunting... You could sense the movement happening right across the water; the bustling of city life... I can't explain it, but you could see it all right there... and depressing... You'd hear women laughing on boats as they passed the island... The voices of the guides on the tour boats... You could hear them... That sure made things tough for a lot of men... They're pulling these long sentences; they're left with the reality of their situation... They lived with only their memories... Some had enough... They made a decision that they were not going to live out their final days rotting away on that island... I don't think people really

Willie Sutton

> understand what it's like to live in that environment for years on end. Most anybody can survive weeks or months living in that state, but think of the mental strain that comes from living that for a continuum of years...
>
> We were told when we could eat...when we could sleep...when we could smoke...when we could read...when we could shit...Alcatraz was harshest in those terms...You could choose the books you read and really that was about it...One way or another, some of these guys were going to taste freedom again...On their own terms...They were going to taste freedom at least one last time...You know...Dead or alive...They figure they're dead anyway...They had nothing to lose...Hell, even the guys who didn't make it, they didn't lose anything..."

Stories and the lore of past escapes on Alcatraz swirled the island and was a daily topic of discussion for many. Coon recounted that all of the involved principals were versed with numerous escapes that occurred in other prisons, some of which they had been involved in. But it was the breakout that occurred in April of 1945 at Eastern State Penitentiary that caught the eye of John Anglin and the others. The escape had been recounted in a book well known to various inmates entitled Smooth and Deadly published in the 1950s, chronicling the criminal escapades and jailbreaks of Willie Sutton, including his grand but ill-fated escape from Eastern State.

While Sutton never served time on Alcatraz and his book was certainly not permitted in the library, he was very well-known amongst the prison population. His stories of spectacular prison breaks were legendary and often talked about over meals and during the men's work hours. Like so many other fellow cons serving time on the Rock, Sutton's inmate case file was bursting at the seams with documents chronicling attempted breaks. In December of 1932, while serving time at Sing Sing Prison in Ossining, New York, Sutton and fellow inmate John Egan cut from their cells using stolen hacksaw blades, wired ladders together and made their escape over the west wall of the prison. Egan was shot and killed at a New York speakeasy only months later, and Sutton would be captured nearly a year later in Philadelphia. He would land at the historic Eastern State Penitentiary. Opening in 1829, Eastern was considered the world's first true penitentiary. It was designed to inspire "penitence" in those incarcerated there. It was also to become a platform for Sutton to better hone his skills in the art of escape.

Sutton would make two break attempts in 1936, another in 1941, then finally a spectacular escape in April of 1945, where along with eleven others tunneled under the towering and massive stone prison wall and into the light of freedom. Up until this point, it was considered one of the most ingenious escapes known to take place from inside an American prison. The break made national headlines and was reminiscent of a dazzling mass escape accomplished by Allied prisoners inside a German POW camp that had been pulled off just a year earlier known as the The Great Escape (their story was later made into a classic motion picture starring Steve McQueen and James Garner).

While Sutton ultimately took credit for the escape, it was the work of a mason and plasterer named Clarence Klinedinst who masterminded the complex scheme. Klinedinst was an experienced stonemason who was well liked by resident officers. While doing authorized work to re-cement and plaster his and other cells at the end of Eastern States' Cell Block 7, he began chipping a small hollow passage from his cell wall, camouflaged with a false removable panel made of cement. It was the birth of a legendary jailbreak.

It would take a year to complete... Every night after lights out and working in shifts, Klinedinst along with his cell mate William Russell, placed dummy heads in their beds (made from Plaster of Paris molds) to counter any suspicions of patrolling guards. It was a slow tedious process, but well-engineered... Most nights they made less than a half foot headway as it involved digging a pathway under the prison yard and then dipping to a depth of 15 feet to get under the massive stone wall that resembled that of an ancient bastion. They would fill their clothing with the loose dirt, and then hide the debris under their beds and just like in a scene portrayed in the epic film The Shawshank Redemption, the inmates would shake the debris from their pant legs as they walked the yard the following day.

Upon its completion, the 97 foot long tunnel was an engineering feat of sorts. The tunnel's size ranged from a small 3 x 3 foot angled shaft, down to an even more claustrophobic 14 x 14 inches at some sections. Despite the rigorous planning and effort, the escape was destined to end in failure...

On the day of the getaway, Klinedinst, Russell and Sutton, along with nine other followers, climbed, crawled and squeezed through the tight passage where they emerged outside the prison, shadowed by the 30-foot-high

(Above) An officer examines the tunnel entrance located in Cell #68 of Cell Block #7 at Eastern State Penitentiary.

(Right) The tunnel excavated and constructed by the escapees. The passage was 12 feet deep and nearly 100 feet in length. The prisoners tunneled under the cellblock, then under the recreation yard and past the massive exterior stone wall. They would exit near a busy street adjacent to the prison.

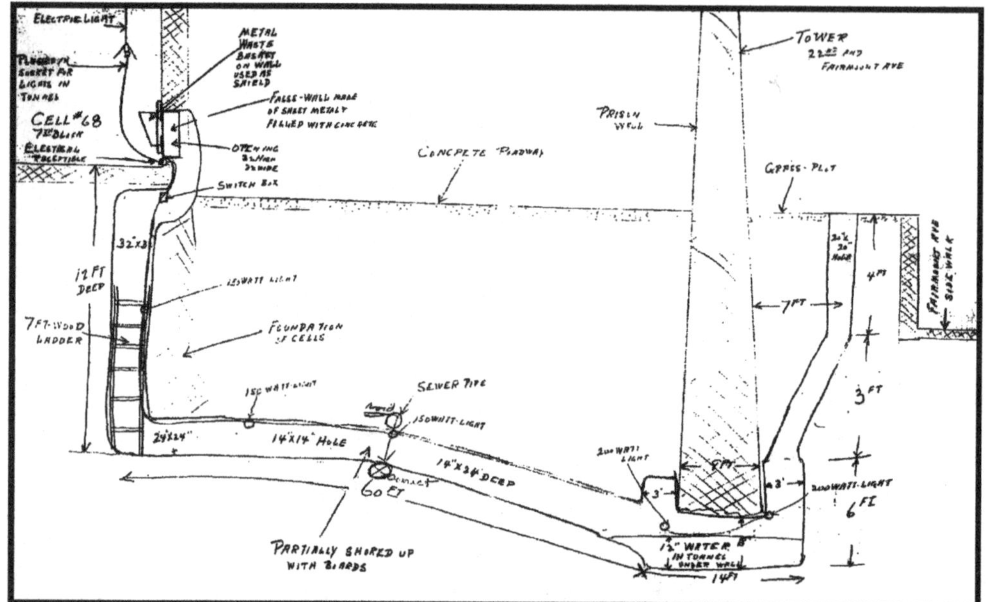

A diagram sketched by a guard representing the escape path and complex construction that took over a year to plan and construct.

Officers inspecting the tunnel exit next to a guard tower.

prison wall they had tunneled under. Sutton made it only two blocks away, coming face to face with a police officer who fired several shots and took him into custody. Five others were also immediately captured and one was shot. The others' short-lived freedom ranged from three days to eight weeks. Klinedinst's cellmate was shot days later while attempting to visit his girlfriend.

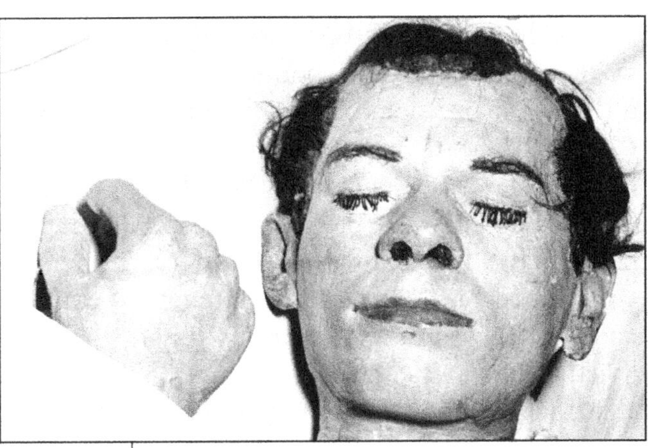

The lifelike dummy head fabricated and used by Willie Sutton during his escape.

Erle Stanley Gardner, a famed author who wrote detective and crime thrillers, examines Sutton's dummy head used in his escape. Gardner was best known for the Perry Mason series.

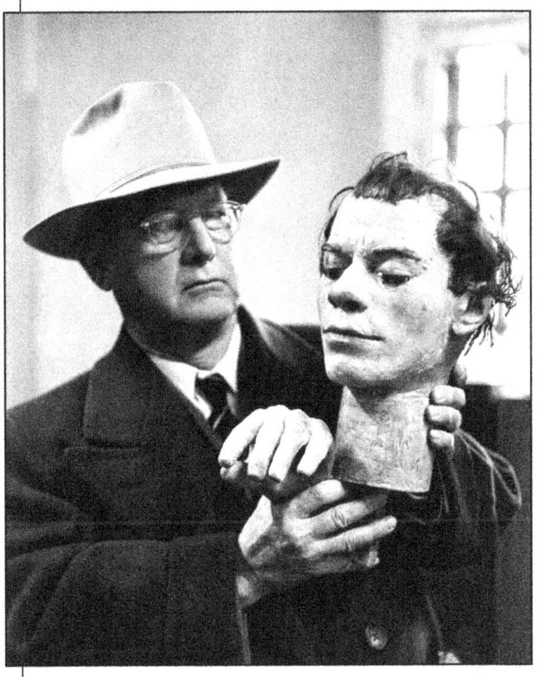

Sutton's desperate thirst for freedom remained unquenched... Less than two years later after being transferred to the Holmes County Prison in Philadelphia, Sutton again with Klinedinst and David Aikens (another inmate involved in the 1945 break who was captured three days later in Delaware) attempted yet another break. Using a smuggled gun and hacksaw blades, the convicts broke from their cells, captured guards and then donned their uniforms. Although the versions vary as to how they made it past the gates, a popular version is that Sutton simply yelled up to an unsuspecting tower guard who opened the gate on their request. His accomplices were captured the following day, but Sutton remained a fugitive until 1952. Sutton was a legend among the convicts at Alcatraz, and the use of fake dummy heads as decoys from his 1945 attempt held great promise.

Surrounded by water and loaded with layers of security, government officials work hard to craft the image of an inescapable fortress. Alcatraz was scarred with headline escape attempts. For the cons, it was the favored topic of discussion, along with sports and current events happening in the free world. The cons only spoke of their families and home lives to their closest friends. It was the old timers that many of the cons looked to bounce ideas off and share opinions...Men like Clarence "Joe" Carnes who was a key figure in the escape known as the Battle of Alcatraz, knew the prison landscape better than anyone. It had been sixteen years since his foiled escape attempt and Carnes was now serving his time quietly, but he was highly perceptive of all of the intricacies and inner-workings of the prison. Even those who had not attempted an escape but had special access to different areas of the prison (usually the result of a special job assignment), or simply having known people involved in previous escapes, there were lessons to be learned from each one. Many of the early escapes had direct ties to the Morris Anglins' break decades later.

The First Escape

"Put me in the dungeon, I do not want to work..."
JOE BOWERS, AZ-210

THE FIRST ESCAPE at Alcatraz during the federal years was known to convicts not for its ingenuity, but rather for how fiercely guards reacted to a breach of boundaries. Prisoners who knew Bowers saw it as nothing more than a desperate act of suicide. The mental strain of a dismal and dreary existence had finally reached its low point. All of the men in population were well aware of Bowers' attempt at taking his own life only a year prior and when news spread of his escape attempt, the cons concluded that it was not a sincere break for freedom. No one would have scaled the perimeter fence in full view of a tower guard. In the eyes of the officers, Bowers had grown desperate to make a run for freedom, regardless of how hopeless his attempt, it was a treasonous act. Alcatraz had not only its reputation to protect, but a responsibility to uphold, and Bowers would test the sacred foundation from which it was built.

FATAL SHOTS HALT ESCAPE IN ALCATRAZ

Prisoner Falls Dead in Bay

Joseph Bowers

Joseph "Dutch" Bowers was thirty-eight years old when he arrived on Alcatraz by a secure prison railcar in September of 1934, as part of one of the first groups of inmates. Just two weeks prior, fifty-two inmates, including the notorious Al Capone, arrived from the Federal Penitentiary at Atlanta. Bowers had been transferred from Leavenworth as part of a group of one hundred six inmates, the third and largest group of transfers during the prison's opening. George "Machine Gun" Kelly, his crime partners Albert Bates and Harvey Baily, Doc Barker (Ma Barker's last surviving son), Roy Gardner (the last of the great American Train Robbers), Floyd Hamilton (driver for Bonnie and Clyde), and several other gangland notables arrived together on the same railcar to become residents of America's new minimum privilege, super-max penitentiary.

In a report submitted shortly after his arrival, Chief Medical Officer George Hess concluded that Bowers was "a man of extremely low mentality upon which is superimposed of an extremely ugly disposition; he is a custodial problem and will probably have to be dealt with by firm measures." Officials had a difficult time piecing together his family background and even Bowers seemed to know very little about his roots.

DIVISION OF INVESTIGATION, U. S. DEPARTMENT OF JUSTICE
WASHINGTON, D. C.

Record from U.S. Prison (Address) Alcatraz Cal
On the above line please state whether Police Department, Sheriff's Office, or County Jail

Date of arrest Rec'd Sept 4, 1934
Charge P.O. Robbery
Disposition of case 25yrs
Residence None
Place of birth Austria
Nationality Austrian
Criminal specialty
Age 38 Build Med
Height 5-11 Comp. Lr Hair Br
Weight 175 Eyes Blue
Scars and marks Sev. small scars back of Rt. Ear. Lg rag cut scar on forehead

210

CRIMINAL HISTORY

NAME	NUMBER	CITY OR INSTITUTION	DATE	CHARGE	DISPOSITION OR SENTENCE
Joe Bowers	43202	USP Leavenworth Kans		Transf to USP	Alcatraz Cal 9-4-34

Bowers arrived on Alcatraz as part of one of the first groups of prisoners in September of 1934.

Records would later show that he was an Austrian citizen and held legal US citizenship. It is unclear whether he ever learned of his actual origins. His prison case file reads:

The Houdini of escape, Roy Gardner, the last of the great train robbers traveled with Bowers from Leavenworth to Alcatraz on a secure prison railcar.

> On this man it has been impossible to get any dependable information. He states that he was born of parents who were members of a traveling circus. On February 18, 1897, at El Paso, Texas, he claims he was immediately deserted by his parents, and was raised by circus people who were traveling about and with whom he has lost all contact. He has been unable to establish his birth as an American Citizen. Claims to have worked in Germany, France, Belgium, Italy, Spain, Russia, Buenos Aires, Mexico, Cuba, and other places principally as an interpreter, as he claims to speak six languages.

In 1928, Bowers was arrested for car theft in Oregon and served ten months in jail. He was arrested again in Washington in 1930 for drunken driving, fined $75, and released. The crime that led him to Alcatraz was committed in 1930 and garnered him a mere $16.63. Bowers' description of the crime, which he claimed he did not commit, was included in Dr. Ritchey's neuropsychiatry summary written while Bowers was imprisoned at McNeil Island (in 1938, Dr. Ritchey left McNeil to replace Dr. George Hess as chief medical officer at Alcatraz). A pertinent section of Dr. Ritchey's report on Bowers reads:

> His present crime he says was committed because he was out of funds and was actually hungry most of the time. He says he met a man sleeping in a park in Sacramento who persuaded him to go along while they robbed a store and post office near Orville, California. He claims that he did not actually go with the man to Orville but that the man himself proceeded with his plan and robbed the store and finally was arrested

> and confessed and lay the blame on Bowers, he himself going free for his testimony.

Dr. Ritchey's report described Bowers thus: "constitutional psychopathic state, inadequate personality, emotionally unstable and without psychosis." Bowers' fellow inmates at Alcatraz considered him insane and in a subsequent report by Dr. Hess, mental illness was suggested. On January 4, 1935, after serving just four months on Alcatraz, Bowers was already showing serious signs of mental strain under the extreme confinement practices. Alcatraz's silence rule and unrelenting routine weighed heavily on him. He refused to work at his assignment in the laundry, and was reduced to a third grade status. This translated to having all privileges revoked and remaining confined to his 9 x 5 foot cell for a period of three months; only being allowed to leave for a single shower once per week, and three meals daily. All other privileges were revoked, including reading.

On March 7, 1935, after spending just two months in lockdown status, Bowers attempted to take his own life by breaking his eyeglasses and using the sharp edge of the lens to cut his throat. He believed other inmates were plotting against him and said that he could "hear" them talking about him at night after lights out and frequently asked to be admitted to the hospital for protection. But each time he was admitted, he quickly demanded to be released.

Edward Twitchell, the consulting psychiatrist was suspicious of Bowers mental and medical complaints. He wrote in a memorandum dated March 22, 1935:

> The more I listened to Bowers, the less belief I had in him. He has been watched now for months and no epileptic seizures have been noted, although he insists that he has them. The recent attempts at suicide have been theatrically planned and have resulted in very little damage to him. Had he been determined at suicide, he had good opportunity to make a success of it. Hence, I believe unsuccessful attempts were for the purpose of gaining opinion favorable to him. Like so many of his kind, it must be admitted first that this is not a normal individual, but he is not so crazy as he is trying to make out.
>
> It is a well-recognized fact that an individual who is insane endeavors to make out his insanity worse than it really is for the purpose of gaining on some end. Bowers, while an abnormal individual, is not truly insane in my opinion and is pretending a mental disturbance for some purpose.

Bowers was placed on suicide watch by Warden Johnston and he had already been moved to cell B-240, the last cell located at the west end of the cellhouse where "guards can keep him under observation while performing their regular duties," but his mental state continued to worsen.

On June 1, 1935, Bowers was waiting to go to work in the laundry when he started shouting, "Put me in the dungeon...I do not want to go to work!" Bowers was punished harshly. He was placed in solitary confinement and put on a restricted diet. Around the same time, a letter from an inmate smuggled to a San Francisco newspaper alleged "cruelty practices on prisoners" at Alcatraz, which were causing inmates to go insane. The letter was rumored to have been smuggled out by a correctional officer and Bowers was one of four inmates named.

Warden Johnston later wrote that he looked at Bowers as "a weak-minded man with a strong back who would get peace of mind by exercising his body." This essentially translated to a trivial but difficult work assignment at the island's incinerator, located on the west side of the island close to the wire fence that lined the perimeter. Bowers appeared to be coping well with his job until the day of the escape.

On April 27, 1936, Erville Chandler was the lookout officer stationed in the road tower. He had a clear and unobstructed view of Bowers as he worked the incinerator detail. From the road tower, Chandler could observe inmates transcending the steep stairs from the recreation yard down into the Industries building, and had clean north and south views of the lower road. He also had a clean shot at any boats that unlawfully approached the island within the 200 yard restricted perimeter. Years later, in a memoir penned by his son Rocky Chandler, he described his father as "a dead shot...Seasoned by years of military rifle competition, cable strong, with exceptional eyesight...a marksman most guards could only wish to be."

United States Penitentiary
Alcatraz, California
3-23-36

DEPUTY WARDEN'S OFFICE

WORK CHANGES

Reg. No. 210 Name Bowers
From Cell House orderly
Guard In Charge Mickelson
To Incinerator
[illegible]
Guard In Charge
Entd
[illegible]
DEPUTY WARDEN

U.S.P.AC.F.77

Bowers was assigned to work the incinerator detail in March of 1936. It was considered one of the least favored work assignments by Alcatraz prisoners.

The incinerator detail was a tough and dirty job; considered one of the worst job assignments by convicts, especially during periods of inclement weather. It was menial work separating garbage, burning refuse, crushing cans, and pitching the non-burnable items down a drop chute which emptied directly in the Bay waters below. Alcatraz had no responsible means of disposing of its waste (even sewage was dumped directly into the Bay), and nearly all of the refuse the prison and residents generated was either burned or dumped.

Chandler's official report written on the date of the escape described the following:

> While on duty in the road tower at about 11:00 A.M., I suddenly looked to see inmate Joseph Bowers AZ-210 on top of the wire fence attempting to go over. I then yelled at him several times to get down but he ignored my warning and continued. I fired two

Views of the incinerator work area located on the west side of the island.

(Above top and right) The road tower had a direct line of sight to the incinerator detail.

(Above left) Correctional Officer Walters shown in the road tower with his Springfield rifle.

(Left) A view of the road tower post with the incinerator detail visible in the lower right. The Golden Gate Bridge is faintly visible in the distance. Bowers was shot and killed from this very location.

> shots low and waited a few seconds to see the results. He started down the far side of the fence and I fired one more shot, aiming at his legs. Bowers was hanging on the fence with his hands but his feet were pointing down toward the cement ledge. After my third shot I called the armory and reported the matter. When I returned from calling the armory, the body dropped into the Bay.

But rumors swirled the island like the currents, and the general opinion by the inmate population, and even some of the officers, believed Bowers was shot in cold blood. That it wasn't at all an attempt to escape, but nothing more than to get the attention of Sanford Bates, the director of the Bureau of Prisons who happened to be on Alcatraz conducting inspections. Bates was examining the prison workshops, accompanied by Warden Johnston. The two were entering the warden's office when they heard the gunfire. James Sargeart (AZ-129), who was serving time for robbery and assault, and had been sent to Alcatraz for a brazen escape attempt while imprisoned at McNeil Island, met with Bates for an interview the previous day. He knew Bowers from Leavenworth, and was on the same chain for transfer to Alcatraz. Sargeart had voiced grave concerns over the harsh disciplinary measures that were being imposed on him and the others under Johnston's harsh rule. Following the shooting, he immediately came forward, claiming that Bowers had been persuaded by fellow inmates to jump over the fence while the director was there to get his attention. Witnesses of the shooting claimed that Bowers was climbing back up the fence and attempting to scale the top when Chandler fired the fatal bullet.

James Sargeart

Roy Gardner, considered the Houdini of prison escapes and the last of the great American Train Robbers, was a fellow inmate of Bowers during the 1930s and also witnessed the shooting. Gardner later recalled:

> Joe Bowers was shot and killed for disobedience of orders. It was reported that Bowers attempted to "escape" but that wasn't the true story. I saw the second shot fired, the shot which dropped him from the fence, dead, to the rocks 50 feet below... Three months before he was shot, Joe Bowers had tried to commit suicide by cutting his throat. He had a big scar there at the time of his

death. Three weeks before his death he slugged a guard without provocation. Joe was sent to work at the incinerator, alone.

He was working there when a garbage truck dumped some papers and the wind blew some of them over the fence. Bowers was under orders to keep the place clean and attempted to climb over the fence to gather up the papers. The guard in the tower overlooking the incinerator ordered Bowers to get down off the fence. Bowers protested that he had to gather up the papers and the guard shot him—twice. The truth of the matter was that Bowers made no attempt to escape, and the inmate body of Alcatraz was so aroused over the killing that the federal authorities transferred the guard to another prison for his own protection. No doubt the guard thought he was doing his duty, as he saw it. However, in the opinion of this writer, he was somewhat overzealous when he fired the fatal shot.

A.R. Archer, a junior custodial officer assigned to the hill tower seemed to share at least some of the sentiments of the prisoner population, or at least suggest that Bowers wasn't making a sincere dash for freedom. He wrote in his official summary:

> About 10:50 A.M. this date, in the company of Mr. Starr in my tower, I heard two shots fired. Running to the door, I saw prisoner 210, Joseph Bowers, standing on the ledge outside the fence by the incinerator. Mr. Chandler was standing outside the road tower on the edge of the platform nearest the incinerator, rifle in hand. As I watched, #210 started climbing the fence, apparently trying to get back inside the yard. He succeeded in getting an arm and one leg over the topmost strands of barbed wire when a third shot sounded. His body stiffened and hung there for a few seconds, when he fell backwards out of my sight, over the cliff.

Headlines of Bowers death spread across the nation's most prominent newspapers. The stories of brutal conditions were surfacing more frequently as inmates who had been transferred off the Rock told of the desperateness it created in men that were already at their lowest point. Chandler's testimony during the coroner's inquest gave light to Bowers impulsive and frantic state of mind:

> I picked up Mary Ann (referencing his rifle) and fired a couple of low ones, thinking I might get him in the leg... When he kept on going and went over the fence I leveled Mary Ann and let him have it. I knew if he got to the Bay, God knew where he'd go next. He might be robbing banks in San Francisco. I had my orders and I followed them. That's what I'm there for. Bowers was over the deadline. He knew what he was doing, and I couldn't go get him without wings..."

In a May 7, 1936, memorandum to the warden by Chief Medical Officer George Hess, he detailed that Bowers had died from a gunshot to the chest.

Bowers's lifeless body is seen being off-loaded from the prison launch and into a San Francisco ambulance.

Irrespective of what Bowers intended to achieve by scaling the fence on that foggy morning, it was a message sent loud and clear to the prisoners that officers would shoot to kill for crossing a limit line and not heeding to a warning. In a later interview, former Officer Clifford Fish, who served on Alcatraz from 1938 until 1962, firmly defended Chandler's actions. He felt anything less would have been seen as breach of duty. In his mind, "Dutch" chose his own fate, not Chandler... He stated in part: "That shooting happened only a couple years before I arrived and I remember it got debated here and there; what would you have done kind of talk... You've got to remember what side of the fence he landed on when he was shot... He landed on the rocks on the other side of the fence. He was an escapee... I would have done the same..."

The escape proof reputation of Alcatraz remained untarnished. Bowers would fade quietly into history... He was buried in an unmarked paupers' grave on May 2, 1936, at the Olive Memorial Park in Colma, California. Ironically, ten years to the day of his burial would mark the islands' most brutal and vicious escape attempt, the Battle of Alcatraz.

Fading Into the Fog

"I don't think I'll like the island...
I doubt if I'll stay there long enough to get bored..."
—THEODORE COLE, AZ-258

TED COLE and Ralph Roe were made of the very fabric that Alcatraz was designed to hem. By December of 1937, Alcatraz had reached its highest population of inmates during the twenty-nine years of operation, housing three hundred twenty of America's most cunning criminals within the federal prison system. The highest inmate register number for men having served or still being housed on Alcatraz now well passed four hundred, with nearly one hundred eighty of those convicts specifically having been sent to Alcatraz for either a past escape or high risk thereof. Men who were considered some of the finest escape artists of that era, accounted for almost half of the prison's populace. Warden Johnston later wrote: "It seemed as if most of the established escape artists had been corralled into the federal net and transferred to Alcatraz..."

The convicts and officers were now deep into a metaphorical game of chess; each studying the moves and patterns of their rival, searching for the slightest oversight that could be used to the others' advantage. Many of the cons working in the industries were the architects to some of the most complex and spectacular bank heists of the century. They were intelligent, deep thinking and experienced in crafting plots that required intricate coordination. On Alcatraz, the patterns and routines of each officer were studied. Their individual style in how they made their rounds, points of focus, faithfulness to count protocols; to how each would react to simple distractions were scrutinized by many inmates examining the feasibility of breaking from the Rock.

In 1934, the same year that Alcatraz opened, the Bureau of Prisons launched the Federal Prison Industries (FPI) work program, also coined "Factories with Fences." The concept had been to provide inmates the experience of working in a formal industrial environment while developing a strong work

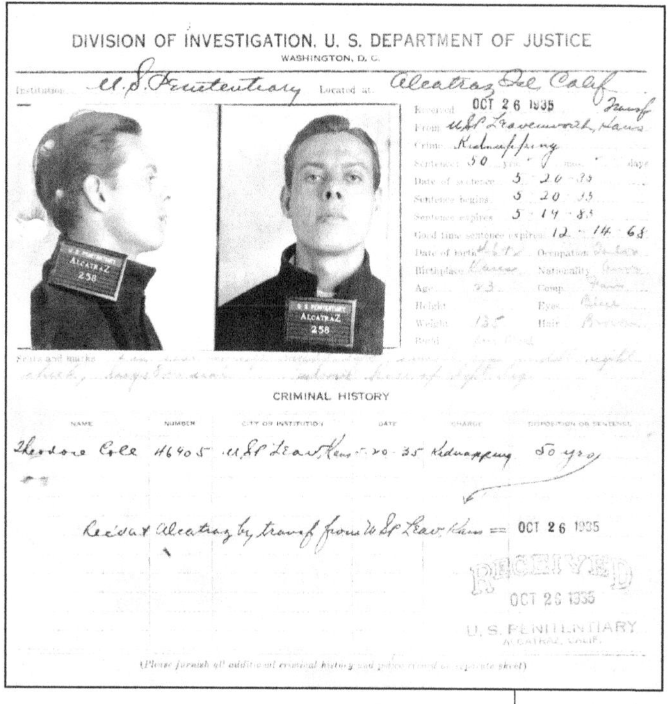

DIVISION OF INVESTIGATION, U. S. DEPARTMENT OF JUSTICE
WASHINGTON, D. C.

Institution U.S. Penitentiary Located at Alcatraz Isl. Calif

Received OCT 26 1935 Transf

From U.S.P. Leavenworth, Kans

Crime Kidnapping

Sentence 50 yrs.

Date of sentence 5-20-35

Sentence begins 5-20-35

Sentence expires 5-19-85

Good time sentence expires 12-14-68

Age 23

Weight 135

U. S. PENITENTIARY ALCATRAZ 258

CRIMINAL HISTORY

NAME	NUMBER	CITY OR INSTITUTION	DATE	CHARGE	DISPOSITION OR SENTENCE
Theodore Cole	46405	U.S.P. Leav. Kans	5-20-35	Kidnapping	50 yrs

Rec'd at Alcatraz by transf from U.S.P. Leav. Kans — OCT 26 1935

RECEIVED OCT 26 1935 U. S. PENITENTIARY ALCATRAZ, CALIF.

(Please furnish all additional criminal history and police record on separate sheet)

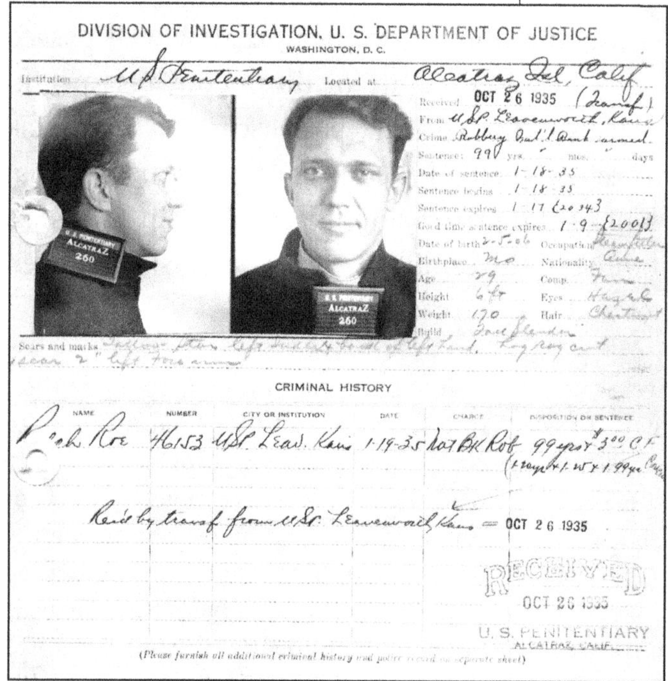

DIVISION OF INVESTIGATION, U. S. DEPARTMENT OF JUSTICE
WASHINGTON, D. C.

Institution U.S. Penitentiary Located at Alcatraz Isl. Calif

Received OCT 26 1935 (Transf)

From U.S.P. Leavenworth, Kans

Crime Robbery Nat'l Bank armed

Sentence 99 yrs.

Date of sentence 1-18-35

Sentence begins 1-18-35

Sentence expires 1-17 (2034)

Good time sentence expires 1-9 (2001)

Date of birth 2-5-06

Birthplace Mo

Age 29

Height 6 ft

Weight 170

U. S. PENITENTIARY ALCATRAZ 260

CRIMINAL HISTORY

NAME	NUMBER	CITY OR INSTITUTION	DATE	CHARGE	DISPOSITION OR SENTENCE
Ralph Roe	46153	U.S.P. Leav. Kans	1-19-35	Nat. Bk. Rob.	99 yrs

Rec'd by transf from U.S.P. Leavenworth, Kans — OCT 26 1935

RECEIVED OCT 26 1935 U. S. PENITENTIARY ALCATRAZ, CALIF.

(Please furnish all additional criminal history and police record on separate sheet)

Theodore "Ted" Cole (Top) and Ralph Roe (Bottom) arrived on Alcatraz together and were shackled on the same chain.

ethic and adherence to a daily routine. For the men who would eventually be released, it would give them an edge to earning an honest living. Alcatraz's third warden, Paul J. Madigan, who also served as an officer on Alcatraz and ironically was taken hostage in the model industries, offered that Alcatraz was designed to instill the "importance of good character, not necessarily intellect," and believed a strong work ethic was essential to successful rehabilitation.

For many convicts, the Alcatraz Industries was a compass to successful employment in free society. It helped prevent inmates from falling back to a state of destitute, which often resulted in criminal recidivism. The Alcatraz Industries provided meaningful job skills that in many cases went beyond generic factory labor. Many job assignments encompassed a level of expertise and craftsman skills that translated to reasonable paying jobs on the outside. By learning gainful skills, they could be afforded steady jobs upon their release with adequate level income to allow comfortable lives in free society. Job assignments included working in the rubber mat factory, the dry cleaning

Aerial views of Alcatraz Island during the same period as the Cole and Roe escape.

plant, the laundry, the tailor shop, the shoe shop, the clothing factory, or the Model Shop, which constructed and reconditioned furniture.

Inherited from the military, the model industry buildings were perhaps the most dangerous locations on the island. During work hours, they held large numbers of inmates, but were estranged from the multiple layers of security that was a constant presence in nearly every other location of the prison. Ironically, during his initial inspections of the prison, Former Attorney General, Homer Cummings identified that if a convict were to make

The Alcatraz Model Shop building photographed in December of 1937.

an attempt at escape, it would likely be from the industries. He wrote:

> As I made my way about the island, the conviction grew with me that here surely was a prison from which no man could escape, but as I reached the far end of the island, where the industrial shops and the laundry are located, I was not quite so sure. If I were to make a break, I decided it would be from the shop area, which is on the crest of a tall cliff; out the window—into the sea. That would be the plan, I felt sure. At my direction, an extra tower was placed on the shop roof. It was also arranged that guards should constantly patrol the shop rooms. I went away satisfied…

Theodore Cole and Ralph Roe did time together both at the State Prison in McAlester, Oklahoma, and at Leavenworth. They were transferred to Alcatraz on the same chain, arriving October 26, 1935. Both were considered serial criminals; both were considered escape risks; both were considered the worst of the worst.

Ted Cole's case file is a chronicle full of violent acts and capital crimes. His case file described him as a "moronic, vicious, and a killer" with "an unusual air of calmness." He would cultivate his youth in the Paul's Valley Reformatory, "robbing and slashing" his way through a series of escapades. In his own words, he had always "gotten the wrong end of every deal."

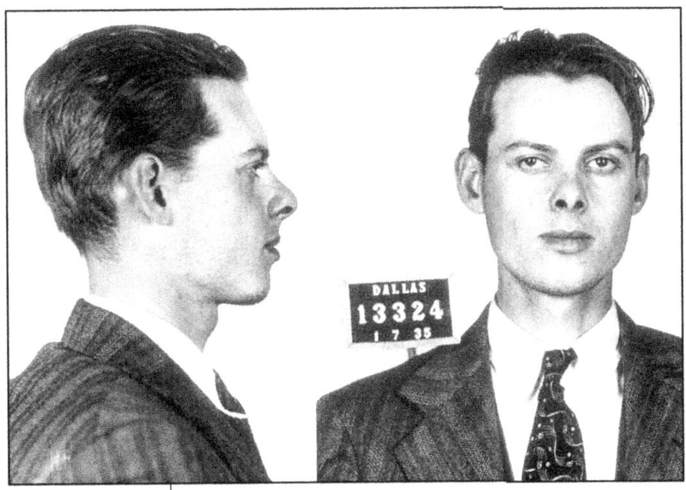

Ted Cole photographed following his arrest in Dallas Texas, October of 1935. He would arrive on Alcatraz less than one year later.

He was born in Pittsburg, Kansas on April 6, 1912, but raised principally in Oklahoma City and Tulsa, Oklahoma. At only 17, he robbed the Dr. Pepper Bottling Works in Tulsa, Oklahoma, and was sentenced to death for the violent nature of the robbery. Since no one had been killed, and Cole was considered "just a foolish and reckless youth," there was public outcry for leniency and his sentence was reduced to fifteen years in state prison. While serving his sentence at the Oklahoma State Penitentiary, he killed his cellmate by stabbing him twenty-seven times, then while waiting to be prosecuted, he escaped the prison by hiding in a laundry bag. In one entry, his file read: "He is a vicious criminal with robberies, kidnapping and other crimes that cross state borders... Several times since he has been incarcerated, awaiting trial on kidnapping charges, he has attempted to escape. He sawed several bars of his cell on numerous occasions and has boasted he will affect his escape..."

Ralph Roe was born in Excelsior Springs, Missouri, on February 5, 1906, and much like Cole, had a turbulent childhood. Roe's mother died of Tuberculosis when he was only nine years old and would drop out of school at fourteen. His case file is riddled with entries of bank robberies, theft and larceny charges spanning over a decade. He was also an associate of the famed outlaw Wilbur Underhill, known during that era as the "Tri-State Terror." Both Roe and Underhill would be taken down together. In December of 1933 as wanted fugitives, federal agents traced their whereabouts to a small cottage in Shawnee, Oklahoma, where they were hiding out. Using the cover of darkness, federal agents surrounded the property and demanded them to surrender. Within seconds, a gun battle erupted and under a volley of bullets, Roe and his girlfriend, Eva May Nichols, were both struck down. Underhill suffered numerous gunshot wounds, but managed to escape. He was found hiding in a furniture store hours later, critically injured having suffered extreme blood loss from numerous gunshot wounds. Underhill was taken to McAlester where

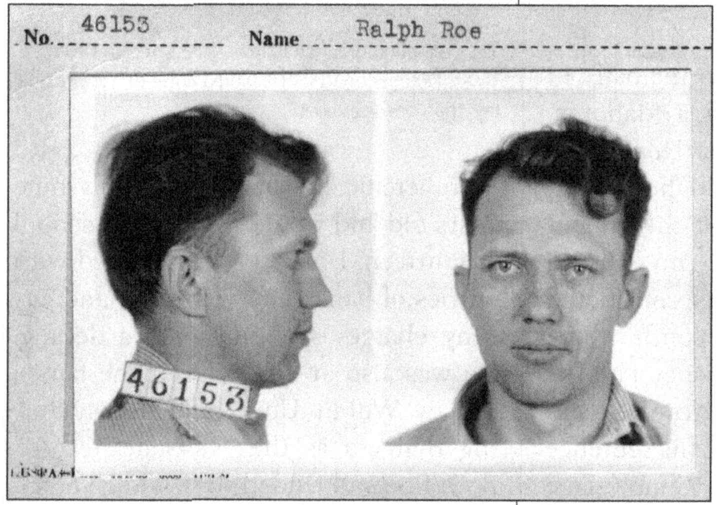

(Top) Wilbur Underhill

(Bottom) Ralph Roe on January 17, 1935, at USP Leavenworth.

he remained, handcuffed in his bed, at the prison hospital until his death on January 6, 1934. His last spoken words were alleged as being: "Tell the boys I'm coming home." Ralph's girlfriend Eva Nichols would also later die from her injuries, but he survived and was sent to prison to serve out a life sentence.

On Alcatraz, Roe was considered a habitual menace, with one report stating: "This prisoner is a constant noise maker, promotes discord among the other prisoners by attempting to keep them from going to work, and by use of the foulest of profane language directed at the officers... To solitary A Block because he was constantly agitating inmates in D Block and also challenging guards to come in and fight."

In March of 1936, after serving nearly three months in solitary confinement, Roe was released back to the general population and assigned to work in the mat shop. Cole would follow to the industries months later, first being assigned a job in the laundry, then a position in the blacksmith shop. Together, they would plot the first successful break from the Rock.

The morning of December 16, 1937, proved to be a perfect storm of sorts... A thick fog layer shrouded the island so densely that when the inmates filed into the recreation yard for work line-ups, the tower officers suspended all morning work details as a result of the poor visibility. Former Correctional Officer Clifford Fish stated that as a general rule, the towers who had line of sight of each other, had to have reasonable visibility or "at risk" job assignments could be canceled. When reporting to work in the old industries buildings, the pathway that prisoners walked to work, only had a chain link fence that separated them from the Bay waters. In addition to the road, hill and model industries towers, an officer on the yard wall catwalk also stood on ready to watch their movements. With limited visibility, the walkway from the yard steps to the industries was considered a high risk pathway and the inmates were all sent back to their cells. This issue was mostly resolved in 1940 with the construction of the New Industries building that included more modern security features, but in the early years, officers didn't take any risks.

Following lunch, the fog, though still thick, had cleared reasonably enough to allow prisoners to return to work. Senior Officer Cochenour estimated visibility was about 50 yards from his station on the roof of the model building. The low resonating fog horns sounded back and forth, and the screeching seagulls lent to a sense of eeriness. The fog was a perfect partner to aid in their escape.

Aside from the roof tower, the old model industries building had escaped security renovations performed on most of the other structures. The security bars that covered the windows were the original soft iron metal left from the military. Using stolen hacksaw blades, and over the course of several weeks, possibly even months, Cole and Roe took turns sawing through bars located in a storage room on the backside of the model industries building. The two convicts had concealed their saw work by filling the gaps with grease, paint chips and other metal shavings. The intense fog would provide the perfect means to slip away undetected.

Roe's work assignment, along with twenty six other inmates, was in the adjacent building on the ground floor of the mat shop. He was permitted to move between the two buildings to enter the storage room for supplies without supervision and without suspicion. Alongside Roe, other notable prisoners who would later make their own attempt at breaking the Rock, watched the events closely. Bernard Paul Coy, the principal of the 1946 Battle of Alcatraz, had just arrived on July 31st, and was facing a bleak future of up to twenty five years in prison. The mat shop detail was his first long term work assignment on Alcatraz. Doc Barker, William Martin, Rufus McCain, and Rufus Franklin would also be observing from the same job assignment, and all men would later make their own desperate attempts at escape. Cole worked alongside a much smaller group of five inmates in a small shop area located on the ground floor of the model building. One of his five

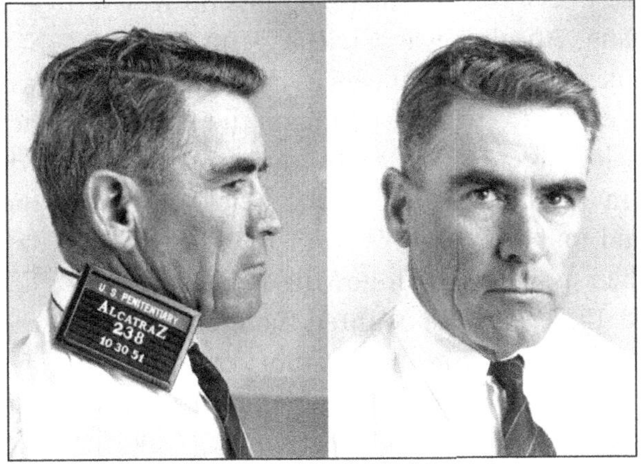

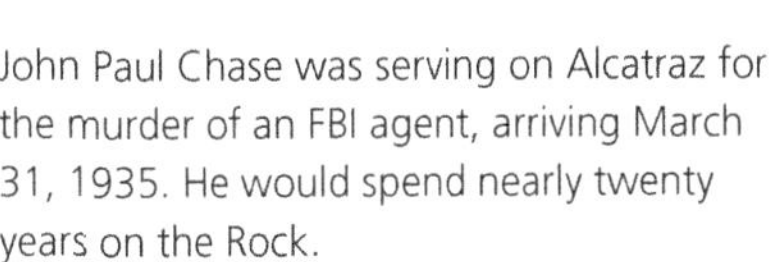
John Paul Chase was serving on Alcatraz for the murder of an FBI agent, arriving March 31, 1935. He would spend nearly twenty years on the Rock.

The interior of the Model Shop area where Cole and Role cut the bars and made their break. These photos were taken following temporary repairs.

coworkers was John Paul Chase (AZ-238), a famed bank robber and Depression-era outlaw, well known for criminal association with Baby Face Nelson and the John Dillinger gang. Another was Charlie Berta, considered by many officers as the toughest prisoner to ever serve time on the Rock.

Joe Steere was a forty-four -year-old junior officer who led the blacksmith and mat shop details from the yard to their assignments following lunchtime. At 12:50 P.M., he counted the men into their shops and then unlocked their tool lockers calling in his counts at 1:00 P.M. Following the initial count, Cole and Roe slipped out of site into the storage room, removed the bars and then dropped from a window on the backside of the model building and then using a Stilson wrench, broke open the secure gate at the perimeter fence where old tires were discarded.

Alvin Karpis, America Public Enemy Number One, who served the longest sentence on Alcatraz, later wrote that in his personal memoir "On the Rock" that he watched the two escape. He wrote:

> Ralph and Ted pop out of the window from the floor beneath us…in work clothes and bare feet…carrying five gallon cans with handles strapped on them and the tops welded shut…Ralph Roe tries to wrestle the padlock off the fence, but he's all nerves. Ted Cole takes the wrench from him and calmly twists the lock open…The two make their way to the water's edge; access is difficult because rubber tires circle the shores of the Rock…Ralph and Ted move cautiously past the barbed wire but as they reach open water they are picked up by the current and taken

The repaired window where the convicts sawed through the security bars and escaped.

> off rapidly in the direction of the Golden Gate Bridge, now safely invisible from the low hanging fog…As Jim Clark and I turn away from the window to an anxious Harvey Bailey, I whisper. "They're gone…"

At 1:30 P.M., Officer Steere initiated his count and reportedly looked perplexed. He wrote in his report: "I looked over the entire window lay-out and found where the window had been cut away. I looked out of the window, but could see nothing." Within minutes, the island went into lockdown mode and for the first time, the escape alarm was sounded…Despite intensive searches, there was no sign of Cole and Roe. Associate Warden E.J. Miller wrote:

> Closer examination of the security window sash of the blacksmith shop revealed that it had been cut with an instrument, which was apparently a hacksaw. Warden Johnston and

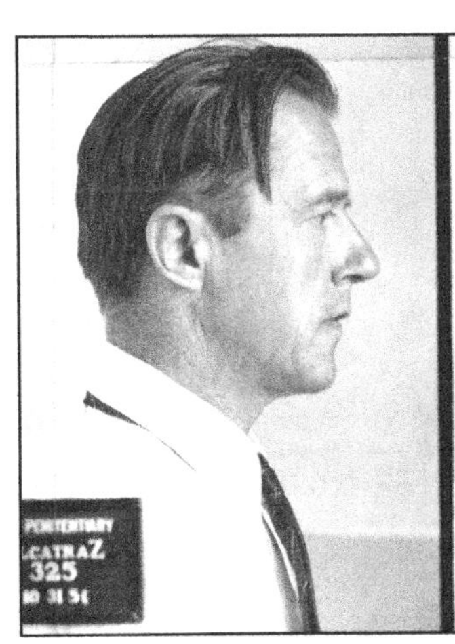

(Above) Alvin Karpis

(Right) James Clark

WARNING

WARNING

Officer Steere advised that hacksaws are only used in the blacksmith shop, and are charged out to the men working therein. As Officer Steere is required to continuously inspect five rooms, it is logical to believe that subject Cole used a hacksaw which is charged to the blacksmith shop to saw the detention sash at such times that Officer Steere was inspecting other rooms, particularly those in the adjoining mat shop.

The window faces the northwest corner of the island, and is immediately above the water-line. There is, however, a 14 foot heavy iron-mesh fence on the edge of the cliff, to prevent prisoners from running to the edge of the island, and diving into the Bay. Between the window where the escape was made, and the iron fence, there is a steel catwalk, which leads to a lower level at the rear of the mat shop, and was used for the purpose of throwing remnants of the automobile tire casings into the Bay after the good portions had been removed for use in construction of the mats. At the termination of the catwalk, is a small iron gate in the fence, which could be opened for throwing the tires over the cliff. Examination of this gate following the escape revealed that the subjects had taken with them a large Stilson wrench, for the purpose of twisting the padlock off. After opening, it was then possible for the prisoners to jump to a ledge a few feet below the gate, which is covered densely with automobile tires, and then to either jump directly into the Bay, or to follow a natural ledge which leads down to within a very few feet of the waterline.

(Opposite pages) A series of photographs taken by investigators from the water of the model industry building. Note the discarded rubber automobile tires all along the cliff and shore areas. The wall of the tires were used to manufacture rubber non-slip rubber floor mats for military vessels.

We searched the area in the back of the model building and found where the lock on the gate where we throw the old tires through, had been broke with the Stilson wrench and was lying beside the gate also. We made a complete search of the area without finding any additional clues or signs of the men, no footprints, no clothing. The caves were searched with lights and the big cave was flooded with tear gas and in the evening with sickening gas and had men stationed to see if there was any movement or anyone came out, without result. We combed the island thoroughly, entered all residences, inspected every nook and cranny, all along the shoreline, in the rocks, the emergency dock, the regular dock, beneath the docks, the sewers, all shrubbery, covering every inch of the island.

US Coast Guard boats were also notified of the escape, and the entire surrounding waters of the island were thoroughly patrolled. It will be noted, however, that on the day of the escape there was heavy fog, and visibility ranged between two and three hundred yards. There was also an exceptionally strong current running in the vicinity of the island at that time, caused by an exceedingly high tide. The current was accelerated

(Above) The prisoners' escape route.

(Below) A tide chart showing the ebb velocity for December 16, 1937.

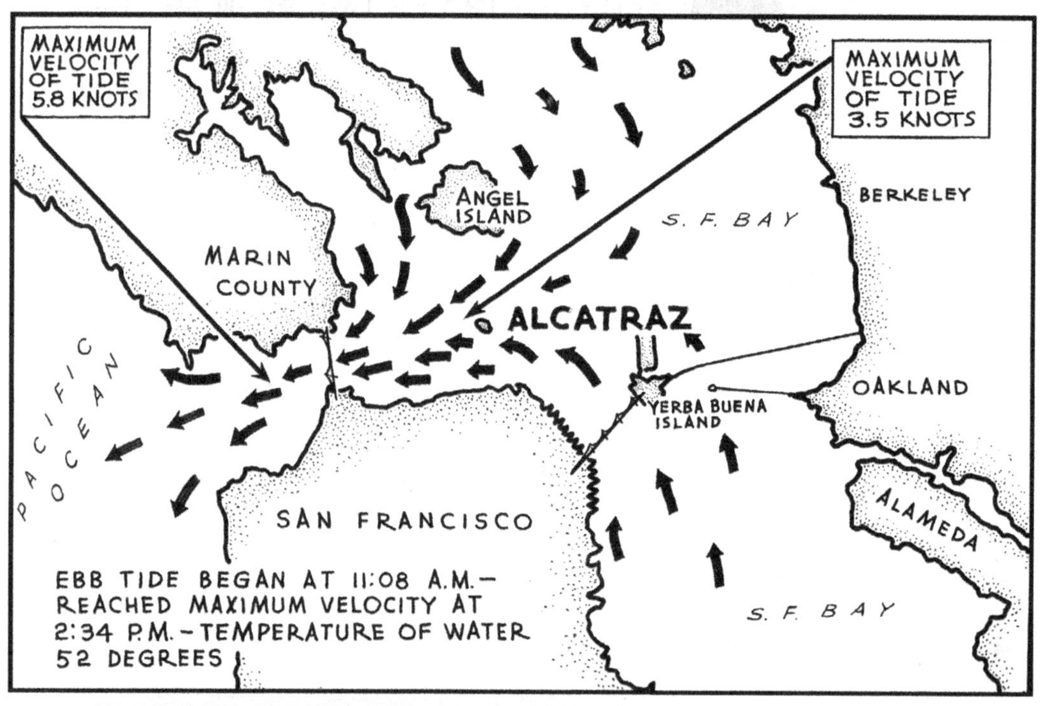

A Coast Guard cruiser patrolling the waters near Alcatraz searching for the two escaped convicts.

> by flood waters from rivers, caused by heavy rains in the valley. Light house keepers and coast guardsmen estimate that the current at the time of the escape had a speed of approximately six knots per hour.

News of the escape quickly swept across the nation in radio broadcasts and newspaper headlines. Within days, scores of tips and alleged reports of sightings flooded the police station switchboards, but to no avail. As the investigation widened, experts started to question whether escape was even possible considering the strong ebb tides the prisoners faced as they made their escape. Lloyd C. Whaley, Assistant City Engineer for San Francisco was quoted in the San Francisco Chronicle stating: "The day Roe and Cole made their getaway was one of the exceptionally high tides…The run-out between 11 A.M. and 4 P.M. was at a speed of about eight miles per hour. A strong swimmer starting at Alcatraz would have found himself going out the Golden Gate in the fog before he had expended sufficient energy to reach shore in still water…Small boats could not have bucked the current. Such a vessel as the Oakland garbage boat could not have entered the Golden Gate against it."

Their trail had completely vanished after entering the water and exhaustive search of the island and various shores revealed nothing. In spite of expert opinions surmising their escape had ended in failure, sightings continued for several months. Newspapers ran stories that ranged from the men showing up in beer taverns, to tying various robberies to the duo. Former Alcatraz inmate William Malcolm "Runt" Ritchey (AZ-99) told Investigator William McMahon of the San Francisco Police Department that he knew they'd made it...He provided details of the empty oil barrels that were stored on the island and confirmed that they would have had access to them. It was also alleged that after Roe and Cole were reported missing, guards punctured large holes in all the containers remaining on the island to prevent them from being used again. A raft using identical barrels had been found the day following the escape by fishermen near the Golden Gate, but experts doubted it had been crafted by the inmates. An FBI report stated that the barrels were sometimes disposed of off Alcatraz by being tossed in the water and later salvaged by fisherman for their own use.

While many fellow inmates had held hope, not all believed their escape was so cunning or even successful. Theodore "Blackie" Audett, the only prisoner to serve three separate terms, under three separate register numbers, gave his own account:

> I was watching from the other end of the shop, and I had seen Ralph jump from the window. He hit the water and come up about 25 yards out, just at the thin edge of the fog. He was only a dozen feet or so from safety behind that shroud of fog when he come up from his dive. Ted had went first and was already into the fog and out of sight when Ralph started swimming.
>
> Ralph began to flounder almost as soon as he come up. I think he hurt himself when he hit the water. He never hollered or anything that might spook them up on the wall. But Ted must have been waiting, out there in the fog. Anyways, Ted come swimming back out of the fog bank to help Ralph. Both struggled there for a few seconds and then began drifting back out into the thick fog mist. Right there the alert signal went off and guards begin yelling. But before they could open up, a big rolling mass of heavier fog moved in between the Rock and the spot where the boys had been struggling in the water. It swallowed them up before a shot could be fired. The heavy fog patch stayed there only about a minute, then lifted enough so we could see clean out to the bell buoy, about 200 yards from the surf line at the Rock. There wasn't a sign of Ralph and Ted.
>
> They couldn't have possibly made it out that far in the few seconds it taken that glob of fog to lift. The riptides got them. I'm sure of that. There has been lots of stories since, though, that Roe and Cole showed up later, here or there around the country. But I seen with my own eyes what happened to Ralph Roe and Ted Cole.

Karpis also later revealed a similar fate...He wrote: "As Jim and I had stood at the window watching, Ralph and Ted picked up speed. They had just passed the buoy straining on its side from the strong current when, less than 500 yards from shore, Ralph disappeared as if someone grabbed him from under the water. The five-gallon can he had been clutching jumped high out of the water

IDENTIFICATION ORDER NO. 1471

December 20, 1937.

FEDERAL BUREAU OF INVESTIGATION
UNITED STATES DEPARTMENT OF JUSTICE
WASHINGTON, D. C.

F.P.C. $\frac{22\ \ 17\ \ W\ \ IM\ \ 16}{27\ \ W\ \ 0\ \ 14}$

WANTED

THEODORE COLE, with aliases: TED COLE, THEADORE COLE, ROY JACKSON.

ESCAPED FEDERAL PRISONER (KIDNAPING)

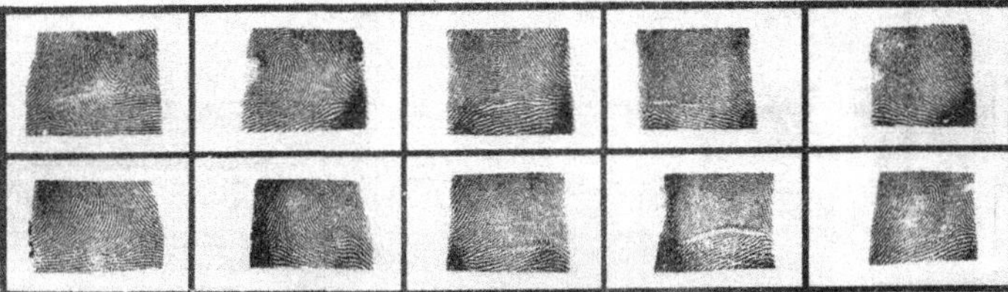

DESCRIPTION

(Photograph taken October, 1935)

Age, 25 (born April 4, 1912); Height, 5 feet 7½ inches; Weight, 135 pounds; Eyes, blue; Hair, brown; Complexion, medium; Build, medium; Occupation, tailor; Scars and marks: 2-inch oblique scar corner right eye; small scar middle right cheek; 8-inch scar above knee left leg; faint oblique scar 1½ to 2 inches above left wrist rear; curved scar ½ inch out from lower lip left; 1½-inch horizontal scar under chin.

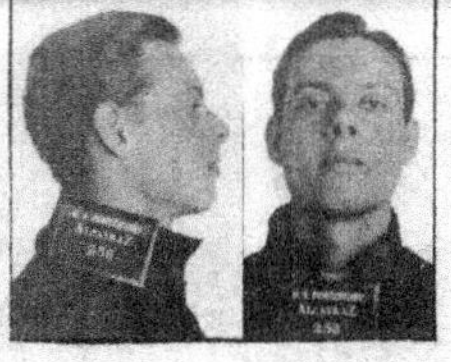

CRIMINAL RECORD

*As Theodore Cole, #--, arrested PD, Tulsa, Oklahoma, 1924, charge not given, sentenced 2 years parole.

As Theodore Cole, #5090, arrested PD, Tulsa, Oklahoma, January 31, 1927, charge burglary, released to County Humane Agent.

As Ted Cole, #26817, received State Penitentiary, Little Rock, Arkansas, August 27, 1928, crime burglary and grand larceny, sentenced two years, released to Sheriff, Tulsa County, Oklahoma.

As Theodore Cole, #4478, arrested Sheriff's Office, Tulsa, Oklahoma, September 26, 1929, crime robbery, sentenced death by electrocution.

As Theodore Cole, #21023, received State Prison, McAlester, Oklahoma, October 22, 1929, crime robbery, sentence death by electrocution commuted to fifteen years.

As Roy Jackson, #13324, arrested PD, Dallas, Texas, January 6, 1935, charge fugitive from Cushing, Oklahoma - kidnaping, released to U. S. Marshal January 10, 1935.

As Theodore Cole, #1824, arrested U. S. Marshal, Dallas, Texas, January 10, 1935, charge kidnaping.

As Ted Cole, #2710, received Sheriff's Office, Oklahoma City, Oklahoma, March 11, 1935, charge kidnaping, sentenced fifty years in Federal Penitentiary.

As Theodore Cole, #46905, received U. S. Penitentiary, Leavenworth, Kansas, May 20, 1935, crime kidnaping, sentenced fifty years. Transferred October 23, 1935, to U. S. Penitentiary, Alcatraz Island, California.

As Theodore Cole, #258-AZ, received U. S. Penitentiary, Alcatraz Island, California, October 26, 1935, transferred from U. S. Penitentiary, Leavenworth, Kansas, crime kidnaping, sentence fifty years.

On May 20, 1935, at Guthrie, Oklahoma, Theodore Cole entered a plea of guilty in Federal Court to an indictment charging him with kidnaping and he was sentenced to serve fifty years in a Federal Penitentiary. He was confined in the United States Penitentiary at Alcatraz Island, California, and escaped therefrom on December 16, 1937.

Law enforcement agencies kindly transmit any additional information or criminal record to the nearest division of the Federal Bureau of Investigation, United States Department of Justice.

If apprehended please notify the Director, Federal Bureau of Investigation, United States Department of Justice, Washington, D. C., or the Special Agent in Charge of the division of the Federal Bureau of Investigation listed on the back hereof which is nearest your city.

*Represents Notation Unsupported by Fingerprints. (over) Issued by: JOHN EDGAR HOOVER, DIRECTOR.

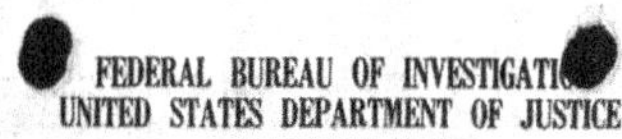

IDENTIFICATION ORDER NO. 1472

December 20, 1937.

FEDERAL BUREAU OF INVESTIGATION
UNITED STATES DEPARTMENT OF JUSTICE
WASHINGTON, D. C.

F.P.C. $\frac{24\ \ L\ \ 1\ \ R\ \ III\ \ 5}{M\ \ 1\ \ U\ \ III\ \ 4}$

WANTED

RALPH ROE, with aliases: PAUL SULLIVAN, JACK SULLIVAN, RAYMOND ROE, RAYMOND ROWE, J. H. REYNOLDS, JACK McCARTHY, JACK McCARTY, RALPH ROWE.

ESCAPED FEDERAL PRISONER (BANK ROBBERY)

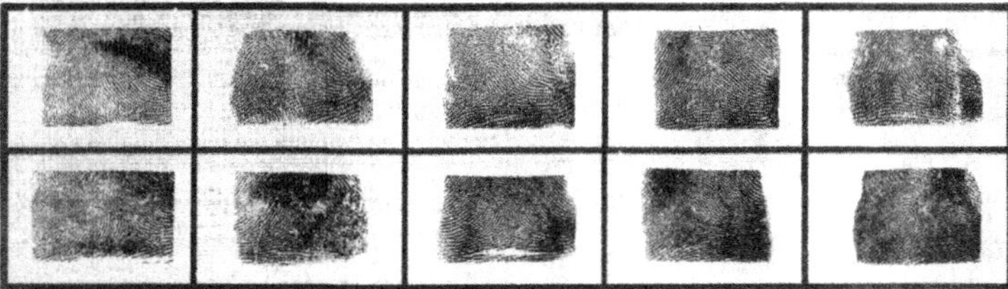

DESCRIPTION

(Photograph taken October, 1935)

Age, 31 (born February 4, 1906); Height, six feet; Weight, 170 pounds; Eyes, grey; Hair, dark brown; Complexion, medium; Build, tall, medium; Scars and marks: blue tattooed small star first joint left index finger rear; blue tattooed two small stars back left hand; faint blue tattoo 4 inches above left wrist rear; oblique scar 1½ to 2 inches below left elbow rear outside; faint blue tattoo 4 inches below right elbow front; horizontal scar 5 inches below left nipple; cut scar 2½ inches above right eyebrow on forehead.

CRIMINAL RECORD

As Paul Sullivan, #93, arrested PD, Pomona, California, April 28, 1923, charge robbery, released to Constable, Pomona, California.

As Jack Sullivan, #21728, received State Penitentiary, Little Rock, Arkansas, September 25, 1924, crime grand larceny, sentenced one to five years, released August 18, 1925, expiration short term.

As Jack McCarthy, #--, arrested Sheriff's Office, Enid, Oklahoma, September 6, 1925, charge theft. No disposition given.

As Jack Sullivan, #6089, received State Reformatory, Granite, Oklahoma, September 20, 1925, crime grand larceny, sentenced two years, released December 16, 1926, expiration short term.

As Raymond Roe, #17578, received State Penitentiary, McAlester, Oklahoma, June 28, 1927, crime robbery with firearms, sentenced twelve years.

As Ralph Roe, #--, arrested PD, Shawnee, Oklahoma, December 30, 1933, charge harboring, no disposition given.

As Ralph Roe, #15589, arrested PD, Oklahoma City, Oklahoma, December 30, 1933, charge robbery with firearms, released to Oklahoma County.

As Ralph Roe, #0-504, arrested Sheriff's Office, Oklahoma City, Oklahoma, January 1, 1934, charge robbery with firearms, disposition not given.

As Ralph Roe, #15589, arrested PD, Oklahoma City, Oklahoma, July 7, 1934, charge vagrancy and investigation, released to Pottawatomie County, Oklahoma.

As Ralph Roe, #--, arrested Sheriff's Office, Bonham, Texas, July 25, 1934, charge auto theft, disposition not given.

As Ralph Roe, #--, arrested Sheriff's Office, Bonham, Texas, August 1, 1934, charge burglary, disposition not given.

As Ralph Roe, #15589, arrested PD, Oklahoma City, Oklahoma, October 5, 1934, charge investigation, released to Muskogee, Oklahoma, County.

As Ralph Rowe, #11900 U.S., arrested PD, Muskogee, Oklahoma, October 6, 1934, charge bank robbery, sentenced 99 years Federal Penitentiary.

As Ralph Roe, #46153, received U.S. Penitentiary, Leavenworth, Kansas, January 19, 1935, crime armed robbery National Bank, sentence 99 years; transferred to U. S. Penitentiary, Alcatraz Island, California, October 23, 1935.

As Ralph Roe, #260-AZ, received U.S. Penitentiary, Alcatraz Island, California, October 26, 1935, transferred from U.S. Penitentiary, Leavenworth, Kansas, crime armed robbery - National Bank, sentence 99 years.

On January 18, 1935, at Muskogee, Oklahoma, Ralph Roe was convicted in Federal Court on charges of bank robbery and was sentenced to serve 99 years in a Federal Penitentiary. He was confined in the United States Penitentiary at Alcatraz Island, California, and escaped therefrom on December 16, 1937.

Law enforcement agencies kindly transmit any additional information or criminal record to the nearest division of the Federal Bureau of Investigation, United States Department of Justice.

If apprehended please notify the Director, Federal Bureau of Investigation, United States Department of Justice, Washington, D. C., or the Special Agent in Charge of the division of the Federal Bureau of Investigation listed on the back hereof which is nearest your city.

(over) Issued by: JOHN EDGAR HOOVER, DIRECTOR.

(Above) A labeled press photo representing distance in miles from Alcatraz to various locations around the San Francisco Bay in 1937.

and sailed off of the swirling surface of the dark water."

In April 1941, years following their escape, John Terrell, a reporter for the San Francisco Chronicle ran a feature length story alleging Cole and Roe had made it to South America. He wrote in part without offering his sources:

> They are now living in South America; have resided for periods in both Peru and Chile. The only prisoners ever to stage a successful break on "the Rock," they have

(Opposite page) FBI agents examine a makeshift raft found adrift by the Golden Gate Bridge. The raft was recovered by a fishing boat and examined for evidence. The fuel canisters used as floats were traced back to Alcatraz, but it was never proven as being used by the convicts in the break (the official FBI report stated fuel canisters from the Alcatraz industries were frequently discarded into the bay and salvaged by fisherman). It was the growing conviction by federal authorities that the prisoners drowned. Dale Stamphill, a co-conspirator in a later escape with Doc Barker commented that someone had passed him a smuggled page from a "True Detective" type magazine that featured an article on Roe and Cole and a photo of their alleged raft. Stamphill considered building a raft but decided they would have to collect whatever they could on their path to the waters' edge and make a go for it.

(Above) Police officers with rifles at the ready searching for the escapees. Alcatraz is visible in the background.

(Below) A photo taken eighty years later in the Model Shop area where Cole and Roe made their escape. Additional security features installed following the break along with steel mesh window coverings that made it more difficult to cut through without detection. The bench and vice plate is still in-place.

> eluded all the law enforcement agencies engaged in one of the Nation's greatest manhunts. Roe and Cole made good their escape with two large air-tight oil cans. The oil cans were securely strapped together. They floated lightly on the swirling waters. All Roe and Cole had to do was hold onto the straps on the cans, one of them on each side of the tossing raft... sealed into one of them were civilian clothes. It was in these clothes that the two Oklahoma desperados fled northward on the Redwood highway. They contacted the automobile of a confederate on a Marin county road, but they drove away alone... The notorious fugitives are reported to have "plenty" of money today, to be living comfortably in their South American hideouts.

After a search of the various industry work areas, Laundry Officer James Halsted came across a poem, the author unknown. He stated that at some point following the escape, he overheard a convict say something to the effect: "They're going to write a book called Gone with the Fog." Special Agent N.J.L. Pieper wrote FBI Director J. Edgar Hoover in jest, providing a copy of the poem that was found which was entitled "Lost in the Fog" that referenced him, though incorrectly spelling his name.

> Twas a few days before Christmas, with the fog like a sheet, when over the fence two boys did leap, with all the Bulls in the towers fast asleep.
>
> With high-powered rifles, tommy-guns and grenades, they said "Old Alcatraz" boys can never be made.
>
> With thousands of dollars spent day by day, I wonder what the public will have to say.
>
> Such tumultuous excitement we have never seen before, all the Bulls in the joint were walking the floor.
>
> As we marched in to supper, there stood, "Ole Meat Head" with a puss that was ashen gray, though they called out the Army, Navy, Coast Guard, Marine Corps, the boys kept swimming for the opposite shore.
>
> Now dear public be very skeptical when you hear Edgar J. Hoover say, all night through we wished the boys luck, while the screws in the joint were passing the buck.

The true fate of Cole and Roe may never be known, but regardless of whether they made it or perished, the San Francisco Chronicle offered one fact that couldn't be disputed:

> With long years of prison ahead of them, Ralph Roe, Muskogee, Okla., robber and Theodore Cole, Cushing, Okla., kidnaper, defied science, the natural hazards and the guns of guards, escaped and shattered a national byword, the legend of "escape proof" Alcatraz.

James Lucas

Thomas Limerick

Rufus Franklin

Murder on Alcatraz

"They intended to fight their way to the boat and sail away..."
—JAMES LUCAS, AZ-224

THE ESCAPE OF COLE AND ROE was the main talk of the prisoners and fueled hope to those strategizing an exit. James Bennett, the Director of the Federal Bureau of Prisons, made assurances to the public emphasizing: "We intend to make Alcatraz as nearly impregnable as the mind of man can conceive... Improvements designed to diminish the chances of escape and to make the prison more easily administered will be recommended..." The improvements, however, wouldn't happen quickly enough...

The layout and design of the old industry buildings left few options that could be implemented to mitigate the security deficiencies in short order. It was clear that a new structure would need to be designed and built to allow for safer custody.

Less than six months after Cole and Roe disappeared into the turbulent Bay waters, another more violent plot was in the works. It would again leverage the weakened security of the model building. On May 23, 1938, James Lucas, Rufus Franklin, and Thomas Limerick, all serving lengthy sentences for bank robbery, conspired in one of the most brutally violent escape attempts in the history of Alcatraz.

Lucas, who arrived on Alcatraz on January 24, 1935, from Leavenworth, offered his memory of the vicious break:

> Limerick, Franklin and I were among fifteen or so inmates who all worked on the third floor of the model building. We were on the top floor. There were shops on the two floors below. Above was the roof there were two armed guards up there. One set in the glass tower who observed the work area and wire fence, while the other patrolled the backside of the building. Every thirty minutes they changed places while the guard in the tower looked out over the yard. While the patrol officer walked to the

The model industries building.

get behind the concrete elevator shaft, throw down the other officer and disarm or shoot him. Limerick claimed that with the high powered rifle he could

end of the building and back to the other end, his back was toward the window for a minute as he walked very slowly. A concrete elevator shaft cut off his view also when he was on the far end of the building.

So for a minute no one could see the window. The plan was to slip up the roof quietly and overpower the guard in the tower, take his guns and

pick off the other two guards from behind the concrete elevator shaft. His associates outside said he was an expert shot. To get on the roof, there were four strands of barbed wire strung along the edge of the roof. Franklin said he intended to get a pistol down on a rope to his buddy on the first floor, Doc Barker. They were close friends I know. There

Senior Officer Royal C. Cline photographed in 1937 while guarding the road tower. Cline was brutally murdered during the escape attempt. In his final moments, Cline refused to cooperate with the escapees and was killed.

were others, but I never knew who exactly…I knew they intended to fight their way to the boat and sail away…

They picked a little after one o'clock at the time the officials in charge of the shop went into the office to check his count sheet. At Alcatraz, each officer must check his men on the count sheet every thirty minutes. He also looked over orders and stayed in the office about fifteen minutes. This routine never varied just as the officers change places every thirty minutes.

When the day of the break came, Limerick said I was to work with him. At one o'clock, Mr. [Royal] Cline went into his office as usual. Limerick got out a wedge he had built to hold the window open [and level] when we stood on it. He put it on and waited. Franklin went into the file room. He was to watch the officer patrolling the backside, and when he started back at the far end of the building, and his back was to the window, he was to walk back out. That would be the signal to go up on the roof. So that was the reason Franklin was in the file room. We stood on the floor near the window watching for Franklin to come out. Then as we stood on the far side of the shop under the window, Mr. Cline came out of the office and walked slowly into the file room. I don't know why he came out of his office so soon; he never had done that before. Maybe he went there to check on an order for supplies. I just don't know. I told Limerick let's put it off. His eyes were as cold as ice as he shook his head. He said he didn't notice anything, meaning Mr. Cline. We waited what seemed like one million years, but was only a minute or so according to the time verified at the trial. Then, Franklin walked out of the file room with a hammer in his hand. Limerick grabbed my arm; let's go he said and crawled-up on a desk. My job was to put a short piece of one-inch board across the window to stand on. I left it lying on the floor. Limerick didn't notice, he crawled out the window and stood on the steel sash of the window. I crawled out the other side. I looked up and could see the officer in the tower, his back towards us, looking out over the work area. The door to the glass tower stood open. He was totally unaware of what was creeping up behind him.

I was supposed to help Limerick cut the barbed wire. Franklin was below us now waiting to crawl out the window as soon as one of us went up. Before I could put up my hand and pretend to cut the wire, Limerick had cut through two strands. I had to act fast as the officer was still sitting unaware of anything. Limerick cut the third strand as I lifted my foot and kicked out one of the windows. I looked up at the officer and he never moved; my heart fell. Below, Franklin jerked my pant leg. I rested the other foot on the steel sash of the window and kicked another pane of glass out. The window was only three panes wide. I looked up and the officer had heard that one break. He slowly turned around and looked back. Limerick was crawling up on the roof. He stood up and charged the tower, throwing everything he could at the tower officer. The officer kicked the door shut and barely had time to bring his gun into action. At that time the other officer was on the far side of the building getting ready to move a scaffold for workers pulling in new steel. I got up on the roof and Mr. Stites was firing at everything and everybody. He fired at me and I was barely able to save my life by crawling under [the raised] floor of the tower. Limerick was killed at the door. Franklin came along flying into action and charged the door and struck several times at the glass with a bloodstained hammer. He was shot down as he struck again and again with the hammer. After everything was over they dragged me out from under the tower. Mr. Miller asked me who hit Cline. I said I did not know he had been hit. Limerick died never knowing Mr. Cline had been hurt. Mr. Ordway, Mr. Pepper shook me down. No blood, no striking weapon of any kind on me.

There was no plan to kill Mr. Cline he just walked out into the room where there was a man who already had a life sentence in Alabama for murder. At the trial, I asked Franklin why he had killed

Mr. Cline. He said when Mr. Cline came into the room he tried to tie him up but was resistant. He said Mr. Cline reached for his sap. Franklin said he hit him several times with his hammer before he fell.

Warden Johnston also recorded the officers' version of the bloody escape. He wrote in a memo to the Bureau Director three weeks following the event:

Almost as soon as Officer Stites saw the prisoners, they rushed the tower from several angles each of them firing iron missiles (note: these consisted of heavy metal objects including hammers and heavy wrenches), their apparent purpose being to try to knock him out and seize his arms.

Officer Stites endeavored to halt them by warning and by firing the first shot into the frame of the

(Right) The guard tower on the model industries building, where Correctional Officer Harold Stites was attacked by the would-be escapees. Stites opened fire on the inmates, fatally wounding Limerick.

(Below) The rooftop gun tower rushed by inmates Limerick, Lucas and Franklin. Lucas hid under the raised floor to avoid being shot after Officer Stites successfully gunned down Limerick and Franklin.

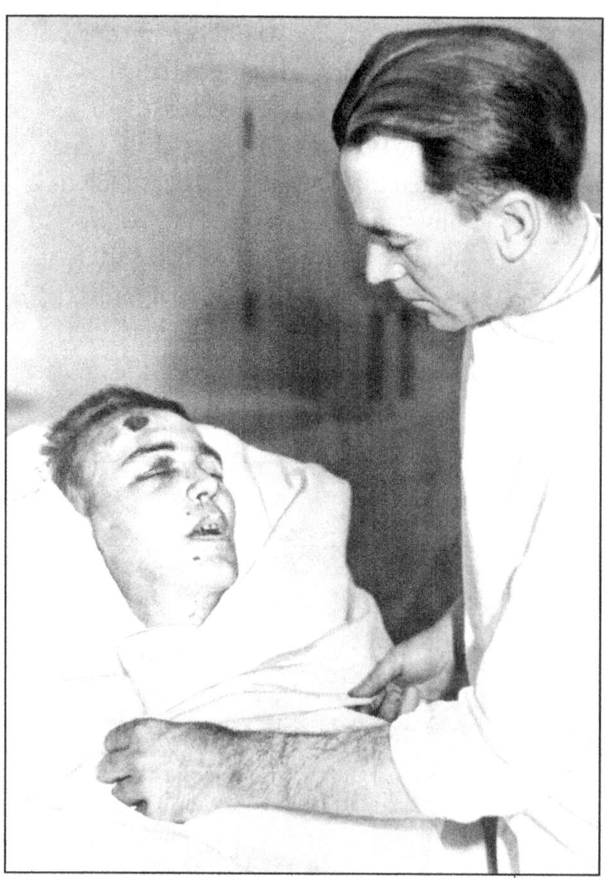

The lifeless body of Thomas Limerick at the San Francisco County's Coroner's Office.

at the time was in the laundry. The associate warden heard the shots and went toward the Model Shop building where he saw prisoner Franklin laying on the barbed wire which goes around the edge of the roof. Lieutenant Culver coming from the laundry also saw Franklin, as did several other officers.

Associate Warden Miller, used the emergency telephone to call all of the officers from the front of the building and instructed the Armorer to get those that were on the island but off duty to go into the work area, and had the launch go to that part of the Bay, not knowing just whether or not anybody had succeeded in getting out. When he learned that Officer Stites and Officer Stewart had the three men under control on the roof, Associate Warden Miller and Senior Officer Nickelson went up to the top floor of the building to see if all of the other prisoners were there and had all of the shops in the building checked.

When they got to the fourth floor where Franklin, Lucas, and Limerick had been assigned to work, they found the remaining prisoners assigned to that shop up at one corner and looking around for Mr. Cline, they found him in a corner of the storeroom with his head battered in and bleeding.

He sent for stretchers and immediately moved Mr. Cline to the hospital, then went to the roof and removed Prisoner Franklin who still had the

window but they kept advancing and then he kept dodging and firing shots through the glass in his tower. Several of the missiles they fired went through the glass in the tower but many others failed to go through, showing that the shatterproof glass is a very valuable protection. Only one of the missiles that went through hit Officer Stites. He did not leave his tower but fired through the glass.

The associate warden happened to be in his work area on the west side near the incinerator. Lieutenant Culver was making his regular afternoon inspection of the work area and

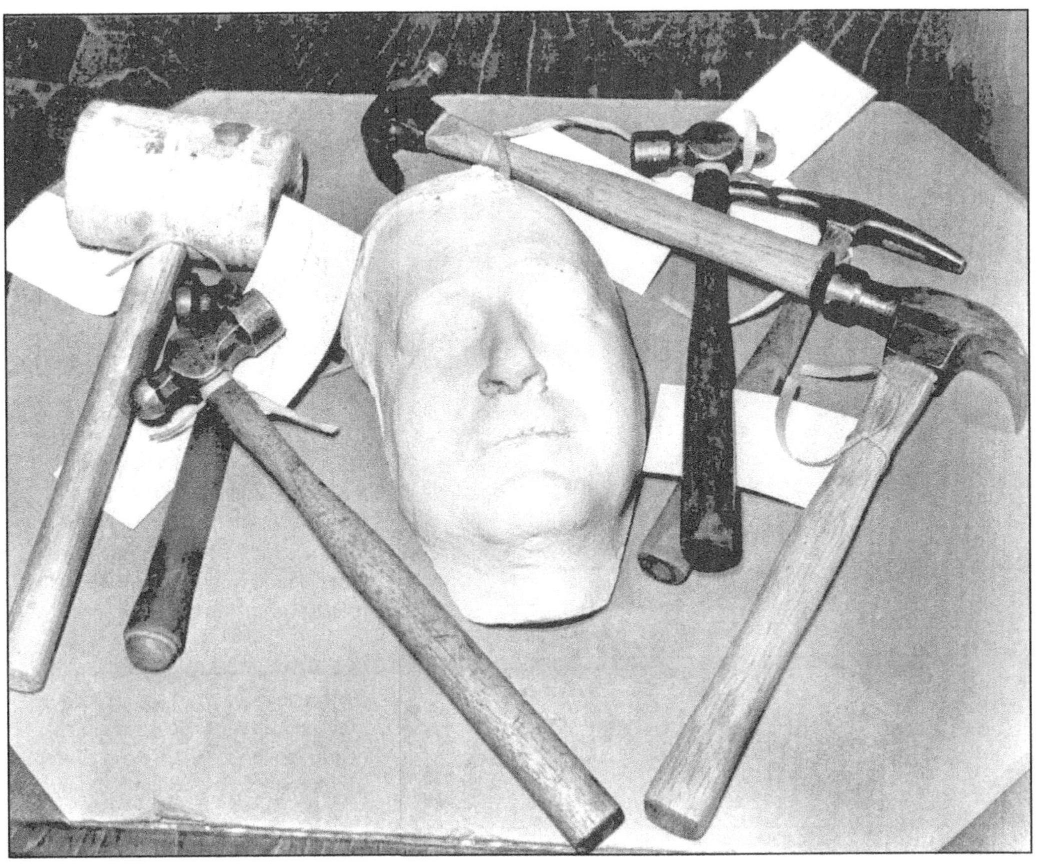

Death mask of slain officer Royal Cline; the hammers used in his murder, and other tools used in the escape attempt that were found in the model building.

hammer in his hand with which he had been trying to hit Officer Stites, and from the blood appearing on it, it appeared that this hammer was used in assaulting Officer Cline. Limerick was lying on the roof, shot in his head, unconscious. Lucas was held in [a] corner, apparently in [an] attitude of surrender, kept covered but not fired upon by Officer Stewart, while Officer Stites was engaged in the battle with Franklin and Limerick.

Limerick and Franklin were then removed to the hospital and Lucas was taken to the cell building and locked up. The associate warden interviewed both Lucas and Franklin. He secured a statement from Lucas which was reduced to writing and signed by the prisoner and afterwards he turned it over to the FBI Agent.

At the request of Dr. Ritchey, arrangements were made to move Officer Cline to the Marine Hospital, San Francisco, and he was moved over there at 5 P.M.

Dr. Creel, in charge of the Marine Hospital, telephoned me during the evening and said that Mr. Cline's condition was very critical and it was doubtful if he would survive the night.

the murder of Officer Cline. The case was followed closely by the media as the convicts voiced allegations of brutal punishment by the officers. Their defense strategy fell on deaf ears and both were convicted of first degree murder and given life sentences.

(Left) Harold P. Stites is sworn in to testify at a coroner's inquest on November 4, 1938. On the table is Limerick's death mask, showing the bullet wound from Stites's fatal gunshot. Stites himself would die in 1946, in the brutally violent "Battle of Alcatraz."

(Below) Lucas and Franklin during their highly publicized court appearances. Both inmates were convicted of first-degree murder for their role in Officer Cline's death.

Just hours after the failed escape while Limerick and Cline lie dying from their wounds, Lucas was brought down into the hallway of the shower room area to be interviewed by Associate Warden Miller. Miller pressed him to help understand why they would make such a foolish attempt knowing that they would encounter a gun gauntlet once they reached the wharf. Lucas stated simply: "I thought it was foolish to start with…I didn't want to go but had been talking about it and just went…"

Limerick never regained consciousness and ultimately died from the gunshot wound. Lucas and Franklin both stood trial for

The Escape and Death of Doc Barker

"I'm crazy as hell; I should have never tried it..."
—DOC BARKER, AZ-268

DOC BARKER played a significant role in the escape of Cole and Roe, and had Limerick, Lucas and Franklin secured weapons, he clearly would have a role in that getaway as well. Unknowing to Barker, his efforts from the early escapes would ultimately aid Morris and the Anglin Brothers in their famed break decades later...

From the first moment he arrived on Alcatraz, Barker conspired to escape. He worked in the mat shop alongside Ralph Roe, and as a fellow Oklahoman, he was considered a trusted friend. Karpis claimed that Cole and Roe were always the first to be counted and then released to their job assignments. While the two men were released to begin their work, Officer Steere would take time to finish counting the other inmates before giving the "all clear" signal... He followed the same practice for every count, every day, and this routine ultimately gave an edge to the escapees.

Although intent on breaking out, Barker reluctantly opted to stay behind... He realized it would be the only way to give the men a reasonable head start before the next count. His absence from his job assignment could create suspicion. It was common for Cole and Roe to secure supplies in the bottom floor storage area of the model building. Nevertheless, Barker had played a crucial role in helping the men acquire essential tools.

Barker knew that his best chance at escape would be to exploit the weaknesses inherit of the military sections that were still being utilized, just as Cole and Roe did. He would turn focus to the D Block section of the cellhouse. Ironically, the cellblocks used to house some of the most problematic inmates in close confinement, were also those that had escaped the tool-proof cell bar retrofits in 1934.

D Block housed some of the highest risk inmates; those who refused to conform to the rules and regulations of Alcatraz. D Block was the main isolation section, and closed front cells on the upper tier of A Block were utilized for solitary confinement. In fact, a daily charge out sheet dated January

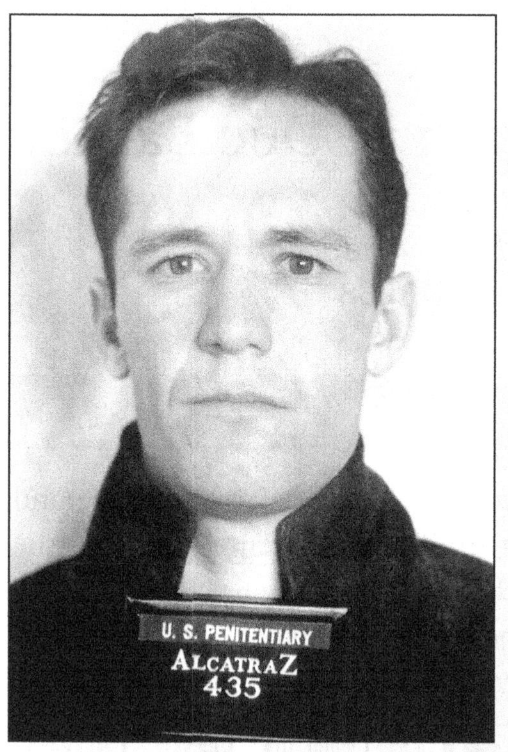

Dale Stamphill

William "Ty" Martin

Henri Theodore Young

Rufus McCain

DIVISION OF INVESTIGATION, U. S. DEPARTMENT OF JUSTICE
WASHINGTON, D. C.

Institution U.S. Penitentiary Located at Alcatraz Isl, Calif

Received OCT 26 1935 Transf
From U.S.P. Leavenworth Kans
Crime Consp. to transport Kidnapped person
Sentence: Life yrs. mos. days
Date of sentence 5-17-35
Sentence begins 5-17-35
Sentence expires Life
Good time sentence expires Life
Date of birth 6-21-99 Occupation Painter
Birthplace Mo Nationality Amer
Age 36 Comp. Ruddy
Height 5-5 Eyes Brown
Weight 150 Hair Dk Br
Build fair Med

Scars and marks 3/4 scar, 2" long under rt ear. 1/2" scar, under left ear.

CRIMINAL HISTORY

NAME	NUMBER	CITY OR INSTITUTION	DATE	CHARGE	DISPOSITION OR SENTENCE
Arthur R Barker	46978	USP Leav., Kans.	5-25-35	Consp to Kidnap	Life
		Recd from Leavenworth Kans (Transfer)			OCT 26 1935

RECEIVED
OCT 26 1935
U. S. PENITENTIARY
ALCATRAZ, CALIF.

(Please furnish all additional criminal history and police record on separate sheet)

Doc Barker

29, 1936, showed that all of the A Block closed front solitary cells had inmates assigned, and the dungeon cells located in the prison basement below both A & D Blocks were also all occupied.

The cells in both A and D Blocks were made of the flat soft iron bars from the original 1912 construction. The window bars of the cellhouse had all been retrofitted with the modernized tool-proof steel, but Barker, consulting with other escape artists came up with an effective solution. On Alcatraz, the tool-proof bars were made of a casehardened steel composite. Hacksaw blades were comprised of an untreated softer metal that would splinter or dull when used against the metal core. Barker decided that he could use the saw blades for the soft iron bars of the cells as well as the joining weld sections of the bars shrouding the windows. They would use a bar spreader to snap the bar from the frame, and similar to Cole and Roe, use paint shavings and other mixtures to conceal the breaks until they were ready to escape.

Dale Stamphill (AZ-435), was described in his case file as a "cool, calculative and methodical thinker," arriving on the Rock in January of 1938. He was serving a life sentence for armed robbery and kidnapping. Years earlier, while a prisoner at the Oklahoma State Reformatory, Stamphill helped orchestrate a mass escape that resulted in the tragic murder of a tower guard. He would evade capture for nearly three weeks and his ingenuity and ability to help coordinate such a break appealed to Barker. He also held a job assignment that could offer considerable advantage in helping procure contraband tools. Along with Barker's recruitment of Stamphill, he also brought in Henry (Henri) Young, Rufus "Roy" McCain and William "Ty" Martin.

On Alcatraz, Stamphill worked as part of a light labor crew and had considerable access to various sections of the prison normally off limits to other inmates. He did odd jobs such as painting, repairs, maintenance and various other tasks. He would be instrumental in helping secure blades and other items that had been carefully planted for him in other areas of the prison, along with the help of other key allies.

Thomas Dugan (AZ-256) was a close associate of Jewish Mafia figure Waxey Gordon. Dugan was from New York and had extensive experience working as an inmate plumber while serving time at Sing Sing Prison, and became friends with Dale after sharing adjacent cells in C Block. On Alcatraz, Dugan worked in the industries steam pressing clothes, but with his plumbing background, he would sometimes be pulled from his day assignment to assist inmate plumber Lee Snyder (AZ-348) on the more complex jobs. Dale would later identify Dugan and Snyder as having been key sources in helping not only acquire hacksaw blades that had been used in cutting pipes, but also having them carefully "delivered" while performing their work rounds. Dale stated that without Dugan's help, they could have never pulled off their break.

William "Slim" Bartlett (AZ-239) would also provide assistance by crafting a bar-spreader. Alvin Karpis would later claim that tools and blades were smuggled past the metal detectors by concealing them in their shoes and keeping them as close to the ground as possible. The snitch box (or stool pigeons as they were affectionately known) would fail to detect them if the metal was kept below the magnetron. Stamphill, however, felt that version was ridiculous. He gave all the credit to the inmate plumbers stating that they carried tools, blades and other fittings without ever being questioned by officers. The plumbers were constantly cutting and replacing leaky pipes, valves and fittings. Their tool boxes were constantly inspected by officers, but everything they carried, including saw blades, were part of their standard array of tools. They were also trusted by officers. Often times, an officer would be assigned solely to supervise the plumber and they would spend an extensive amount of time together. The shower room, which was also where the clothing issue area was located, was an area that required constant attention of the plumbers. Passing hacksaw blades and other contraband items could easily be concealed in clean laundry that was passed to inmates. It

Thomas Dugan

William "Slim" Bartlett

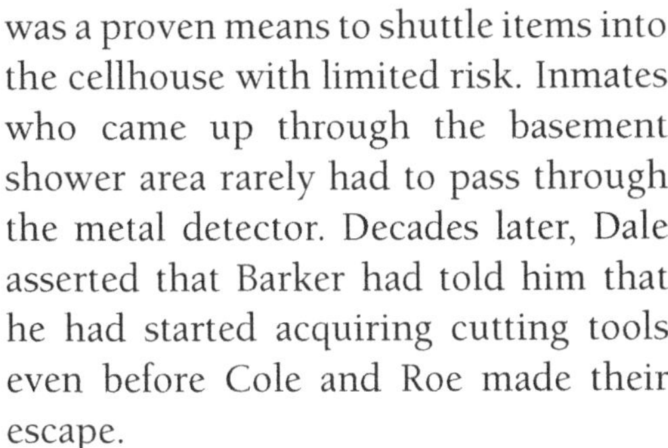

was a proven means to shuttle items into the cellhouse with limited risk. Inmates who came up through the basement shower area rarely had to pass through the metal detector. Decades later, Dale asserted that Barker had told him that he had started acquiring cutting tools even before Cole and Roe made their escape.

There was a lot of debate on the best method for reaching the mainland. Since the escape would involve climbing through a cellblock window, it would land them on the exterior wall catwalk that officers patrolled during their rounds. One of the first ideas had been to breakout before the midnight count and ambush the west gun gallery officer as he reported for duty on the exterior catwalk. After stealing weapons, they could enter the warden or family residences, take hostages and then take over the prison launch. The more they debated, the more they realized that things could have a fatal outcome if they were detected too early in the plan. It was too risky and too close to the counts... Each time they considered their options, they always circled back to their original plan of escaping undetected just like Cole and Roe. Their model for escaping after the midnight count seemed to hold the most promise.

As part of the labor crew doing odd jobs, Stamphill moved about the cellhouse with little supervision. On weekdays, most of the cellhouse population was down in the industries and during his rounds he drew little attention from the officers. The west gallery officer spent the majority of his time on the D Block side during the day when the majority of the prison population was at work in the industries. The plumbers would plant tools in other cells along the flats, as well as other places that were easy for Stamphill to access. Additionally, the plumbing in D Block was already a quarter century old, and work in this area was common.

Once the bar-spreader was finally delivered to Barker, work on cutting the interior bar of the window began. The soft flat iron bars of D Block had rivets that were not only easy to saw through, but by leaving one rivet intact, the bar could be swung from side to side making egress easy. It also allowed the bars to be moved back into place with little detection.

Three times each day, the main prison population would enter the mess hall for meals, and the west gun gallery officer would post in that section to watch over inmates and provide safety to the officers walking the floor. This provided just over ten minutes each meal period for the inmate to squeeze between the bars, first peering around the corner of the cellblock to ensure that no other officers were roaming the cellhouse, then to begin work on loosening one of the window bars to allow the escapees to break from the main prison. The clanging sounds of the gates opening and closing would give warning that an officer was entering the main floor of the cellhouse and allow just enough time for the convicts to sprint back into their cells. Henry Young would go to the edge of the cellblock and stand watch for the gallery officer. It was a good alert system in the event an officer broke routine...

While the hacksaw blades were no match against the tool-proof steel, the blades were highly effective in cutting the welds from where the bar met the iron framing. The bar-spreader was used to break the bar from the frame, and this would provide just barely enough space to squeeze through the opening. The spreader was in some respects similar to the device that would later be used by Bernard Coy in the 1946 escape attempt: small, with two bolts with a cross thread. Used in combination with a crescent-style wrench, it could exert enough force to break the bar from the frame. Once a bar had been snapped free from its foundation, they used a putty mix to set it back in its place.

As considerable progress was being made in D Block, Stamphill would make his move to be placed into isolation. On November 24, 1938, Stamphill staged a fight to be removed from the general population, but things didn't go exactly as planned. Instead, the officers placed him in a closed front solitary confinement cell on the upper tier of A Block, and he remained there for fifteen days before finally being moved to isolation in D Block. He would be given a cell on the flats for closer supervision, giving him the perfect placement for his role in the escape.

On the night of Friday, January 13, 1939, Barker and the other conspirators were ready to make their dash for freedom. At 3:00 A.M., there was only one officer working the cellhouse floor. The main counts always started in D Block and progressively worked to the

D Block as it appeared at the time of the 1939 escape. Note the spread bars on one of the cell fronts. Also note the extended cell front toward the rear of the cellblock. This was one of the early solitary confinement cells.

other sections of the prison. The gallery officers on each side of the cellhouse followed the movement of the officer as he migrated to each cellblock performing his counts.

Henri Young would be the first to exit his cell and quietly peer around the corner to visualize the officer. As they gave the signal that the coast was clear, the men crawled through the spread flat iron bars and made their way to the window. Stamphill had cut the rounded bars on the door section of his cell and simply pushed them down outward to make his exit. One by one, the men squeezed through the bar section of the window, dropped down to the edge of the exterior of the building, then while staying low to the ground, they hiked cautiously down to a small beach area at the water's edge.

Under the cover of heavy fog, the inmates struggled to find wood and other debris that could be used into making crudely fashioned rafts. As they worked desperately to find materials, the officer made his way back into D Block to begin his 3:30 A.M. count and almost immediately, he noticed the cell bars amiss. It was only a matter of minutes before the chaotic sounds of

A typical cell in D Block, prior to the 1940 remodeling. Note the soft 'flat iron' bars.

ringing telephones, sirens and yelling officers resonated throughout the cell-blocks. At the water's edge, with sirens blazing overhead, the inmates became separated and hurried to complete their improvised wooden rafts.

Off-duty officers poured into the armory to pick up guns, then began combing the island in groups as the prison launch was sent out to search for the escapees. It was well known among the staff that in their desperate quests to be free, inmates would try to take hostages, so officers were also sent to search every conceivable hiding spot around the living quarters, including the warden's basement. As they walked quietly along the roadway, one of them heard voices coming from the cove below, but was unable to see anything because of the fog. Finally, the road tower guard shined the powerful searchlight into the cove and picked up two figures running for the water. One of the officers observing from the roadway yelled at the inmates to halt, and fired several warning shots ahead of them. Ignoring the command, the two men hit the water, and the officers, now able to target the inmates, opened fire, raining a shower of machine gun and rifle bullets into the cove.

The first to be captured was Young and McCain, both naked and suffering from exposure. They were brought up to the visitor's area of the administration and wrapped in blankets until they could be escorted to the prison hospital. Less than two years later, Young would murder McCain in what some speculated as a revenge killing for the failed escape.

Navigating the cove proved too dangerous for the launch, so two officers took a small row boat into the shallow water and pulled the wounded inmates Stamphill and Barker, into the craft. Stamphill, who had been shot in the legs, was lethargic; one bullet had gone through his left leg just above the knee, severing an artery, and the wound bled profusely. He also had a gunshot wound

(Above and below) Rufus McCain and Dale Stamphill's cells following their escape.

to his right leg near the ankle, which some estimated may have been a result of the same bullet. Barker was pulled into the boat and was also found to be critically injured. He had suffered gunshot wounds to the head and thigh, and had an obvious fracture of his left leg, most likely the result of a stray bullet. Ty Martin was found wearing only a pair of water-soaked socks, bleeding from

several cuts and bruises and nearly frozen. He was brought immediately to the hospital upstairs and interviewed by Associate Warden Miller. When questioned as to how they cut the window, he stated: "With saw blades…had three files, three homemade hacksaw blades and a kind of a jack. I am in so much pain now, but I'll tell you more later on after I get warm. I'm

The area where the escapees entered the water, known today as Barker Beach.

awful sick now; got terrific pains, cramps, can hardly walk..." Similar to Cole and Roe's escape, some of the tools that had been acquired had perplexed the administration. When Johnston had given a statement to the press about the Cole and Role escape, he acknowledged that no tools or blades were missing from the inventory. He stated: "The instrument with which Cole and Roe cut the bars of the machine shop was not, apparently, prison property. A careful check has revealed no such tool missing." Alvin Karpis had also made a claim that Bartlett crafted the bar-spreader and hid it inside a Dobro style guitar to smuggle it inside the cellhouse. Miller interviewed Bartlett regarding this claim. He asked: "What about fixing musical instruments and planting saw blades in them and getting them smuggled into the cellhouse?" Bartlett replied: "Deputy as sure as I'm standing here, I absolutely didn't do it and anyone else that said I done it is a damned liar...That was planted down there in the clothing room..."

Uninjured, McCain and Young were immediately sent to solitary confinement in A Block. Martin was also treated and placed back in solitary confinement.

Henri Young being led into the courtroom during his famous 'Murder in the First' trial for the fatal stabbing of Rufus McCain.

Barker, who was semi-conscious when he arrived at the hospital, complained that he was in severe pain. Warden Johnston noted that they tried to get a formal statement from Barker; his last words were documented in a report by Junior Officer George Hoag:

> "While in the hospital, after Stamphill and Barker were laying on the operating tables, at approximately 5:25 A.M., Barker started to roll and twist...I stepped to table and held him, while doing so, Mr. Pepper, being on the opposite side of the inmate, Barker spoke to me, saying, 'I'm crazy as hell, I should have never tried it...' "

James Boarman

Harold Brest

Floyd Hamilton

Fred Hunter

The Bloody Bay

"The last time I saw your son he was swimming towards Sausalito on his way to freedom. Don't think ill of the boy, he wanted to go and all your prayers wouldnot st op him . . ."

ALCATRAZ OFFICER BOB BAKER

(sent to Prisoner James Boarman's mother, April 14, 1943)

WITH EACH PLOT, valuable lessons emerged exposing both the strengths and weak points of security. Prison officials mapped new design features that would ultimately lend to more secure and safer work areas for officers patrolling the industries.

In 1940, construction would begin a new and larger Industries building that would merge all of the workshops in the two existing buildings into a single structure. The new building would incorporate better visibility both to the interior and exterior, and most significant, the dual level building would include a gun gallery to allow for an armed officer to quickly walk the length of the building with excellent visibility of all of the work areas. It would prove to be one of the most significant enhancements to the prison since the transition in 1934. Additionally, in 1941, D Block was completely redesigned to incorporate larger steel encased isolation cells better suited for long term confinement, along with six closed front solitary detention cells that included a standard set of tool-proof bars on the interior of the cell for safer custody of the prisoner. This was a major improvement over the A Block closed front cells. The A Block cells were considered a serious safety hazard for officers as they were located on the top tier with no protective barrier between the outer door and the inmate. Additionally, the eastern cell section of the old D Block was removed and a cement wall was built to completely isolate the cellblock from the rest of the prison. Enhancements were also made to the west gun gallery, and doors were installed at each level to isolate noise from the opposite section of the cellhouse. A remote panel was installed to allow the officer the ability to open and close cell doors in this section of the prison.

By 1943, the old model industries building had been almost completely phased out of use. The New Industries

The New Industries building (visible in the lower right of the aerial view) was completed in 1941. It boasted new high security features including a fully enclosed dual level gun gallery. Following its opening, the upper floors of the Model Shop were abandoned and used only for storage.

building merged nearly all of the factory workshops into a single structure and the new design features provided better security and safer conditions for the officers. The upper levels of the old model building were now only used for storage and off limits to the convicts, but the lower level still housed a small repair and carpentry shop, a paint shop and a small cement works where convicts fabricated custom cement blocks to be utilized on the sea walls around the island. Despite being the site of two prior escapes, only moderate enhancements had been made

A contemporary view of D Block (the Treatment Unit) that was remodeled in 1941. This section of the prison was used solely to isolate violent and other disciplinary prone inmates.

to improve security. James Boarman, Harold Brest, Floyd Hamilton, and Fred Hunter were assigned to this work detail. The men would again, leverage both the gaps in security and lack of visibility. On April 14, 1943, the four men took Captain of the Guards Henry Weinhold and Officer George Smith hostage while at work in the industries area. The men had created float devices that were a reverse surfboard concept, as they would use their belts and wire to strap them to their backs. The boards included a sealed compartment for their clothing, and incorporated snorkel type hoses for breathing underwater, and were camouflaged with dark paint to match the murky hue of the Bay waters.

A dramatic account which included a surprising wealth of accurate information appeared in a 1943 Startling Detective article. It described the Alcatraz Officer being taken hostage:

> From the west a droning sound rushed suddenly into a roaring crescendo from dawn patrol far offshore brought the Pacific war home to Smith's mind. He glanced up. The ships were invisible and the fog shrouded sun did not hurt his eyes. A faint breeze stirred the waters of the Pacific. The fog might clear in an hour or so, he decided today is the day with a shiver, pulling his overcoat closer about his throat.

Convict Hamilton rose stiffly from a form. Smith turned watching cautiously from long habit as the criminal moved slowly toward a grease pail 10 feet away. That instant as though by prearrangement, Hunter picked up several loose boards. He started toward a pile of wood on the other side of the guard. Shuffling methodically over the rocky ground, the convicts converged on the officer.

Hunter stooped, slowly laying the boards on the pile near the guard. He crouched in an instant, bony fingers fumbling in a pocket. He gave an almost imperceptible nod to Hamilton facing the unarmed guard, then leaped silently. A prison made knife flashed in the convict's right hand.

In that split second, Hamilton from the front also charged Smith, who jumped backward involuntarily. That reflex movement took the guard just beyond the glittering arc of the prison made "shiv" in Hunter's clenched fist. Before he could cry out an alarm the hapless guard was overpowered and crushed to the ground. "Keep quiet," Hunter gritted, holding the razor sharp point against Smith's throat. The officer was helpless.

Fanatical gleams of hatred in the eyes of the desperate criminals told Smith that failure to obey their ruthless orders meant swift, certain death. He was under no delusions. They would kill remorselessly if it would serve their purposes. But they were too cunning to kill a guard if they could help it. Penalty on the American Devil's Island for murder might be virtual burial alive in a solitary vault if the murderers escapes actual execution. Smith ceased his struggles. "Look," he got out in a low voice, "You can't win. You haven't a chance for a clean break. Use your heads, men."

Smith was tied-up and gagged and the four turned to capture the Captain of the Guards, Henry Weinhold. The captain was making his rounds and when he entered the building, he immediately noticed something amiss. Smith was absent and things seemed "more quiet than normal." He slowed his entry into the workshop, but before he could retreat to call for additional officers, he was ambushed by the four convicts. Weinhold, an ex-marine, fought back hard and struggled. Though not seriously wounded, he suffered minor stab wounds to various parts of his extremities, most significantly his right arm. Weinhold later identified Harold Brest as being the main conspirator. After he was tied-up alongside Smith, the convicts made their break.

Brest and Boarman quickly stripped down to their underwear and attempted to harness the makeshift floats onto their backs. They realized that there wasn't enough room to maneuver them through the small cutaway opening in the security bars, and there wouldn't be enough time to saw through another bar to help widen the opening. They decided to continue without the floats and make the mile and a quarter swim with only engine grease smeared over their bodies to serve both as insulation and camouflage as they swam under the cover of dense fog. A makeshift plank was used to reach the top of the fence, along with a large section of a heavy canvas painting drape to place over the barbed-wire fencing. One by one, the convicts climbed through the window where the security bars had been severed, negotiated the barbed wire, scaled the fence and then hurried down to the rocky shore. For Brest and Boarman, it was an ill-fated plan, as the floats also contained stolen military clothing and if they did make to shore; they'd certainly be identified without clothing.

Hunter suffered a minor injury when dropped from the fence and retreated to a small cave that had been filled with large rubber tire sections to help reduce erosion and went far back into the cave to take cover. The other convicts made their dash for freedom, attempting to swim north to remain out of view of the tower officer.

Frank L. Johnson was the officer on duty in the roof tower of the model industries building. After not being able to reach Smith, Johnson immediately contacted Cliff Fish in the armory. Fish, who had just been relieved from this assignment, hurried to the model tower using the long catwalk that passed the hill tower with fellow officers Phil Bergen and Earl Long. Smith, while unable to undo his gag, was able to position himself against Weinhold, who managed to maneuver Smith's whistle into his mouth. The shrill whistle blasts were clearly audible from Johnson's post.

Johnson stepped outside the tower booth and immediately spotted several figures in the water, swimming away from the island. Lifting his rifle, he strained to see through the fog. Keeping his eye on the figures moving in rhythm with the sea, he aimed his Springfield .30-06 and squeezed the trigger, then repeated the process. With each round, the caustic smell of burnt gunpowder mixed with the damp salt air. The water around Brest and Boarman erupted in geyser-like splash patterns, and they could hear the distant sharp crack of a high-powered rifle. As the two men swam almost side-by-side a few hundred yards from shore, Boarman's thrashing suddenly stopped. As Brest reached out to his fellow inmate, he saw that the water around them was stained red with Boarman's blood; he was bleeding heavily from what appeared to be a bullet wound behind his left ear. As the prison launch McDowell pulled alongside, Officer Robert Sutter aimed his gun at Brest's head, while Brest struggled to hang on to Boarman's belt. The officers attempted to catch it with a boat hook, but the belt broke, and Boarman slowly disappeared underwater. Brest was pulled into the launch and wrapped in blankets, then returned to the island, where he was taken to the prison hospital and examined. He had sustained only a minor bullet wound to his elbow.

Hamilton had been able to swim to Little Alcatraz using a large wood plank as a float, but when he heard the bullets whizzing past his head, he tried stay submerged for as long as he could hold his breath. He apparently clung to the small top of Little Alcatraz, and then swam back to the island, lifting his head out of the water just long enough to take a breath. Once there, he made his way to the cave where Hunter was hiding. Warden Johnston had already assembled a team of three officers to explore the shoreline in an attempt to

The cave entrance where Hamilton successfully hid for three days. Cold, exhausted and without food or water, he finally made his way back to the industries and surrendered.

locate the missing inmates. Associate Warden Ed Miller walked the island perimeter, while a boat with a powerful spotlight covered the officers from the water. Standing near the mouth of the cave, Miller noticed a blood smear on one of the rocks. He yelled into the small cavern, demanding that the men surrender or be fired upon. When he received no response, he decided to fire a round from his colt .45 into the void. Fred Hunter, hiding behind some tires and nearly neck deep in water, immediately raised his arms to surrender. Unknown to Miller, Hamilton was still in hiding under several tires.

Officer Johnson reported back to the warden that he had fired upon at least three inmates, and that Hamilton had probably met his death. The prison launch patrolled the waters around the island for hours, but when there was no sign of Hamilton, Johnston began to feel confident that the inmate had perished in the gunfire alongside his accomplice. He was so convinced that he released a statement to the press that read in part: "Hamilton is dead. He was shot, and we saw him go under."

Hamilton remained barricaded far back into the cave for another two days. After many close calls, he decided to give up. He climbed a fence and was again able to breach the security perimeter without being detected. Additionally, he located an unsecured window and was able to climb back inside the old model building and seek shelter in the old electric shop. Captain Weinhold, who had returned to reexamine the scene

Boats patrolling shores of Alcatraz searching for any signs or evidence of the missing convicts.

of the escape, found Hamilton curled up, weak from hunger and exposure. In the press, Warden Johnston announced that he had presumed Hamilton dead. It was an embarrassment to the Bureau of Prisons and even J. Edgar Hoover criticized the lapses in security. Following a detailed inspection of the model building, they found numerous articles of army clothing, a $5.00 bill, a map of the Bay Area, a 50-foot coil of insulated wire, an inflated rubber tire tube that could be utilized as a float, a small wooden raft, and even two bars of soap for use to clean up when they reached the mainland. Former Officer Cliff Fish recalled that following the escape, the officers performed an intensive and thorough shakedown of the cellhouse. He stated the biggest surprise was the

Huron "Terrible Ted" Walters

Walters and Hamilton were friends prior to their transfer to Alcatraz. Both men were involved in a spectacular break from a Texas jail in 1938. Hamilton had once been a driver for Bonnie and Clyde in the early 1930s. Decades later in 1971, Walters would be shot to death by Texas Rangers after taking a family hostage following a violent crime spree. Ironically, Walters died only three hundred feet from where Bonnie and Clyde had slain two police officers on April 1, 1934.

amount of money they located in prisoners cells. The soldiers when sending in their laundry were leaving sums of cash that made it past the metal detectors. Had the prisoners made it to the mainland, they would have easily blended in as it was during the war period and San Francisco was a popular liberty location for those on leave.

As officials examined opportunities to deepen security measures, the convicts continued to plot their paths to freedom. Less than four months after the attempt by Brest, Boarman, Hamilton and Hunter, Huron "Terrible Ted" Walters would slip away from his work assignment in the New Industries building laundry. During the war years, the increased demands of laundry created the necessity for weekend work for the convicts. The Model Shop tower was not manned on the weekends and is located in a section of the perimeter that lacked visibility by the officer stationed in the road tower. On a Saturday, when the road tower officer moved to the recreation yard catwalk to observe the prisoners, Walters slipped from sight, scaled a barbed-wire fence and then walked down a flight of steps near the old "Rock Dock," an old wharf section used during the military period.

Ted's escape was halted as he entered the water. A watchful officer noticed him missing from his work station and soon the sounds of the wailing escape siren created a frenzy as officers scattered to locate him. Less than fifteen minutes after he slipped away, he was located by Officers Bob Baker and Ed Stucker, attempting to hide behind rocks in a little cove along the western sea wall. It would be the last escape attempt from the laundry...

While Alcatraz recorded only fourteen official escape attempts over its twenty-nine year history as a federal prison, there were scores of other plots

(Above) John Knight Giles

(Left) Over the course of several years, John Giles lifted all the elements of a complete army uniform from military laundry sent to Alcatraz. This photo was taken at Alcatraz immediately following his capture and return to the island.

and schemes that never materialized. The security in the industries intensified, but the ramifications of Barker's break was profound and still resonating amongst the prison population. He had proven that escape from the main cellhouse was possible, and with patience and careful study, it could be pulled off again, even with the enhanced security features. When Stamphill looked back, he'd felt that if they'd used dummy heads and did a better job concealing their exit, they could have eluded capture…

There would be three more escape attempts where inmates took officers as hostages, and some of the less violent attempts were even more clever and cunning, as was the case with John Giles who was assigned a job at the Alcatraz dock. Giles, a quiet and soft spoken convict serving a life sentence for murder, spent over a decade

Giles later returned to Alcatraz following his release from prison as a tourist in 1968, prior to the island's opening for public tours. He reflected on the mindset and fixation to escape: "A man with a long time, he's only got one thought; he wants to escape... You need to escape... You think it's the end of your life... You don't want to die in prison... You have that obsession. That's all you think about... It fills your waking hours from morning until night."

stealing clothing articles from the laundry bags containing military uniforms. He eventually pieced together a tech sergeants' uniform and once complete, he snuck onboard a military launch headed for Angel Island. Tragically for Giles, his escape ended as quickly as it began... Giles was immediately noticed missing during the dock count and officers sprung aboard the prison launch and intercepted him after the boat docked on Angel Island.

In addition to his own attempt, Barker's role in the early escapes would directly tie back to the 1962 break of Morris and the Anglin Brothers. Decades later, tools procured by Barker would land directly in the hands of Clarence "Joe" Carnes, one of the most respected convicts on the Rock, one of the early players in the '62 escape, and also one of the principals in the most bloody escape attempt ever on Alcatraz.

The Battle of Alcatraz

"When they decided to die, I was there...It was on the bottom steps of C Block, and they were talking about it like ordinary conversation. That struck me...I didn't know what I expected but I didn't expect them to casually talk about dying. Coy said, 'Well...they're not going to get me...' Hubbard then said, 'Well...they're not going to get me either...' Cretzer then said, 'Well, we better save some bullets for ourselves..."

—CLARENCE "JOE" CARNES, AZ-714

CLARENCE VICTOR CARNES (AZ-714) was only eighteen years old when he arrived on Alcatraz in July of 1945. He was serving a life plus ninety-nine year sentence for murder, robbery and kidnapping, and was considered to be "aggressive" and a "viciously savage fighter" when challenged. To friends, he was known simply as "Joe." Carnes was a full-blooded Choctaw Indian who endured a tough childhood growing up in a poverty-stricken Oklahoma household. At only sixteen, Carnes and a school friend attempted to hold up a small gas station. Carnes threatened the station attendant with a stolen pistol, but he refused to take the youths seriously. He tried to disarm Carnes, and the struggle ended with a fatal gunshot wound to the station attendant's chest.

Both youths were quickly apprehended and locked up in the county jail and charged with first-degree murder. Not long after, they managed to overpower their jailer and escape, but both were recaptured within hours. In October 1943, Carnes was found guilty of first-degree murder and sentenced to serve life in prison. While at the Oklahoma State Reformatory in Granite, Carnes escaped once again. As part of a hard-labor chain gang working in a rock quarry, he and two accomplices escaped, stole a vehicle and kidnapped the owner and committed additional crimes. Their freedom was short-lived and following capture, Carnes received an additional ninety-nine years for larceny and abduction. He was sent first to Oklahoma State Penitentiary in McAlester, and then later to Leavenworth. He became a serious disciplinary problem and the warden recommended that he be transferred to

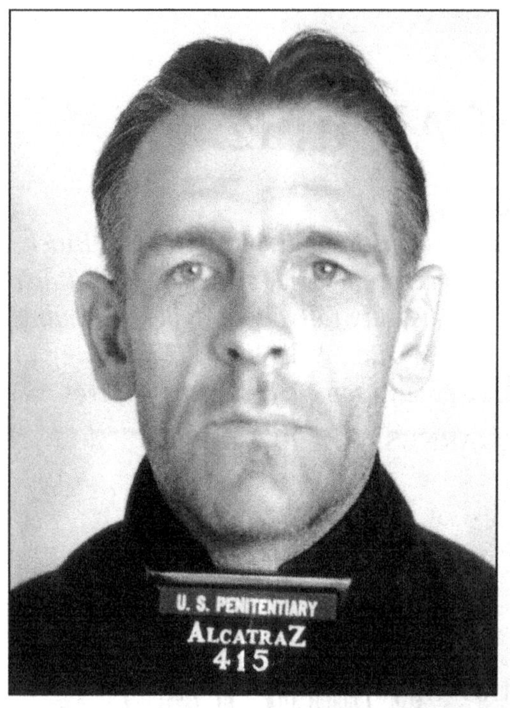

Bernie Coy

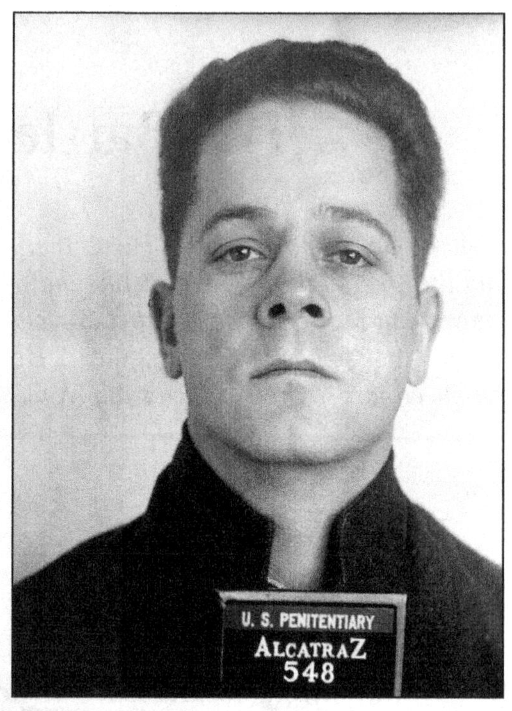

Joseph Cretzer

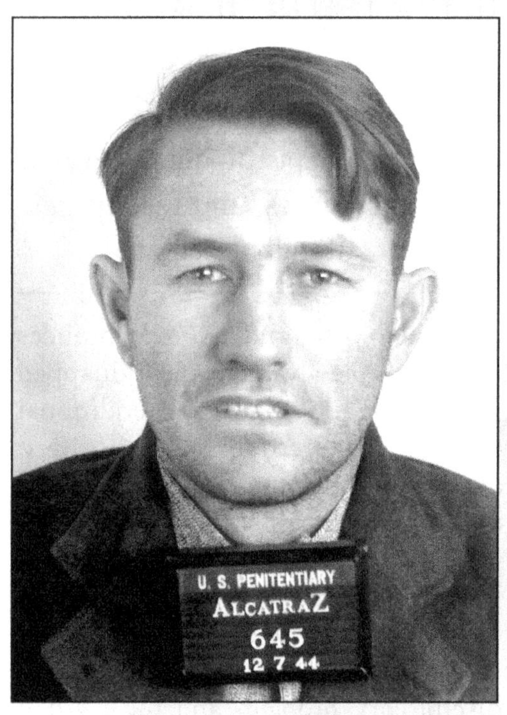

Marvin Hubbard

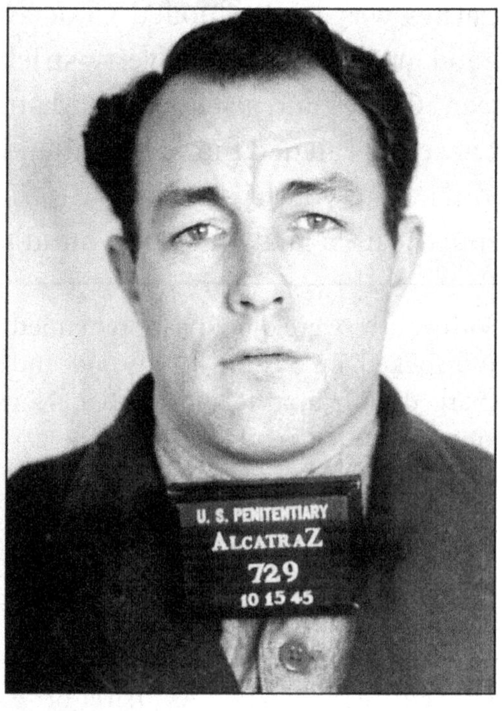

Miran Thompson

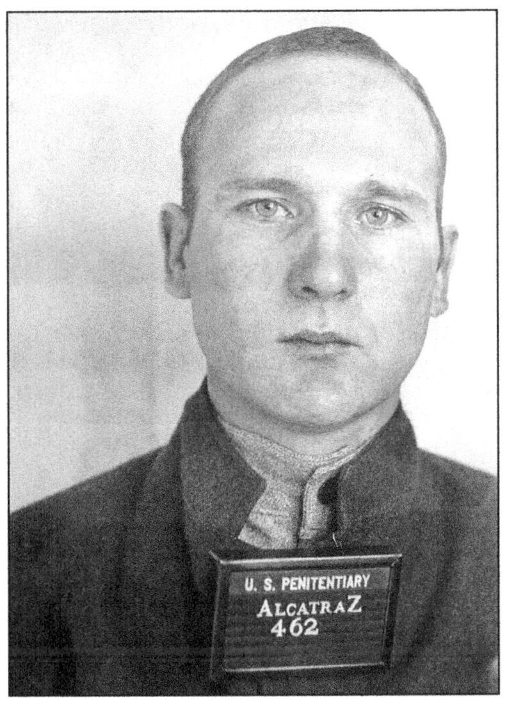

Sam Shockley

Clarence "Joe" Carnes

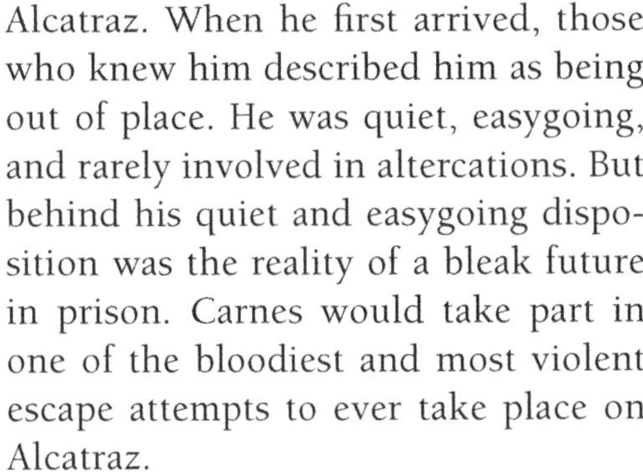

Alcatraz. When he first arrived, those who knew him described him as being out of place. He was quiet, easygoing, and rarely involved in altercations. But behind his quiet and easygoing disposition was the reality of a bleak future in prison. Carnes would take part in one of the bloodiest and most violent escape attempts to ever take place on Alcatraz.

The Battle of Alcatraz was perhaps one of the most significant escape attempts in the Rock's history. It was an extremely complex escape plan, and much like Barker's scheme, it leveraged taking advantage of the routines by individual officers. The key element of this plan was to breach the gun gallery and acquire weapons to be used by the conspirators. It would be the only escape to successfully secure weapons and attempt to breakout using brutal violence against officers and taking hostages.

Over the years, there were several plots to gain entry into gun galleries and take weapons. James Lucas, who was part of the failed escape plot with Franklin and Limerick, claimed that he found a weakness where he could have acquired a rifle while isolated in D Block, but decided against it. He described:

> Only one inmate was allowed out of his cell at a time. Cretzer was in isolation for attempted escape. He noticed a weak spot and carelessness of the officer in the gun gallery with his rifle. The officer left the rifle in the corner when he came around to work the [door] switches. To step from the top of the cabinet to the gallery was

The violent battle scene of Alcatraz in May of 1946. Armed with mortars, United States Marines used heavy artillery to bomb the cellhouse in an effort to regain control.

> easy. Cretzer wanted me to hook out the rifle that was left in the corner. He gave me a hook, but I quickly destroyed it.

During the same time period, Franklin who was also in held in D Block for his escape attempt with Lucas, devised a scheme that would involve cutting the floor level gun gallery bars. By 1942, Franklin was allowed out of his cell for limited periods to help deliver meals and perform light janitorial work along the tiers and flats of the cellblock. His plan was to cut through two bars to gain entry, then sneak to the second floor while the officer was in the main cellblock section and then daze and overpower him. It was over as quickly as it began. Franklin was caught with a file in hand attempting to cut at the bars, but regardless, the plan resonated with Bernard Coy and Joe Cretzer and would surface again...

On May 2, 1946, the Battle of Alcatraz took San Francisco by storm. All eyes would be focused on the island as the battle raged. James Bennett, Director

A correctional officer firmly warns an approaching vessel to maintain its distance from the island.

of the Bureau of Prisons wrote a summary of the escape to give insight of the events for his select staff. Also included in this transcription are handwritten passages from Carl Sundstrom, one of the officers held hostage by the inmates. It's an important chapter to the island's history.

> The revolt was engineered by six of the most dangerous and desperate of the institution's most intractable inmates, and seems to have been led by a former bank robber and dishonorably discharged soldier who was serving a twenty-five year sentence.
>
> This individual by means of a diabolically clever combination of toilet fixtures and a pair of pipe pinchers succeeded in widening the space between two of the bars which protected the gun gallery.
>
> Gaining access to the protected passageway which ran through and above the various cell housing units, the prisoner was able to slug and disarm the officer on-duty as he passed from one unit to another. With the firearms, thus obtained, the prisoners forced unarmed officers to turn over keys with which they released other prisoners and locked up a number of officers as hostages.
>
> The escape plot was frustrated at the outset because the prisoners could not obtain the keys to the

(Right) An excerpt of the letter and diagram from James Lucas describing an earlier plot by Joe Cretzer to climb on top of the cabinet located under the gun gallery (inside D Block), reach in and steal the officer's rifle.

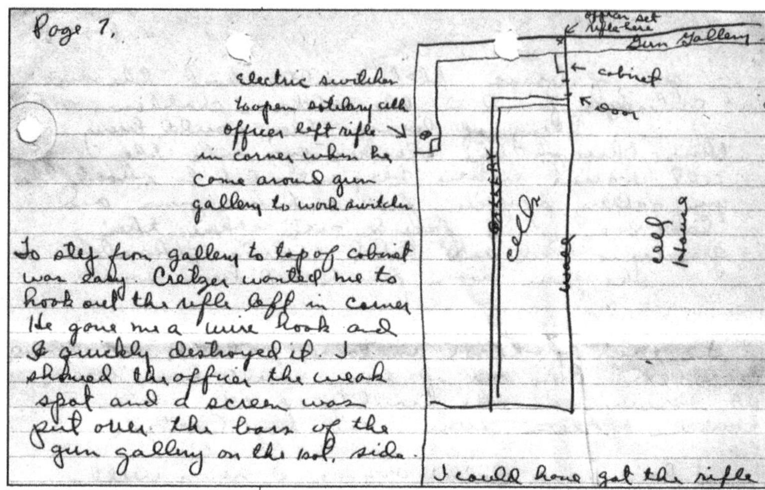

Page 1.

electric switches to open solitary cells

officer left rifle in corner when he come around gun gallery to work switches

To step from gallery to top of cabinet was easy. Cretzer wanted me to hook out the rifle left in corner. He gave me a wire hook and I quickly destroyed it. I showed the officer the weak spot and a screen was put over the bars of the gun gallery on the sol. side.

(Below) The cabinet at the entrance of D Block in 1946. Lucas claimed they had planned to use it as a platform where they could stand close enough to reach inside the gun gallery. He alleged an officer often left a rifle next to the door and against the wall. Also visible is the door located on the second tier that Coy hid behind in wait; overpowered the officer and stole the cache of firearms.

door leading to the outside yard. But they nevertheless, refused to give up their firearms. Thus, the mass escape became a revolt and a gun battle between inmates inside and prison officers and law-enforcement authorities outside the main cellblock. This ended as it had to, by the surrender of the prisoners, but only after two days of serious rioting. Three prisoners were killed, including the one who had gained access to the gun gallery, and a number were injured.

Alcatraz had been unusually quiet until about a week before the revolt took place on Thursday, May 2, 1946. There had been no strikes of concerted action all during the war, but about a week before the outbreak, some of the prisoners in D Block had smashed their toilets and created

WANTED FOR BANK ROBBERY

Photographs taken June 8, 1931

Photographs taken August 20, 1927

Photographs taken June 10, 1931

Photographs taken November 17, 1929

Photographs taken August 22, 1931

Photographs taken September 26, 1932

ARNOLD THOMAS KYLE, with aliases: SHORTY AYERS, DAN HARRINGTON, THOMAS HOLT, THOMAS MARSH, SHORTY McKAY, THOMAS McKAY, A. T. KYLE, ARNOLD KYLE, "SHORTY", "RUSTY", ARNOLD T. KYLE.

DESCRIPTION: Age, 28 years (born October 12, 1909); Height, 5' 6½"; Weight, 140 lbs; Build, slim but compact; Hair, light brown; Eyes, grey; Complexion, sandy, freckles over nose and under eyes; Dress, neat dresser, often wears riding boots and breeches; Speech, slow and calm; Occupation, truck driver; Marital Status, married; Scars and Marks: tattoos - nude woman, upper right arm outer side; girl's head, right forearm inner side; nude woman, left forearm outer side; 1½" cut scar palm left hand. (Kyle is the subject of Identification Order #1453 issued by this Bureau on August 7, 1937.)

JOSEPH PAUL CRETZER, with aliases: JOSEPH P. BENNETT, JOSEPH P. BRENT, PAUL CRETZER, J. P. CRETCHER, JOE PAUL CRITZER, JAMES HAYES, JAMES HAYS, JOSEPH P. KRETCHER, JOE PAUL CRETZER, JOE P. KRETCHER, GEORGE FRANK THOMPSON, DUTCH WHITE, "DUTCH", "JOE", "J. P.", JOE CRETZER, JOE P. CRETZER, JOSEPH CRETZER, JOE CRITZER, "STEVE", JOSEPH KRETZER, JOE JACKSON, JOE P. CRETZER, DICK LITTLE, JOSEPH PAUL GRETZER.

DESCRIPTION: Age, 27 years in 1937 (born Denver, Colorado); Height, 5'7"; Weight, 170 lbs; Build, medium heavy, with noticeable stomach; Hair, dark brown or black; Eyes, brown; Complexion, olive; Dress, unusually neat dresser, often wears polo shirt and slacks; Nationality, American; Occupation, hotel keeper; Marital Status, married; Scars, vaccination scar left arm. (Cretzer is the subject of Identification Order #1450 issued by this Bureau on July 27, 1937.)

Arnold Thomas Kyle and Joseph Paul Cretzer are wanted by the Federal Bureau of Investigation for the robberies of the following banks:

40th and Piedmont Branch of the American Trust Company, Oakland, California, January 23, 1936.
Bank of America National Trust and Savings Association, Melrose and Bronson Branch, Los Angeles, California, March 2, 1936.
Seaboard National Bank, Wilshire and Vermont Branch, Los Angeles, California, July 1, 1936.
Bank of America National Trust and Savings Association, Vineyard and Washington Branch, Los Angeles, California, January 24, 1936.
Security-First National Bank of Los Angeles, Ambassador Hotel Branch, Los Angeles, California, November 29, 1935.

Arnold Thomas Kyle is also wanted for the robbery of the Rose City Branch of the First National Bank, Portland, Oregon, March 29, 1937.

Joseph Paul Cretzer is also wanted for the robberies of the following banks:

Broadway Branch of the Seattle First National Bank, Seattle, Washington, July 27, 1936.
United States National Bank, Branch 30, Portland, Oregon, January 31, 1935.

An indictment was returned by the Federal Grand Jury at Los Angeles, California, on April 28, 1937, charging Kyle and Cretzer with the robbery of the Bank of America National Trust and Savings Association, Melrose and Bronson Branch, Los Angeles, California, on March 2, 1936. Other Federal processes are also outstanding against them.

If you are in possession of any information concerning the location of Arnold Thomas Kyle and Joseph Paul Cretzer, please communicate by telephone or telegraph collect with the undersigned or with the nearest division of the Federal Bureau of Investigation, United States Department of Justice, the local addresses and telephone numbers of which are set forth on the reverse side of this notice.

JOHN EDGAR HOOVER, DIRECTOR,
FEDERAL BUREAU OF INVESTIGATION,
UNITED STATES DEPARTMENT OF JUSTICE,
WASHINGTON, D. C.
TELEPHONE, NATIONAL 7117.

November 23, 1937.

An early era FBI Wanted Poster of Joseph Crezter and crime partner Arnold Kyle. Both men would later be sentenced to life in prison and transferred to Alcatraz.

a mild disturbance. Repairs were being made to the plumbing, but all seemed orderly and quiet.

The officer in the west gun gallery had, however, been instructed to devote much of his time and attention to the prisoners segregated in their cells in D Block, since there was some feeling that perhaps there might be another demonstration.

When the noon meal was over on May 2nd, the main body of the prisoners had been sent to the work area, only one officer was on-duty on the floor of D Block, and the steward and an officer were in the kitchen and dining room supervising the prisoners at work in the culinary department. The few prisoners in "B" and "C" Blocks were locked in their cells, with the exception of Bernard Coy, who was the orderly.

Bernard Coy was a Kentucky bank robber, a dishonorably discharged soldier, and escapee from several prisons, serving a sentence of twenty-five years in the federal institution and with a pending life sentence in Kentucky. He could not adjust himself in the Atlanta Penitentiary, where he was first committed, but when he got to Alcatraz he seemed to be making a better adjustment and for that reason was made a cellhouse orderly.

Joseph Cretzer was known to almost everyone in the federal prison system, since he had previously attempted to escape from the McNeil Island Penitentiary. Also, he was the murderer of the Unites States Marshal Chitty during an abortive attempt to escape while being tried in Tacoma on the escape charge. He had a long record dating back to the time when he was thirteen years of age. He had boasted that no prison could hold him, and proved that six could not. He had gone down the long, ugly road to Alcatraz before he was thirty years of age.

He was a ruthless killer who had committed nine daylight bank robberies, including the Bank of America on Wilshire Boulevard in Los Angeles. He had a period of confinement in D Block, but was being given a trial on the "main line" when he participated in this revolt.

Marvin Hubbard was an escapee from Alabama prisons and jails and a desperate gunman who had, on several occasions, battled it out with the police. He was a merciless and ruthless gunman. The others where in the same category. Sullen, aggressive, and beyond the reach of prison officials, psychiatrists, and all who had labored with them.

At about 1:45 P.M., Coy apparently approached Officer Miller, who was on-duty on the floor of the main cellhouse. At the same time another prisoner, Marvin Hubbard, apparently came to the door of the dining hall and indicated that he wished to return to his cell. The door was opened, and then Coy and Hubbard captured Officer Miller. Hubbard helped Coy overpower Miller, tied him and took his keys except 107, which he had hidden in his pocket.

Miller was locked in a cell at the end of C Block, and Cretzer and Coy (possibly others involved) unlocked cells releasing Cretzer, Carnes, and Thompson. Rioters' unlocked utility corridors and secured tools and parts for the improvised bar spreader. Coy and Hubbard climbed to the west gun gallery to spread the bars. Carnes was on the cellhouse floor, Mr. Bristow headed for the kitchen and was overpowered by Carnes who was armed with a pair of artists' dividers, and was locked in the cell with Officer Miller.

An officer looks up toward the area where Bernard Coy scaled the west gun gallery. Using plumbing fixtures that had been fashioned into a makeshift bar-spreader, Coy was able to enter and secure weapons.

Once Bernard Coy had managed to get through the bars of the gun gallery, it was easy for him to slip down the ladder to the first tier of the gun gallery and hurry along to the soundproof door leading into D Block, behind which he would crouch. When one of the prisoners on the main floor attracted the officer's attention as he passed through the door, he was slugged by Coy with a blackjack or wrench which he had somehow contrived to obtain. Thus, he got possession of the officer's revolver and rifle and considerable ammunition. He passed the revolver down to Cretzer and, armed with the rifle, hurried along the gun gallery into D Block, where he could threaten the officer on duty on the ground floor.

The officer, when he heard a mysterious noise in the gun gallery, was prevented from getting to the telephone by the inmate orderly in D Block. Under threats of Coy to shoot,

(Above left and right) An interior view of the east gallery. Correctional officers considered the gallery post assignments the most desirable. Until the 1946 Battle of Alcatraz, it was also thought to be the safest. The chain link fencing was one of many security features added following the '46 events. Additionally, the entrances were fortified as it had proven to be a weakness during the revolt as they were unable to gain access when attempting to enter under heavy gunfire.

(Below) The D Block section of the west gun gallery.

the officer was compelled to open the door between D Block and the main part of the cellhouse. Although the prisoners then had possession of Officer Miller's keys to the control boxes in D Block, they were unable to release some of the more desperate prisoners who they knew would join them.

Coy entered the D Block section of the gallery and threatened Corwin with a rifle. Corwin opened the door to the cellhouse, and Cretzer entered armed with a .45. He opened the second and third tier with captured keys, liberating all of the convicts except those on the electronically controlled lower tier which the convicts were unable to open.

The whole plot was frustrated at this point because they could not find the key to the door leading to the yard. Miller had retained this key [failing to pass it back to the gallery officer as dictated by protocol], and apparently, he had hidden it so it could not be found by the prisoners. It was an alert and courageous action which spoiled the plan for the inmates to get out into the yard, pick off tower officers with the Springfield rifle, of which they were in possession and thus capture the entire island. When they found they could not get out of the cellblock and into the recreation yard, a complete change in their plans was necessary. They apparently decided then and there to fight it out in the main cellblock.

While the hostages were in the cells, the rioters Coy, Carnes, and Hubbard fired rifle shots at the towers from the dining room. Two rounds at the road tower; two at the dock tower and another two at the hill tower from the bakery. Six empty cartridges were found there. Shockley, Thompson and Cretzer came up to the cells where the hostages were being held. Shockley urged Cretzer to kill all the witnesses. Cretzer emptied the .45 clip into cell #2 hitting Captain Weinhold and Corwin. The others were not hit. Shockley and Thompson kept urging Cretzer to kill all of the witnesses. Cretzer fired three shots into the cell where Simpson, Baker and I [Sundstrom] were being held. He hit Simpson and Baker. He then returned to cell #2 and fired at Mr. Lageson. He was not hit, just grazed. His ear lobe was fiery red. He pretended he was dead. Close shot.

Rioters left the hostages and went elsewhere in the cellhouse, returning at three intervals to see if any hostages were alive. All this time they were still hunting for key #107, the key to the outside cell door. Officers Long, Cochenour, Mullen and Zubke were placed in the east gun gallery. They were able to drive the inmates away from the C and D corridor and away from the hostage cells, but they stayed at the west end of the cellhouse, protected by the cellblock C. Other officers were placed at various posts. Attempts were made at reentering the west gun gallery but they failed as Coy shot at them with the rifle. O'Brien and Green posted in the visitor's room.

Up to this time, it was impossible to locate the cells where the hostages

(Above) A rare photograph of William Miller being loaded into an ambulance at the Van Ness Street Pier.

(Left) Correctional Officer Carl Sundstrom entering the court during the officers' murder trial in December of 1946.

were being held. It was considered necessary to take the cellhouse by assault. The outside entrance to the west gun gallery is an exposed position, offering no cover until the upper gun gallery is reached. Finally, the door was opened and the manning of the gallery was accomplished under direct fire. It was during this action that Officer Stites was wounded fatally and several others less seriously.

In the gallery, the assault team located the officer who had been slugged and tied up, but not wounded. He was set at liberty and armed. From him, they gained definite knowledge of what guns the prisoners had and how they acquired them. Despite the firing of Coy and Cretzer, five armed officers managed to drive the inmates to cover. They were, of course, able to dodge in and out of darkness and scramble to the tops of the blocks; they seemed, in fact, to be everywhere sniping at our officers.

At about 10:00 P.M., Thursday night it was decided to attempt to rescue the hostages. The armed prisoners had apparently gone to the top of the blocks, from where they could fire down on anyone who attempted to enter the main cellhouse. Notwithstanding this, a group of officers in the west gun gallery and other officers accompanying the rescue squad were able to take out all of the wounded officers.

From that time on, the battle was directed at driving the prisoners out of the utilities corridor, in which they barricaded themselves. Holes were punched in the roof of the cellblock and demolition grenades dropped into the utilities corridor.

The entire cellhouse was, of course, shrouded in smoke and darkness and with escaping steam from broken pipes and a haze of tear gas. It seemed an almost impossible job to dislodge the prisoners.

On Saturday morning, after two days of gun fighting, a search of the utilities corridor in C Block was started. The door was opened and volleys of shotgun and rifle fire was directed into the corridor. About four hours later, when there was no answering to the gun fire, two officers with searchlights entered the corridor and found two prisoners dead and one dying. The guns were recaptured and returned to the armory. Of the fifty rounds of rifle ammunition, twenty-five were recovered, but apparently, all of the rounds of revolver ammunition had been used.

Finally, the prisoners were brought under control. The mass escape attempt was over. Every officer did his duty intelligently, and courageously. The federal prison system is proud of their devotion to duty and those who sacrificed themselves to prevent the release of nearly three hundred desperate prisoners. Alcatraz remains impregnable...

In the final hours, with no place left to hide from the ceaseless gunfire, Cretzer, Coy, and Hubbard retreated to the utility corridor in C Block for shelter. Carnes later remembered:

> I wanted to quit right after the siren went off. But I felt if I did—you see, Cook, one of the main participants in this thing, was supposed to have a hole going through the roof. They talk about the key 109 (correctly 107) now on the tour, that had nothing to do with the break. That was just bullshit...The way to go was up through that skylight. There was a scaffold, right by this radiator here, and Cook was supposed to be in charge of getting that thing up there, call the guard on the roof and tell him the maintenance crew's gonna

(left) An officer standing in front of the cells (the end of C Block) where the officers were held hostage and shot.

(Below) Warden Johnston peers into Cell #403 where Officer William Miller was fatally shot.

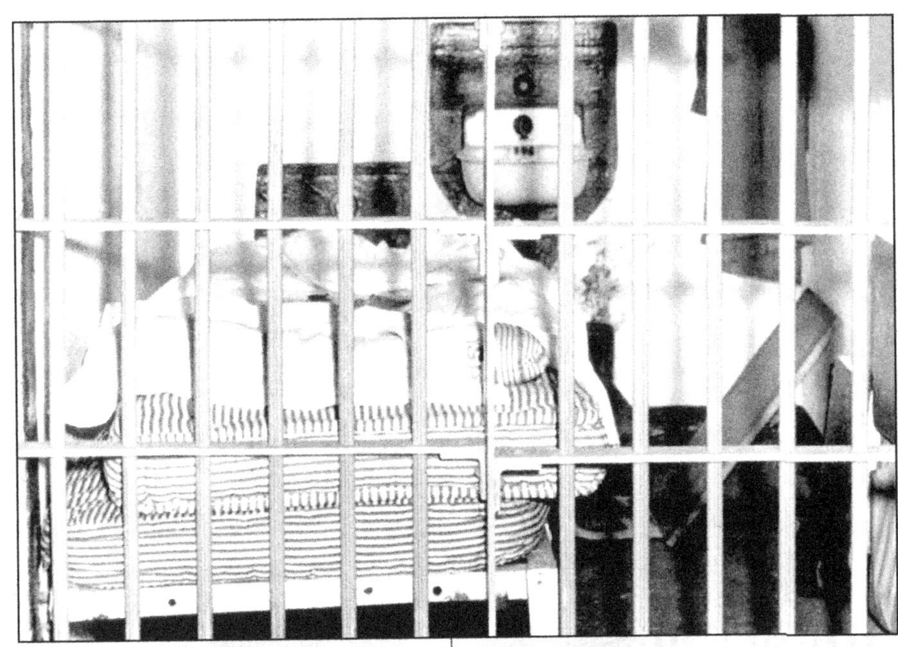

(Above and left) Views of the bloodstained walls of cell #403, where several officers were shot in cold blood by Joseph Cretzer.

(Below) Behind the bed frame to keep it concealed, Correctional Officer Ernest Lageson scrawled the names of the conspirators on the cell wall, circling the names of the ringleaders. This would prove to be a key piece of evidence in the trial of the surviving inmates.

(Top) Marines firing anti-tank mortars into D Block. The mortars were fired from the grassy slopes and loud explosions could be heard on the mainland as they slammed into the exterior walls of the prison.

(Middle) Armed Marines guarding prisoners from the yard wall catwalk. The prisoners who were at work in the industries when the escape attempt took place were rallied into the recreation yard and given blankets and boxed meals until they could safely reenter the cellhouse on May 4th.

(Bottom) Officers carefully peering into D Block through the mangled steel wreckage; aftermath of the military artillery fired into the prison.

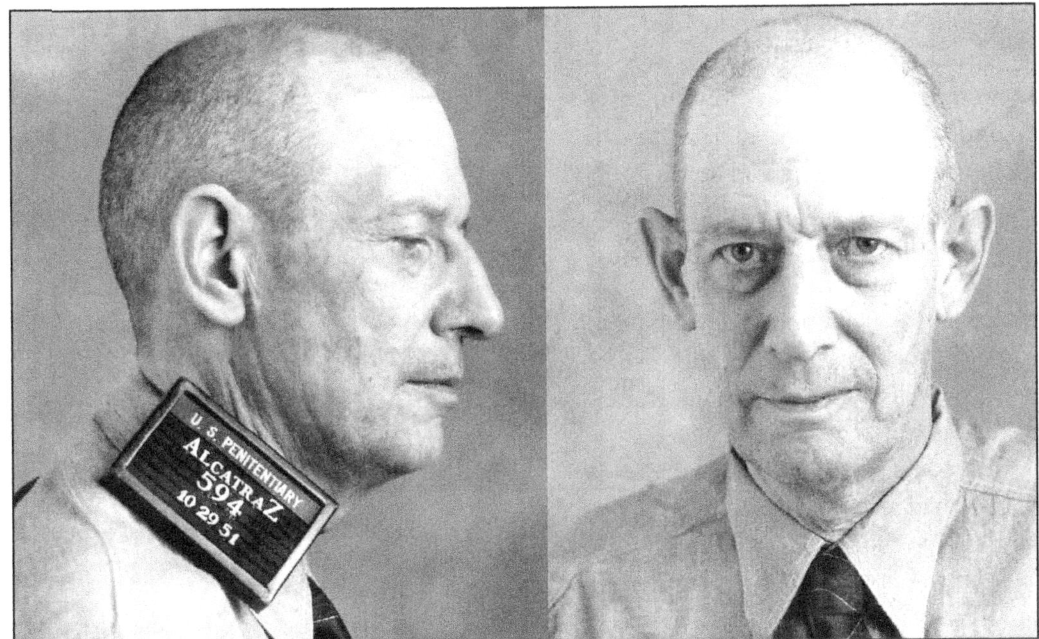

be working on the skylight, and then after we got into the skylight, call him again so we'd know exactly where he was, and look at him through one of the cracks—that are still in that skylight, by the way—and there would be two guys in that skylight. One would get a hammer and knock a hole in the skylight and put a rifle through it and take over the roof; then come down, take over the armory and cut off all communications, so that by the time we reached Frisco nothing would be stirring over there until we hit land and started getting cars, for transportation out of there.

When the siren went off, Hamilton was up there with me, and Cook was hiding behind some boxes. We didn't know where he was at that time. And then the siren went off and I knew it was over and I should go back to my cell, but I also knew when the siren went off and they said, "Where's

(Above) Robert Stroud, the infamous "Birdman of Alcatraz" was barricaded in Cell #41, located on the upper tier of D Block during the battle.

(Below) Edgar Cook

Cook? Where's that goddamned son-of-a-bitch at?" that they were gonna be looking for him, and if I go ahead and quit without saying anything and go back to my cell, then maybe they'll be looking for me too. So I just held on until finally they did have the talk around in C Block. And Shockley said "I'm going to my cell," and Thompson said "I'm going to my cell..." and I had some papers and maps that Coy had given me and I burnt those on the floor.

It was at that point the guys decided to die, and they even saved some bullets for themselves. Very calmly, Coy, who always called me 'Old Man,' says "Well, Old Man, what are you going to do?" and I said, "Well, I was just thinking, if I do ten years in lock-up, I'll still be young when I get out – twenty nine. I think I can stand that and maybe get another chance." And he says, "I think that's a good idea... I'm going to be going myself." So there were gun guards up there (east gun gallery) by that time, and I ran across Broadway before anybody had a chance to shoot me. And then he'd told me to unlock the door, which had been locked when I came out. So I worked the levers like he told me, and I raised my hand like that (good-bye gesture) and that was the last time I saw them. They died that night...

A prisoner held in A Block during the Battle of Alcatraz scratched the message "Hell Broke Luce" into one of the soft iron bars.

Cretzer, Coy, and Hubbard were killed in the corridor by bullets and shrapnel. Carnes later confided to James "Whitey" Bulger (AZ-1428), that he thought he was going to be shot dead in his cell. Bulger remembered:

"Joe said he was sitting on the toilet, heard a noise and looked up; Mahan had a .45 caliber pistol pointed straight at him through the bars. He thought it was the end of him, but Mahan just stoically gestured with a wave of the pistol and walked him over to A Block. Mahan just walked casually through the cellhouse with the pistol in hand for all the convicts to see... He felt like Mahan was looking for a reason to take him out..."

Carnes remembered after being removed from his cell:

They (guards) took me to the top of the A Block cells and stripped me down and came in yelling with guns pointed at me. And then one Lieutenant with a pistol and Jughead

(Above and right) Bodies of the dead convicts being loaded for transport to the coroner's office.

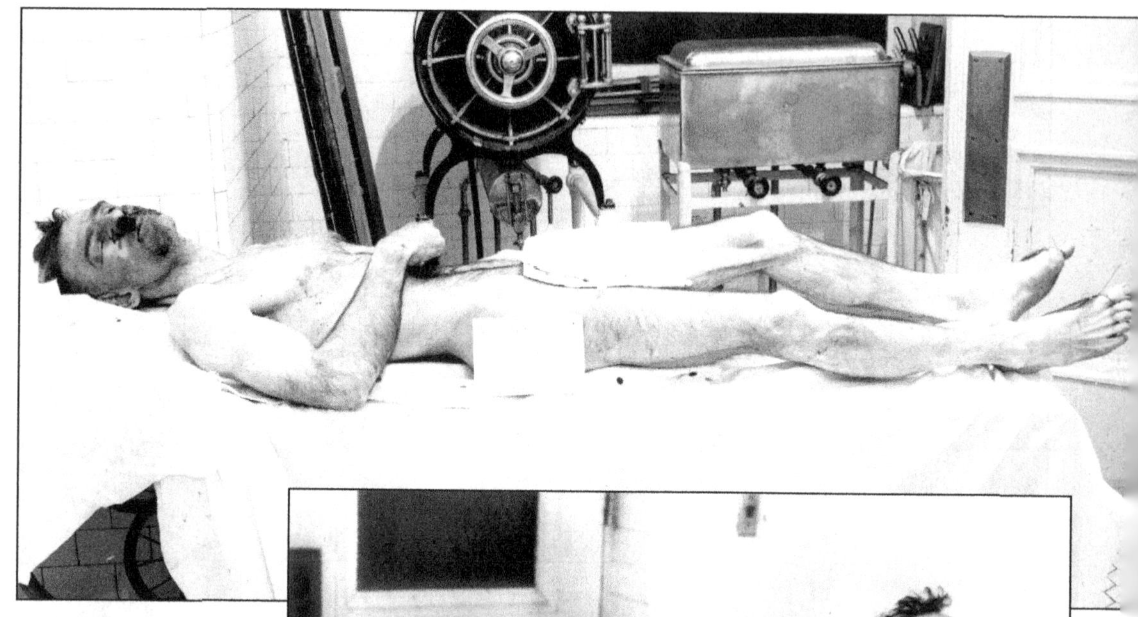

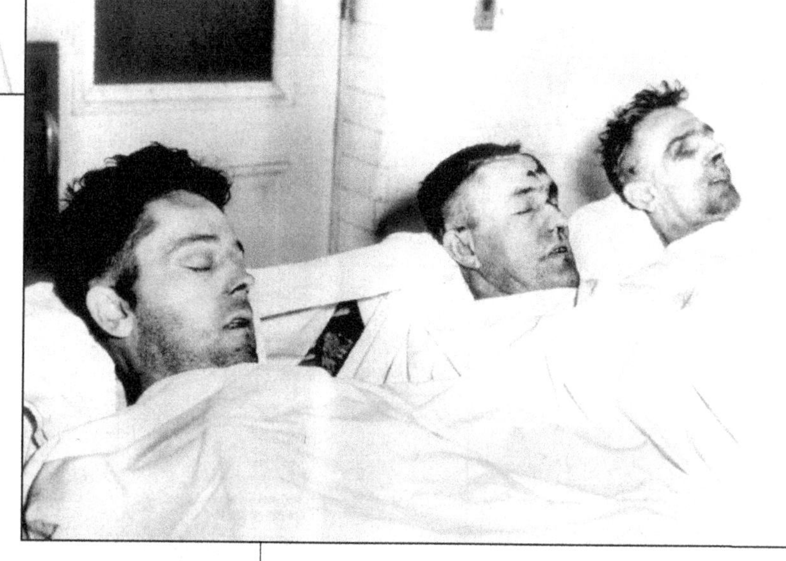

Coy, Cretzer and Hubbard at the San Francisco County Coroner's Office just prior to their autopsies. The photographs showed the brutality of the events and their deaths. Of special interest is the state of Coy's body. He had used extreme dieting to slip between the bars of the gun gallery.

(Associate Warden Miller), and also another associate warden took me up there and Jughead started beating on me. I thought they took me up there to kill me, because only one person came up with a pistol, and I thought, they're going to say that I tried to take the gun away and they shot me... So when Jughead started beating on me, it was the first time, and the only time in my life I was glad to be beaten, cause I knew then they weren't going to shoot me.

Officer William Miller died from his injuries, and Officer Harold Stites was killed by friendly fire during the attempt to regain control of the cellhouse. On December 22, 1946, Shockley and Thompson were sentenced to death following a month long trial for their role in the murder of Officer Miller. As Thompson was being led from the courtroom he commented to reporters: "It's just as well! I'd rather have it that way than go back to the Rock!" Both men were later executed seated side by side in the gas chamber at San Quentin.

Clarence "Joe" Carnes being led to court during a later appeal. Carnes, along with Shockley and Thompson were convicted of the first-degree murder of William Miller. Shockley and Thompson were given the death penalty for their role in the crime, and sentenced to die in the gas chamber at San Quentin. Carnes was spared the death penalty; instead he received an additional life sentence. Among the mitigating factors cited was the leniency he had demonstrated toward the officers held hostage, which ultimately saved their lives. Shockley and Thompson were transferred from Alcatraz to San Quentin, the State Penitentiary in Marin County to serve until their date of execution.

Joe Carnes was only a teenager when he took his place in the escape, and jurors extended leniency to him based on his age and inside accounts that he was told to finish off any officers who moved, but he showed mercy... Carnes later acknowledged that he attempted to spare the lives of the officers. He remembered:

> Weinhold's belly was laying wide open. He had no pants on and his shirt flapped up and his white belly was going up and down. Simpson was unconscious but breathing... And it was obvious that the mail clerk (Carl Sundstrom) was holding his breath. So I knew they were alive. I didn't know if they were all alive, but I knew that that some of them were. But I went back and said, "They're all dead," because at the age of nineteen I couldn't see any purpose in this...

Carnes would receive an additional ninety-nine year sentence to run concurrent with the life sentence he was already serving.

Thompson and Shockley were executed seated side by side on December 3, 1948.

Record Form No. 8
(July, 1936)

CONDUCT RECORD

DEPARTMENT OF JUSTICE
Penal and Correctional Institutions

U. S. PENITENTIARY (Institution) ALCATRAZ, CALIFORNIA (Location)

Record of THOMPSON, Miran Edgar No. 729-AZ

FPI—LK—4-7-42—6M—888-6

Date	Prison Violations	Days Lost
5-4-46	Joining in desperate escape attempt, and riot with other inmates attacking officers, with use of firearms & other weapons, causing death to officers & wounding others, May 2, 1946. TO SOLITARY A-BLOCK, 5-4-46.	
5-10-46	OUT OF SOLITARY INTO SEGREGATION D BLOCK	
12-21-46	FOUND GUILTY OF MURDER IN FIRST DEGREE BY JURY AT SAN FRANCISCO, CALIFORNIA AND SENTENCED TO DEATH, SAME DAY. 12-27-46 TRANSFERRED TO SAN QUENTIN, CALIF. ST. PRISON. Date of Execution set for Sept. 24, 1948, by Judge Louis Goodman, on June 29, 1948. Executed 12-3-48 S.Q. gas chamber	

Following the bloody battle, the Bureau of Prisons took quick action to facilitate security enhancements to the main cellhouse structure. Gun ports and vision panels were installed around the various exterior walls, in addition to the visitors' room, administration area, library, and outer wall of the barbershop. Gun ports were also installed in the gun galleries, along with wrapping the barred sections in a steel mesh wire to remove the ability for weapons to be passed through the bars. Steel bracings were installed to strengthen the bars that wrapped over the top of the galleries to prevent future attempts at spreading them open. A stairway shielded by a steel plate was added on the south wall to connect both tiers of the east gallery, and the stairway entrances to the hospital and down to the basement were strengthened with a steel wire mesh.

Carnes carried with him the stories of the battle, and he served his time quietly, mostly as a model prisoner. But some officers remained suspicious of him... Behind his soft-spoken and calm demeanor, he still watched the officers; studying their routines; studied the failures of the other later escapes, and he became one of the most trusted convicts on Alcatraz. In 1962, when Frank Morris, John and Clarence and West were plotting their epic prison break, Carnes was brought in as a partner. He knew Alcatraz better than anyone...

> "One of my motives to help them was that once convicts escaped from Alcatraz and stepped foot on San Francisco soil; that would be it... They would close Alcatraz..."

Band of Brothers

"There was a lot of talk... a lot of bullshit talk... You don't know how to separate the wheat from the shaft, like the saying goes. But these two kids, these guys, were solid son of a bitches. I wanna believe they made it..."

—MICKEY COHEN, AZ-1518

ALFRED, JOHN, AND CLARENCE ANGLIN were the middle children of fourteen; seven boys and seven girls. Their siblings remembered them as being fun loving, energetic and playful brothers, but all three with an adventurous and mischievous streak. The three shared an extraordinary bond... Their mischief as teenagers eventually evolved into serious crimes and spectacular prison breaks, but it was a single bank robbery that would change their course in destiny...

They were born in succession; Alfred Ray on October 12, 1928; John William on May 12, 1930; and Clarence on May 11, 1931; the latter two, exactly one year and one day apart. All were born in Donalsonville, Georgia. They did everything as a trio. They roller-skated; watched movies; worked the crop fields; worked on cars; chased girls; swam the turbulent waters of Tampa Bay; robbed banks; and in prison, they even plotted to breakout together...

The Anglins' were a large and close knit clan... Their mother and father, George and Rachel were married in Henry County, Alabama, in 1919. George was twenty-two, a carpenter and farmer by trade, and his young bride, Rachel, was only sixteen years of age when they married. Both had been raised on farms in rural Georgia, and were only afforded first grade educations. They had worked their entire lives farming. George had honorably served in the United States Army during the end of World War I, and using the little money he had from his military service, he bought a small farm just outside of Donalsonville, Georgia, where they started their family. They were simple, modest and hard-working people. George was a pillar of faith and considered in the community as a man of his word. He was active in the church, and the importance of instilling good values into his children was paramount to everything. Rachel's

The Anglin children in Ruskin, Florida, during the 1940s. John Anglin is seen sitting center on the hood of the automobile and Clarence on the left.

cousin was a preacher and George took on the task to help build a neighborhood church just outside of Colquitt, Georgia, milling the lumber from pine trees cut on his own property. He took a lot of pride in doing something so noble. Each week, he loaded his children into a buggy that was pulled by the family mules to attend services. The Anglin sisters remembered it was a loving and idyllic childhood despite the severe hardships they encountered during the Great Depression. In 1936, Rachel lost her baby, Tommy, right after giving birth and she was sick thereafter for a long period.

By 1938, the family had grown to eleven, and with Rachel again pregnant, George was struggling to keep food on the table. Farming communities were hit hard by the Great Depression and advancing technology. The introduction of motorized farming machinery resulted in massive job cuts and plummeting crop prices. The work that was available paid near poverty wages, and when the children were not in school, they were forced to work the fields to help support the family. The backbreaking work was exhausting...The older daughters were tasked with babysitting, laundry and meals, while the boys

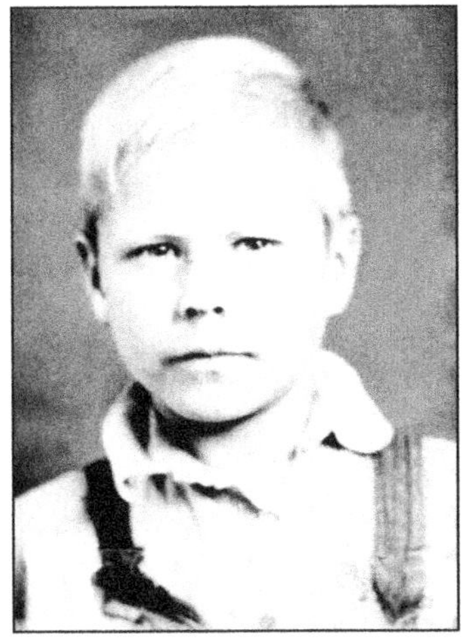
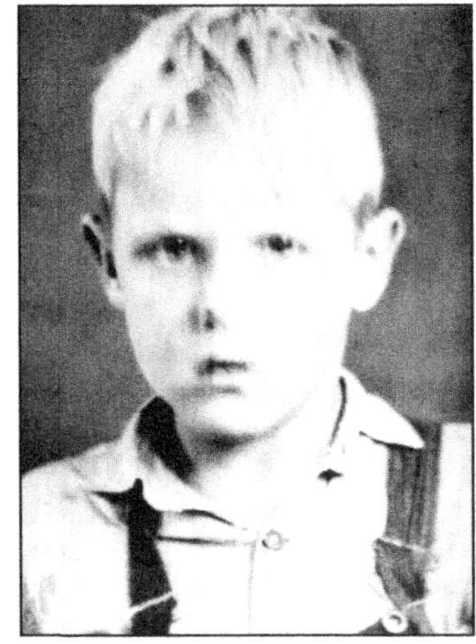
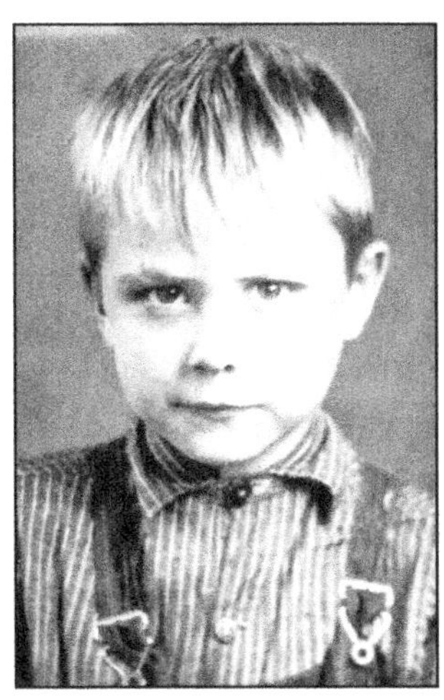

(Left to right) Alfred Ray Anglin at ten years of age; John William Anglin at nine; Clarence Anglin at eight.

worked in the fields. Rachel would spend most of her time at the sewing machine making all of the children's clothing. The soft cloth from flour sacks was used for shirts, pillow cases, and underwear. No fabric was wasted... Even the bags of fertilizer were used to make overalls for the boys. On occasion, the Salvation Army helped provide secondhand clothing that the children usually wore for school and Sunday services. The family also generated most of their own food supply, and what they couldn't produce on their own like sugar and coffee; they bartered with meats from animals they raised on the farm, along with eggs, cultivated crops and berries. As the children grew older, and the costs of raising their family swelled, they followed the crops in spring and summer, migrating as far north as Michigan and south into Florida.

In 1939, a year after moving to the Donalsonville property, Rufus, the oldest brother was struck with tragedy. Rufus left home at seventeen to work in a construction battalion at Fort Benning in Georgia. While using a sling-blade to clear brush, he struck an undetonated explosive that had been dropped during an air bombing practice run. It was a life changing event for both Rufus and the family. He lost one of his legs and after nearly a year in veteran hospitals, he came home and assumed a working role on the farm with the family. It was a difficult adjustment for Rufus as he was high-spirited and the handicap made work more difficult.

There were other pressures that also had been mounting... Years earlier, George's father died unexpectedly of influenza at only fifty-two. In destitute, he took in his mother, sister and brother adding burden in having to provide for them. In the same year that Rufus was injured, George's mother died of a heart attack... Verna, the oldest daughter, now seventeen, married and left home... She remained close by, and continued to work the crop fields, but with the loss of Verna and their grandmother, most of their daily chores to

Clarence Anglin at thirteen.

Born only a year and one day apart, brothers John and Clarence Anglin were very close throughout their lives. In this childhood photo, they are posing in front of one of the many rivers they swam during their youth.

keep the household running shifted to the younger children.

George and Rachel moved the family to Brandon, Florida, attempting to provide a better quality of life, but as the children grew older, so did their awareness of their hardships. There was mounting frustration and embarrassment of their poverty. As the children went to school, they were embarrassed by their clothing, and one by one, they started to shift their focus from future to present. They dropped from school to work and help with the finances. The older siblings tried to provide nicer clothing and other luxuries to the younger ones.

Despite so many hardships and the poverty stricken conditions that surrounded them, they all remained close. All of the children looked back at their childhood in the Anglin home with reverence and admiration of their parents. Jeanette Anglin, the wife of Alfred remembered: "There was a lot of love and harmony in that home. There was so much laughter; they were all really close. I admired them that way... You could sense the goodness in those people. They made me feel like I was family the minute I walked through their door..."

In 1944, Verna and her husband migrated to central Florida and brought back news of the prospering economy. Field work was plentiful and there was a lot of money to be made harvesting oranges, strawberries and other varieties. George had received back funds from the military and decided to purchase a plot of twenty acres located on Shell Point Road in Ruskin, Florida. The property lined with tall pine and palm trees, was located less than a few miles from the ocean and was an ideal climate for cultivating vegetable crops.

Using lumber from trees cut on the property, he built a small two-bedroom, 900 square foot home. It was functional, but meager at best.

The Shell Point roadway was a long straight stretch that dead-ended at the ocean waters of Tampa Bay. Bahia Beach was just walking distance and offered a welcome diversion from the financial instability that had plagued them throughout their lives. Bahia Beach became a favorite hangout for the boys. There were girls sunbathing during the spring and summer months, and there were close-by lakes and waterways that offered a means to cool off during the extremes of heat, and competitive water sports to feed their adventurous spirits. Less than ten miles from home was Lake Wimauma, which also became a favorite swimming hole for the boys. John had become even more adept in the water

The entire Anglin family worked the family farm and together helped cultivate seasonal crops.

(Above) The brothers were inseparable and rarely seen apart.

(Left) Even in work, the boys were together. Rufus Anglin overlooks John (left to right), Robert, Alfred and Clarence as they plant strawberries.

(Right) Clarence (left) showing John (right) a pistol during a work break.

(Left) The house on Shell Point in Ruskin built by George and his older sons.

(Below) The Bahia Beach Resort, located at the end of Shell Point Road. The beaches of the resort on the Tampa Bay was just a short walk from their home. It was a favorite hangout for the brothers.

and during one trip he won a competition for swimming across the 650 yard lake in record time.

They also continued to travel and work with the family helping provide support. Wherever they traveled, you could find the brothers either in or close to the water. Their sister Marie Anglin, born only a few years apart from John and Clarence, had fond memories watching them jump from a dock on Lake Superior's southern tip in Michigan and breaking the ice. In late May they would travel to Michigan to pick cherries. They were strong swimmers and would jump in and out of the water in subfreezing temperatures challenging each other to see who could endure the freezing cold the longest. Marie also remembered another time where a fisherman had lost his outboard motor down in deep waters.

(Left and right) Clarence as a teenager.

He offered $20.00 to anyone who could locate the motor and tie a rope so that it could be salvaged. John went on a mission, and after long searches holding his breath underwater, he located the motor and claimed his prize. There was another time when their sister Christine almost drowned during an outing at Lake Wimauma. The boys sprung to action and pulled her from water. As she gasped for air, the boys who were unfazed, simply wrapped her in a towel and after ensuring her safety, went straight back into the chilled water.

The boys were always competing and showing off. They jumped from high bridges into the deep waterways, and even during the winter months when the waters of Bahia Beach dipped in to the low 50's, the boys swam deep into the bay waters. But life in Ruskin would also be a turning point for Alfred, John and Clarence...

School for the boys became increasingly difficult. They were the new kids in Ruskin and picked on constantly. Academically, they received excellent grades. So proud was their mother, she saved their report cards even into their adulthood, but socially, all three struggled. Their sister Verna remembered:

> "They hated school because they were always getting teased because of their clothes. None of us had nice clothes and the boys were especially ashamed. My mother often had to patch their trousers in the worn spots

(Top) The Florida Industrial School for Boys, in Marianna where Clarence was sentenced to serve time for various crimes during his youth.

(Middle and bottom) The Adam's Cottage where Clarence was housed at the Industrial School for Boys.

and it got to the point where they were too embarrassed to be seen in them. They were just teenagers and got fed-up with being cackled at every day. I think they just decided that enough was enough...They started skipping school and would swim all day and then only come home at night. They started stealing and getting into trouble about that time. It was really difficult for them being constantly tormented by the other kids at that age. My parents did the best they could, but times were hard back then...They really loved them boys and gave them the best of what they could, but it just wasn't enough. Those boys were not hurtful to anyone...They just didn't want to be seen as being poor...And our family being as big as it was, we were as poor as it gets..."

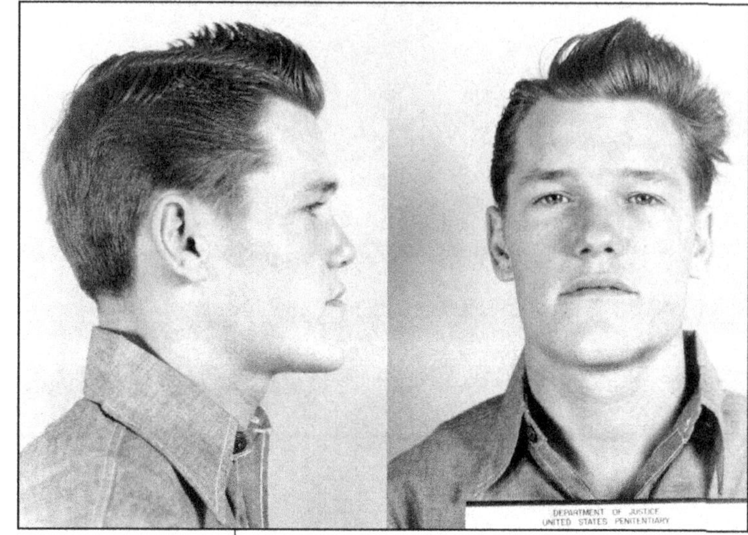

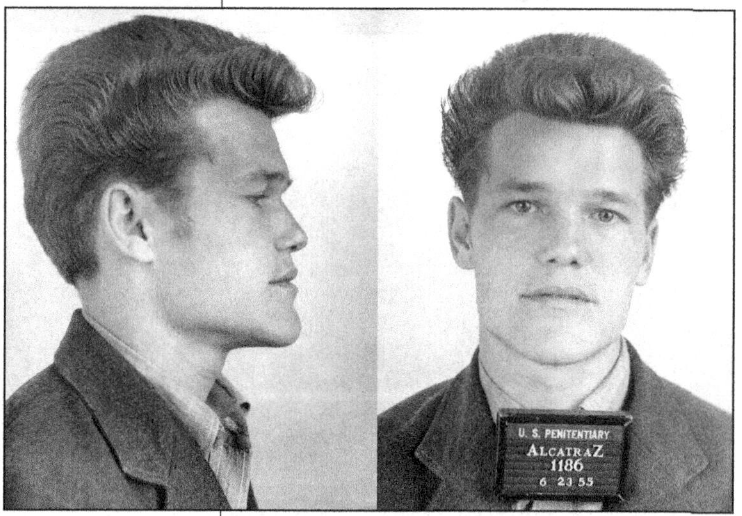

(Top and bottom) Charlie Hopkins was a childhood friend of Clarence and both served time together at Marianna (both were housed in the Adam's Cottage). Hopkins would later serve time on Alcatraz for robbery and kidnapping charges.

By 1945, Alfred, John and Clarence were playing hooky from school almost daily. By day, they were breaking into homes when people were away at work, and at night, they were breaking into businesses stealing items in order to buy things like clothes and cigarettes.

On June 19, 1945, Clarence now only fourteen years of age, was committed to the Hillsborough County, Florida, Juvenile Court and charged with "truancy, incorrigibility, breaking and entering, and grand larceny."

(Top, middle and bottom) Photographs of John Anglin and Clarence in the late 1950s. Clarence was an avid guitarist and later played extensively in his cell on Alcatraz.

On July 6, 1945, Clarence was officially deemed "incorrigible" (based on both his crime and truancy) by a juvenile court judge, and sentenced to serve one year at the Florida Industrial School for Boys, in Marianna. John followed right behind Clarence and was sentenced to serve nine months at the reformatory.

The school housed about six-hundred boys, all committed throughout the State of Florida for "delinquent and incorrigible acts" by juvenile courts. The facility was located just over 350 miles north of Ruskin, making it difficult for family visits. It was considered a

Alfred and John Anglin.

tough reformatory, especially for such young boys.

The institution was housed at the center of a 1,200 acre plot of land, and provided occupational training primarily in industrial and agricultural subjects. The focus was on work and education, teaching the boys usable skills they could use once released, and the living conditions were grim at best. It included a building for severe disciplinary cases, known as the "White House," as its exterior and interior were painted all white, and the interior housed isolation cells for extreme cases.

Clarence was housed in the "Adam's Cottage," along with Charlie Hopkins, a friend he'd known on the outside who also later wound up serving time on Alcatraz. The cottage was a small, overcrowded building that consisted of an open space dorm style room upstairs where the boys slept. At Marianna, Clarence was constantly plotting to escape. When Special Agent Charles Carroll from the FBI examined his case file in 1962, he found Clarence had made three attempts to escape from the school in 1945 alone. He was released to his mother on August 26, 1946, but charged again with similar crimes and was returned on January 25, 1947, and served there until December 10, 1947. His sisters remember Clarence remarked that all his time was spent with other thieves, and he was mentored in the art of theft and robbery. He learned skills such as picking locks and hot wiring cars.

Upon their release, the boys went back to their conflicted lives working in the fields, and without ever once complaining, gave their money to the family to help with expenses. Billie Anglin, the wife of their brother Robert recalled about the Anglins' mother and their early crimes:

> "They were on her mind every day of her life. They were good boys she would say with tears in her eyes... 'I just don't understand why they do the things that they do. They're good boys.' What they made working was just not enough to help the family and have enough left over for their needs and wants. You can't give them everything they need, much less the things they want. It is really hard to see your children going down the wrong path in life and all you can do is pray for them, and keep hope that God will help turn them around before they get into something too big they can't get out of..."

As the three brothers spiraled deeper into a life of crime, their family was left powerless and could only watch from the sidelines... They bought cars, new clothes, and expensive dinners, but when questioned they would answer that they had jobs and worked for the money, but everyone else knew better. Their sister Marie remembered her brothers fondly and was especially close with John. Whenever he was home, he would take her and her sisters shopping to buy clothes, shoes and other luxury items that they were otherwise not able to afford. She recalled when John took her to dinner at Kelly's Bar & Grill Restaurant in Ruskin. Their specialty was a stacked ham sandwich and it was a favorite of the boys. On this occasion, John and Marie both enjoyed a large

(Above and left) In 1950, John, Clarence, Alfred along with childhood friend Kenneth Busbee embarked on a cross-country trip to California. Armed with only a stolen camera, syphon hose (to steal fuel) and a BB gun, they traveled across the United States committing petty crimes to help fund their travels and mischievous adventures. Pictured is Kenneth, Alfred and John.

(Right) John Anglin and Kenneth Busbee at the Antelope Buffalo Refuge in Arizona in 1950.

steak dinner with all the trimmings. When they were ready to leave, John pulled from his pocket a wad of cash and dumped it on the counter and walked out without taking his change. The act caught the attention of everyone. When she asked him why he did that, he said simply, "I want them to know I was there . . . " The boys wanted to give their family a better life.

In November of 1948, John and Clarence were again arrested for petty larceny, but the charges were dropped and they were released from custody after only a few days. A year later, when John was nineteen, he landed a well-paying job as the manager of a roller-skating rink. The owners, impressed by his demeanor, placed him in charge and he soon became popular with locals also taking part in various skating competitions. He was a natural on skates, and the Anglin clan enjoyed coming to watch him compete.

(Above) Clarence, Kenneth and John (Alfred snapped the photo).

(Left) Alfred, Kenneth and John.

(Below) Clarence photographed in Arizona.

The Florida State Penitentiary at Raiford.

But when the roller rink moved out of Ruskin, John fell back into his former lifestyle along with his brothers.

In 1950, Alfred, John and Clarence along with their friend Kenneth Busbee, decided to go on a trip cross country to California and back. With no money, and armed only with a syphon hose, a gas can, a stolen camera and a BB gun, they headed west in John's 1936 Ford Deluxe Sedan, committing numerous late night burglaries to finance their trip. It would be the trip of a lifetime, and one they'd reminisce about during their later years in prison.

The boys continued in and out of trouble, rotating in and out of jail. However, whenever arrested, they would take responsibility for their crimes and never protest their sentencing. In late 1950, Clarence was arrested again for a burglary charge and sentenced to serve hard time in a labor camp, which usually translated to work on a chain-gang in soaring hot and humid temperatures. They were no longer juveniles, and now being treated as adult felons.

On November 19, 1951, John pleaded guilty to grand larceny and was sentenced to serve two years at the Florida State Penitentiary in Raiford. His case file read:

> He and accomplices John D. Miller and William Earl Pryor stole batteries, oil, and tools from tractors parked in fields of Ruskin Florida farms. Batteries were sold near Tampa. Pryor's license plate was noted by the purchaser which led to his arrest.

On May 3, 1951, Clarence burglarized a dry cleaning establishment in Tampa, and got away with a small sum of money, but would soon be arrested. In June of 1951, Clarence would get

During one of his bold escapes, Clarence was able to evade capture by running through rough swampy terrain and hiding in the black waters of the Suwannee River.

four years for his burglary related crimes, simultaneously with a five year term from neighboring Hillsborough County for additional breaking and entering charges. Clarence would again be sent to serve his time working hard labor road camps, and again, he would escape. His FBI file reads:

> He escaped on January 6, 1952 from the State Road Prison, Perry Florida, and was recaptured on April 3, 1952. He made another escape (the file contains no details of date missing) and on April 29, 1952, he broke into an office at the Mayorette Drive-In Theatre located in Tallahassee, Florida, and stole a typewriter. He was recaptured by the Sheriff's Office, Hernando County, on May 14, 1952. On July 19, 1952, Clarence Anglin and Roger James Hill escaped from the State Road Prison, Pompano, Florida. They remained together after the escape and stole a car. Apprehended by North Miami Police Department July 19, 1952. He received an additional five years for this auto larceny on July 22, 1952. As of 1959, Roger James Hill was in the Nevada State Penitentiary, Carson City, Nevada. Clarence Anglin escaped the State Road Prison, Floral City, Florida, November 29, 1953. Recaptured same day, had one buckshot wound to his left arm. His final escape was made on February 14, 1957 from the State Road Prison, Fort Myers, Florida, and he was never again returned to the Florida State Prison system.

In May of 1952, Clarence talked about his escaping the road camp in a letter to his mother dated May 5, 1952. He had evaded capture by running through rough swampy terrain and hiding in the black waters of the Suwannee

The "Sweat Box" at Raiford. Clarence would be forced to serve time inside this device as a punishment for his escapes.

River near Perry, Florida. In an act of desperation, as a bloodhound closed in and began barking to alert searchers of his find, he lured and silenced the dog, then sent his carcass floating quietly down the river. Keeping a low profile in the water, Clarence floated along the downstream current making his way to the other side. He recalled his capture in a letter written to his mother in 1952:

> "After running from that camp, and going right back there, they put chains on me, put me in the sweat box, and shot tear gas on me. They tried to make me say I killed a dog, but they never found out... I tried to write you all, but they put me in the sweat box every time I wrote. So if you all blame me for leaving, well I can't help it..."

His time served at the State prisons and road camps proved to be hard time. During the same year, the State of Florida had 3,860 prisoners being held in its road camps and penitentiaries, with more than half of that number serving time at Raiford. Frank Lee Morris had also served time at Raiford a few years earlier in 1949 for similar charges, and it would be at Raiford that John would meet one of the co-conspirators of their Alcatraz escape, Allen West, who was also serving time there for breaking and entering charges.

In some of Clarence's prison letters to home, he would ask his mother to bring his guitar, but in the next letter, would tell her not to bring it, as if it were an indicator of another planned escape. Billie Anglin remembered the 1957 Valentine's Day escape:

> "We took Granny down to Fort Meyers to see Clarence. We took dinner and had a picnic with him. We left about 4:00 in the afternoon coming back home. At 7:30 that evening Clarence called Verna to go tell Robert to come to the Hubba Hub Drive-In in Palmetto and pick him up. He left right after we did and almost beat us back home. Robert went to and picked him up and JW

took him to Haines City, where Alfred was. He was wet from head to toe. He had waded through all the swamps and rivers between Ruskin and Fort Meyers. Robert took him some dry clothes to change into. It's a blessing he didn't get shot at . . . The law didn't even come to the house looking for him. He had been out about a year when they done the bank robbery. Alfred had been out about five years."

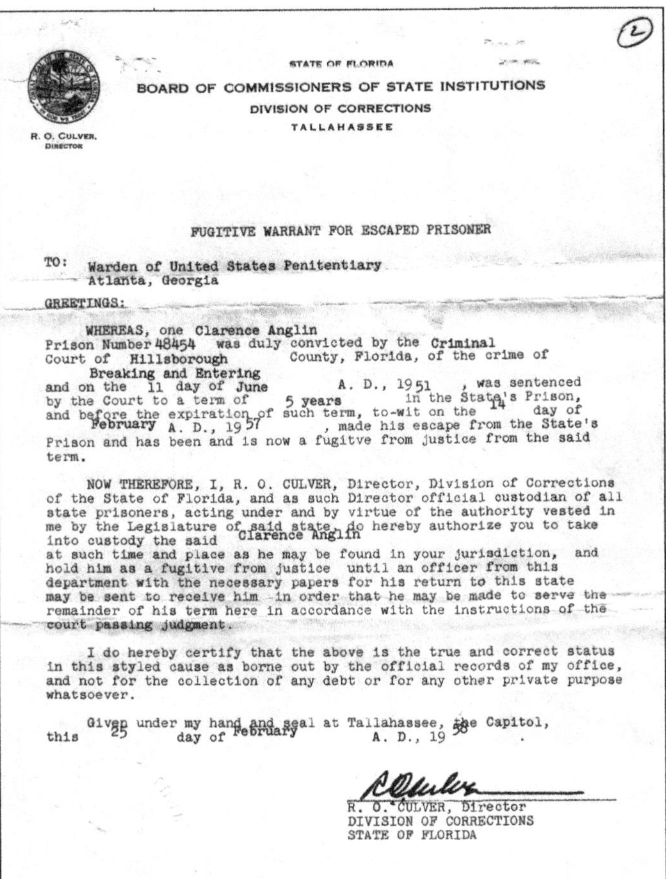

(2)

R. O. CULVER, DIRECTOR

STATE OF FLORIDA
BOARD OF COMMISSIONERS OF STATE INSTITUTIONS
DIVISION OF CORRECTIONS
TALLAHASSEE

FUGITIVE WARRANT FOR ESCAPED PRISONER

TO: Warden of United States Penitentiary
Atlanta, Georgia

GREETINGS:

WHEREAS, one Clarence Anglin Prison Number 48454 was duly convicted by the Criminal Court of Hillsborough County, Florida, of the crime of Breaking and Entering and on the 11 day of June A. D., 1951, was sentenced by the Court to a term of 5 years in the State's Prison, and before the expiration of such term, to-wit on the 14 day of February A. D., 1957, made his escape from the State's Prison and has been and is now a fugitve from justice from the said term.

NOW THEREFORE, I, R. O. CULVER, Director, Division of Corrections of the State of Florida, and as such Director official custodian of all state prisoners, acting under and by virtue of the authority vested in me by the Legislature of said state, do hereby authorize you to take into custody the said Clarence Anglin at such time and place as he may be found in your jurisdiction, and hold him as a fugitive from justice until an officer from this department with the necessary papers for his return to this state may be sent to receive him in order that he may be made to serve the remainder of his term here in accordance with the instructions of the court passing judgment.

I do hereby certify that the above is the true and correct status in this styled cause as borne out by the official records of my office, and not for the collection of any debt or for any other private purpose whatsoever.

Given under my hand and seal at Tallahassee, the Capitol, this 25 day of February A. D., 1958.

R. O. Culver
R. O. CULVER, Director
DIVISION OF CORRECTIONS
STATE OF FLORIDA

A 1950s fugitive warrant for Clarence following an escape in 1957. Ironically, Director Richard O. Culver who signed the warrant, once served under Warden Johnston as a lieutenant on Alcatraz Island.

Alfred Anglin came close to matching his brother's record of jail breaks. Alfred was already twenty-two when he was first arrested for burglary and auto theft, and received consecutive terms of four and five years, and ran away three times before his final break in December of 1954. At that time he had fifteen years of sentences to serve. He assumed his brother Robert's name and identification. Robert and Alfred were exactly two years apart in age, and their appearance was close enough to fool law enforcement. No one knew Alfred by his own name, not even his future wife Jeanette Anderson who met Alfred when she was only fifteen years of age. She remembered:

> Back in 1957, during spring break, I was staying with my sister Thelma in Haines City, Florida. It was during this time that I'd met Alfred Ray Anglin, but I knew him as Robert Ray. One Sunday my sister let me go to the movies with him. He took me to the Ritz in Winter Haven, and we watched the movie Purple Mask with Tony Curtis. After that, we started dating and became inseparable. We went everywhere together. We went to so many drive-in movies.
>
> Then one day, I can't remember the month, but when I was at school, the FBI came to talk to me. I acted dumb,

Alfred and his future wife Jeanette Anderson.

but I knew that it was really serious if the FBI was coming to ask questions. They wanted to know if I knew Alfred. I told them that I didn't know an Alfred Anglin. I only knew Robert. I warned him by sending a note to JW's girlfriend Helen that the FBI had come to my school to interview me. I didn't see Alfred for a while after that incident, but then sometime later, I noticed JW's Thunderbird drive by in front of the school. I was so nervous that the FBI would still be around, so I hid. That night, Alfred came to my house and hid in the orange grove across the road. I came out on the porch and I heard him whisper my name from across the street. I snuck over to the other side of the road and we talked... We made plans for him to pick me up at the school bus stop in Helen's car. We went to her house in Tampa and right away made plans to get married. The following day we drove up to Statenville, Georgia, got married, then came back to stay in a small cabin in Tampa.

Not long after, JW's girlfriend Helen insisted that I travel to Ohio with her... I really didn't want to go but she was so insistent, and kept on-and-on until I went. She knew what was going to happen. I can't prove it, but I think she knew... We stayed at her dad's house for a few days and then the boys met up with us. Alfred and I stayed in the upstairs apartment next door. JW stayed at Helen's dad's house, and Clarence, who had just bought a brand new Pontiac Convertible, stayed in a close by motel. I honestly had no idea of what was to come...

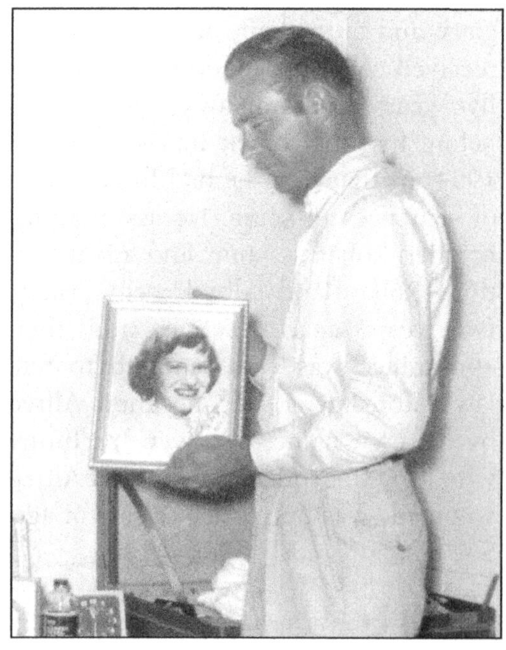

Clarence holding a photo of his girlfriend Ruth. John was dating Ruth's sister Helen.

The Robbery

"When I come out of Lewisburg, I intended to go straight. I got me a job and did go straight. I lost that job, and couldn't find another one for hell. I tried to join the Army, the Navy, and the Marine Corps and didn't get in, so I went and got me a gun and started robbin banks."

—JAMES A. BOARMAN, AZ-581

BY 1958, the three brothers had their sights on pulling off a larger, more complex heist; a single robbery that could reap enough money so that they could relocate and start anew. They desperately wanted to escape their criminal lifestyles. As their sister Verna remembered: "They didn't want to live the life of outlaws... They wanted to break away from their past. I think they wanted to settle down to live normal and comfortable lives... That's all they really wanted... They were just getting in too deep..."

While Alfred and Clarence were still fugitives (with Alfred having been on the run for nearly five years and Clarence about eleven months), John had served his time and had remained out of prison for almost five years. He had fallen deep in love, but in an extremely complicated relationship with young Tampa native, Helen Taylor-McIntosh. Helen was married and the mother of three, and in the process of separating from her husband. They were living in separate parts of the house, and it appeared to be an amicable parting as her husband James was well aware that John and Helen were making plans to spend their lives together. "She was sweet, vibrant and vivacious..." remembered one of the Anglin sisters. "She had a way about her that turned heads... JW was mad for her... I believe that drove him to take risks I guess most of us will never be able understand... He wanted to give both her and her children a better life... It was all that simple... We loved our brothers so much, but our family didn't excuse or tolerate their crimes. You have to understand in his eyes he wanted to give Helen and her kids, you know, a better life than he had... He just didn't have the means to do it properly..."

Located about 350 miles north of Ruskin, Columbia was a small rustic town in rural Alabama, with a history going back into the 1820s. By the later part of the century, Columbia had become a major trading post for steamboat travelers navigating the Chattahoochee River, and saw little change even a hundred years past. During a brief period while on the run, Alfred lived with his Uncle Charlie, a well-respected farmer who had inherited a large farmstead from owners of an affluent mill and grain company. His uncle was reasonably wealthy and had opened his home to Alfred, not knowing he was on the run from the law... Alfred had become aware that he kept his savings at the small community bank downtown, and being criminally observant, he noticed that virtually all of the local business dealings were accomplished using cash. At the end of most days, local store owners and businesses drove to the small community bank to deposit their daily earnings. Alfred figured that its holdings at any given time would likely be substantial, but especially on Friday mornings, just before locals started showing up to cash their paychecks.

The Bank of Columbia was seen by the brothers as a perfect hit. It was the main depository for all of the town's cash holdings. The small community bank was situated in a modest red brick building located on the corner of South Main and State Highway 52, and along with its president and his wife, it boasted only one other employee. This was an ideal scenario for the three brothers who had resolved that a daytime robbery would be the only option. Casing the vault afterhours would be too risky. The safe was protected by a then state-of-the-art warfare chemical gas system. The system utilized a heat and linkage based detector that would trigger a caustic gas to thwart any robbery attempts using cutting torches. For its time, it was considered a sophisticated safeguard.

On Tuesday, January 15th, only days before the robbery, Helen took Jeanette up to her father's home in Hamilton, Ohio. It was a significant road trip, nearly a thousand miles from Tampa. Though Jeanette was resistant, Helen was insistent she go with her as the brothers would meet up with them the following week. Jeanette didn't want to be separated from Alfred for such a long period, but as Helen wouldn't take no for an answer, and with Alfred also urging her to go, she conceded...

January 17, 1958, was a typically busy Friday morning for Walter F. Oakley Jr., the bank president, his wife Florrie Fields Oakley who worked as the bookkeeper, and Charles L. Williams, Jr., who worked the front as cashier. It was payday for most of the working locals, so things usually got busy starting around the lunch hour. At about 10:00 A.M., Alfred, John and Clarence now twenty-nine, twenty-seven and twenty-six years old respectively, pulled in front of the small bank armed with toy Wyandotte metal "Crack Shot Target Pistols," and waited for the moment when no patrons were inside. In a flash flurry, Alfred and Clarence rushed into the bank taking the unsuspecting employees by complete surprise. John remained the lookout sitting in the getaway car on ready. Oakley commented to a reporter: "He had a rusty looking gun in his hand and appeared to be about 10 feet tall. He made me get in the corner and tied my hands. I tried to holler but he said, 'If you holler, I'll kill you.' I said 'For God's sake, don't kill me.' At this point I fell to the floor." The bank employees were scurried into the back area while Williams was ordered to open the vault. Mr. Oakley became so distressed that he fainted, and Clarence tended to him by ordering Williams to get a glass of water and based on family accounts, they halted the robbery until they could confirm he was alright. The official FBI summary of the robbery read in part:

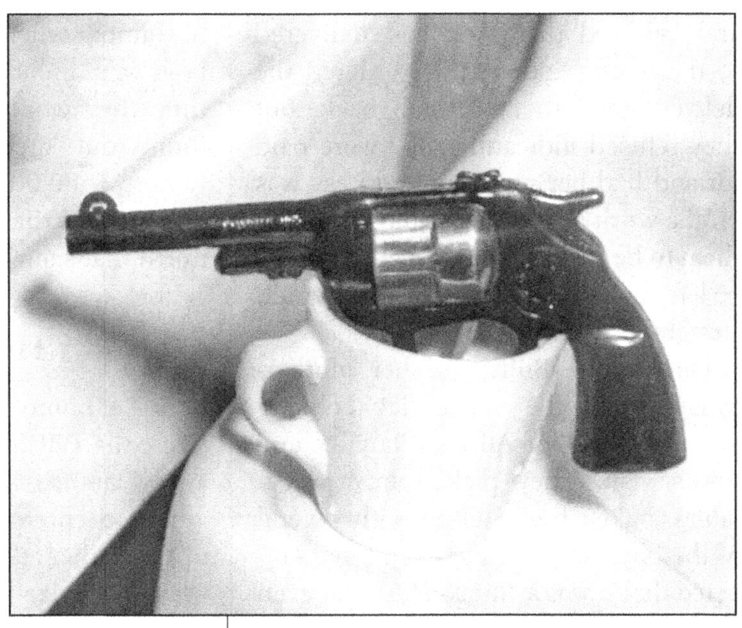

An evidence photo from the State of Alabama trial. The family would later state that John was the only one carrying a real gun. This trial photo of one of the recovered pistols is a toy metal replica of a .32 caliber revolver.

> "...after Mr. Oakley had somewhat recovered from that brief fainting spell, [Clarence] did force Mr. Oakley to cross his hands behind him, then tied the hands of Mr. Oakley with 16-inch length of plastic covered copper wire, and then forced Mr. Oakley at gunpoint to face a wall in the back office of that bank while the robbery was in progress. He also held two other bank officials at gunpoint in the same back office after those two officials had been brought to that room by Alfred Ray Anglin during the progress of the robbery..."

The men filled heavy money sacks with cash, traveler's checks, pocket watches and other sorted valuables, then scurried to the getaway car and sped off down Highway 52. They made off with over $18,000 in cash and valuables. The shaken employees filed statements and within hours, Montgomery FBI Agents Spencer Robb, John Lill and Myron Turner immediately starting working to identifying the suspects.

On the same evening of the bank robbery, John called the family home and told Billie, Robert's wife, they would stop in on Sunday evening to have supper together. This was a big surprise and would be a special evening to have all three brothers together for a meal. The following afternoon, a brand new, top of the line electric washer and dryer was delivered to the doorstep of their parents' home. Their mother was perplexed and believed that they had delivered to the wrong address. She ordered the delivery men to take them back, but they refused indicating they were paid for and had her name and address was on the work order. She would not allow them to be installed and asked that they be left on her back porch until she could straighten things out.

On Sunday, Billie and her mother-in-law spent the entire day cooking and preparing for Alfred, Clarence and John's visit. They picked fresh vegetables, baked bread along with several of the boys' favorite pies. Billie remembered that it was a "king's feast that even rivaled a Thanksgiving meal."

When the boys arrived at the house, Billie remembered that they all seemed nervous and not themselves. Rachel wasted no time and confronted John about the washer and dryer. She knew they "weren't bought with good money" and demanded to know what they had got themselves into this time? John responded that he had made some extra cash and he just wanted to make life easier for her. But Rachel stood firm...She demanded he get them off her porch by morning. She would not have them and she knew they didn't earn the money to buy them properly. The conversations remained tense and all three had unusually brisk appetites. They spent little time inside and most of the evening was in secret conversation with their brother Robert on the porch. They left early, driving away in a 1956 Crown Victoria, the car that would later be identified as their getaway car from the robbery. The following day, Robert and his wife would drive to a cabin located in a rural wooded area outside of Tampa, where unknown to her, the boys were in hiding. It would be the last time they would ever see them. Billie found out later that John had given Robert $500.00 for safe keeping, and commented they would be heading up north that same afternoon.

The Arrest

Using a photo album of known fugitives, the FBI quickly identified Alfred and Clarence as being the two men who had entered and robbed the Bank of Columbia at gunpoint. Not only did they recognize Alfred and Clarence as the conspirators in the robbery, but had also identified John's flashy Ford which had caught the eye of several in the community as it was seen pacing the streets only hours before the heist. The FBI launched a massive search for their suspects, sending bulletins out across state lines widening their net.

The boys arrived in Hamilton, Ohio, on the night of January 21st, and met up with the girls at the home of Fern Taylor, Helen's father. John and Helen would stay there for the evening, while Alfred and Jeanette rented a small nearby apartment located at 190 Dayton Street, and Clarence stayed just down the road at a motel. The men were exhausted from their trip and after a quick meal together, each of them went back to their rooms to sleep.

In early morning hours of January 22, 1958, without any warning, FBI agents rushed into the small one bedroom apartment of Alfred and Jeanette with machine guns drawn while they were both still asleep. Jeanette remembered:

The scene of the arrest on January 22, 1958, at 190 Dayton Street in Hamilton, Ohio. Alfred Anglin is sitting handcuffed while Jeanette looks on in disbelief. Nearly $14,000 was found in one of the trunks on the lower left.

> "They woke us up poking machine guns into our chests... I was so scared... I didn't know what was going on. They took us completely by surprise. I knew it was something big... I had no idea that in one of the trunks we had in the room was full of money. I just figured it was full of clothes or something. I honestly had no idea whatsoever..."

John, Helen and Clarence were all arrested within the same timeframe. There are several theories to how law officials traced them to Ohio so quickly. Some speculate Helen's husband tipped them off, to others simply chalking it up to good police work in the tracing of John's car. Verna later recalled one of the FBI agents stated that they had left a trail a mile long...

Helen was released within hours without any charges filed against her. Jeanette would remain in jail for two days under intense questioning before they finally identified her young age. She was then freed with no charges being filed. A sympathetic employee seeing she had no means to get home, drove her to a Greyhound bus station and bought her a ticket. Jeanette's father was so angry and unwelcoming, the Anglin family took her into their home to live and work alongside them.

The Trial

Immediately following their arrest, federal indictments were filed against the three brothers. They were transferred to Montgomery, Alabama, to stand trial on federal bank robbery charges. The trial was highly publicized and photos of the brothers were spread across the front pages of local papers. Without funds to hire their own lawyers, the court appointed William B. Moore, Jr., a public defender to represent the three brothers. He was given only a few days to confer with them and prepare his case. The brothers appeared in court on February 10, 1958, which was presided by District Court Judge, Frank M. Johnson. It was a packed courtroom and local interest was so great that even a high school civics class teacher brought her students to watch the proceedings. Johnson was later to become an iconic figure for his values and rulings relating to civil rights causes during the 1950s and 60s. Robert F. Kennedy, Jr., later wrote a detailed biography on Johnson and his profound impact on human rights. He was described by another biographer:

> Thrust into the center of a raging storm over civil rights, Frank M. Johnson, Jr., was the youngest federal judge in the country at the time of his appointment in 1955. During his twenty-four years on the district court in Montgomery, Alabama, Johnson handed down a string of precedent-setting decisions that were vastly unpopular at the time but that would prove to have profound consequences for America's future. Not only did Johnson's trailblazing opinions greatly expand the access of

7589

No. 57 Page

A TRUE BILL

Forman of the Grand Jury

Presented to the Court by the Foreman of the Grand Jury in the presence of 17 other Grand Jurors.

Filed Feb. 15 1958

Clerk

Writ of arrest ordered issued and amount of Bail to be required of the Defendant

No bail

Judge

The State of Alabama
HOUSTON COUNTY

CIRCUIT COURT

THE STATE
vs.
John William Anglin, Clarence Anglin, and Alfred Ray Anglin

INDICTMENT
Robbery

No Prosecutor

STATE WITNESSES

Walter F. Oakley
Mrs. Walter F. Oakley
C. L. Williams, Jr.
John Lill
(Spencer Robb)
(Myron Turner)
FBI AGENTS, MONTGOMERY

STATE SUBPOENA—ORIGINAL

NO. 7589 Docket Page

THE STATE OF ALABAMA
CIRCUIT COURT
HOUSTON COUNTY

To Any Sheriff of the State of Alabama:
You are hereby commanded to summon Mrs Walter F. Oakley

in a case pending in said Court, wherein The State of Alabama is Plaintiff, and John Wm. Anglin et al Defendant

personally to be and appear at 9 o'clock a.m. on the 14 day of March, 1958 before the Circuit Court to be holden for said County, at the Courthouse thereof, and from day to day of said term and from term to term thereafter, until discharged by law, to give testimony in behalf of THE STATE

and have you then and there this Writ; With your return thereon. Witness my hand, this 3 day of March 1958

Clerk

SHERIFF'S RETURN

Received in office 19

Executed 3-4 1958

by serving a copy on above-named witness.

Sheriff

Deputy Sheriff

The original court indictment and subpoenas for the bank robbery trial.

District Court Judge Frank M. Johnson presided over the federal court trial. He was later to become an icon in the civil rights movement.

African Americans to their constitutional rights, but his opinions also helped to dismantle discrimination against women, prison inmates, and the mentally ill. Johnson paid a heavy price for his judicial vision, however, for he had to endure public scorn, death threats, and the outrage of a society that felt itself and its values to be under siege. Eventually Johnson prevailed, winning honor even in his native Alabama and a respected place in the history of the civil rights movement.

In the courtroom, Johnson was strict and fiercely tough on those who broke the law... The Anglins' attorney advised the trio not to contest any of the charges. In fact, statements that seemed in complete conflict of the actual events were never challenged or opposed. As one example, when Judge Johnson read charges to John (as derived from the court transcript) he stated:

"All right. John William Anglin, do you understand that you are charged with, on or about January 17 of this year in this District, that you did by force and violence and intimidation take from the presence or person of Walter Oakley a sum of money approximately thirteen thousand, six hundred dollars that was in his care and custody and control and management and possession in the Bank of Columbia at Columbia, Alabama; do you understand that you are charged with that, John William Anglin? 'Yes Sir...' And do you understand that the Bank of Columbia was at that time insured by the Federal Deposit

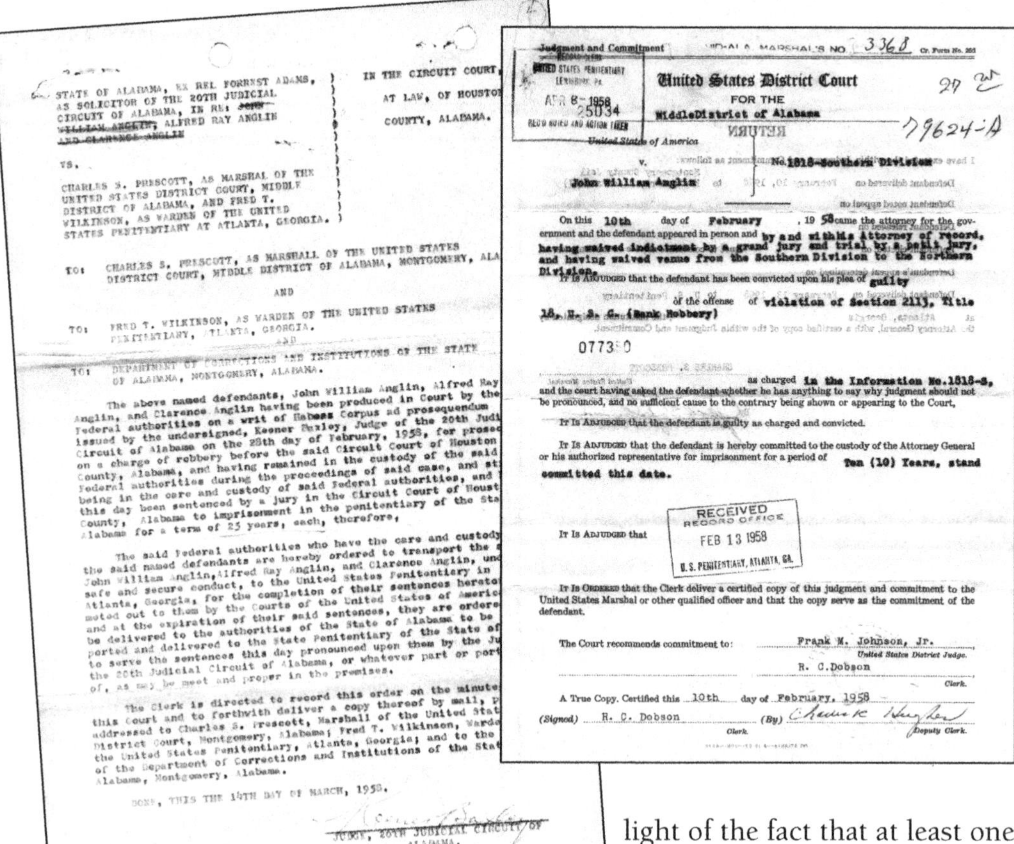

STATE OF ALABAMA, EX REL FORREST ADAMS, AS SOLICITOR OF THE 20TH JUDICIAL CIRCUIT OF ALABAMA, IN RE: ~~JOHN WILLIAM ANGLIN~~, ALFRED RAY ANGLIN ~~AND CLARENCE ANGLIN~~

VS.

CHARLES S. PRESCOTT, AS MARSHAL OF THE UNITED STATES DISTRICT COURT, MIDDLE DISTRICT OF ALABAMA, AND FRED T. WILKINSON, AS WARDEN OF THE UNITED STATES PENITENTIARY AT ATLANTA, GEORGIA.

IN THE CIRCUIT COURT, AT LAW, OF HOUSTO[N] COUNTY, ALABAMA.

TO: CHARLES S. PRESCOTT, AS MARSHALL OF THE UNITED STATES DISTRICT COURT, MIDDLE DISTRICT OF ALABAMA, MONTGOMERY, ALA

AND

TO: FRED T. WILKINSON, AS WARDEN OF THE UNITED STATES PENITENTIARY, ATLANTA, GEORGIA.

AND

TO: DEPARTMENT OF CORRECTIONS AND INSTITUTIONS OF THE STATE OF ALABAMA, MONTGOMERY, ALABAMA.

The above named defendants, John William Anglin, Alfred Ray Anglin, and Clarence Anglin having been produced in Court by the Federal authorities on a writ of Habeas Corpus ad prosequendum issued by the undersigned, Keener Baxley, Judge of the 20th Judi[cial] Circuit of Alabama on the 28th day of February, 1958, for prose[cution] on a charge of robbery before the said Circuit Court of Houston County, Alabama, and having remained in the custody of the said Federal authorities during the proceedings of said case, and st[ill] being in the care and custody of said Federal authorities, and [having] this day been sentenced by a jury in the Circuit Court of Houst[on] County, Alabama to imprisonment in the penitentiary of the Sta[te of] Alabama for a term of 25 years, each, therefore,

The said Federal authorities who have the care and custody [of] the said named defendants are hereby ordered to transport the s[aid] John William Anglin, Alfred Ray Anglin, and Clarence Anglin, und[er] safe and secure conduct, to the United States Penitentiary in Atlanta, Georgia, for the completion of their sentences hereto[fore] meted out to them by the Courts of the United States of Americ[a] and at the expiration of their said sentences, they are ordere[d to] be delivered to the authorities of the State of Alabama to be [trans]ported and delivered to the State Penitentiary of the State of [Alabama] to serve the sentences this day pronounced upon them by the Ju[dge of] the 20th Judicial Circuit of Alabama, or whatever part or port[ion there]of, as may be meet and proper in the premises.

The Clerk is directed to record this order on the minute[s of] this Court and to forthwith deliver a copy thereof by mail, p[ostpaid] addressed to Charles S. Prescott, Marshall of the United Stat[es] District Court, Montgomery, Alabama; Fred T. Wilkinson, Warde[n of] the United States Penitentiary, Atlanta, Georgia; and to the [Director] of the Department of Corrections and Institutions of the Stat[e of] Alabama, Montgomery, Alabama.

DONE, THIS THE 14TH DAY OF MARCH, 1958.

JUDGE, 20TH JUDICIAL CIRCUIT OF ALABAMA.

Judgment and Commitment — MID-ALA. MARSHAL'S NO. 3368 — Cr. Form No. 203

UNITED STATES PENITENTIARY LEWISBURG, PA. APR 8 - 1958 25034 REC'D NOTED AND ACTION TAKEN

United States District Court
FOR THE
Middle District of Alabama

27

79624-A

United States of America

v.

John William Anglin

No. 1818-Southern Division

On this 10th day of February, 1958 came the attorney for the government and the defendant appeared in person and by and with his Attorney of record, having waived indictment by a grand jury and trial by a petit jury, and having waived venue from the Southern Division to the Northern Division.

It Is Adjudged that the defendant has been convicted upon his plea of guilty of the offense of violation of Section 2113, Title 18, U. S. C. (Bank Robbery)

077330

as charged in the Information No. 1818-S, and the court having asked the defendant whether he has anything to say why judgment should not be pronounced, and no sufficient cause to the contrary being shown or appearing to the Court,

It Is Adjudged that the defendant is guilty as charged and convicted.

It Is Adjudged that the defendant is hereby committed to the custody of the Attorney General or his authorized representative for imprisonment for a period of Ten (10) Years, stand committed this date.

It Is Adjudged that

RECEIVED RECORD OFFICE FEB 13 1958 U.S. PENITENTIARY, ATLANTA, GA.

It Is Ordered that the Clerk deliver a certified copy of this judgment and commitment to the United States Marshal or other qualified officer and that the copy serve as the commitment of the defendant.

The Court recommends commitment to: Frank M. Johnson, Jr., United States District Judge.

R. C. Dobson, Clerk.

A True Copy. Certified this 10th day of February, 1958

(Signed) R. C. Dobson, Clerk. (By) Charles K. Hughes, Deputy Clerk.

Insurance Corporation, and that the Government says in committing this offense that you did assault and put in jeopardy the life of Walter Oakley by the use of a dangerous weapon, that is, a thirty-two caliber pistol; do you understand what you are charged with, John William Anglin?"
'Yes Sir...'

John had never entered the bank and remained in the getaway car on watch. The single evidence photo (later used in the State of Alabama trial), showed only a toy metal replica of a .32 caliber revolver. The replica looked convincingly real and there is no record showing that during the trial anyone made light of the fact that at least one weapon used during the robbery was confirmed as being replica. The Anglin family has made clear that of the three weapons used during the robbery, John was the only one who had carried a real pistol, and it stayed with him in the car. Walter Oakley the bank president, stated during his testimony that he had been tied up and threatened during the robbery, but there was no statement of an assault by him or the other witnesses.

One by one, the judge asked each defendant, "Do you understand what you are charged with?" and quietly each responded, "Yes, Sir..." Before imposing his sentence, he commented: "All right... Now, I am not going to sentence you all now; I am going to come back to this case later on. I am going to, in the

The Anglin brothers handcuffed outside the courthouse. (L-R) Alfred, Jeanette (she was not tried in the case), Clarence and John.

meantime, give each of you and your attorney an opportunity to confer with me regarding any sentence that is to be imposed on these pleas of guilty..."

When Judge Johnson returned to the court for sentencing, he questioned each one about their time served in prison:

JUDGE JOHNSON: John William Anglin, Clarence Anglin, Alfred Ray Anglin...John William Anglin?

JOHN: Yes, Sir.

JUDGE JOHNSON: Do you have any statement that you would like to make prior to the time I impose sentence on your plea of guilty in this case?

JOHN WILLIAM ANGLIN: No, Sir.

JUDGE JOHNSON: Let me ask you this: How much of the time did you serve when you were convicted in the State of Florida in 1951 -- in 1951 for grand larceny, how much of that time did you serve?

Anglin Boys Face Second Robbery Trial

ANGLIN BROTHERS IN BANK ROBBERY TRIAL
Left, John and Clarence of Ruskin, Alfred, of Tampa

JOHN WILLIAM ANGLIN: Twenty-two months.

JUDGE JOHNSON: Did you have any escapes at that time?

JOHN WILLIAM ANGLIN: No, Sir.

JUDGE JOHNSON: That is your only prior conviction?

JOHN WILLIAM ANGLIN: Yes, Sir.

JUDGE JOHNSON: All right. Upon your plea of guilty in this case, John William Anglin, it is the order and judgment of this court that you be committed to the custody of the Attorney General for a period of ten years, to stand committed this date. You can stand in the hands of the Marshal.

JUDGE JOHNSON: Clarence Anglin?

CLARENCE: Yes Sir.

JUDGE JOHNSON: Do you have any statement that you would like to make to the court prior to the time I impose sentence on your plea of guilty?

CLARENCE: No, sir.

JUDGE JOHNSON: Do you know of any reason why I should not sentence you at this time on your plea of guilty?

CLARENCE: No, sir.

JUDGE JOHNSON: How much of the last thirteen years have you spent in the penitentiary?

CLARENCE: About seven.

JUDGE JOHNSON: About half of it?
CLARENCE: Just about.
JUDGE JOHNSON: And all of them have been State penitentiaries, haven't they?
CLARENCE: Yes, sir.
JUDGE JOHNSON: And you have three or four convictions?
CLARENCE: Yes, sir.
JUDGE JOHNSON: For breaking and entering and burglary and larceny; is that correct?
CLARENCE: Yes, sir.
JUDGE JOHNSON: Do you have any commitments pending against you at this time, unserved time that has been imposed on you?
CLARENCE: Yes, sir; Florida.
JUDGE JOHNSON: How much?
CLARENCE: About six years.
JUDGE JOHNSON: Six years is pending against you now?
CLARENCE: Yes, sir.
JUDGE JOHNSON: Do you know whether or not they have placed a detainer against you?
CLARENCE: No sir; no, sir; I don't.
ATTORNEY W.B. MOORE: If it would please the court, I might partially answer that.
JUDGE JOHNSON: I would like to know.
ATTORNEY W.B. MOORE: There was a hold order out, the FBI had a pick-up on unlawful flight, and when they were apprehended on this of course that was withdrawn, but I understand the time is still --
JUDGE JOHNSON: The time is still against him?
ATTORNEY W.B. MOORE: Yes, sir.
JUDGE JOHNSON: Uh, huh. And that is for the offense that he was sentenced on and escaped from the penitentiary in February of this year; is that right?
ATTORNEY W.B. MOORE: That is my understanding.
JUDGE JOHNSON: Now, I've discussed this matter with your lawyer, Clarence Anglin, and gone into it with him. If you have nothing to say, it is the order and judgment of this court that you be committed to the custody of the Attorney General for a period of fifteen-years, to stand committed this date. You can stand in the hands of the Marshal.

Bank Robbers Sentenced

ONE FROM TAMPA, TWO FROM RUSKIN—Alfred Anglin (left, from Tampa) and John Anglin from Ruskin, were sentenced yesterday in Montgomery, Ala., to robbing a Columbia, Ala., bank Jan. 17 after pleading guilty. Alfred and a third brother, Clarence got 15 years; John 10 years. Alfred and Clarence are escapees from Raiford.

Alfred's sentencing read nearly identical to Clarence. The three men took full responsibility for their crimes and pled guilty to all counts. One reporter described them as "quiet surly-appearing defendants, who gazed at the floor looking defeated." They were placed into custody of the United States Marshal and all three brothers were transferred to the Federal Penitentiary in Atlanta, arriving just a few days later on February 13, 1958.

On the same date of their arrival at the federal prison in Atlanta, the Houston County Prosecutor (for Alabama) filed indictments for a State trial, setting their court date for March 10, 1958, exactly one month from their original sentencing.

As newspapers aptly pointed out, the ramifications for prosecution in Houston County held potentially dire consequences. In the State of Alabama, the maximum punishment for bank robbery carried the death penalty. The brothers were panic stricken when they were served with the indictments. While at Raiford Penitentiary in Florida, insolent prisoners were sometimes paraded past the electric chair as a crime deterrent. It was a valid fear, as several men were put to death there during the same period the boys served time there. Records show that in 1951 alone, nine men had been put to death in the electric chair at Raiford. During interviews with the Associated Press, State Prosecutor Forrest L. Adams confirmed that the boys could get the death penalty under state charges.

William Moore, the attorney who handled the federal case, advised the family that he believed the brothers were immune from a second prosecution as it placed them in double jeopardy. He provided a prior legal ruling, stating:

> "In the absence of extraordinary circumstances, where the offenses are substantially the same, such double punishment should not be inflicted, and, of course, where the accused was prosecuted in the state court and no federal offense was committed and it appears that the jurisdiction is in the state and not in the federal government, accused should not be again be put in jeopardy."

While in their case it was the reverse (their first trial was held in a federal court), the ramifications were identical. The State, however, interpreted the law differently, and despite their legal protests the court ordered the U.S. Marshal Service to deliver the brothers back to Houston County to again stand trial; again with defense attorneys appointed by the State. The State's prosecutor defended their ability to bring the boys back to court. He stated: "Those indictments constitute a separate offense altogether from the federal offenses."

News of the second trial created a frenzy among locals, with many, including their own uncle, demanding that the boys receive a harsher punishment for their crime. In a small town with few to draw from, jury selection proved challenging. The jurors were selected from a pool of sixty people. Juror number #53 was excluded as he was bank employee Charlie Williams. Jurors #59 and #60 were exempt because they were immediate relatives of the Oakleys', and eleven others were excluded for being either a witness, family member, or having close associations with the victims of the robbery. Many people of the community felt the courts didn't take stern

The electric chair at Raiford Penitentiary in Florida. Problematic prisoners were often paraded past the electric chair as both a deterrent and means to instill fear.

enough action against the brothers in the first trial, and despite no one being injured during the robbery, several were vocal in their desire to see the boys put to death. The Anglins' sister Marie remembered:

> In the courtroom, people were chanting "electrocute, electrocute" and our mother became so ill she had to leave. I remember the prosecutor pacing back and forth in front of everyone shouting in his southern drawl: "They came here from Florida to rob us good people... They should be put to death... This will teach people from Florida to stay out of our state..." When he started shouting "electrocute them!" John became so sick, he threw-up. Even my own

> uncle told reporters he wanted to see them get life sentences for the robbery. Growing-up, my brothers never hurt anybody, and I don't remember them ever even being mean to anyone. They were just mischievous, like young boys sometimes are. They were good boys and good people...

The brothers didn't testify in either trial, nor did they protest any of the charges or allegations made against them. It remains unclear as to why the use of toy pistols was never referenced during proceedings. The single evidence photo from the robbery was a Wyandotte toy metal revolver (a period replica of a .32 caliber pistol), but to an unskilled eye, it may have looked convincingly real to the jury, or simply not mattered as the victims believed they were being threatened with deadly weapons. On March 14, 1958, jury foreman Otis Mendheim read the verdict of guilty and the brothers were sentenced to an additional twenty-five years, not to run to concurrent, but to begin at the expiration of their federal sentence. They were led out of the courtroom crestfallen. It would be the last time Jeanette would ever see her husband Alfred...

On May 28, 1959, a petition in the case was filed by the United States Attorney stating in part: "...two .32 cal revolvers seized in this case and held as evidence will be turned over to the FBI by the Marshal of this District." Another entry dated only days later ordered that the "United States Marshal destroy certain articles in his possession." A follow-up reference dated June 1, 1959, confirmed the articles had been destroyed. There are no records as to what final evidentiary items were disposed.

Federal Prison

"My brain is the key that sets me free."
—HARRY HOUDINI

SULLEN AND DEFEATED, the brothers were transferred under heavy guard back to the federal prison in Atlanta. They carried with them collective sentences totaling more than a hundred years. Despite legal and lobby support by the American Civil Liberties Union in Washington D.C. to have their State (double jeopardy) sentences overturned, each attempt was met with a refusal for consideration. Their fight for freedom was hopeless.

On March 27th, a classification committee convened to discuss the long confinement of the brothers, specifically addressing their proneness to escape. The committee wrote in part:

> Clarence is the larger man physically; appears to be much rougher than the other two (2); and likely is the leader. Clarence Anglin and Alfred Ray Anglin, have served in the State Prison Camp in Georgia together and also served a term in Raiford, Florida together. Clarence escaped from Raiford three times.
>
> The Classification Committee felt by all means they should be in separate institutions as they are both definite escape risks and quite capable of planning and executing several kinds of overt acts. In separate institutions they should be able to make better adjustments and certainly they could be better supervised individually and would not be able to plan anything together.
>
> The Committee has recommended that Alfred Ray Anglin #79625-A be retained in Atlanta; Clarence Anglin #79622-A transfer recommended to Leavenworth, and John William Anglin #79624-A be sent to Lewisburg.

The three brothers had enjoyed a brief period serving together at USP

The United States Federal Penitentiary in Atlanta.

Atlanta. Alfred wrote his mother on April 7, 1958, the day his brothers were transferred:

> Dear Mom,
>
> Just a few lines to say hello. Hope these few lines find everyone at home well. As for us, we are ok. Mom, I wanted to write you and let you know that Brothers John and Clarence are being transferred to different places. Brother Clarence is going to Leavenworth, Kansas, and Brother John is going to Lewisburg, Pennsylvania. They leave today. We were hoping that we could stay together, I am being left here, and it will make it harder for you, us being at different places. Mom, if Jeanette is there tell her I said hi. I am going to write her as soon as I finish this letter. In one of her letters she said she was staying there through the week, and was going home on weekends, so I thought she might be there. Tell all we said hello, as news is short at this time, I will close for now. Hope to hear from you all soon.
>
> Love always your sons,
>
> Brother John, Clarence and Alfred Anglin

With little fanfare, both Clarence and John were transferred to the federal facilities recommended by the classification committee. John arrived at the Federal Penitentiary in Lewisburg, Pennsylvania the following day, and Clarence at USP Leavenworth in Kansas on April 14th. Because of his escape risk, he remained shackled on his journey of more than 800 miles.

Immediately following their transfers, their mother begged Bureau Director James Bennett to consider returning them both back to Atlanta. She pled that due to her and her husband's age and meager finances, they would not be able to travel long distances to visit them. Bennett stood by the recommendations of the classification committee. He responded in part:

FEDERAL BUREAU OF INVESTIGATION, UNITED STATES DEPARTMENT OF JUSTICE
WASHINGTON, D. C.

Record from .... Address ....
(On the above line please state whether Police Department, Sheriff's Office, or County Jail)

USPA 79624 2 13 58

Date of arrest
Charge
Disposition of case
Residence
Place of birth
Nationality
~~Criminal specialty~~ OCCUPATION

F. B. I. NO. 4 745 119

Age
Date of birth
Height
Comp.
Hair
Weight
Eyes
Build
Scars and marks

CRIMINAL HISTORY

NAME	NUMBER	CITY OR INSTITUTION	DATE	CHARGE	DISPOSITION OR SENTENCE

49025

ACCOMPLICES

NAME	NUMBER	NAME	NUMBER

(Please furnish all additional criminal hi

USPA 79622 2 13 58

"I have gone into the situation carefully and while I understand the desire to have your three sons at the same institution, we feel it to their best interests that they be kept separated. This situation works a hardship on you, I realize, and I am sorry

John and Clarence's inmate case file photos taken on February 13, 1958, the day of their arrival at USP Atlanta. The overlay photo on John's admission card was taken at Raiford in December of 1951.

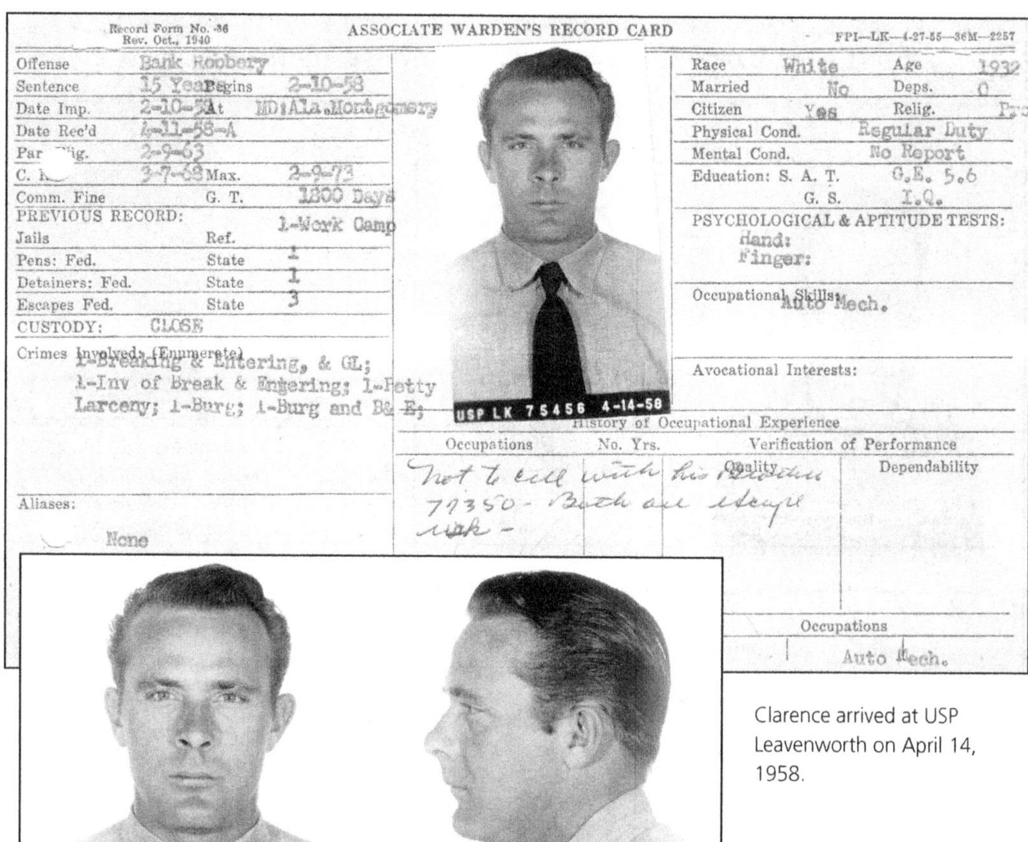

Record Form No. 36
Rev. Oct., 1940

ASSOCIATE WARDEN'S RECORD CARD

FPI—LK—4-27-55—36M—2257

Offense Bank Robbery
Sentence 15 Years Begins 2-10-58
Date Imp. 2-10-58 At MD: Ala. Montgomery
Date Rec'd 4-11-58-A
Par. Elig. 2-9-63
C. R. 3-7-68 Max. 2-9-73
Comm. Fine G. T. 1800 Days
PREVIOUS RECORD: 1-Work Camp
Jails Ref.
Pens: Fed. State 1
Detainers: Fed. State 1
Escapes Fed. State 3
CUSTODY: CLOSE
Crimes Involved: (Enumerate) 1-Breaking & Entering, & GL; 1-Inv of Break & Entering; 1-Petty Larceny; 1-Burg; 1-Burg and B& E;

Aliases:
None

Race White Age 1932
Married No Deps. 0
Citizen Yes Relig. Pro
Physical Cond. Regular Duty
Mental Cond. No Report
Education: S. A. T. G.E. 5.6
G. S. I.Q.
PSYCHOLOGICAL & APTITUDE TESTS:
Hand:
Finger:
Occupational Skills: Auto Mech.
Avocational Interests:

USP LK 75456 4-14-58

History of Occupational Experience

Occupations	No. Yrs.	Verification of Performance: Quality	Dependability
Not to cell with his brother 77350 - Both are escape risk -			

Occupations
Auto Mech.

Clarence arrived at USP Leavenworth on April 14, 1958.

that circumstances do not permit me to be any more encouraging now than I have been in the past..."

The Federal Penitentiary in Lewisburg was one of four high-security prisons established by the Bureau of Prisons in 1932. Of the four, it held the lowest ratio of guards-to-inmates; so while the criminal records of those institutionalized there were typically significant, the men were generally not considered high-level escape risks. Over the course of the prison's history, Lewisburg held many notable figures including, James "Whitey" Bulger, John Gotti, Henry Hill, Jimmy Hoffa and Al Capone (though only for a minimal period during his release phase).

As John didn't carry any significant history of escape, the classification committee likely felt he would serve his time quietly and not become a security risk. But with the bleak reality that upon completion of his federal term he would face serving out his twenty-five year state sentence, John quickly began plotting his break. Just over a year later, the officials discovered his activities. A report by a lieutenant offered details:

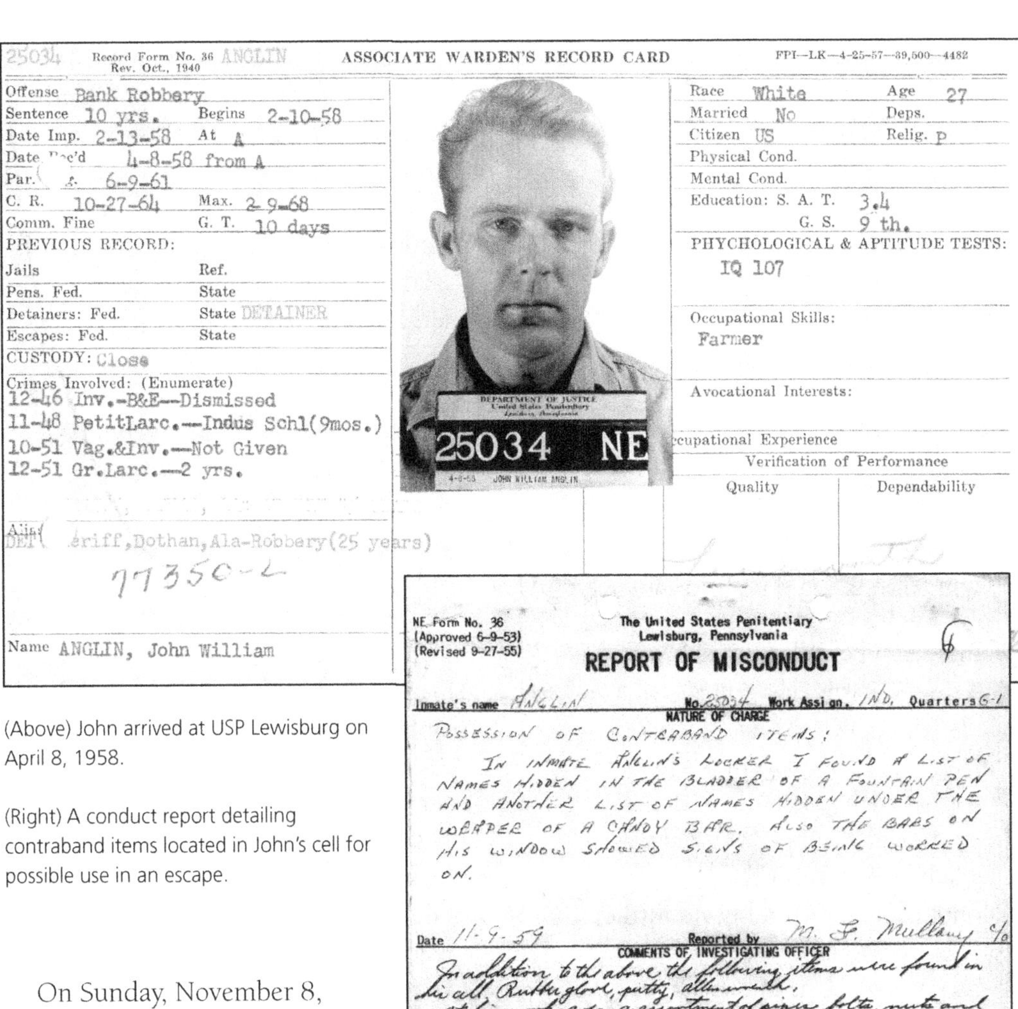

25034 Record Form No. 36 ANGLIN Rev. Oct., 1940 **ASSOCIATE WARDEN'S RECORD CARD** FPI—LK—4-25-57—39,500—4482

Offense Bank Robbery
Sentence 10 yrs. Begins 2-10-58
Date Imp. 2-13-58 At A
Date Rec'd 4-8-58 from A
Par. 6-9-61
C. R. 10-27-64 Max. 2-9-68
Comm. Fine G. T. 10 days
PREVIOUS RECORD:
Jails Ref.
Pens. Fed. State
Detainers: Fed. State DETAINER
Escapes: Fed. State
CUSTODY: Close
Crimes Involved: (Enumerate)
12-46 Inv.-B&E—Dismissed
11-48 PetitLarc.—Indus Schl(9mos.)
10-51 Vag.&Inv.—Not Given
12-51 Gr.Larc.—2 yrs.

DET(eriff,Dothan,Ala-Robbery(25 years)
77350-L

Name ANGLIN, John William

DEPARTMENT OF JUSTICE
25034 NE
4-8-58 JOHN WILLIAM ANGLIN

Race White Age 27
Married No Deps.
Citizen US Relig. P
Physical Cond.
Mental Cond.
Education: S. A. T. 3.4
G. S. 9 th.
PHYCHOLOGICAL & APTITUDE TESTS:
IQ 107
Occupational Skills:
Farmer
Avocational Interests:
Occupational Experience
Verification of Performance
Quality Dependability

NE Form No. 36
(Approved 6-9-53)
(Revised 9-27-55)
The United States Penitentiary
Lewisburg, Pennsylvania
REPORT OF MISCONDUCT

Inmate's name ANGLIN No. 25034 Work Assign. IND. Quarters G-1

NATURE OF CHARGE

POSSESSION OF CONTRABAND ITEMS:
IN INMATE ANGLIN'S LOCKER I FOUND A LIST OF NAMES HIDDEN IN THE BLADDER OF A FOUNTAIN PEN AND ANOTHER LIST OF NAMES HIDDEN UNDER THE WRAPPER OF A CANDY BAR. ALSO THE BARS ON HIS WINDOW SHOWED SIGNS OF BEING WORKED ON.

Date 11-9-59 Reported by M. F. Mullany c/o

COMMENTS OF INVESTIGATING OFFICER

In addition to the above the following items were found in his cell. Rubber glove, putty, allen wrench. At his work area an assortment of pipes, bolts, nuts and grey paint. Anglin denied any intentions of escaping. Attitude good. Placed in A/S.

Date November 10, 1959 Investigated by Lt J Kusheh

INMATE'S STATEMENT TO BOARD

Admitted that he used to think of escaping but dismissed this from his mind. He feebly denies that he was planning to escape but all the evidence indicates that he had advanced plans and equipment to escape.

Date 11-13-59 DISCIPLINARY BOARD ACTION

Punitive segregation. Recommend forfeiture of 100 days statutory good time. His case should also be referred to the Reclassification committee for consideration of transfer.

H. J. Shaffer, Lt. — Member
R. Bolliger, Captain — Chairman
J. D. Riggsby, Chief, CP — Member

(Above) John arrived at USP Lewisburg on April 8, 1958.

(Right) A conduct report detailing contraband items located in John's cell for possible use in an escape.

On Sunday, November 8, 1959, information came to me that Anglin was planning to escape during the next fog. He was supposed to have hacksaw blades in his cell with which to saw the bars in order to affect his escape from quarters. At his place of work in the industries, he was supposed to have parts of a makeshift ladder with which to scale the wall.

Immediately after I received this information I searched the area in [the] industries where he worked and found hidden under the punch press that he worked on several short pieces of threaded ½ inch pipe, several elbows, a plastic bag containing a large quantity of bolts and nuts, a large Allen wrench to fit these bolts, several sheets of sand paper, a small container of grey paint to match the

> paint on the bars of his cell, a small bottle of kerosene and several pieces of flat metal bolted together with small bolts.
>
> Anglin's cell was searched thoroughly on Monday morning while he was at work where we found names and addresses concealed in the rubber tube of a fountain pen and some in a candy bar, one rubber glove and some putty. Several bars were found loose in the concrete but none were sawed through as I had been informed. My information indicated that subject had several hacksaw blades in his cell but none were found. Another Allen wrench was also found in his cell to fit the smaller bolts with which the flat pieces of metal were bolted together with.
>
> A thorough search of the department in which subject worked was made by six officers during the Monday lunch period but no further pieces were found.
>
> According to the information I received, Anglin was going to use angle iron to construct a ladder and use a piece of reinforcing steel for the hook to hang onto the top of the wall.
>
> There is plenty of small angle irons of various lengths with holes already drilled in them available in the industries. It appears quite obvious that Anglin was planning an escape, but was apprehended before he could complete his preparations.

John would lose all of his privileges and be placed into administrative segregation for "maximum custody control." He vehemently denied any of the items were intended to be used in a plot to escape. John wrote the warden pleading for leniency and to have his privileges restored while being held in segregation:

> Warden Hagen,
>
> I think I've done as much as any man can do to keep a clean record here. I worked as hard as I knew how. I have went out of my way to avoid trouble when I seen it coming my way. I worked very hard on my job over in Industry and liked it. I had worked my way up to a second grade job and pay. It took me two long years to get there, and I would like to say that it meant plenty to me. No one has spoken up for me or did anything in my favor.
>
> I feel that my two years here has been in vain to all of you. I think that I have earned the right to let all of you know how I feel. I'm not guilty of the charge against me and I want my job back. I've got thirty-five years hanging on me and I can't do it over here in segregation. I'm being punished for something I knew nothing about and I wish that some of you would come up with that same idea. I can't just sit here and watch everything that I've worked for go down the drain without saying something.
>
> This might not sound like much to you but here is one of my main reasons for trying to keep a clean record here.
>
> I wrote my mother last year and told her that I would have a photo made to send her. I lacked just a few days having in enough time to qualify. So I wrote and told her that I would have to wait until next Xmas.

DNA | Record Form No. 36 Rev. Oct. 1940 | ASSOCIATE WARDEN'S RECORD CARD | FPI—LK—4-24-59—66M—6640

Offense: Bank Robbery
Sentence: 10 yrs | Begins: 2-10-58
Date Imp.: 2-10-58 | At: MD:ALA
Date Rec'd: 1-22-60-MR
Par. Elig.: 6-9-61
C. R.: 12-28-64 | Max.: 2-9-68
Comm. Fine | G. T.: 1200
PREVIOUS RECORD: 38 EGT
Jails | Ref.: 1-SIS
Pens. Fed. | State: 1
Detainers: Fed. | State: 1
Escapes: Fed. | State
CUSTODY: CLOSE
Crimes Involved: (Enumerate)
1-Inv B & E; 1-PL; 1-Vag; 1-GL

Aliases:
None

USP LK 77350 1-25-60

Race: White | Age: 29 1931
Married: Single | Deps.: None
Citizen: U.S. | Relig.: Prot.
Physical Cond.: Reg. Duty
Mental Cond.: No Report
Education: S. A. T. 3.8
G. S. 10
PSYCHOLOGICAL & APTITUDE TESTS:
Occupational Skills:
Labor
Avocational Interests:

Occupational Experience

Occupations	No. Yrs.	Verification of Performance: Quality	Dependability
5-9½ 160 lbs Escape Risk Not to Cell with his Brother 75456-			

Name	Number	Residence	Occupations
ANGLIN, John William 1476	77350-L	Ruskin, Flor.	Labor

John arrived at USP Leavenworth on January 25, 1960. Note the handwritten entry on his case file indicating that he shouldn't be celled with his brother.

She asks me about that in her letters. It doesn't mean all that much to me, but it do to her. I haven't had a visit since I've been here. My people don't have that kind of money. I was planning on sending her a photo this Christmas and make a phone call.

I would like to know how and where I stand on all this. I'm only asking for what I have earned here. I would also like some kind of consideration on my case. Please.

Yours Truly,
John William Anglin

His pleas fell on deaf ears and he remained under strict watch in isolation. A month later as the administration convened a committee to review his progress, it was determined that he should be transferred to a higher secure facility. The committee stated in their recommendation: "Recommend transfer to another institution to be selected by the Bureau, to provide maximum custody, noting his codefendants are presumably still at Atlanta." John was transferred to USP Leavenworth in Kansas on January 22, 1960, and would arrive three days later.

By the time John arrived at Leavenworth, it had been nearly two years since he'd last seen his brother. It was a welcome reunion as previous classification reports stated Clarence was "rather bitter" for having been transferred so far away from his family. Up to this point, Clarence had been serving hard time at the Kansas prison. Nicknamed the "Hot House" for its lack of ventilation, Leavenworth was home to some of America's most dangerous and violent men. Its horrid conditions were considered some of the most repressive in the prison system. His institutional report showed that Clarence was placed in isolation on three occasions, with minor reprimands for offenses mostly related to not following orders and wandering from his assigned work areas.

When John arrived, everything seemingly changed to a positive course. Clarence was assigned to the kitchen as a "Pudding Man" which was part of the crew who held responsibility for preparing the desserts menu for the prison population. He resided in the A Block section (cell #313) and John in the adjacent B Block section (cell #297). John was first assigned to work in the laundry and then later earned a job with his brother in the kitchen.

Both men received accolades from their supervisors and on July 1, 1960, Clarence received a meritorious good time award for going six months without any write-ups for misconduct. John worked in the adjacent bakery, where bread and other goods were baked for not only the internal population, but also distributed to prison camps and other institutions. Their good behavior was only a ruse...

On Monday, August 8, 1960, John wasn't scheduled to report to work, but later told officials that Clarence had asked him to come in to assist him. The official summary of the escape was provided by J.P. Hatfield, the associate warden's secretary:

> At approximately 9:45 A.M., August 8, 1960, Inmate Clarence Anglin, Register Number 75456-L was apprehended in an escape from this institution. He was assisted by brother John William Anglin Reg. No 77350-L. Clarence Anglin had ingeniously hidden himself inside two metal bread boxes which were being prepared for the Honor Farm in Missouri. The boxes which were stacked on top of the other had the bottom cut out of the top box, and the top cut out of the box under that one, leaving just enough room for a person to conceal himself in the cavity. Bread had been stacked in front of Anglin to conceal him inside one of the boxes that were shaken-down. They were constructed in such a manner, that even though stacked together, a small space still existed between them. When the boxes were being pushed toward the elevator in the kitchen, Mr. Author Davidson, Food Supervisor, noticed a movement in this area between the two boxes. At this time the loading stopped and called Food Supervisor Sidney Sexton Jr. to assist him while he investigated the irregularity. A check revealed that someone was concealed in these boxes and when ordered to dismount, Inmate Clarence Anglin emerged from the bread boxes holding an improvised knife and iron bar in his hands. Upon seeing that the Food Supervisors were present, he immediately dropped these weapons and offered no resistance.
>
> It was evident that Clarence Anglin had received assistance from some other person(s) in helping to place the loaves of bread in front of him. During the investigation of this incident it was discovered that Clarence's brother, Inmate John William Anglin, Register Number 77350-L, who is assigned to the kitchen, was not

Admin... Form No. 66
No...mber 1938

UNITED STATES
DEPARTMENT OF JUSTICE
WASHINGTON

September 6, 1960

To the Warden, United States Penitentiary, Leavenworth, Kansas

WHEREAS, in accordance with the authority contained in title 18, sections 4082, 4085, and 4125, U. S. Code, the Attorney General by the Director of the Bureau of Prisons has ordered the transfer of John William Anglin #77350
from the United States Penitentiary, Leavenworth, Kansas
to the United States Penitentiary, Alcatraz, California ✓

NOW THEREFORE, you, the above-named officer, are hereby authorized and directed to execute this order by causing the removal of said prisoner, together with the original writ of commitment and other official papers as above ordered and to incur the necessary expense and include it in your regular accounts.

And you, the warden, superintendent, or official in charge of the institution in which the prisoner is now confined, are hereby authorized to deliver the prisoner in accordance with the above order; and you, the warden, superintendent, or official in charge of the institution to which the transfer has been ordered, are hereby authorized and directed to receive the said prisoner into your custody and him to safely keep until the expiration of his sentence or until he is otherwise discharged according to law.

By direction of the Attorney General,

JAMES V. BENNETT,
Director, Bureau of Prisons.

FRANK LOVELAND
Assistant Director.

Safer custody R-1

ORIGINAL.—To be left at institution to which prisoner is transferred

FPI—LK—4-22-60—400 pads—7974

John's transfer order to USP Alcatraz.

supposed to be on-duty at the time this incident occurred, but was present and was assisting in pushing the food cart on which the boxes were stacked, to the elevator to be taken to the farm truck. He emphatically denies that he was aware that his brother had intended to escape and did not know that he was concealed in the boxes. He admits he was not supposed to be working on this particular day, but had been requested to come to work by his brother.

Upon questioning Clarence Anglin, he readily admitted that he thought he could escape from within the walls by this method, but refused to implicate anyone else as being involved. He indicates that he procured the tin snips from the Machine Shop which he used to cut the aluminum bread boxes. Anglin, who was also assigned to the kitchen, states that he had been observing the process by which food is shipped to the Honor Farm and it appeared to him that he could successfully use this means of escaping. He states he had not necessarily planned on any specific date for trying this attempt, but intended to take the most opportune time. He had stated that he had been successful in getting by all of the shakedowns and through the rear gate on the truck, he would have used the iron bar to pry the lock off of the truck as it traveled down the highway on the way to the Farm Dormitory.

It is quite evident that John William Anglin assisted his brother in this escape attempt and the board found him guilty as charged.

The brothers were both stripped of privileges and placed in the segregation unit. Within weeks, it was discovered that they again were plotting another break. Senior Officer Allen Preston who was in charge of the administrative segregation unit, intercepted a letter written by Clarence. The letter was concealed in a library book that was in the process of being delivered to John. The letter indicated that a prisoner who worked on the laundry loading dock was acquiring tools for them to use in another escape plot. Paired with their long sentences and their aggressive efforts to break from prison, Alcatraz was recommended for both brothers. The final entry in John's case file simply read: "Anglin is now in segregation and cannot be returned to the population inasmuch as he is a serious escape risk. He will remain a potentially dangerous individual because of his substantial sentence and the detainer involving a twenty-five year term. Transfer to Alcatraz is recommended where he may serve his sentence under the maximum supervision which he will require for some years to come..."

Welcome to Alcatraz

If you disobey the rules of society, they send you to prison; if you disobey the rules of the prison, they send you to us. Alcatraz is not like any other prison in the United States. Here, every inmate is confined alone…to an individual cell. Unlike my predecessors, Wardens Johnston and Blackwell, I don't have good conduct programs, I do not have inmate councils. Inmates here have no say in what they do; they do as they're told. You're not permitted to have newspapers or magazines carrying news; knowledge of the outside world is what we tell you. From this day on, your world will be everything that happens in this building.

—ALCATRAZ WARDEN

(from the Classic Motion Picture *Escape from Alcatraz*)

ON SEPTEMBER 6, 1960, Assistant Director of the Bureau of Prisons Frank Loveland on behalf of the Director James Bennett, issued an executive order to transfer both brothers to the United States Federal Penitentiary on Alcatraz Island.

Following years of prison and bold breaks, the brothers were now being transferred to America's toughest and most secure prison. Designed to hold the most notorious enemies of society; the most dangerous and infamous, Alcatraz served a bitter menu of hard time with the only rights being food, clothing, shelter and medical care. Everything else, including work, was an earned privilege. On the Rock, prison regulations were rigidly enforced and violations even of the most trivial nature were swiftly punished. Alcatraz was the ultimate punishment for men with histories of brazen escape attempts, as its reputation as being escape-proof remained untarnished. Alcatraz had successfully silenced the criminal voices of men like Al Capone, Machine Gun Kelly, and Alvin Karpis who was still imprisoned on the island, only now a skeleton of his former self after decades of the harsh regimen.

John departed Leavenworth on October 22, 1960, arriving at Alcatraz two days later. His first cell assignment was C-239, located on the second tier of the main corridor known as Broadway. Sitting in his new cell he wrote his

mother stating in part: "I guess all of you will be surprised to hear from me here in California, but don't let it worry you if you can help it. It's really a nice place to build time, and I like that part of it...I dig this sea breeze, it reminds me of home...It stays cool here most of the time. The boat ride was too short and we were going the wrong way for me to enjoy it...Guess I caught the wrong boat..."

When John arrived on Alcatraz nearly three decades after its opening, it was still being operated under strict rule, but the stone face regimen had started to soften. Alcatraz had now become the spirit of a different era. Through the decades, the prison had seen only slight changes in the daily regimen, but in January of 1955, when Paul J. Madigan became its third warden, hard-fisted rules transitioned to a more measured hand, and he tempered some of the more harsh regulations. He would also face fiscal challenges and staffing shortages that would force his hand to laxer security.

Described by Correctional Officer Pat Mahoney as a "jewel of a superior" and a "distinguished man of integrity," Madigan had been handpicked by then Warden James A. Johnston to serve as one of four lieutenants when the prison opened in 1934. A devout Irish Catholic, Madigan often smoked a pipe and was the most visible among the inmate population than any of his predecessors. Darwin Coon remembered that Madigan would come into the dining room almost daily and sit in the small officers' dining area to enjoy a fresh baked pastry and coffee.

United States Federal Penitentiary Alcatraz Island located in the San Francisco Bay. Angel Island is visible in the background.

He had been personally mentored by Johnston during some of the most strict policy periods, and during his reign, he reformed many of the harsh standards that were considered trademarks of the prison. He had abolished the bread and water diets for prisoners confined in isolation, and most popular, installed radio jacks in all of the general population cells in October of 1955, offering prisoners for the first time to hear the sounds of freedom.

One of the most notable aspects of his career was that he had been credited with thwarting Joseph Cretzer and Sam Shockley's first escape attempt in May of 1941 after being held hostage in the model industries building. He kept his cool during the desperate break attempt and talked the convicts into surrendering, promising that they would be treated justly by the administration. Madigan also would later take a shared responsibility of loosening some of the essential security elements of Alcatraz. In the face of extreme budget cuts, he began to reduce guard posts that would

Department of Justice
P[illegible]NAL AND CORRECTIONAL INSTITU[illegible]IONS

ANGLIN, John William — U. S. Penitentiary (Institution) — Alcatraz, California (Location)

Received 10-24-60
From Leavenworth
Crime B ank Robbery
Sentence: 10 yrs. ....mos. ....days
Date of sentence 2-10-58
Sentence begins 2-10-58
Sentence expires 2-9-68
Good time sentence expires 10-27-64
Date of birth 5-2-30 Occupation Laborer
Birthplace Georgia Nationality American
Age 30 Comp. Light
Height 5' 10" Eyes Blue
Weight 140 Hair Blonde
Build Med.

Scars and marks Small scar on left side of cheek Round scar on left side of forearm

CRIMINAL HISTORY

NAME	NUMBER	CITY OR INSTITUTION	DATE	CHARGE	DISPOSITION OR SENTENCE
John William Anglin	77350-L	Leavenworth	(Transferred to AZ on		10-24-60)
		TRANSFERRED TO THIS INSTITUTION BECAUSE HE WAS INVOLVED IN AN ESCAPE ATTEMPT AT LEAVENWORTH.			

[...]y and police record on separate sheet)

(Above) John Anglin arrived at Alcatraz on October 24, 1960.

(Left) Paul Joseph Madigan, Alcatraz's third warden.

later be cited as a significant security breach during the '62 escape.

Madigan's associate warden was Olin Guy Blackwell, a Texas native who had arrived in April of 1959 and was only forty-four-years-old. He had been nicknamed "Gypsy" by the convicts for the turquoise jewelry he commonly wore, but friends and associates called him "Blackie." Blackwell had been a college dropout, and he started his career as a correctional officer in 1941, working at a minimum security federal prison in La Tuna, Texas. In 1951, he was promoted to a federal jail inspector position in Washington D.C., and then two years later became Captain of the Guards at USP Lewisburg, and finally to an associate warden position before his transfer to Alcatraz. Officers who worked under Blackwell remembered him as a heavy smoker and social drinker, with mixed popularity among the correctional staff.

On November 4, 1960, John was delegated his first work assignment inside the cellhouse on the maintenance detail. It was here that John would meet a thirty-one-year-old bank robber from South Boston named James "Whitey" Bulger. Known as "Jimmy" to his closest friends, he was serving a twenty year stint for a string of bank robberies and had also earned his ticket to Alcatraz from a failed prison break at USP Atlanta. He was later to become one of the most influential crime figures in American history.

Jimmy Bulger had arrived on Alcatraz a year earlier in November of 1959, and had been working the cellhouse maintenance detail for less than a week when John received his first assignment. Jimmy had just finished working a ten month stretch in the clothing room, the same area Al Capone once worked and held court reminiscing about his days when he ruled the criminal underworld. Bulger commented that he had remembered seeing John walking the recreation yard a few days prior to formally meeting him. Everybody on the yard summed up the new faces among them, and decades later Bulger called to mind that John's looks reminded him of Hollywood actor Steve McQueen. "He walked among the men with a certain air of confidence..."

Olin Blackwell served as the associate warden under Warden Madigan and was promoted to warden in November of 1961.

The maintenance detail involved a range of duties including everything from polishing the cement floors of the cellhouse to special cleaning assignments in the hospital. It was one of the least favored work details with high turnover, since it was comprised mostly of unskilled labor and most days the men were confined to the cellhouse where it offered little to no change in scenery. As an example, for the convicts working in the prison industries, they were able to walk outside to and from work, and take in the sights and smells of the sprawling landscape visible during the walk down

BULGER Record Form No. 36 Rev. Oct., 1940 1428-AZ **ASSOCIATE WARDEN'S RECORD CARD** FPI—LK—6-1-56—65M—3414

Offense Robbery of FDIC Bank
Sentence 20 Years Begins 6-21-56
Date Imp. 6-21-56 At Boston, Mass.
Date Rec'd 11-13-59 fr Atlanta
Par. Elig. 2-20-63
C. R. 11-24-69 Max. 6-20-76
Comm. Fine None G. T. 2400 days
PREVIOUS RECORD:
Jails 6 Ref.
Pens: Fed. State
Detainers: Fed. State
Escapes: Fed. State
CUSTODY:
Crimes Involved: (Enumerate)
Investigation 2; Unarmed Robbery 1; Grand Larceny 1; Vagrancy 1; AWOL 1;

Aliases:

BULGER JAMES J. JR

U.S. PENITENTIARY ALCATRAZ 1428 11 16 59

Race White Age 9-3-29
Married no Deps. none
Citizen Yes USA Relig. Cath
Physical Cond. Regular Duty
Mental Cond. High Average Intellig
Education: S. A. T. 10.2
G. S.
PSYCHOLOGICAL & APTITUDE TESTS:
IQ 113
Occupational Skills:
Laborer
Avocational Interests:

History of Occupational Experience

Occupations	No. Yrs.	Verification of Performance	
		Quality	Dependability

Investigation at Atlanta disclosed that subject furnished a hacksaw blade to 3 men in B Cellhouse. Two of these men were subsequently transferred here. (Names not given) On 8-24-59 subject was again returned to Adm Sed when information received that subject was again plotting with others to escape.

Number	Residence	Occupations
1428-AZ	Mass.	Laborer

Legendary fugitive James "Whitey" Bulger served on Alcatraz from November 1959 until July 1962 for a string of bank robberies. After serving nine years in federal prison, he returned to Boston where he rose to the highest and most influential echelon of crime figures, ultimately reaching number one on the FBI's 10 Most Wanted list. After sixteen years at large, Bulger was arrested in an ocean side neighborhood of Santa Monica, California, on June 22, 2011.

the stairwell from the recreation yard. As former prisoner John Banner (AZ-1133) later remembered: "It was a short burst of freedom lasting only minutes, but you relished that walk…"

Another downside of the work assignment was that it varied in levels of supervision, but most often it was closely supervised when working in less secure areas of the prison. While there were some seasoned convicts working the detail, it was usually reserved for new arrivals getting acclimated to the general routine, or men integrating back into the general population from the segregation unit.

Though he was assigned to Bulger's work detail for only a week, it was a critical study time for John Anglin. It was here that he was able to survey his new surroundings, and all the while Jimmy Bulger provided him crucial insight to the dissident politics needed to survive the cloak and dagger underworld of Alcatraz…On November 10th, John was awarded the culinary assignment working inside the kitchen. He also moved down to C-205, which was a section populated by those who worked the same assignment. The culinary workers were assigned to the same section as they were released from their cells two hours before the main population in order to prepare the morning breakfast, and generally the last to return after clean up following the evening meal.

Darwin Coon lived close to John on Broadway and also was assigned the culinary detail. His cell was located on

One of John's first cell assignments was C-205, located on the second tier of C Block. This photo was taken from B Block looking towards the section where John was housed.

the same tier (C-223) and like John, he had served time at Leavenworth prior to his stint on Alcatraz. Coon arrived on Alcatraz in September of 1959, at only twenty-six years of age, he had a long and violent prison record which included a bold break from the Nevada State Prison in 1958. So brutal were the circumstances of his escape that the jacket of his inmate case file was stamped in bold black letters: "WANTED DEAD." During their ruthless break, Coon and four other convicts stabbed a prison guard and took a civilian hostage at knifepoint. It sparked a nationwide manhunt with Darwin evading capture for nearly a month.

On Alcatraz, Darwin was serving out his time quietly and keeping a low profile. The culinary assignment had perks not afforded in other work details. The dining room was considered the most dangerous area of the prison as during each meal, the entire general population prisoners would congregate into a single common area. Only those confined to D Block and the hospital would be served meals in their cells, and the remaining population of America's worst criminal minds would assemble three times daily to enjoy a cafeteria style meal. Fourteen permanently fixed tear gas canisters were mounted on the walls and ceiling structures to keep order. The tear gas release panel was mounted on a catwalk outside the dining room and the population was always cautious and aware of the grave consequences.

The culinary fare on the Rock was considered the finest in the entire federal prison system and the convicts rarely complained. Public Health Service nutritionists approved the menus to ensure they met dietary standards and convicts were allowed to take as much as they wanted within the allotted amounts listed on the menu board, but were expected to eat all that they took.

John's first assignment in the kitchen was working in the dish and dining rooms. Located on the ground floor of the north wing of the main prison building, the kitchen was considered a prime work assignment.

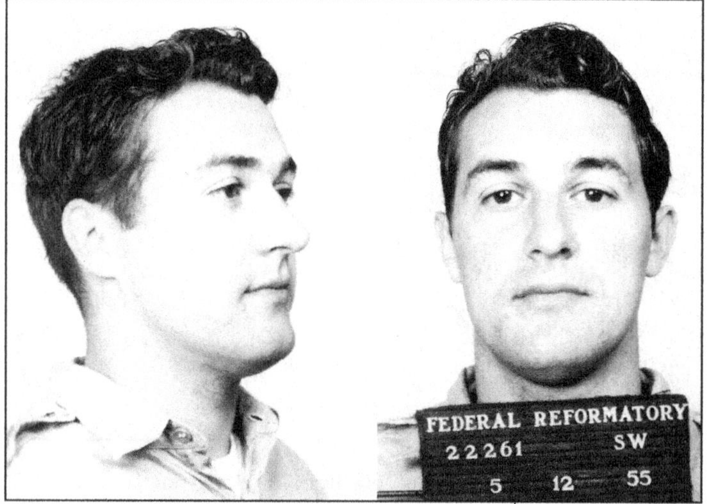

Darwin Coon during his early criminal years. He was assigned to the kitchen along with John Anglin and they were to become good friends. Coon resided in the same section of C Block as John when he worked in the kitchen.

Darwin on April 30, 2007, standing inside his old cell on C Block.

(Above) A photograph taken in 1960 of Darwin working in the Alcatraz bakery.

(Right) The second warden, Edwin Swope is pictured in the bakery looking over a baking tray of freshly baked dinner rolls made from scratch by convicts.

Darwin remembered:

The guys who worked in the dish and dining rooms had to work only about an hour after each of the meals. After shower time in the morning, they were allowed to go to the yard. After the evening meals, they helped with sweeping and mopping the floors. When our work was done, we could sit together, snack on baked goods and drink coffee. I got to know John well since we swapped stories over coffee when we finished our work. Before Alcatraz, we both worked in the kitchen at Leavenworth so we had a lot of things in common to talk about. We knew a lot of the same guys. It helped pass the time to share stories and you developed close friendships working in such a close setting every day.

Within only weeks of his new assignment, John wrote Associate Warden Olin Blackwell, pleading his assistance in moving to an industries job where he could earn both money and good-time credits. While he liked the work, he quickly realized that time would pass slowly unless he could get work where he could earn back his good time credits. John wrote:

> I just want to remind you Sir that I would like very much to have a job in the industry here. I prefer the tailor shop, but I will take any of the others if there is no openings there. I need the money, and I want to start earning my good time back as soon as possible. I would appreciate your help. I don't mind working in the kitchen, but I had rather have a job so I can earn some money and extra good time. I thank you very much, Sir.
>
> John William Anglin, 1476

Darwin would comment during an interview:

> There were downsides to the kitchen detail. It wasn't a paid assignment, and you had to work 7-days a week. It didn't offer many breaks to stay idle in your cell [on weekends] like the others. This didn't matter to me much, but there were days on the weekends where you wanted to relax and listen to the radio like everyone else. The money was the biggest problem for a lot of guys working the kitchen. You couldn't buy much on Alcatraz anyway, but without money, you couldn't subscribe to magazines or buy a musical instrument. When Blackwell got promoted to warden, he changed those rules. We got meritorious pay and meritorious good time. The pay was about $35.00 per month and it made a big difference. John worked maybe a year in the kitchen, but we remained good friends and always talked out in the yard on weekends.

John seemed to do well in his work assignment and didn't suggest any serious hardships in his letters home to family. He was well liked by his supervisor, and so much so that he successfully lobbied the classification committee and Warden Madigan to allow time worked to be considered for good time credits. Food Supervisor C.V. Bray wrote on December 22, 1960:

> It is recommended that the above named inmate be given consideration at this time for meritorious good time on the basis of his work and conduct since being assigned to the Culinary Department. Anglin entered the department on November 10, 1960. He was assigned to the dining room where he continues to work. He is doing a very good job, is a good worker and tries hard. He keeps his section of the dining room neat and clean. He is dependable. He gets along with everyone. He works seven days a week. He has had no disciplinary problems at this institution.

In the committees' approval, they provided John two days of good time per month to be effective on January 1, 1961. It was welcome news, but he still lobbied for an alternate assignment.

(Above) A view down Broadway looking towards the Alcatraz dining room.

After spending his first Christmas on Alcatraz he wrote home in January of 1961:

Hello Mom,

Received your letter and cards. Hope all of you had a big Christmas and Happy New Year to all of you. I had a pretty good Christmas myself. I just didn't have the spirit to go with it. I got more Christmas cards than I expected, so I guess someone out there knows where I am.

You should be proud of the cold weather you're having down there that goes with Christmas you know. It doesn't ever snow here. It gets pretty cold some times. It does snow on up in the mountains, but not here. I have never seen weather like we have here. It can be seventy degrees over in town and on this island it's forty five or fifty. We have to wear our coats year round here. Some days are pretty nice, but not many. I kinda like it myself, but I prefer Florida.

Well…I'll be on my fourth year next month. I know Alfred and Clarence is thinking the same thing. I wrote Clarence last week, so I'm expecting him to write me this week. I'll write Al too. You can tell everyone hello for me. I didn't have enough Christmas cards to send to all of you, and I hope it didn't hurt anyone's feelings. I don't like to send cards if I can't send to everyone, but it just don't work that way here. I got the pictures you sent. This one of Sue looks just like Marie when she was

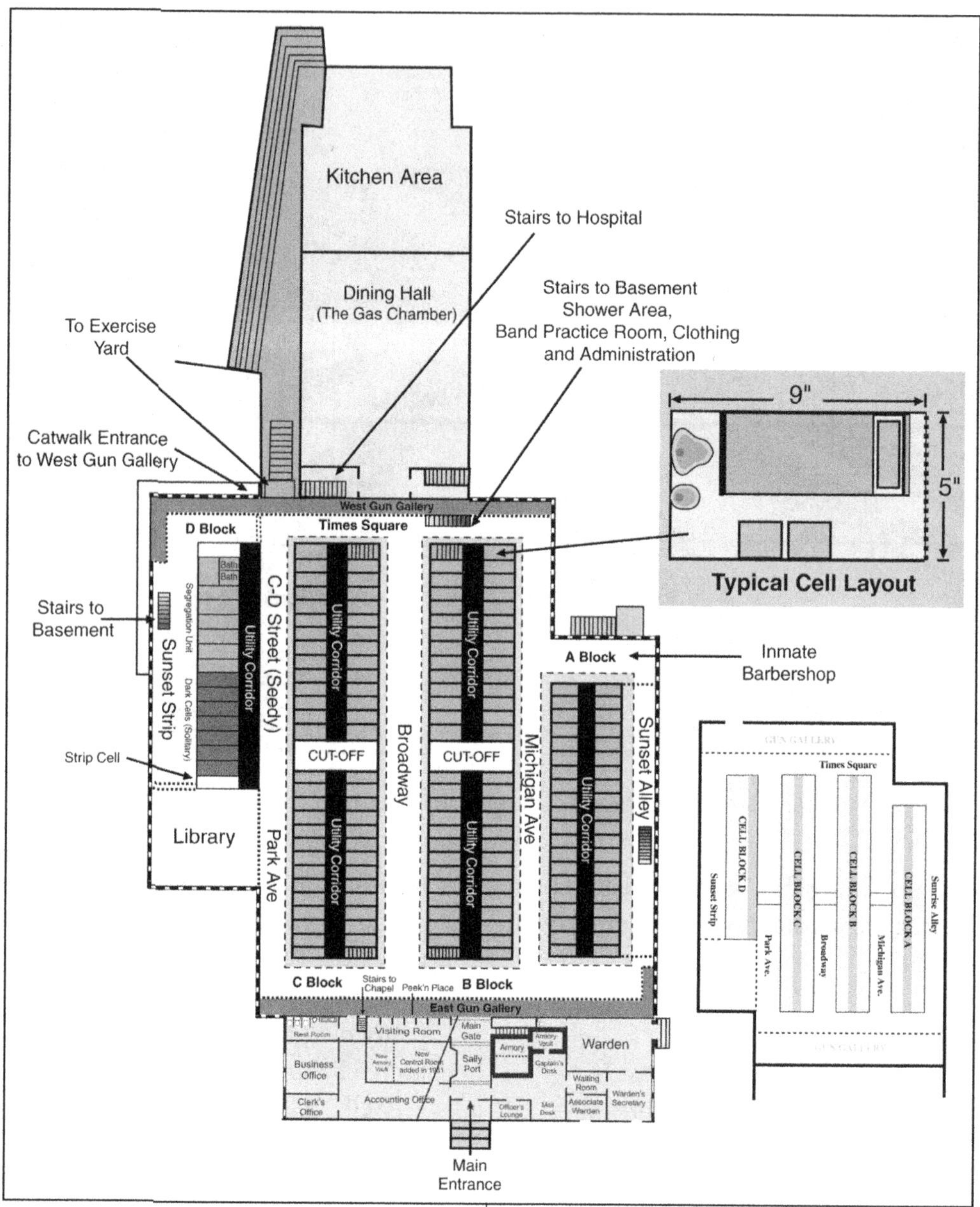

small. I know you were thinking of us. That was enough to make my Christmas a pretty fair one. I wish I could have been there with all of you, but it will have to be later. I just might be down there in three more years, or at least in Alabama. Well I guess I better close for now. Take care and don't forget to write real soon.

Love, John

Clarence finally arrived at Alcatraz on January 16, 1961, and bypassed the traditional cell assignment on Broadway, and was placed in B-140. Ironically, it was the very cell that fellow conspirator Allen West would later occupy during the escape. On the same day he arrived, Clarence penned a letter to his mother stating in part:

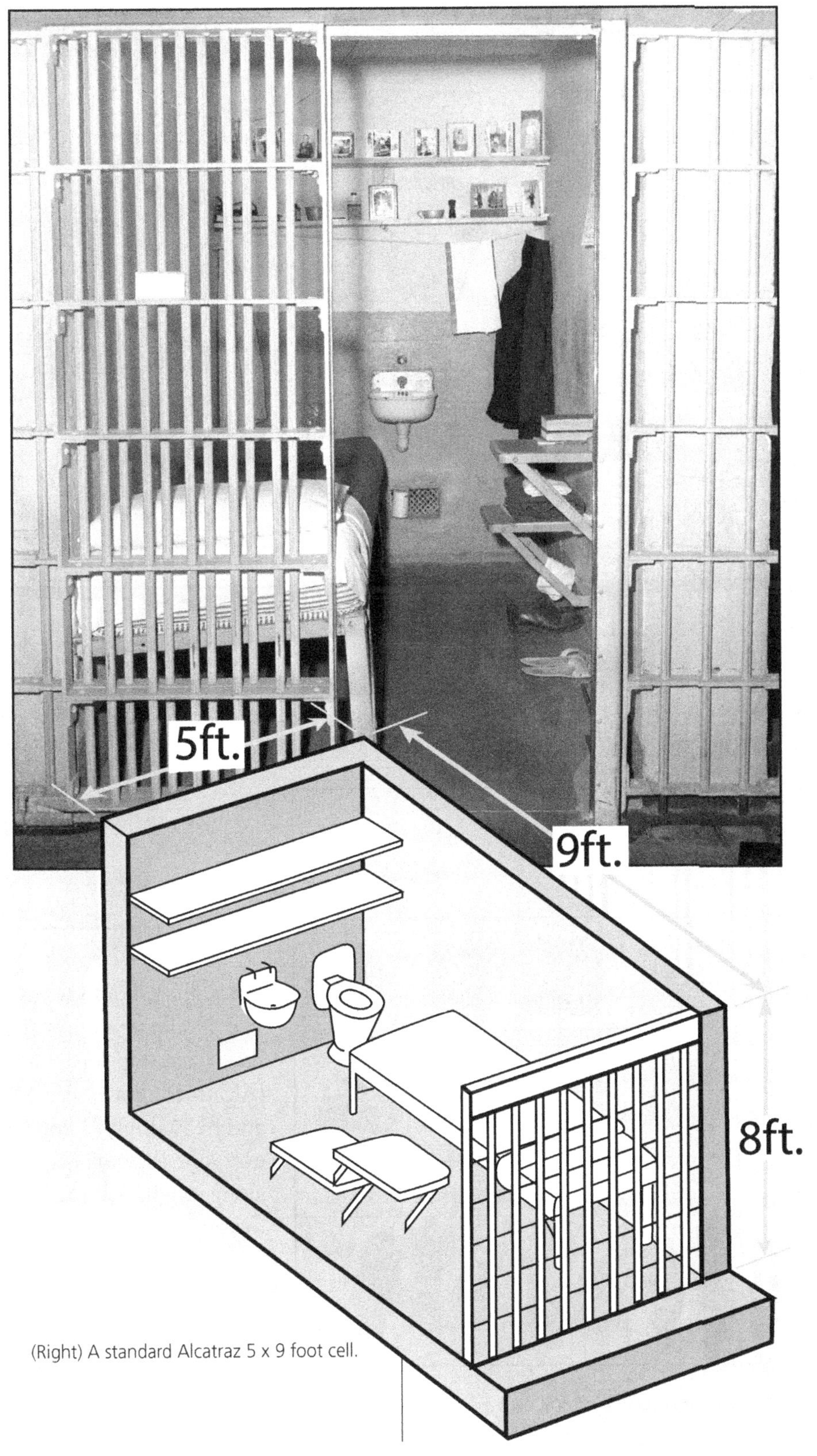

(Right) A standard Alcatraz 5 x 9 foot cell.

UNITED STATES DEPARTMENT OF JUSTICE
PENAL AND CORRECTIONAL INSTITUTIONS

U. S. Penitentiary (Institution) — Alcatraz, California (Location)

Received: January 16, 1961
From: USP, Leavenworth, Kansas
Crime: Bank Robbery & Attempt Escape
Sentence: 17 yrs. ... mos. ... days
Date of sentence: 2-10-58
Sentence begins: 2-10-58
Sentence expires: 2-9-75
Good time sentence expires: 6-19-70
Date of birth: 5-11-31 Occupation: Carp.
Birthplace: Georgia Nationality: Amer.
Age: 29 Comp.: Light
Height: 5' 11½" Eyes: Haz
Weight: 168 Hair: Brown
Build: Med.

Scars and marks: Tatt "Zona" left wrist; Tatt "Nita" right 4 arm

CRIMINAL HISTORY

NAME	NUMBER	CITY OR INSTITUTION	DATE	CHARGE	DISPOSITION OR SENTENCE
ANGLIN, Clarence	75456-L	USP Leavenworth (Transferred to Alcatraz 1-16-61)			

record on separate sheet)

Record Form No. 7
July, 1950

LEAVE THIS SPACE BLANK

Name
Alias Class.
No. Color. Sex. Ref.

RIGHT HAND

1. Thumb	2. Index Finger	3. Middle Finger	4. Ring Finger	5. Little Finger

LEFT HAND

6. Thumb	7. Index Finger	8. Middle Finger	9. Ring Finger	10. Little Finger

Classified. Assembled.
Searched. Verified.
Index Card. Answered.

Note Amputations

Prisoner's Signature: Clarence Anglin

Four Fingers Taken Simultaneously — Left Hand | L. Thumb | R. Thumb | Four Fingers Taken Simultaneously — Right Hand

Clarence arrived in January of 1961 and was immediately placed in B-140 along Michigan Ave.

I thought I should write you and let you know that I have been transferred here (Alcatraz). I have seen John and he is alright. I hope everyone at home is getting along alright. I am making out here ok. It sure is a long ways from home. It took about twenty hours to come out here on the train. It would take about a week drive out here from there. It will be hard on you when you want

A nighttime view of Michigan Ave.

> to visit, but I like it better here than I did at Leavenworth. It's sure not as cold as it was there either and I haven't been assigned any work yet, but there's nothing to worry about. I'll get along alright out here.

Located along the flat of B Block, his cell faced the old A Block section of vacant cells left over from the military era. Although not used, the cells were semi-maintained for potential use in the event of disaster or urgent need. They had escaped the retrofitting in 1934 during its transition to a federal prison. The flat bars were the remnants of a different era, and the same as those that allowed Doc Barker and accomplices to make their break from the cellhouse in 1939. The flats and general location was not overly popular with the prison population. There were only a handful of convicts residing in this section, but a familiar face would look down from the end cell (B-356) on the top tier. Frank Lee Morris (AZ-1441) was the familiar face from USP Atlanta. He would soon play a key role in their destiny, but most who knew him claimed that Morris likely would have nodded or offered a simple hand gesture to wave hello, as he generally kept to himself and engaged in very little conversation with casual associates or those he didn't know well.

As Clarence was confined to his cell without a work assignment, he would remain in lockdown twenty-three hours out of the day with the tedium broke only by the occasional officer or convict assigned the maintenance detail, walking past his cell. Of those men was another familiar face from Atlanta

Convicts entering the dining room for their morning meal.

(Above) A ground view towards the main cellblock from the dining room.

(Right) Frank Morris would occupy B-356, the end cell on the third tier of B Block from October of 1960 until January of 1961. He was able to examine the roof vent whenever he entered or exited his cell.

named Allen West (AZ-1335). In fact, during a brief few months in early 1958, James "Whitey" Bulger, Frank Lee Morris, Allen West, and the three Anglin brothers, Alfred, Clarence and John were all serving time together at USP Atlanta.

Clarence observed activities of the prison through the bars of his new home on the flats of B Block. The atmosphere of Alcatraz seemed to have softened and likely didn't live up to the harsh reputation whispered among cons

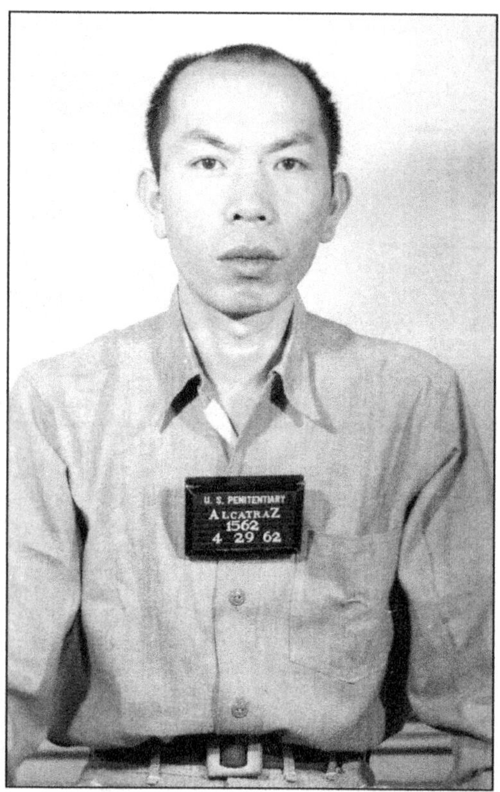

Wayne Fong resided in B-156, the end cell of B Block and only two cells away from Clarence Anglin's cell during the escape. Described as quiet and non-social by those who knew him, he denied any knowledge or awareness of the escape plot when later interviewed by officials.

at other prisons. Frank Sprenz (AZ-1414), the prisoner dubbed "The Flying Bandit" by J. Edgar Hoover, commented in 2012: "Alcatraz wasn't all hard time and grim faces. There were many humorous happenings to blunt the loneliness and isolation. I made great friends and great memories. There were times you'd hear loud laughter echoing in the cellblock, then an officer yelling to quiet down..."

The extreme redundancies in security measures that were once considered the trademark of the infamous prison had slowly faded with time. There was now a slow bleed of rust oozing from the colossal structure and the once solid cement foundation had begun to crumble following decades of standing against the harsh salt winds of a bitter sea.

When Alcatraz opened as federal penitentiary in 1934, the Bureau of Prisons not only renovated the interior cellhouse, but also enhanced security with strategically placed guard towers around the island that were manned around the clock. Structures were built at the dock, the hill tower between the recreation yard and industries buildings, powerhouse, and the road tower, located on the west access road next to the recreation yard overlooking the incinerator. Two years later in 1936, towers were built on top of the model building, and the main tower on-top of the cellhouse. They were part of the Rock's foundation and reputation of being escape proof and harnessing the nation's most volatile prison population. By the 1960s, the era of America's fight against public enemies had also started to fade and severe budget cuts paired against difficulty in the recruitment of officers had forced Warden Madigan to cut corners in security. Alcatraz's second Warden Edwin Swope who took office in 1948, had closed and dismantled the main tower located on top of the cellhouse, as well as the tower next to the powerhouse on the eastside of the prison. Ironically, the escape path of 1962 would align with both locations.

George DeVincenzi, an officer who worked on Alcatraz from 1950 to 1958 commented: "After I was there four or five years, I began to notice that security was starting to get a little bit lax. They

Emil Rychner, Captain of the Guards, is seen in a portrait photograph with guard tower located at the powerhouse in the background. This tower was removed several years prior to the escape. Over the course of several years, several towers were permanently closed as the once iron strict security measures were gradually softened over the decades.

put radios in the cells, this was unheard of before, and they started closing the gun towers, including the one on the roof of the cellhouse. If that tower had been there on the night of the escape, they never would've got anywhere."

Madigan, who had been mentored under the measured but firm style of Warden Johnston, discontinued staffing two more of the original six gun towers that once provided armed and keen eyes to guard the island perimeter. Only one tower would remain staffed 24-hours per day, and the road tower, the only post left to guard the west side of the island was only manned during the daytime hours. Walking patrols around the island had been reduced as did the coverage of geography. The east gun gallery, the interior post most visible to the prison population and also one that several officers felt created the greatest compromise to prison security, had been down staffed by second Warden Edwin Swope, but now was almost completely abandoned. By 1962, the east gallery was only to be staffed during inclement weather periods on winter weekends when heavy rains prevented convicts from spending time in recreation yard.

Warden Edwin Swope talks with prisoners secured in their cells along the C Block corridor known as "Seedy Street," the location between C and D blocks.

Despite the eroding security obvious to prisoners and officers, there was still a false sense of faith that once the convicts were deadlocked into their cells at night, the prison was at its most secure state. There was no exterior wall of a cell adjacent to an outer prison wall, and along with the case hardened steel bars and frequent convict counts, there was the belief that escaping from the cellhouse at night was mostly impossible.

Warden Madigan had placed his full confidence in this security model as no prisoner in its history had ever escaped from a main retrofitted cellblock. So firm in his faith, he completely ignored the direct warnings from Fred Aiken, the associate warden at Leavenworth, cautioning officials that the Anglin brothers should not be allowed to cell in proximity of each other. The cautionary warning was present in both their casefile records and Warden Notebook reference documents. But this was Alcatraz... Madigan felt that allowing the brothers to cell next to each other would make it easier on both the men and their families, and help make the passage of time go easier. Most importantly, they could sit together during meal periods and pass the time reminiscing. Clarence would move onto Broadway into C-227, then a month later (February 23rd) over to C-217, in the cell next to his brother John who was now residing in C-219. The brothers were again reunited.

Frank Lee Morris

"Morris is unlike any inmate with whom I've dealt... Morris has eleven prior escapes from custody that are of record here and appears he has escaped from every institution to which he has been committed..."

—FRED T. WILKINSON,
Warden, USP Atlanta

IN KEEPING PACE with the Anglins, Frank Lee Morris had spent nearly his entire lifetime affiliated in crime. Morris was no boy scout. More than half his life was spent either institutionalized or as a fugitive, but his years in prison never dulled his intellect. With an IQ of 133, placing his intelligence in the top two percent of the population, his life was much more textured than most of his criminal associates. It was a hard luck story rooted well before his birth, with his mother allegedly suffering from substance abuse and other misfortunes. James "Whitey" Bulger first met Morris while serving time in segregation at Atlanta and remembered him talking about his past:

I knew Frankie Morris at Atlanta. I had arrived at the federal prison in Atlanta in July of 1956 as USPA #77607, and Frankie got there in September of 1956 as USPA #77796. We called Frankie "Paco," short in Spanish for "Little Frank." Frankie, Richard Sunday and I served time across from each other in the segregation unit at Atlanta, just before shipping out to the Rock. We were housed in separate open front cells and got to know each other well. I was serving time in segregation for my role in helping friends in an escape plot.

I remember Morris recounting a lot of stories about serving time in the Louisiana State Prison at Angola. He feared being sent back... Morris had already escaped from Angola once. Not easy by any means. He had several escapes in his past. Freedom was so important that he risked his life each time, and each time he got better at it. I remember him saying "If I go back to Angola I'm escaping... I'm dead if they send me back." He felt

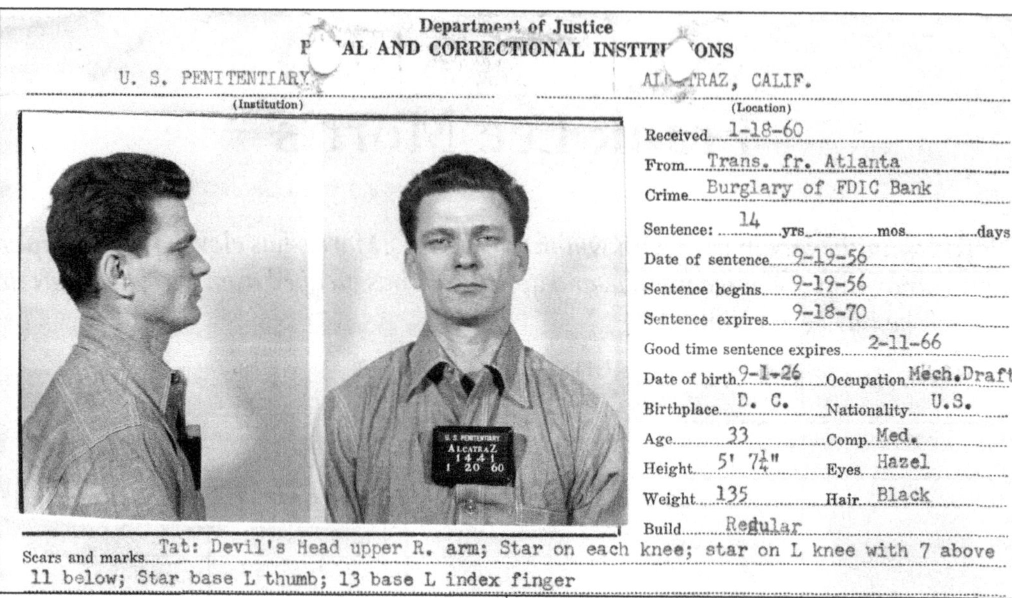

Department of Justice
P[illegible]AL AND CORRECTIONAL INSTIT[illegible]ONS

U. S. PENITENTIARY (Institution) — AL[illegible]RAZ, CALIF. (Location)

Received 1-18-60
From Trans. fr. Atlanta
Crime Burglary of FDIC Bank
Sentence: 14 yrs ... mos ... days
Date of sentence 9-19-56
Sentence begins 9-19-56
Sentence expires 9-18-70
Good time sentence expires 2-11-66
Date of birth 9-1-26 Occupation Mech. Draft.
Birthplace D. C. Nationality U.S.
Age 33 Comp. Med.
Height 5' 7¼" Eyes Hazel
Weight 135 Hair Black
Build Regular

Scars and marks Tat: Devil's Head upper R. arm; Star on each knee; star on L knee with 7 above 11 below; Star base L thumb; 13 base L index finger

Frank Lee Morris

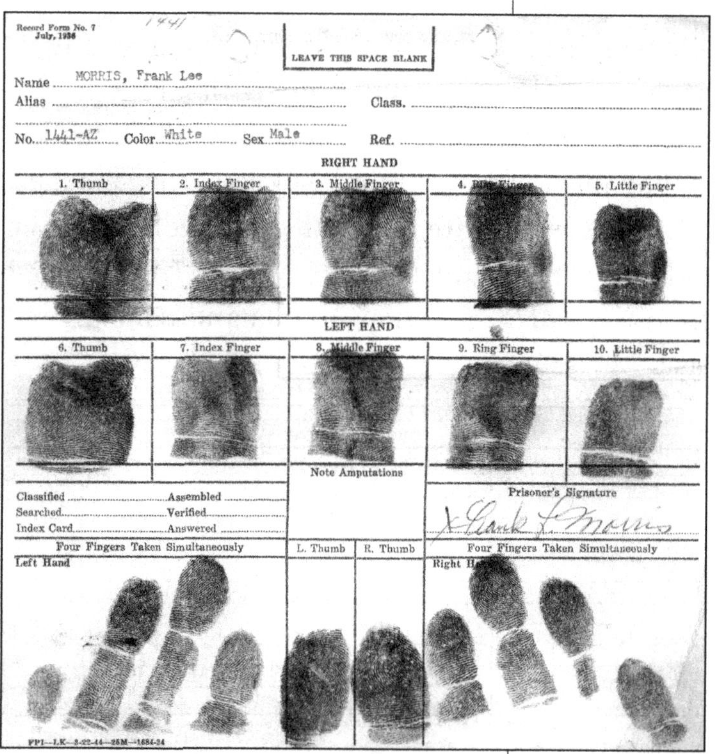

Record Form No. 7
July, 1936

1441

LEAVE THIS SPACE BLANK

Name MORRIS, Frank Lee
Alias
Class.
No. 1441-AZ Color White Sex Male
Ref.

RIGHT HAND

1. Thumb	2. Index Finger	3. Middle Finger	4. Ring Finger	5. Little Finger

LEFT HAND

6. Thumb	7. Index Finger	8. Middle Finger	9. Ring Finger	10. Little Finger

Note Amputations

Classified ... Assembled ...
Searched ... Verified ...
Index Card ... Answered ...

Prisoner's Signature
X Frank L. Morris

Four Fingers Taken Simultaneously	L. Thumb	R. Thumb	Four Fingers Taken Simultaneously
Left Hand			Right Hand

FPI—LK—3-22-44—25M—1684-24

because he had already made a successful break that they would kill him. He told us lots of stories of how violent and corrupt the place was.

Back in the 1950s in the Southern prisons, they used armed convict trusties as guards, and in Texas they used "Barn Bosses." Some of them were real tough, armed with black jacks and straight razors to keep law and order in the barracks. These guys were allowed weapons since they were in prison for non-violent crimes and usually had pending release dates. If they thwarted an escape, it would often earn them their own release. As I said, these prisons were rough places. I remember hearing the stories from Frankie of guys being placed in a cell and the door was actually welded shut for several months. They put titles on cons "Texas Bad Boy," etc., and then set them up to be shot down. In Kilby, convict guards would get a pardon if they killed a convict trying to escape. We used to hear a lot of those stories in Atlanta. I read some of the documents written in his youth. Kind of shakes me up reading the things he wrote at such a young age. He had a hard life…

His family history was a complicated puzzle that officials would later try to piece together in helping to understand the depth of his criminal background. A collection of Department of Justice case files chronicled his troubled early years:

The Washington Field Office determined through the Bureau of Vital Statistics, Washington, D.C., under Certificate of Birth No. 296351, that one Frank Morris was born on September 1, 1926, at Gallinger Municipal Hospital in Washington D.C., to seventeen-year-old Thelma Marie Phillips from Rockville, Maryland. He was her first and only known child. The father was listed as Edward Fred Morris, age thirty-six, occupation – marine engineer, address 1310 D Street SE, Washington D.C., however, it is believed that he is the product of a broken family constellation, his birth coming as a result of the union with a fugitive father named Frank Toanker. According to prior reports, Morris was born into the home of his stepfather, Edward, and as a result Frank took his name. He claimed his father's name was Frank William Lyons and indicated he believed his mother's name was Mary. Little is known about the family unit, though Edward is reported to have drank heavily and was abusive towards Frank's mother and beat her frequently. It is known she was a troubled teen, and had been committed to the National Training School for Girls in Washington D.C., and was known to be untruthful, dishonest, sly, and constantly in trouble. After the birth of the boy, she was returned to the National Training School for white girls at Muirkirk, Maryland. The mother suffered from G.C. and in July 1933, she was in Gallinger Hospital at which time her illness was diagnosed as pulmonary tuberculosis. The whereabouts of his mother have been unknown since that time.

Frank admits that he has no knowledge of his parents, and previous summary reports indicate that he reported both parents died when he was eleven-years old. Morris has claimed that his only living relative was Edith Wilson, his aunt who was residing in Elizabeth City, North Carolina. The Charlotte Division at that time conducted extensive investigations to establish the identity and location of Wilson, but were unsuccessful. He states that he was reared in various homes from which he continually ran and had been reared also in several other juvenile institutions, those being the Industrial Home School for Boys at Blue Plains Virginia, as well as the National Training School for Boys, and the Federal Reformatory at Chillicothe, Ohio.

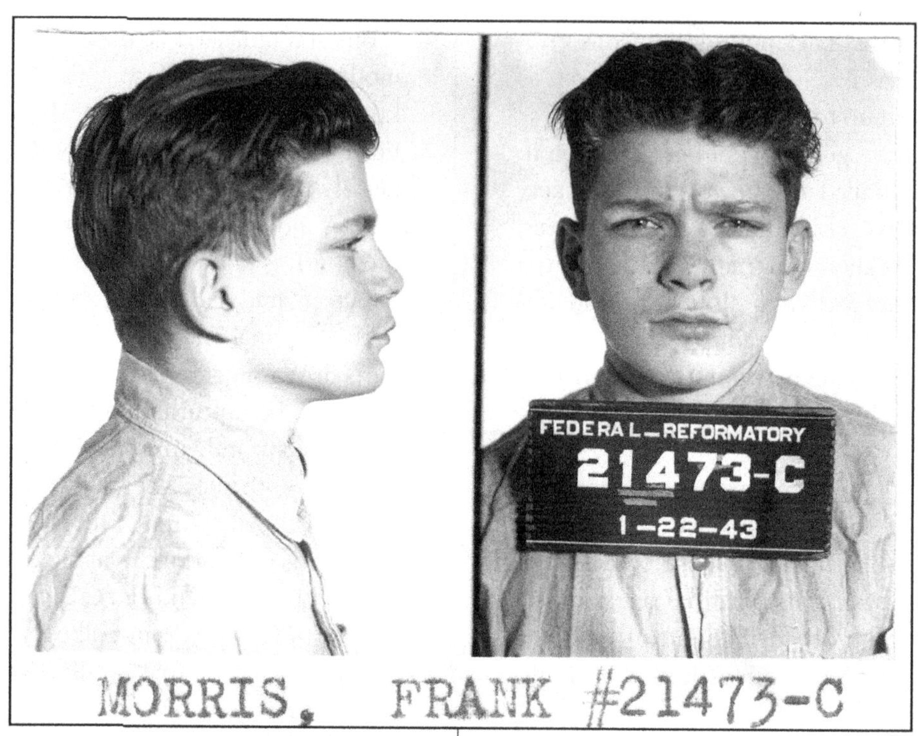

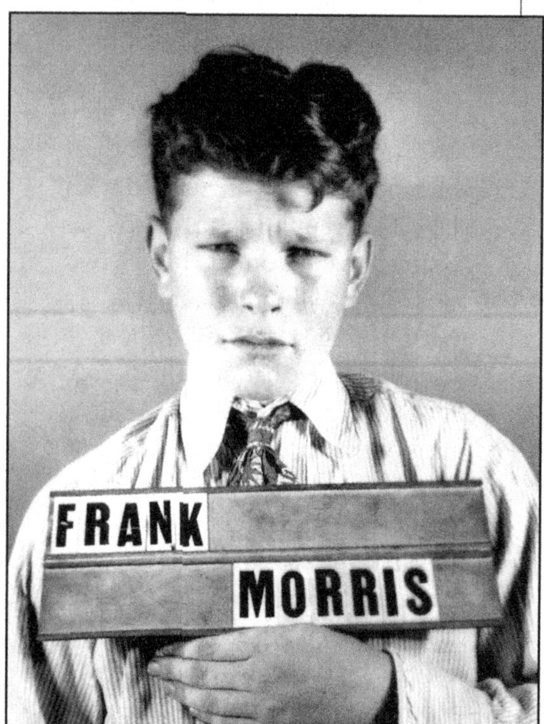

Morris's case file represents a tragic and troubled childhood. His criminal history dated back to grammar school. His early crimes were primarily centered on burglary and theft.

A 1940 social history report provides insight to Frank's tragic childhood:

Stealing appears to be the boy's outstanding problem. This habit began as early as 1933 when Frank was accused by his first grade teacher at Sherwood School, of stealing small articles from other children in the school and from his teacher. First he stole change from the teacher and then food from the lunch boxes of other children. On one of these occasions the boy stole an orange and a slice of cake. The teacher was very sympathetic and cooperated with the caseworker in attempting to properly guide the child. Again, in the summer of 1936, the caseworker received a complaint from the foster mother that the boy had been stealing small amounts of money but later placed it where the foster mother could

Miscellaneous Form No. 63

REPORT OF CUSTODIAL OFFICER — **Nº 183154**

U. S. PRISON SERVICE

DEPARTMENT OF JUSTICE

14-D

Date

Betterment of service — Purpose

Building or equipment — Suggestion — Location

Conduct of Inmate: Frank Morris (Name) 10934-4 (No.) — (Cell) — School (Detail)

Details: Refusing to work or cooperate. Insolence, prevaricating, and drawing obscene pictures—Frank denies this picture but prevaricates on any occasion. Frank has wanted to get out of school this may be his way of doing it. A. Michaelis (Officer)

Disposition: Trans to segregation cottage
Loss of 50 Points
EWB

FPI INC—FLK—2-26-38—4000 BOOKS—11250

find it. Both the foster mother and the caseworker spoke to the child this time, stressing property rights, etc. and it was thought the boy would overcome this habit.

Later, while in the foster home, the boy stole little trinkets, medals, beads, pencils, etc. He did not want them for himself, but gave them away or took them to school and hid them in his locker. At this time he also showed a poor attitude and was difficult to handle. He was quite stubborn, whistled and sang in the school corridors and started fights with other children. He continued to exhibit these traits and was transferred to a new foster home and school.

In 1937, while in this new home, he stole several bars of candy from one of the People's Drug Stores. Also, on June 9, 1937, Miss Driver, the principal of the Bernard School, informed the caseworker that Frank and another boy stole a pocketbook containing $1.81 from the desk of one of the teachers.

In 1938, Frank was placed in what was believed to be a better foster home. On September 14, 1938, it was learned that the boy had broken into a car and taken papers from the dashboard compartment. The boy was given a paper route to from which he would be able to earn sufficient spending money. On his first collection day, however, he collected $2.00 and ran away. He was apprehended shortly after and placed in another foster home and again ran away. Numerous other escapes and references of similar conduct are too excessive to list, however, following another runaway attempt, he made his way to Virginia Beach. While at the amusement park, he dislocated his right thumb while in the Fun House. He went to St. Vincent's Hospital for treatment and when leaving the hospital, stole a purse containing $18.00.

After being placed in July of 1939 at the Industrial Home School, Morris again established an escape pattern of running away, as well as the foster homes into which he has been placed.

He has never been able to develop socially acceptable values, ideals and attitude. He has been unable to benefit by any of the training and treatment programs at any of the numerous institutions to which he has been assigned. Frank has never really enjoyed the close friendship of anyone. He seems to prefer to be alone and read or plan trips on his road maps. Following another series of escapes and burglaries, he was apprehended in September of 1940 in Lawrenceville, Virginia. Frank had entered a home stealing a shotgun, a ring and $4.05. He also had a 22 rifle and a box of cartridges.

He regards his permanent vocation as being that of a draftsman, as well as working in blueprints, or in the printing, plumbing and mill as a mechanic. Apparently, all of his vocation skills were acquired during his incarcerations in the various state and federal penitentiaries. He has considerable skill in drafting. His case entry at Chillicothe, Ohio, states he was doing work of superior quality and had special interest in drafting and also exploited and explored many other related subjects. He was regarded as having an unusual ability to read blueprints. His original work assignment was with the Chief of Mechanical Service office because of his drafting experience and superior intelligence with his educational grade standing at 10.7 and an I.Q. of 133. He is a quiet individual on the job and displays a good attitude toward his duties and is considered to be an energetic worker. He makes good use of the library facilities reading both fiction and non-fiction novels along with different magazines. There is no indicated interest in the religious or recreation programs.

A progress report from Chillicothe in 1943 offered mixed grades on his adjustment status with multiple write-ups in February and March. In one incident, during the exercise period, Morris engaged in some "horseplay" with another youth. When he was reprimanded and told that he would miss a meal, he grumbled under his breath and acted in an insolent manner. He had never been respectful or cooperative with the staff, therefore, it was decided that a stay in therapeutic segregation might be beneficial. He was placed in segregation. He broke the small glass panel in the door frame and screamed that he wanted something to eat. He was placed in the strip cell. In April of 1943 he was released from segregation and back into population. In July during a routine shakedown, a razor blade was found in his room and he was returned to segregation.

Morris graduated to larger crimes and in 1955 was charged robbing the Bank of Slidell in Louisiana on the night of November 24th, 1955. He was sentenced September 19th, 1956, receiving a fourteen (14) year term on count one and a five (5) year term on count two.

Morris stated that he, as well as his codefendant, owed "a lot of time" here and there in various states for crimes they had committed. He indicated that he wanted the money in order to live and had planned to upon leaving the country. He indicated that he had planned to go to Mexico and then to South America. It was felt that Slidell was the best place to secure the cash. He was not successful because the safe of the bank contained gas and they were unable to work in the gas due to the fact that they had no gas masks. He indicated that they were using an acetylene torch as well and it took too much time. They received about $6,500.00 in change and a few bills. Several other persons, Junior Bradley, and a Barbara Tootful, were charged with aiding and abetting and assisting his co-defendant, receiving stolen goods and charges of that nature. Bradley received a five year sentence at Tallahassee and the girl received a two year sentence at Alderson.

In addition to the aforementioned, Morris has been incarcerated at the State Penitentiary, Angola, Louisiana, and also the State Penitentiary,

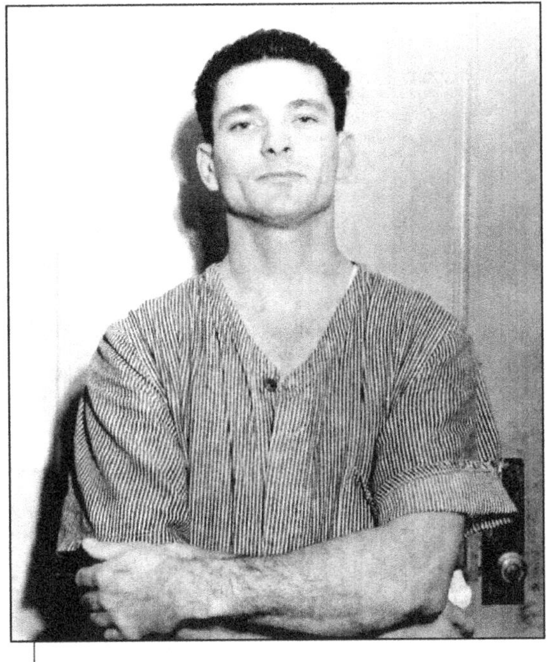

(Above and below) Morris in June of 1952 at Angola, the State Penitentiary in Louisiana.

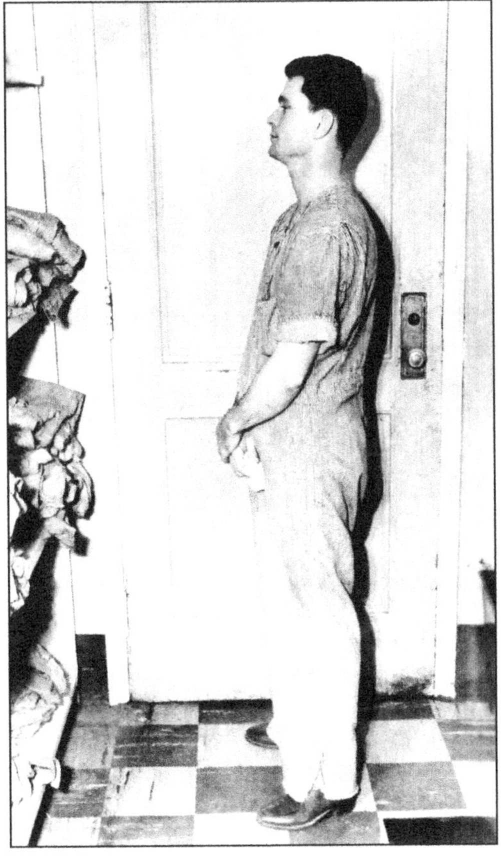

BOARD OF COMMISSIONERS OF STATE INSTITUTIONS

LEROY COLLINS, GOVERNOR
CHAIRMAN
R. A. GRAY, SECRETARY OF STATE
RICHARD W. ERVIN, ATTORNEY GEN.
RAY E. GREEN, COMPTROLLER

J. EDWIN LARSON, STATE TREASURER
THOMAS D. BAILEY, STATE SUP'T. OF PUBLIC INSTRUCTION
NATHAN MAYO, COMM. OF AGRICULTURE
MRS. LEAH S. BATTLE, SECRETARY

FLORIDA STATE PRISON
DEWITT SINCLAIR, SUPERINTENDENT

RAIFORD, FLORIDA

TELEPHONE STARKE 799

September 29th, 1956

ESCAPE RECORD OF FRANK LYONS FSP # 44399-46298, WM.:

On February 14, 1949 escaped from a State Road Department Squad working near the Prison. Recaptured and returned a few hours later after escape.

On March 31, 1949 escaped from State Road Department Camp near Fort Myers, Florida. Recaptured and returned the same date.

On January 25, 1950 escaped from State Road Department Camp near Fort Myers, Florida. Recaptured by Sheriff's Office, of Stuart, Florida. Stole an automobile after his escape from Camp. Received an additional sentence of three years on the charges of escape and larceny of automobile.

On November 6, 1950 escaped from State Road Department Camp near Fort Myers, Florida, recaptured by Chief of Police, Punta Gorda, Florida. Returned to Camp same day of capture.

On June 16, 1951, escaped from the barracks of State Road Camp #8510, Fort Myers, Florida. About 10:30 P M the night of June 16th, 1951, prisoner cut a hole in the Camp barracks floor and escaped. Not recaptured to this date.

Very truly yours,

Milo Seigler

Milo Seigler, Director
Records and Personnel.

MS:mrc

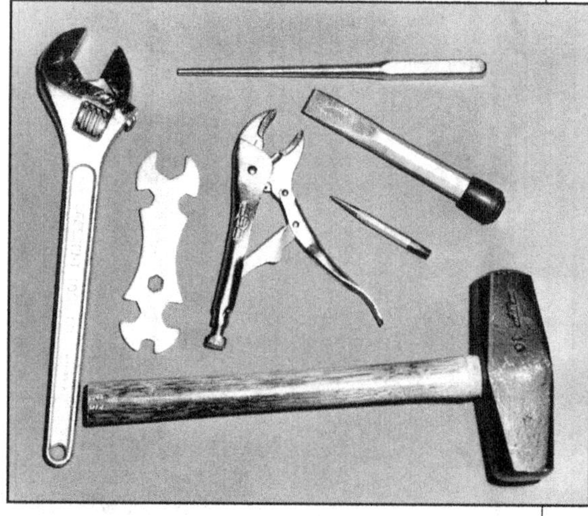

(Above) A 1956 report from the Florida State Penitentiary at Raiford illustrating Morris's extensive history of escapes. He escaped from nearly every prison to which he was ever committed.

(Left) The headline read: "'Have you seen these tools?' These tools were used by the burglars who pulled the $7,000 Bank of Slidell job Thanksgiving night and were left at the scene of the crime, says Morton Chiles, special agent in charge of the New Orleans FBI field office. If you recognize any of them, get in touch with the FBI office, Tenth Floor, Masonic Temple Bldg., Your tip may help catch the burglars."

Raiford, Florida. He escaped from that institution three or four times and presently owes time. There are four detainers outstanding against him and he also has a long record of escapes, having escaped last in April 1955, from the State Prison, Angola, Louisiana. While incarcerated at the Orleans Parish Prison, New Orleans, Louisiana, on bank robbery charges, Morris was placed in solitary confinement. On January 11, 1956, he was discovered to have sawed through two bars by using a piece of copper tubing and concrete from the floor, used as an abrasive. He was subsequently charged with attempted escape. The New Orleans Police Department knows Morris to be erratic, potentially violent, daring and capable of any crime. They further advised they were well acquainted with this subject's proclivity toward escape and his potential as a cunning and clever criminal.

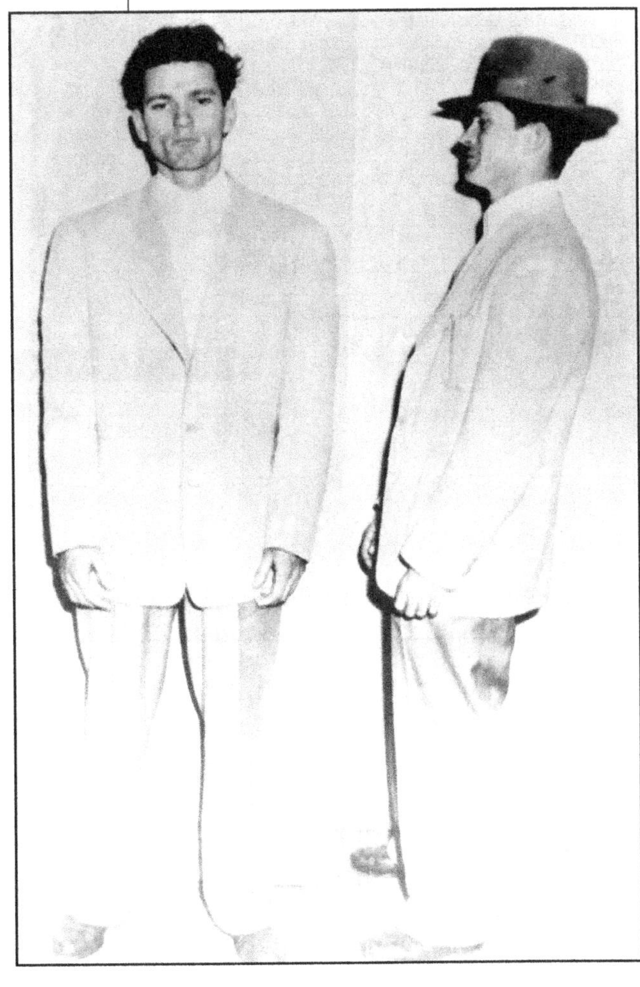

Morris makes a very engaging, frank, appearance and is careful while admitting to his various crimes. He indicated that he had been on the run from the law and incarcerated ever since he was a kid and that this was his final attempt to make a clean start.

Frank Lee Morris was committed to the United

(Right, top and bottom)) Morris following his capture in New Orleans, January of 1956.

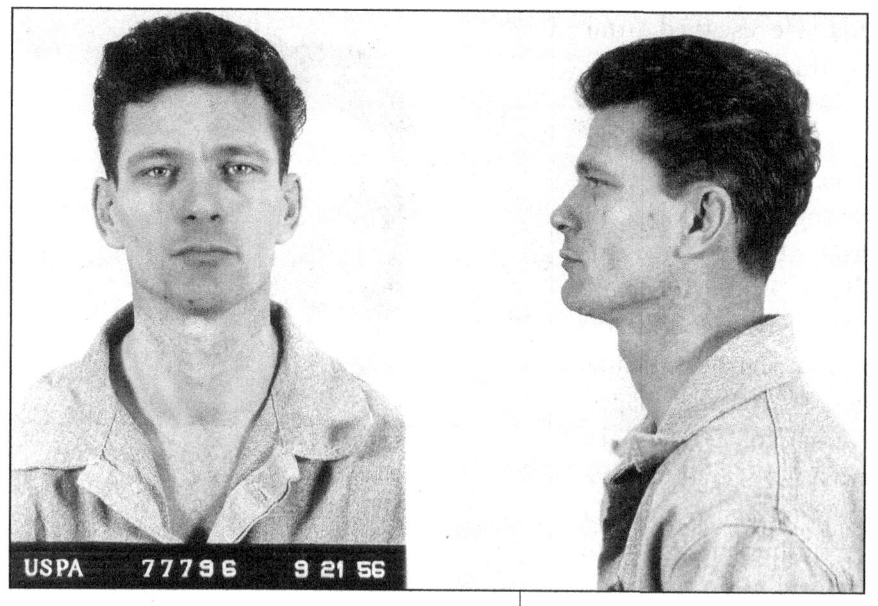

(Left and below) Frank Morris arrived at USP Atlanta on September 21, 1956.

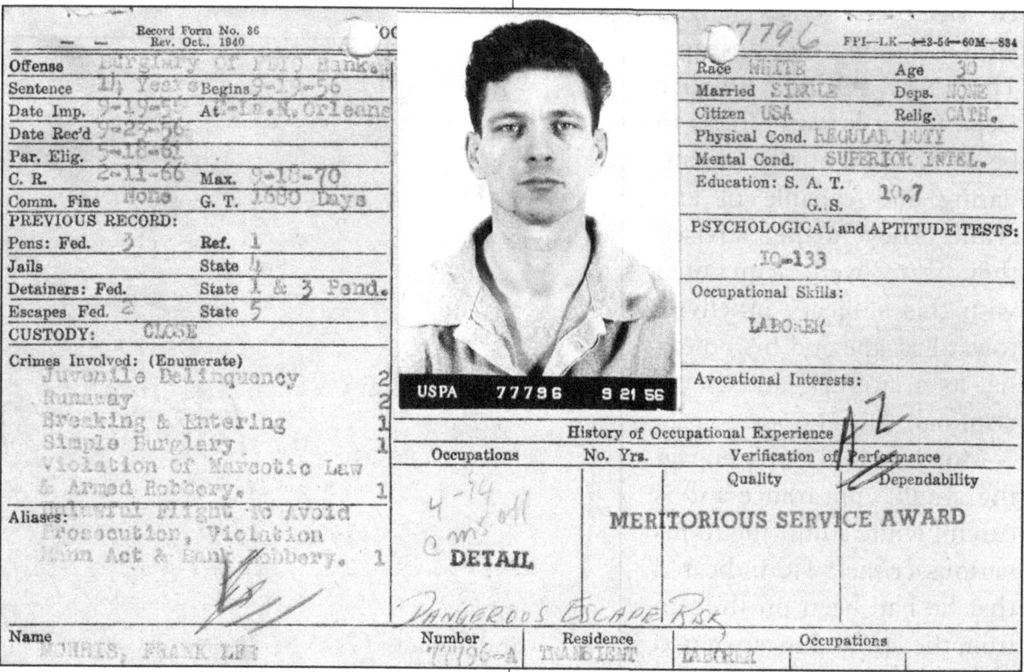

Record Form No. 86
Rev. Oct., 1940

77796 FPI—LK—4-23-54—60M—834

Offense Burglary of FDIC Bank.
Sentence 14 Years Begins 9-19-56
Date Imp. 9-19-56 At E-La. N. Orleans
Date Rec'd 9-23-56
Par. Elig. 5-18-61
C. R. 2-11-66 Max. 9-18-70
Comm. Fine None G. T. 1680 Days
PREVIOUS RECORD:
Pens: Fed. 3 Ref. 1
Jails State 4
Detainers: Fed. State 1 & 3 Pend.
Escapes Fed. 2 State 5
CUSTODY: CLOSE
Crimes Involved: (Enumerate)
Juvenile Delinquency 2
Runaway 2
Breaking & Entering 1
Simple Burglary 1
Violation of Narcotic Law & Armed Robbery. 1
Unlawful Flight to Avoid Prosecution, Violation Mann Act & Bank Robbery. 1
Aliases:

Race WHITE Age 30
Married SINGLE Deps. NONE
Citizen USA Relig. CATH.
Physical Cond. REGULAR DUTY
Mental Cond. SUPERIOR INTEL.
Education: S. A. T. G. S. 10.7
PSYCHOLOGICAL and APTITUDE TESTS:
IQ-133
Occupational Skills:
LABORER
Avocational Interests:

USPA 77796 9 21 56

History of Occupational Experience

Occupations	No. Yrs.	Verification of Performance: Quality	Dependability
4-54 Comm. Detail DETAIL		MERITORIOUS SERVICE AWARD	

DANGEROUS ESCAPE RISK

Name	Number	Residence	Occupations
MORRIS, FRANK LEE	77796-A	TRANSIENT	LABORER

States Federal Penitentiary in Atlanta in September of 1956. Warden Fred T. Wilkinson, who later became the Assistant Director of the Bureau of Prisons, wrote the following summary to Director James Bennett providing his recommendation of Morris being sent to Alcatraz. It stated in part:

The case of Frank Lee Morris is being referenced to you with the recommendation that he be transferred to Alcatraz. Since he was committed here in September of 1956, Morris has been frequently identified with groups of who's plans to escape from this institution have been frustrated for one reason or

Custodial Form No. 5

REPORT OF CUSTODIAL OFFICER
U. S. PRISON SERVICE
DEPARTMENT OF JUSTICE

AWB
№ 21971

Date: 9-20-59

Betterment of service — Purpose: DISICIPINARY REPORT
Building or equipment — Suggestion — Location
Conduct of Inmate — Name: MORRIS — No.: 77796 — Cell: 6-4 — Detail: ORD.

Details: SUSPICION OF ATTENPTING TO ESCAPE:
At 8:30 P.M. this day heard a loud crash. I ran to the south side of the cellhouse and saw Morris 77796 running from the west end of the cell house toward me, he turned at the cut off to the north side of the cellhouse. I ran to that side and saw him go into his cell.

Paul C. Legg — Officer

FPI—LK—12-21-43—1000 Bks—1868

Disposition: Punitive Seg. Modified Priv. 30 days
see memo
Refer to GTFB.

W.H. York
W.H. YORK, Assoc. Warden

another and usually official surveillance and intervention prior to completion of full scale arrangements. In February, 1959, Morris was found to have some lock picks in his personal belongings and, following a period of isolation, he was quartered in administrative segregation. After a few weeks in this status, he was returned to population but he lost little time in becoming re-affiliated with his old cronies and on September 20, 1959, when two inmates escaped from B cellhouse through spreading the bars of one of the window grills in this housing unit, Morris was observed, by one of our officers, running from the area when one of the windows became loosened and crashed onto the cellhouse floor. Morris was undoubtedly planning to leave with the others, but from all indications, he was either unable to squeeze himself through the narrow opening that was made by the bar spreader or else he became frightened and ran into his cell when he feared the noise of the falling window would hastily attract the attention of officers to the scene. He is now again in administrative segregation where he awaits good time forfeiture action and where we feel he should remain until he is transferred.

Morris has eleven prior escapes from custody that are of record here and appears he has escaped from every institution to which he has been committed. As early as his original classification, some thought was given to the transfer of Morris to Alcatraz, but it was judged best to keep him here and try to work out a suitable program for him here. His response, however, has been so persistently unfavorable that we can see no alternative to recommending that he be sent to Alcatraz.

These were the forces that molded Morris and as Bulger remembered:

> I never considered Morris or the brothers as dangerous people. Frankie and the Anglins were all exceptional guys... They never hurt anyone, but paid a hefty price with years of slow time in prison. Their plan of escape was not that of a "Do

MORRIS Record Form No. 36 Rev. Oct., 1940 #1441-AZ **ASSOCIATE WARDEN'S RECORD CARD** FPI—LK—5-1-56—55M—8414

Offense Bank robbery
Sentence 14 years Begins 9-19-56
Date Imp. 9-19-56 AtE-LA New Orleans
Date Rec'd 1-18-60 (Fm. A)
Par. Elig. 5-18-61
C. R. 2-11-66 Max. 9-18-70
Comm. Fine None G. T. 1680 days
PREVIOUS RECORD:
Jails Ref. 1
Pens: Fed. 3 State 4
Detainers: Fed. State 5
Escapes: Fed. 2 State 5
CUSTODY: Close
Crimes Involved: (Enumerate)
Juv. Deliq.-2; Runaways-2; Breaking & Entering-1; Burglary-1; Narcotics & Armed Robbery-1; Unlawful Flight, Mann Act, & Bank Robbery-1

Aliases:

U. S. PENITENTIARY ALCATRAZ 1441 1 20 60

Race White Age 9-1-26
Married No Deps. None
Citizen U. S. A. Relig. Cath.
Physical Cond. Regular duty
Mental Cond. Superior Intel.
Education: S. A. T. 10.7
G. S.
PSYCHOLOGICAL & APTITUDE TESTS:
I. Q. - 133

Occupational Skills: mech - Draftsman, Laborer, Blue Printman
Avocational Interests:

History of Occupational Experience

Occupations	No. Yrs.	Verification of Performance: Quality	Dependability
An escape artist.			

Name	Number	Residence	Occupations
MORRIS, Frank Lee	1441-AZ	Transient	Laborer

Frank Morris arrived on Alcatraz on January 20, 1960, from USP Atlanta. On his associate warden notebook card, officials listed one of his formal occupations as "an escape artist" and noted his superior intelligence. Whitey Bulger who served time with Morris both at Atlanta and Alcatraz, recalled that he loved to do newspaper crossword puzzles. He was skilled at solving complex brainteasers and was a "really well spoken and bright guy."

or Die" plot like Coy and Cretzer in 46'. Also, Paco robbed banks, not with a gun, but by burglary and a cutting torch. He didn't use violence. Looking back I remember Paco sizing everyone up and not saying or revealing much. He was always suspicious of others around him. I expect he must have been burnt by so many of those he trusted in his younger years. In regard to the brothers, they were a credit to their families. Clean living and adventurous. That's how I remember them. They were quiet and fixated on one thing—to leave Alcatraz. Their actions helped close the Rock, not to mention helping many of the old timers get their freedom. I believe that if Alcatraz were to have remained open, they would have been forced to live out the rest of their lives there. As a general rule, men were never paroled directly from Alcatraz, and a life sentence meant just that. Many fellow convicts who were serving hard time benefited from the trio. Allen West was a different story all together.

Allen Clayton West

"Sneaky, demanding and belligerent...
West is a definite detriment to the morale of this institution..."

—1960, Alcatraz Inmate Case File

ALLEN CLAYTON WEST first arrived on Alcatraz in April of 1954, on the same chain as the King of Harlem, Ellsworth "Bumpy" Johnson (AZ-1117). West carried with him a notorious reputation of being a prolific instigator and always at the center of racial conflicts. Despite receiving favorable conduct reports just prior to the escape, Correctional Officer Irving Levinson disliked him. When asked in 1994 if he knew the escapees, including West, and what he thought of them, he commented about West specifically: "What was he like? I didn't like him. I thought he was a piece of shit... What you might not believe is that I liked most of the guys there. Almost every one of them was civil towards to me. I remember West's smirk whenever I'd say hello... He didn't acknowledge me and I remember that about him. Most all of the men were actually very pleasant to be around, but West was the kind that carried a grudge against the uniform... I remember West..."

Allen was born on March 25, 1929, in New York City. His mother, Marie, was a city native, and his father, Roland, was raised in Savannah, Georgia. He had two older brothers and one younger sister, and while his parents were described as loving and nurturing, they lived mostly off a military disability pension and they struggled to raise their four children on limited income. His father had lost his left leg when he was only nineteen years old as a soldier fighting in World War I. His disability sometimes made work more difficult and though money was tight, he managed to supplement his income by doing both commercial and

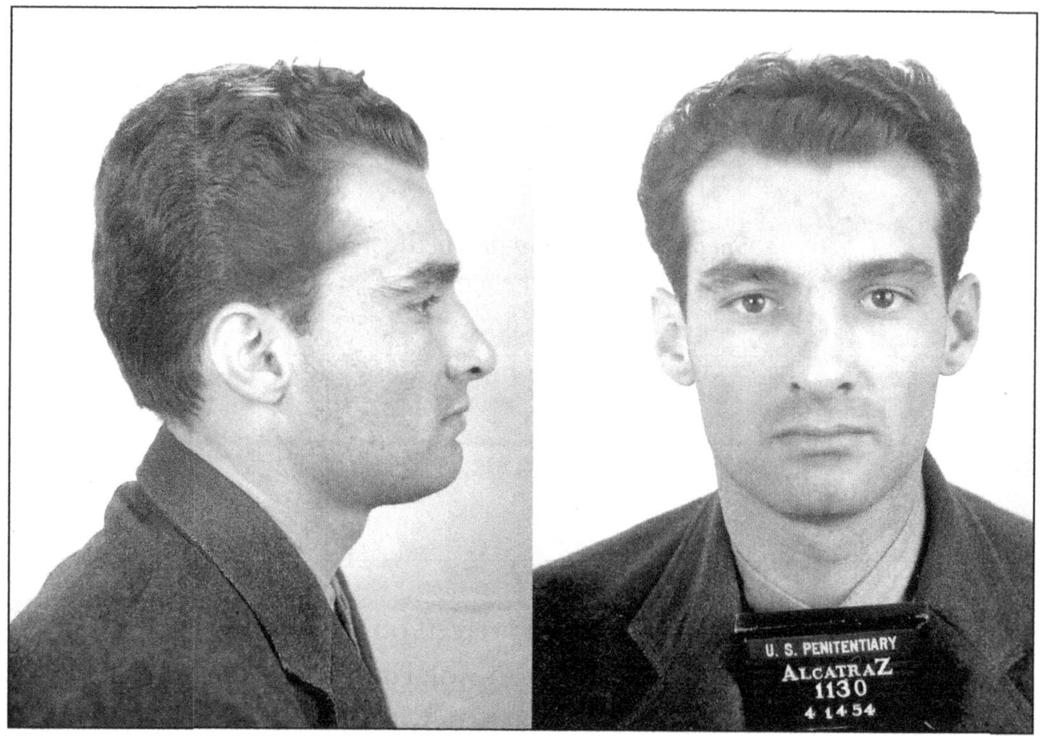

Allen West. He would later claim to authorities that he masterminded the entire escape.

residential electrical work. Despite not owning their home, he earned enough money between his pension and extra income to rent a small but comfortable home on Lincoln Street, in Savannah Georgia. Some records indicate that the father was a heavy drinker, but never abusive or absent.

The oldest sibling Roland, Jr., joined the Army when he turned eighteen in 1931, and his brother Kenneth joined the Navy at the same age in 1944. His brothers were both described as good role models who encouraged Allen to also join the military. Kenneth taught navigation and radar procedures at the Naval Base in San Diego, California, and his oldest brother Roland became a Major in the Army. Both his brothers encourage him and felt it would secure his future and set him on the right path. An early case file entry described Allen as being a "rebellious" youth, and a "delinquent" from the age of eleven. A collection of summaries from various casefile records read in part:

> This man moved with his family to Savannah and attended school until he was 14 years old, completing eighth grade. He claims he had no particular reason for stopping school, but it is noted from the FBI record that the subject received a sentence to the Georgia State Training School for Boys for the theft of an automobile at age fifteen. He ran away almost immediately and was returned the next day, but escaped five times total from this institution. In 1943 or

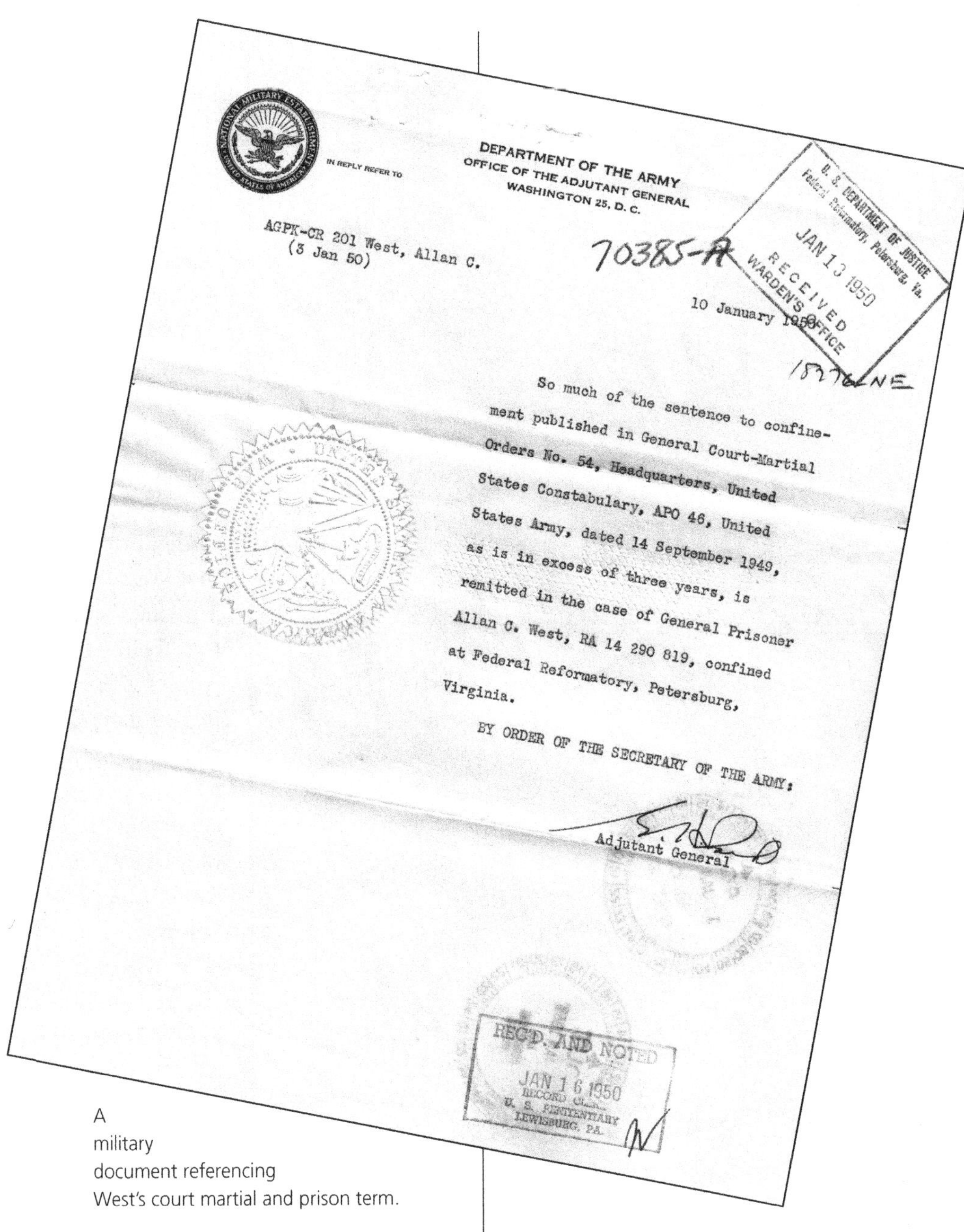

DEPARTMENT OF THE ARMY
OFFICE OF THE ADJUTANT GENERAL
WASHINGTON 25, D. C.

IN REPLY REFER TO

AGPK-CR 201 West, Allan C.
(3 Jan 50)

70385-A

U. S. DEPARTMENT OF JUSTICE
Federal Reformatory, Petersburg, Va.
JAN 13 1950
RECEIVED
WARDEN'S OFFICE

10 January 1950

So much of the sentence to confinement published in General Court-Martial Orders No. 54, Headquarters, United States Constabulary, APO 46, United States Army, dated 14 September 1949, as is in excess of three years, is remitted in the case of General Prisoner Allan C. West, RA 14 290 819, confined at Federal Reformatory, Petersburg, Virginia.

BY ORDER OF THE SECRETARY OF THE ARMY:

Adjutant General

REC'D. AND NOTED
JAN 16 1950
RECORD CLERK
U. S. PENITENTIARY
LEWISBURG, PA.

A military document referencing West's court martial and prison term.

1944, he was sent to the Georgia State Penitentiary in Atlanta with a three year sentence for the theft of an automobile and he escaped while serving on that sentence also. In 1945, he received a six to fifteen year sentence for burglary and automobile theft and served about four years of it before finally being released. He admits that he tried to escape on one occasion by digging a hole under the wall. While in Atlanta, he was continually in difficulty and claims that he was involved in several cuttings and fights. When in isolation, he was overheard by officers more than once, bragging that he

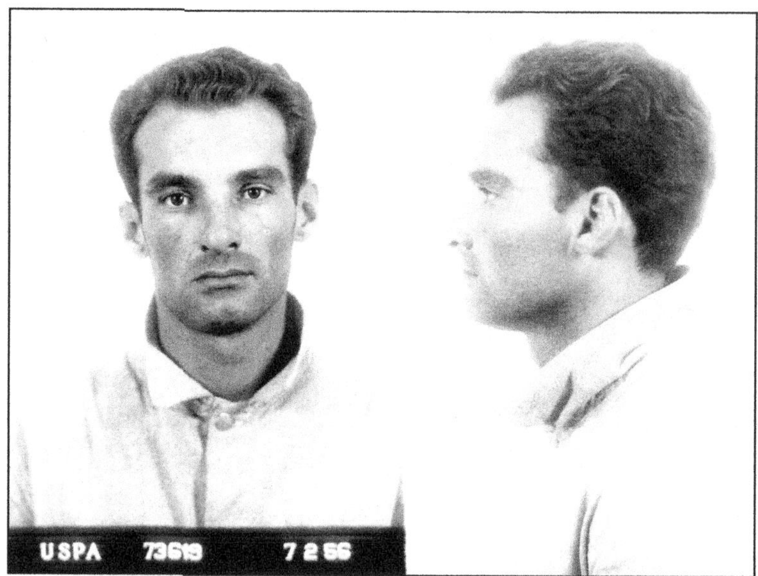

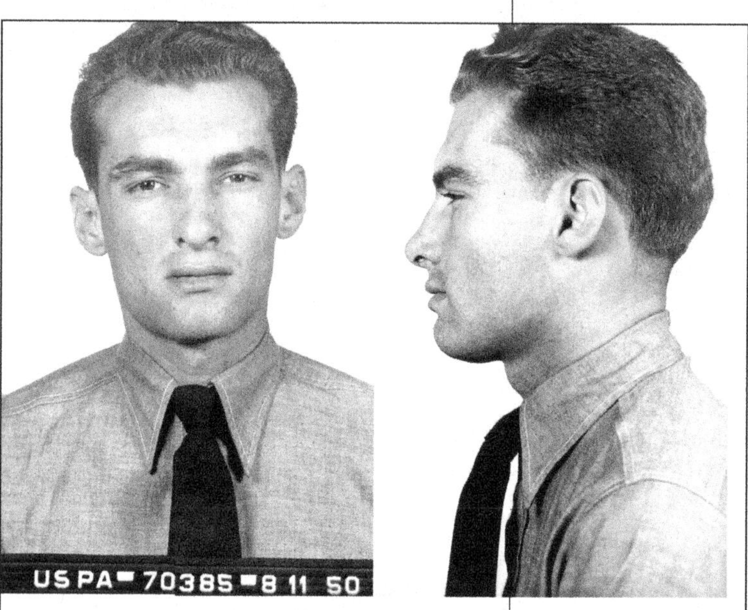

(This page and opposite) Early file photos of West during his multiple terms at USP Atlanta.

will "break out of this place as soon as he hits population." He complains of severe headaches frequently and is a known narcotics user for more than five years.

On September 16, 1948, after serving his state prison term, he enlisted in the United States Army and in December of that same year, was sent overseas to Germany. A United States Army memorandum dated September 14, 1949, referencing a General Court Martial Order, indicated that West was arraigned and tried before two Army Colonels in Stuttgart, Germany for a sodomy charge occurring in May of 1949 at the Wildflecken Training Area. West was also charged and found guilty of numerous AWOL offenses while assigned to Company "I", 3rd Battalion, 2nd Armed Calvary, from his station at Augsburg, Germany. Following his arrest, he escaped from military authorities and was assigned to the Federal Reformatory at Chillicothe, Ohio. Prior to deportation, he was confined at the Command Military Prison in Mannheim, Germany.

Department of Justice
PE[illegible]L AND CORRECTIONAL INSTITUT[illegible]NS

UNITED STATES PENITENTIARY, ATLANTA, GA.
(Institution) (Location)

USPA 70385 7 26 50

Received
From FBI 4-229 558
Crime
Sentence: ... yrs. ... mos. ... days
Date of sentence
Sentence begins
Sentence expires
Good time sentence expires
Date of birth ... Occupation
Birthplace ... Nationality
Age ... Comp. medi.
Height 5'7½" Eyes Dk. Br.
Weight 145 Hair Brown wavy.
Build med

Scars and marks T.T.S.: Baby TRUE back of fingers both hds. good luck back R hand. 3 ... on R 4 arm. Tattoo on left dagger & heart front R 4 arm. Kaye on front left 4 arm.

CRIMINAL HISTORY

NAME	NUMBER	CITY OR INSTITUTION	DATE	CHARGE	DISPOSITION OR SENTENCE

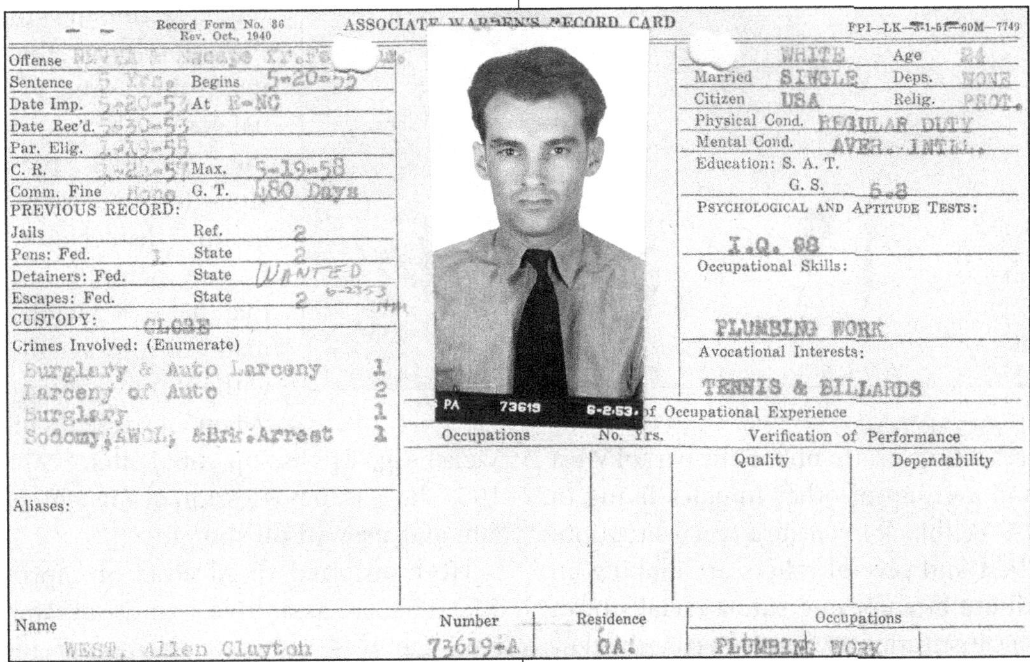

Record Form No. 86
Rev. Oct., 1940

ASSOCIATE WARDEN'S RECORD CARD

FPI—LK—3-1-51—60M—7749

Offense [illegible]
Sentence 5 Yrs. Begins 5-20-53
Date Imp. 5-20-53 At E-NC
Date Rec'd. 5-30-53
Par. Elig. 1-19-55
C. R. 3-21-57 Max. 5-19-58
Comm. Fine None G. T. 180 Days
PREVIOUS RECORD:
Jails Ref. 2
Pens: Fed. 1 State 2
Detainers: Fed. State WANTED
Escapes: Fed. State 2 6-23-53
CUSTODY: CLOSE
Crimes Involved: (Enumerate)
Burglary & Auto Larceny 1
Larceny of Auto 2
Burglary 1
Sodomy, AWOL, & Brk. Arrest 1
Aliases:

PA 73619 6-2-53

WHITE Age 24
Married SINGLE Deps. NONE
Citizen USA Relig. PROT.
Physical Cond. REGULAR DUTY
Mental Cond. AVER. INTELL.
Education: S. A. T.
G. S. 5.8
PSYCHOLOGICAL AND APTITUDE TESTS:
I.Q. 98
Occupational Skills:
PLUMBING WORK
Avocational Interests:
TENNIS & BILLARDS

[illegible]of Occupational Experience

Occupations	No. Yrs.	Verification of Performance: Quality	Dependability

Name	Number	Residence	Occupations
WEST, Allen Clayton	73619-A	GA.	PLUMBING WORK

Subject has been considered a custody risk at every institution he's been confined. Since he has been in this institution, several instances have arisen which pointed to him as being not only an agitator in general institutional troubles, but in addition is considered one of our strongest and most aggressive racial agitators. Two group incidents have occurred in the last three days

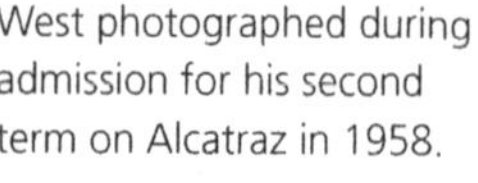
West photographed during admission for his second term on Alcatraz in 1958.

indicating an attempt on the part of West and a group of other inmates living in "A" cellblock to create a racial situation. West and several others are making an all-out attempt to create a racial riot in this institution and considering the tension left over from the recent black and white assault affairs, we find the situation potentially quite dangerous. Since this subject has been in this institution he has not made any attempt to better himself, not make any advantage of a worthwhile program here. He is aligned with a group who became involved in every anti-social and derogatory activity possible, and aids in keeping tension alive among the great majority of inmates who are trying to behave themselves and make good adjustments here. West is a definite detriment to the morale of this institution and a dangerous factor in the potential precipitation of serious group disturbance. It was pointed out that he is a vicious man given to assault without provocation. When arrested in Vicksburg, Mississippi on January 27, 1953, he was in possession of a machine gun and a sawed-off shotgun.

He transferred to Alcatraz on April 14, 1954, as assaultive and an escape risk. He was returned to Atlanta in June of 1956 and he was conditionally released of his federal prison term on December 20, 1956, and custody was immediately turned over to state prison officials for commitment to Raiford, the State Penitentiary in Florida, on a detainer for a prior escape. He again escaped on July 16, 1957, with two other inmates and he was involved in robberies and car thefts while a fugitive. He was returned to Alcatraz in 1958, because of the poor prognosis in view of his prior criminal record including multiple escapes, record of assault, detainers and poor prior institutional adjustment.

Fellow convicts nicknamed West 'Eagle Eye Fleagle' based on a syndicated cartoon character from the popular Lil' Abner comic strip.

With the exception of forty-six days, when he worked in the Culinary Department and Clothing Room, he has been quartered in the Treatment Unit since December 21, 1959. Since that date he has incurred three disciplinary reports. The last one is dated October 2, 1960, when he was cited for assaulting an officer. In June of 1961, he was contacted and advised his eligibility for parole consideration. His first response was to complete the parole application in a frivolous manner in which he indicated his future plans was to join a tribe of natives on the Amazon River. He was advised to either prepare a realistic parole application or sign a waiver. Since this time he has become more withdrawn, and keeps to himself and his cell very clean. He has been more cooperative and is not regarded as a troublemaker. He seems to be making improvement and is trying to better himself by doing extensive reading and studying Spanish.

On Monday, April 24, 1961, West was assigned to work as a painter in the cellhouse. He was released back to the general population on May 5, 1961, and assigned to cellhouse maintenance as a painter. The Lieutenant in charge reports that subject has done an outstanding job. He works seven days a week, including all weekends. He is showing a strong interest in his work and is cooperative and gets along well with officers and inmates. He prefers to work alone.

A portrait photo taken for family while West was imprisoned on Alcatraz in the 1950s.

Little did authorities realize that when the April 19, 1961, casefile entry was written, the escape plot was already in motion. After West's release from the Treatment Unit, he was assigned ironically to B-152, the very cell that Clarence Anglin would occupy next to his brother during the escape. James Bulger commented:

> All of us gave him the nickname "Eagle Eye Fleagle" a cartoon character out of that era. West played a crucial role in the escape. He had figured out how to do some cleaning and also paint the top of B Block and the cellhouse ceiling. He was permitted to put up old blankets to prevent dirt and paint from getting on the tiers and people below. More importantly, it blocked the view of the guard in the gun gallery.
>
> I don't know the particulars, but I remember that Morris was upset with West. The rumor was that West was bragging to someone about the escape plot. Morris and the Anglins told him from now on when you're out of your cell, you're on watch with one of us. This might be why West dragged his feet and was stalling on the night of the escape because he was nervous about the other guys having plans for him. I was aware that Paco and the Anglins had a knife with them and they intended to use it if things went south and they ended being set-up. I'm not saying that was the plan to take West out, but had he proven to be a liability, you know, if he'd laid a trap for the trio and it had been sprung, right then West would go down, because if they were taken alive, they would never get out of D Block, and like I told you, Morris feared Angola. He always thought they'd send him back there eventually.

Plotting The Great Escape

"I just found a way out. I just found an escape route on top of B Block. I think it could be made. There's a vent up there that I think could be opened. We could get out through the back of the cells and put dummies in the beds some night."

—Allen West, AZ-1335

WHEN CLARENCE ANGLIN first arrived at Alcatraz and was assigned to cell B-140, he carefully surveyed the other convicts who stood outside their cell each time the doors were racked open. He would stand in the corridor awaiting the signal to march into the dining room, and each time carefully examined his surroundings taking a mental inventory. Looking up towards the east end of the cellblock, Frank Morris who occupied the last cell on the upper tier, B-356, covertly and unsuspectingly examined the utility space above the cellblock. It was likely not immediately obvious to Clarence that Morris had an ulterior motive for requesting residence on the top tier of B Block. Morris was already looking for a way out, and right above his cell was something captivating his interest.

On January 29, 1960, only eleven days after arriving on Alcatraz, Morris was assigned a job in the prison library which was located on the west side of the cellhouse next to D Block. His primary responsibility was helping shelve and retrieve books for the continuum of requests, and also arrange the titles on carts in preparation for delivery. It was a busy job, since reading was the main pastime for most of the prison population.

Working alongside Morris was Thomas Kent (AZ-1443), a convicted bank robber and brazen escape artist from Boston, which had arrived at Alcatraz on the same chain and same day as Morris. He had been assigned to the library only a few days later, and was a considerable contrast to Morris. Kent was fast and overly talkative with a nervous and jittery presence. He would serve on Alcatraz from 1960 to 1963, and was described in his inmate case

The enclosed roof of B Block visible from the east gun gallery.

file as being "manipulative, shrewd and untrustworthy."

Morris was the complete opposite. He was quiet, cautious around other prisoners and measured in his demeanor. Another convict in the library was Clarence "Joe" Carnes (AZ-714), the co-conspirator and now only remaining survivor of the 1946 failed break. Carnes was also similar in personality to Morris. He was soft spoken, well read and respected by fellow convicts. Joe Carnes had been released from isolation in 1952, he was now working as the chief librarian, and part of his responsibilities was delivering books from to cell to cell. Joe was considered by fellow convicts as one of the solid few. James "Whitey" Bulger remembered:

When Paco (Morris) first arrived on Alcatraz he worked in the prison library and lived in C Block on the second tier right below me for a short period. In the library, he became friends with Joe Carnes who been on Alcatraz since 1945. Joe knew the layout and workings of the prison better than anyone. Joe was more than willing to help a fellow convict to beat the System. Carnes' job assignment was to distribute books to all the cells. Convicts would order books from the library using a catalog that was issued to each cell, and then when finished reading, cons would place the book on a cart located at the entrance of the mess hall at breakfast. Joe knew all of the guards and their personalities. He knew who was most alert and who was lazy. So many things could

The Alcatraz prison library.

have gone wrong... In any other prison they would have been betrayed.

Allen West had been permitted a temporary work assignment out of segregation painting the group of unoccupied cells along the second tier of C Block. Kent later described him approaching the four convicts working in the library telling them what he'd found:

> We all heard it together from him... In February of 1960, we were working in the library... Frank Morris, myself, and Joe Carnes. Outside the library, Allen West, carrying a paint can, who was painting the cells, came over to the library screen and called us over. In a whispered voice, he says: "I just found a way out. I just found an escape route on top of B Block. I think it could be made. There's a vent up there that I think could be opened. We could get out through the back of the cells and put dummies in the beds some night."

From an FBI report:

> West advised that after he was released from the Treatment Unit at Alcatraz he began to think about looking for ways to break out. It was general knowledge among the

(Above) Thomas Kent

(Below) Clarence "Joe" Carnes

inmates that above the cellblocks were eight ventilator holes to the roofing which had not been used in several years.

These holes had been covered up; however, it appeared that the one above cellblock "C" had not been according to information among the inmates. When painting in that area about nine to ten months ago, he was able to verify that the lid covering this ventilator hole to the roof was not cemented like the others. He believed then that it was possible to break out that way. Around this time plumbers were working in the utility corridor which separates the cells in "B" cellblock. This corridor contains all of the plumbing facilities which lead into back of all cells in that block.

After the plumbers had finished working, West was instructed to

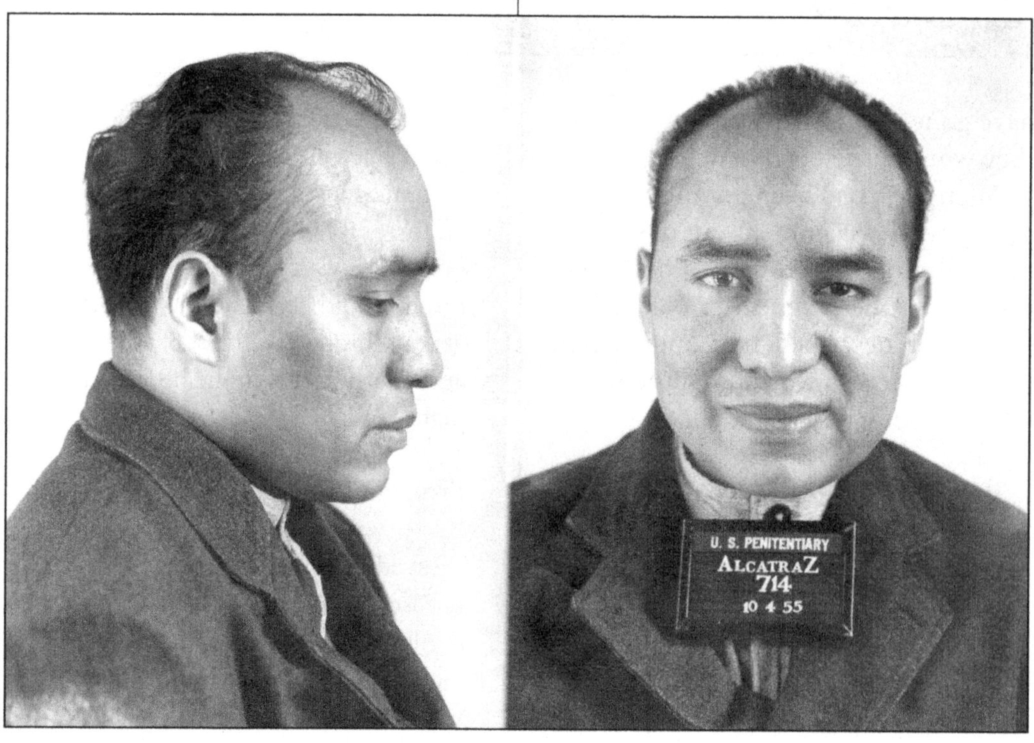

clean the refuse from the utilities corridor. This corridor is approximately 3 feet wide and extends to the roof of the building. While cleaning the floor, West was scraping up some material while on his hands and knees. Underneath a cement support, he noticed something wrapped in an oil paper. When he opened it, he found that it contained some rusty saw blades and little pieces of files, all makeshift and which had evidently, from their condition, been secreted there for some ten to twenty years. He left this material where he had located it. He mentioned to John Anglin, an inmate in Block "B". He had become acquainted with John Anglin previously when they were both in the Florida Penitentiary in Raiford, about 1952. When discussing this with John Anglin, it was apparent that he was already aware of the possibility of escaping through the ventilation area in the roof. They discussed about the possibility of breaking out of Alcatraz and swimming to the mainland. West said that swimming to the mainland was impossible. They considered cutting a couple of the front cell bars and possibility going up the left front part of the cell area, and working on this as a means of exit, then they decided that this could not be accomplished.

On October 15, 1960, Frank Morris was finally given approval to move into B-356, and each time the cell doors racked open for meals and work, he would study the roof vent assembly looking to determine if it could be a viable means of escape. Even during the early years of the federal prison, rumors swirled that many of the exhaust blowers, large industrial size forced air systems (several were still intact but no longer functional) mounted on the roof of their respective cellblock offered a potential way out. There were eight roof vents, and all were thought to have been capped and cemented shut, but might still be a viable access point to the roof. The blowers dated back to the opening of the federal prison, and after decades of use, they had either failed or were noisy and in disrepair. Finally in 1946, during the Battle of Alcatraz, a marine demolition expert drilled small fist sized holes in the ceiling, and with the skill of a puppet master, lowered grenades into the cellhouse and detonated them over the utility corridors. The explosives damaged several blower units beyond repair. Several of those damaged were dismounted and stripped apart, and then disposed of into the San Francisco Bay. Another factor was since the upper sections of cellblocks were incased by steel bars, it made the removal of the remaining inoperative blowers a near impossible endeavor. Several of the blower units had been parted out and then lowered using a makeshift winch to lower them down to the floor, but some remained. Blackwell later indicated in one of the escape reports that none of the blowers had been functional for at least ten years.

Willard "Red" Winhoven (AZ-772), a convicted robber and escape artist who'd arrived on Alcatraz in 1947, had also made a similar observation while attempting to repair a blower years earlier. He had served time alongside Frank Morris at the Federal Reformatory in

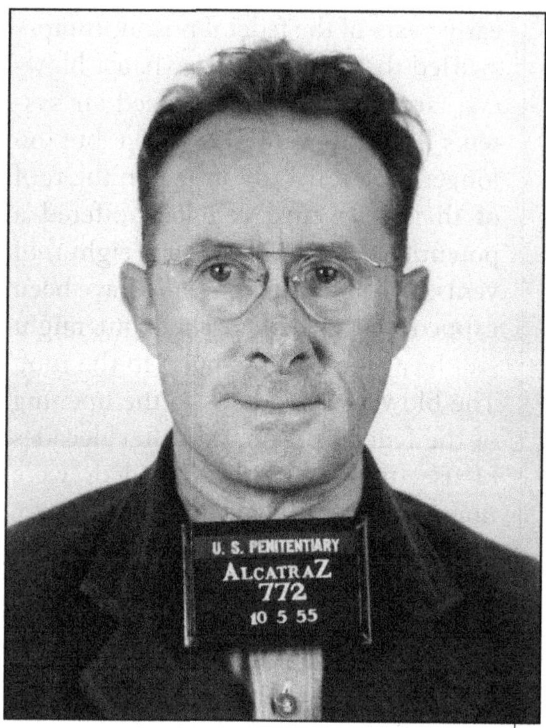

Willard "Red" Winhoven

Chillicothe, Ohio, and like Morris, had several escapes under his belt. He had also served time at San Quentin, Folsom and Leavenworth prisons. In 1947, following another attempted escape, he was sent to Alcatraz. Red served his time quietly and trained to become an electrician while on the Rock. In 1957, he was tasked with repairing one of the blowers; he exposed the fan assembly and was able to visualize the exhaust ducting to the roof. The blower was not fixable and he ultimately abandoned the project, but not without realizing the potential and plotting to use the hallowed opening as a means of escape. The guard assigned to supervise him kept too close of a watch and after running out of excuses to delay the repair, he finally abandoned his idea for a break. Though he wasn't successful in his own attempt, he would spread the word that the open ducts left great promise for a potential way out.

By 1960, all the blowers had been disconnected, dismounted and a few were left on-top of the cellblocks. The majority of vent ducts were cemented over and permanently sealed, and the other reversed "J" shaped ventilation ducts were slowly replaced with passive air vent systems that required no power and utilized a circular hood fan powered solely by rising air from inside the cellhouse. The circular housing duct was reinforced with steel grills boasting large prison style bars, but what officials failed to realize is that the bolts attaching the assembly could be sawed through and removed. Winhoven and West had discovered a weakness that could be exploited. Carnes later remembered the beginning of the escape plot during a National Park interview conducted in 1980:

> It was morning and I was delivering magazines to different cells. I passed by West's cell and he starts talking, He says "When are you going to get transferred out of here, you think?" and I say, "Well, I don't know, maybe five years from now." He said, "Would you be interested in leaving this place?" I said "Shit! You have to ask that?" And right away I got a little leery, because I know West, and too many people know his business. But I thought, well, I'll hear it...And he said, "We can get it together," and he gave me a brief outline of the plan. I said "Well, I don't think that's so good," and I told him "The best way

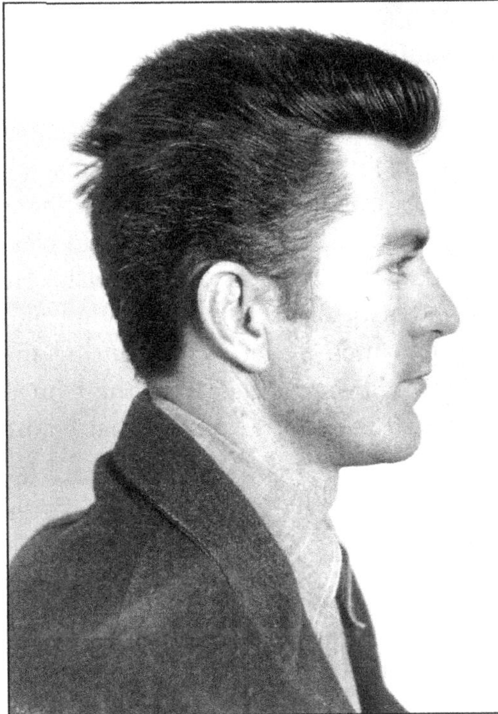

June Heyward Stephens

is to go up through A Block, that way you don't have to contend with concrete. There's ways of getting through concrete, but it's too noisy, too time consuming, you have to make acid, and anything you do with concrete is gonna take a long time. You go up through A Block and cut those bars and beat that rubber hammer. The guards came along and beat on the bars with a rubber hammer to see if any of them are loose, and we can get in the utility corridor of A Block, and this depends on nobody seeing us or rats on us, or 'The Man' don't see us." I say, "That's the best way to go." and he thought about it, and we argued about that, but we did make a commitment to work on it. Me and him.

At this point, the idea just starts, and I don't know how long he'd been thinking about it. But he didn't know anything I didn't already know. I know this place, every inch of it. I mean that literally. There are times when I can close my eyes and see the cracks in the floors. And I knew A Block ventilator's the best way. And the thing is, I was the only man in this institution who had a key to that door. And I gave West a copy of it and said, "Well, you make a key and see that it'll work." I had an original key that would open that door and during the strike I lost it. But I had a sense enough to make copies. You take the key and put it on a piece of paper and cut it out with a razor blade, and use that as a pattern. That way, you have it whenever you want to make a key. I had about seven of those stashed in the covers of library

> books so I wouldn't lose it. So West took one of those copies and made a copy of it and that was the beginning.

On January 23, 1961, Clarence Anglin was assigned the culinary detail working alongside his brother, and both men were already looking for a way out. In March, more than a year before the actual escape, one of the first documented pieces of evidence surfaced that indicated the Anglins were engaged in the plot. Lieutenant Lloyd Miller wrote a memo to Associate Warden Blackwell, alerting him to that fact that there was something suspicious happening with the interactions of Carnes, the Anglins, and June Stephens, who was also assigned to the culinary detail.

June Heyward Stephens (AZ-1225), was a thirty-one-year-old bank robber from Lawton, Oklahoma, and had become a trusted friend to Clarence Anglin. While serving at USP Leavenworth during his original tenure in November of 1955, Stephens, along with Earl Smith (AZ-1224), Bernard LaClair (AZ-1220), Robert Weaver (AZ-1226) and Charles Langford (AZ-1221), plotted an escape using officer uniforms. They bound and gagged both fellow inmates and staff members, then attempted to escape over the rooftop of the dining hall. Stephens was identified as the primary assailant, as he was armed with a knife and threatened to kill anyone who attempted to stop them. All four were immediately captured and after their trial, they were sent on the same chain to Alcatraz in 1956, but due to legal proceedings, Stephens was returned to Leavenworth in 1959 for court and again made another attempt at escape. During his court appearance in August of the same year, he was found to have a lock pick and the filed end of a handcuff key hidden in a fountain pen tube that was stuffed up into his left nostril. In January of 1961, Stephens was ordered back to Alcatraz and classified as an extreme escape risk. He was shackled to Clarence Anglin, and the two men became close during the 1,700 mile train ride across the United States. It is entirely possible that before the men arrived together on January 16, 1961, they had already been discussing the odds of escaping, and June providing Clarence a complete layout of the prison.

On Alcatraz, June kept a seemingly low profile. An adjustment report written just months before the escape noted: "The cellhouse officer comments that subject is a very quiet, soft-spoken person who does nothing to draw attention himself. He has no very close associates or known enemies." During the evening meal on March 9, 1961, Lieutenant Lloyd Miller noticed something awry and Carnes and Stephens were seen covertly passing information. Miller reported his observations to the associate warden in a memo. He wrote:

> During the latter part of the evening meal tonight I noticed Carnes talking to Stephens in what appeared to be a very serious and confidential conversation. As I moved to try and overhear it, Stephens broke it off and moved to the rear of the steam table. Carnes was seated eating and Stephens, a dining room orderly, was going through the motions of clearing the empty table near Carnes.

After the dining room was cleared and the remainder of the culinary detail turned into the dining room I noticed that Stephens met the two Anglin brothers as they entered and took them over to one side. There, he became engrossed in a serious and confidential conversation with them where no Officers or other inmates could overhear. This conversation last several minutes.

After the cell house was counted I entered the culinary dept. and saw 1476 Anglin in a heavy conversation with [OMITTED] near the dish room. A few minutes this [OMITTED] had Burbank off to one side and they were talking quietly and seriously.

As the inmates finished their work the following formed a group away from the rest of the inmates and continued a serious discussion. Stephens, both Anglins and [OMITTED], Burbank kept clear of them at this time.

I have no idea what it was all about, but it certainly was no usual inmate conversation. They were always on the alert and watching Mr. Mills and me very closely. It appeared to me that Stephens was getting the word from Carnes for something that Stephens is the leader for the culinary crew for whatever they have up their sleeve.

L. Miller

The memo marked what would likely be the first article of evidence that the escape was set in motion with Carnes, Stephens and the Anglin brothers exchanging information. Additionally, Charles Burbank (AZ-1369), a bank robber with a violent history of escape, would later be identified as having a potential role in the John Paul Scott and Darl Dee Parker escape that took place in the kitchen basement. In fact, many serving time on Alcatraz during that era remain adamant that Scott and Parker inherited the escape from Burbank, and it's possible that the origins of the escape started in the kitchen basement but later abandoned. One thing was clear, they were all looking for a way out.

After West was released from the Treatment Unit, he was now obsessively plotting the escape. During a later interview with the FBI, West admitted that he had been reading civil engineering books as to how to break down cement and had set his sights firmly on the rooftop vent. Only a month prior, John had taken a job working in the clothing issue located inside a steel fenced section of the shower area in the cellhouse basement. There was a lot of history here, as it was the area where Al Capone once worked, as did Jimmy Bulger less than a year prior. The clothing issue was also considered a freeway for passing contraband weapons, tools and notes. It was an ideal assignment to acquire fabric and other items including money. Laundering for the army was the main and largest industry on Alcatraz. This included both general washing and dry cleaning services. Many of the officers and their families also took advantage of the prison services. Soldiers were notorious for leaving cash in their pockets. While coins typically set off the metal detectors and was confiscated by officers in quick fashion, paper currency was commonly found by convicts and easily placed into the clean laundry and routed to the clothing room. Then in July of 1961, there was another

Mickey Cohen

turn of events that may have helped John play his hand.

Mickey Cohen (AZ-1518) was a famous and well known principal of the Jewish Mafia out of Los Angeles. On July 1, 1961, Cohen was convicted of federal tax evasion, and as he was considered one of the most influential figures in organized crime of his era, he was sent directly to Alcatraz to serve out his fifteen year sentence. He arrived on July 28th, and only eleven days later was assigned to the clothing issue located in the cellhouse basement to work alongside John. There were typically three convicts assigned to work this detail, and two others in the shower area to keep things orderly and clean. For Cohen, he considered it a great assignment and later wrote in his own memoir that it saved his life.

Cohen's stature in crime, along with his reputation gave him immediate credibility among the other convicts at Alcatraz. Although never proven, many have theorized that Cohen was also a conspirator in the escape by leveraging his powerful contacts on the outside. It was a plausible theory in that Cohen was the only convict in the history to make bond while on Alcatraz (during an appeal) and was released in October of 1961. He would return in May of 1962, more than seven months later and assume his former role alongside John back in the clothing issue. Richard Sunday, a trusted friend of Morris and Bulger, had also worked in the clothing issue early into his arrival on Alcatraz, was of the belief that Mickey Cohen did somehow have a role in the escape.

Although entirely speculative, there were also rumors that Cohen negotiated on behalf of the conspirators with another famed Alcatraz convict Bumpy Johnson. On weekends, Cohen and Johnson occasionally walked the yard together and this always generated

(Above and below) The Alcatraz Clothing Issue. Several famous convicts worked in this area of the prison including Al Capone, James "Whitey" Bulger, Mickey Cohen and John Anglin.

suspicious interest. Known as the "Al Capone of Harlem," Ellsworth "Bumpy" Johnson was an African American serving his second stint on Alcatraz. In the 1950s and 60s era, prison officials maintained racial segregation within the cellhouse and the African American prisoners were all confined along the Broadway corridor with some men residing directly behind the conspirators. It was considered the least popular area in the cellblock as it lacked privacy and faced highly populated sections of C Block. Broadway also had the highest volume of foot traffic with officers walking back and forth at various times both during the day and night. The convicts assigned to the kitchen detail were celled nearest the dining room gate in the area known as Times Square and they typically started their workday a couple of hours earlier than the rest of the population. The racking of their cells at early dawn was considered a major nuisance and disruptive to those residing in this section.

Bumpy Johnson lived in cell B-111 along the flats of Broadway, along with numerous other African American prisoners. There have been many unsubstantiated rumors relating to Johnson's role (if any) in the escape plot. The rumors were numerous, and ranged from him helping secure cash for the escapees from a civil liberties group (who frequently had attorneys visiting the island

Ellsworth "Bumpy" Johnson

to investigate claims of abuse and institutional crimes violating human rights and allegedly wanted Alcatraz closed), to rumors that Johnson, leveraging his contacts on the outside through a corrupt officer arranged for a boat to wait for the convicts. None of these theories have ever been proven, but there is evidence in his case file revealing that he likely had some influence with at least one officer. Culled from official prison records and a memo dated February 9, 1962, from Warden Blackwell to the Director of the Bureau of Prisons, they indicated that Johnson has been sent to solitary confinement for possessing contraband items that had likely been secured from an officer. The reports read in part:

> It has been brought to the attention of the officials that there was every reason to believe, beyond any reasonable doubt, that this man had been, for some time getting contraband brought into the institution and distributing it to other inmates, such as chewing gum and cigars. These items were acquired as a result of his known dealings with an officer, although we could not prove it.

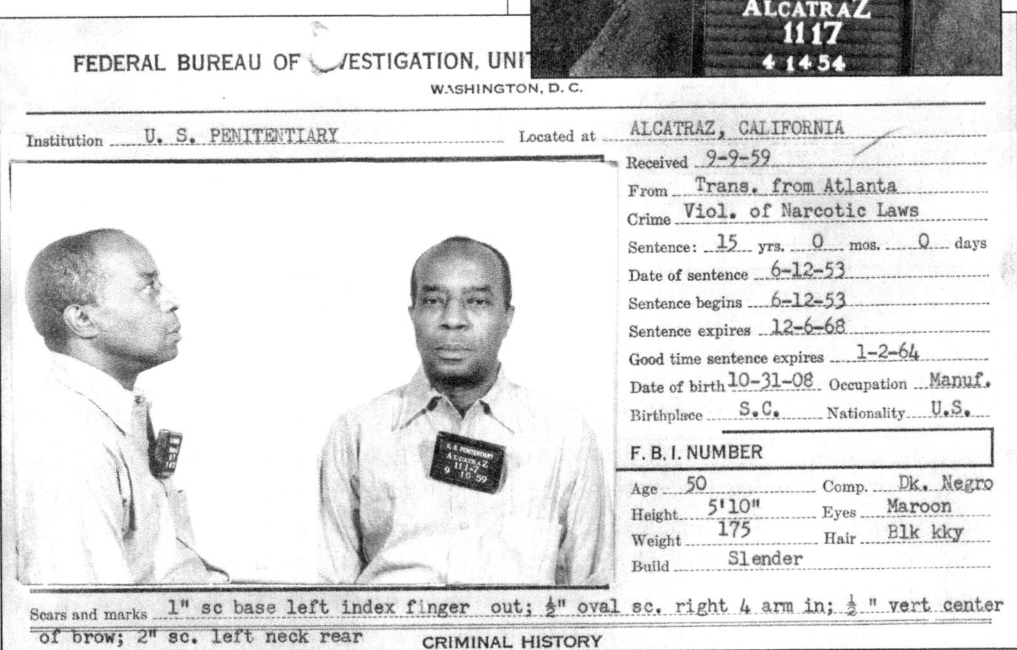

FEDERAL BUREAU OF INVESTIGATION, UNI[TED STATES]
WASHINGTON, D. C.

Institution U. S. PENITENTIARY Located at ALCATRAZ, CALIFORNIA

Received 9-9-59
From Trans. from Atlanta
Crime Viol. of Narcotic Laws
Sentence: 15 yrs. 0 mos. 0 days
Date of sentence 6-12-53
Sentence begins 6-12-53
Sentence expires 12-6-68
Good time sentence expires 1-2-64
Date of birth 10-31-08 Occupation Manuf.
Birthplace S.C. Nationality U.S.

F. B. I. NUMBER

Age 50 Comp. Dk. Negro
Height 5'10" Eyes Maroon
Weight 175 Hair Blk kky
Build Slender

Scars and marks 1" sc base left index finger out; ½" oval sc. right 4 arm in; ½" vert center of brow; 2" sc. left neck rear

CRIMINAL HISTORY

(Above and below) Ellsworth "Bumpy" Johnson

(Above left) Nathaniel Harris resided in B-149 located on Broadway, directly behind John Anglin's cell, B-150. He denied ever hearing any noises on the night of the escape or any knowledge of unusual activities happening in the utility corridor or cell behind his over the course of several months.

(Above right) Henry Banks occupied B-137, the cell directly behind Frank Morris's cell, B-138. He also denied every hearing any suspicious activity happening behind his cell or in the utility corridor.

(Right) David Johnson resided in B-135, next to Banks and in close proximity to Morris. He also denied hearing anything out of the ordinary during the months of the escape plot.

A reasonable theory of Bumpy's role was that he helped negotiate the silence of the African American prisoners living in the cells behind the escapees. A convict would have had a lot to gain by tipping off prison officials of the escape plot. They could have negotiated a transfer off Alcatraz or other subtle benefits. The rumors that Johnson had arranged contacts with the outside or any evidence to substantiate the civil liberties group claim have never been directly sourced or validated. Regardless, there were some that adamantly believed that a civil liberties group had interest in aiding in the escape. It was rumored that an underground force and "possibly members of a human rights organization helped fund the escape in an effort to close Alcatraz."

What's known about Johnson is that he was a leader among this population of inmates and a respected figure in organized crime. His early classification reports illustrate his early life growing up and stature on Alcatraz reading in part:

> As a child, Johnson's father was gainfully employed and the subject attended private schools up through eighth grade then taking to the streets, entering criminal enterprises. In later life, he was considered the crime boss in the Harlem area, controlling numerous rackets in a large section of that part of town, ran numerous gambling establishments and handled the distribution of narcotics to wholesalers in that area. It is also alleged that Johnson used this reputation to sell protection to smaller number operators or others engaged in criminal activity and would charge them for the privilege of using his name or would accept a fee to "straighten out" someone who had gotten a little out of line. This "straightening out" process could involve anything from arbitration to a beating or shooting. In view of his mode of living and apparent wealth, subject was certainly having a rather large income from someplace. There is no question that he was engaged in illicit narcotic traffic for monetary gain and is considered one of the most vicious individuals to come to the attention of the law enforcement agencies for many years. Although he has been arrested on numerous occasions, Johnson has always been able to "beat the rap" due to his "connections" and reluctance of various witnesses to appear against him. He was the arbitrator in disputes between colored criminals in Harlem and Italian East Harlem criminals. He was an impeccable dresser, talked with a smooth well-modulated voice and gave the impression of being a substantial business man in his community. However, he was one of the most dangerous and vicious criminals in Harlem.
>
> Under confinement he has been an extremely difficult individual to control, bitterly resenting the fact that he has to be confined, has refused to conform to institutional regulations. He has had a stormy career in and out of prison and the reports show that he has been shot several times and has frequently boasted that bullets can't harm him.
>
> He was originally transferred to Alcatraz in April of 1954, and after exhibit a favorable adjustment, was approved for transfer back to the federal prison in Atlanta in 1958. His negative social influence amongst the prison population created enough concern for officials that he was transferred back to Alcatraz in September of 1959, for closer custody and Johnson having had a reputation of being assaultive and dangerous. The cellhouse officer states he is known to everyone as a sort of "jail house lawyer" but that he is very shrewd and has a very good influence upon other colored inmates.

> He seems to have been a leader of the colored population. He has used his influence on one or two occasions in keeping down the trouble. He was reported as being a stabilizing influence during a period of racial tension. A stable individual who is highly respected and looked upon as an advisor by our colored population. He is on good terms with all inmates and is courteous and respectful to personnel at all times.

His main work assignment during the period of the escape was in the brush factory where Frank Morris would later take employment. His record also listed him as having worked as a skilled barber and he served in a relief capacity that would have placed him working alongside Clarence Anglin. In both cases, it would provide him significant opportunities to talk with both Frank and Clarence. It was his relationship with Cohen and their quiet walks on the rec yard that fueled the claims of his role in the escape plot, but clearly the African American convicts looked the other way and must have had some knowledge of what was happening in the cells right behind them. Former Correctional Officer George DeVincenzi later commented: "It remains a mystery to me that they didn't say anything. The cells butted back to back with the corridor in between. The black inmates were opposite the whites. They knew what was going on. When those inmates were crawling up there, night after night, bringing supplies up there, the black inmates, could hear it. They never said a word…"

Assigned with Anglin and Cohen in the clothing issue was Daniel Duane Maness (AZ-1402), a bank robber from Carthage, North Carolina. Large framed and loud mouthed, Maness was only twenty-seven-years-old when he was captured by the FBI and eventually routed to Alcatraz to serve out his twenty-five year sentence. Those who knew Maness disliked and avoided him. It's unlikely he would have earned the trust of Cohen and Anglin despite working closely together.

Daniel Duane Maness

Cohen, Anglin and Maness were locked inside their work area daily and maintained a busy schedule of sorting, labeling, ordering, issuing and maintaining clothing for the entire prison population. Every Tuesday and Saturday, the mainline prisoners would file into the shower room and after bathing, present to the open section of the issue counter to be assigned a clean set of clothing. There were also special bath lines for specialty work assignments such as the culinary workers. Men who worked in the kitchen were permitted to bathe three times a week, though the cooks, bakers and men handling the meat preparation were allowed to shower and secure clean clothing daily.

In later FBI reports that chronicled the brothers activities on Alcatraz, it characterized them as loners and not

129	130	
131	132	
133	134	
135	136	
137	**138**	Frank
139	**140**	Allen
141	142	
143	144	
145	146	
147	148	
149	**150**	John
151	**152**	Clarence
153	154	
	156	

(Right) A cell number diagram of the base tier (B1 Section) of B Block and cell assignments of the four escape principals.

(Below) The Alcatraz barbershop where Clarence worked from July of 1961 until the escape. Clarence acquired human hair by creating small cuffs in his pant legs and would drop the hairs into the pant cuffs to retrieve them when no one was looking. The cells of West, Morris and the Anglins were across from this area.

138

(Opposite page, top) An officer at the end section of C Block standing watch in the late 1950s.

(Opposite page, bottom) A contemporary photograph of the Alcatraz cells occupied by the principals in the escape plot.

(Right) Frank Morris's cell and work assignments.

MORRIS - #1441-AZ

1960			1961			
DATE	DETAIL	CELL	DATE	DETAIL	CELL	DA
1/18	Idle	C-139	1/11	Brush	B-356	
1/22	C.H. Mt.	C-224	9/10	"	B-138	
1/25	"	C-256		...1962...		
1/29	Library	"	1/19	1/21 to		
6/9	"	B-220		1/27 - FURLO		
10/15	"	B-356	6/12/62 ESCAPE			
			Rp'td 7:15am Count			

overly social. One report summarized their activities in the recreation yard on weekends. It stated that John typically enjoyed lifting weights (a program that didn't start until the 1960s and many credit with having been initiated by James Bulger), but mostly, the brothers typically stayed to themselves and didn't associate with other convicts during their yard time.

A Perfect Plot

The critical elements of the plot started to fall into place in July of 1961. On the 21st, John moved to B-150, next to Allen West who was residing in B-152. The day before, Clarence had started his new job assignment working in the Barbershop, and moved into cell B-154. John, Clarence and Allen were now all celled next to each other, all three in a row, and the planning of the escape was set in full motion.

On September 10, 1961, Morris moved from his third tier cell down to the flats into B-138, only five cells away from John. The cells along the flats of Michigan Avenue were scarcely populated, and afforded the convicts some degree of flexibility with who they sat next to in the dining room. The meal periods in the dining room were the most crucial in the escape. Three times a day, the men would convene to discuss and debate the rudiments of the scheme.

Robert Schibline (AZ-1355), a fellow bank robber was also residing on the same flat in B-110 and more than a half century later still had a clear memory of the conspirators and early workings of the plot. He was serving a fifteen year sentence for robbery and had gained notoriety for a brazen Milwaukee bank heist in 1955. During a bleak winter storm and armed with revolvers, Bob and his crime partner Roy Kuehn, held up a small bank by storming in and catching the manager off-guard. As the two men filled their bags with cash and start to make their getaway, the manager (an avid hunter and rifleman), grabbed a .32-caliber revolver which he'd hid inside the vault and opened fire

Robert Schibline

as the felons hustled to their getaway car. Unsuccessful in stopping the duo, the manager then retrieved his .30-caliber Remington deer rifle from inside the vault and like a scene from an epic Hollywood film, he took a steady aim at the cream and red colored 1954 Pontiac and fired off several rounds as the two men sped away. The FBI eventually captured both men, and Schibline would arrive on Alcatraz less than three years later. Bob held a clear memory of all the conspirators involved in the escape and he would also have an essential role in the plot. He remembered:

> I'd come over to Alcatraz from Leavenworth in October of 1958. I was on the chain arriving just after Allen West. He'd only been on Alcatraz a few months when I'd arrived. He was 1335 and my number was 1355. I talked to West more than I did anybody…I didn't care for him much though. He had a big mouth and was always bragging.
>
> In the dining room, we all sat close to each other. West sat right next to Morris and they always sat right across from me. The Anglin Brothers also always sat right next to us. I was usually the third or fourth to enter the dining hall depending on how many men occupied the cells before me. I always ate at the first table on the right when you entered the mess hall. We were always in the first group that entered the dining hall. We were on the floor or base tier, and since there wasn't many guys along that section of cells, all of us filled up the same table back when we had the ten-man tables. The cells along the flats were the least popular among the cons. They were cold and didn't have much privacy. I was in #110 right across from the barbershop where Clarence worked, and they were in the next block of cells along the same flat as me. Morris and West were always the first two to walk in, get their food and then sit next to us, and then the Anglin Brothers. The bench seating was John Landin (AZ-1472) on the far right, Morris and West, then John and Clarence sitting at the far end nearest the isle. I sat across with John Rouwenhorst (AZ-1354) on my left and Defoye Inman (AZ-1191) on my right. When we had the four man tables we were always right next to each other.

Another significant event occurred that would give the convicts an advantage not afforded to prisoners prior to the installation of the four-man tables in the dining room. Since opening as a federal prison in 1934, the dining room had ten-man dining tables. On October 9, 1961, the original ten-man tables and benches were replaced with four-man tables and chairs. The prisoners would continue to sit in the same areas as they had before, but now with fewer men and more privacy. Warden Madigan explained in a 1961 memo to the BOP Director: "It should be a little easier for inmates to be seated with those men they can get along with quite well." This was important, as fights occasionally broke out "because of the ill feeling existing between inmates seated at the same table." Three times a day, Allen West, Frank Morris, and the Anglin brothers could now sit together without six other convicts being able to overhear their scheme. They were afforded an hour each day to discuss their progress. It was here in the dining room where the major planning and debate of methods came into play. The decision for the construction of a raft and life preservers, the tools and dummy heads, and their ultimate direction of travel once they reached the mainland.

By the end of September, all of the convicts had made their final cell moves along the Michigan Ave (B Block) corridor and were now able to employ the mechanics of the plan they'd been deliberating for months. Clarence was in B-152, John in B-150, Allen in B-140, and Frank in B-138.

Another critical aspect was in-play, all four men had transitioned into their final work assignments. Earlier in January, Morris had taken a job in the Brush Factory, located on the ground floor of the New Industries building. More likely than not, it would have given Morris access to others who could easily secrete specialty items such as paints, tools, adhesives and solvents that could be used on constructing both the raft and life vests.

John Landin worked in the library and resided in B-148, the cell next to John Anglin during most of the plot. While he denied any knowledge of the plans for escape, he later confessed to knowing that tools and other contraband items were kept in numerous hollowed out books in the Alcatraz library. He indicated the process was simple. The book title would simply be removed from the catalog and then kept on the shelf. The books could be placed on the cart and then delivered and picked-up during the normal delivery periods.

The New Industries building had opened in 1940 and during the weekday daytime hours was where the majority of the prisoners worked. The entire second floor of the building housed the laundry facility, where men like James "Whitey" Bulger worked, but the

In October of 1961, the original ten man bench style tables were replaced with four man tables. This would prove to be a major advantage in the escape planning as the four men could discuss their progress in private.

SHAKE DOWN LOG

MARCH 1961

DATE	SHOP	OFFICER	LIEUTENANT	REMARKS
1	LAUNDRY	TUNSTALL	Valentino	
2	Clothing Fact	Tunstall	Ordway	
3	Clothing Fact	Brown	Ordway	
4	Glove	Rogers, L.	Ordway	
5	Shoe Shop Laundry-Dry C.	Ammons	Ordway	Shiv found, weights found
6	Brush	Hart	Ordway	Bar spreader + file found.
7	BRUSH	CROPPER	VALENTINO	
8	LAUNDRY	AMMONS	VALENTINO	
9	Clo Fact	Ammons	Ordway	
10	Clo Fact.	Ammons	Ordway	Lifting weights in electric shop
11	Dock	Ammons	Ordway	
12	Glove	Ammons	Ordway	

A "Shake Down Log' from March of 1961. Morris was employed in the Brush Factory during this period and it's possible the bar-spreader and files recovered had belonged to him.

ground floor consisted of the clothing factory, dry-cleaning plant, machine shop, furniture plant, brush factory, and a small variety of workshops and offices. For men working in the industries, it was their compass to learning meaningful job skills that in many cases went beyond generic factory labor. Many job assignments encompassed a level of expertise and craftsman skills that translated to reasonable paying jobs in free society. It also provided a pathway for quicker transfers off the Rock. The inmates accrued "good time" credits that deducted time from their sentence. Inmates assigned to the prison industries could acquire two to four days additional industrial credits per month as well as pay. Prisoners were allowed to talk quietly and socialize, with less strict standards than what was permitted in the cellhouse. Inside the prison, officers controlled every movement, but working in the industries allowed more freedom. There were also numerous civilian shop employees who supervised the work prisoners and often looked the other way at the smaller infractions of prison policies. The pay and access was what likely would have interested Morris. It was here he earned money to purchase magazines, musical instruments and art supplies.

The brush factory assignment was mostly menial work, and it consisted of manufacturing brooms and brushes. The brush frames and handles were constructed from wood, and then using stiff fibers made from a corn husk and wicker material were glued into place to create the final brush. Working in the brush shop would provide abundant access to one of the most important materials used in the escape. The brush ends were sealed into the wooden base using a durable liquid bonding agent and had inherent water resistant properties. Morris worked as a puller and would have had immediate access to the adhesives used to seal and bond the bristles into the wood base. Authorities

Record Form No. 8
(July, 1936)

UNITED STATES DEPARTMENT OF JUSTICE
BUREAU OF PRISONS

CONDUCT RECORD

U. S. Penitentiary (Institution) — Alcatraz, Calif. (Location)

Record of MORRIS, Frank Lee No. 1441-AZ

FPI—LK—4-1-53—43M—9789-4a

DATE	PRISON VIOLATIONS	DAYS LOST
5-10-60	DRINKING CONTRABAND COFFEE IN CELL: About 7:30 P. M. this date while making a routine check of the cellhouse I observed the above named inmate with what appeared to be a cup of coffee. I said to Morris, that looks like coffee to me, he replied that's what it is. The aroma to me was that of instant coffee. R. Jimerson INMATE'S VERSION: Admitted he had been drinking coffee. Claimed he had carried it from the dining room in a small varnish bottle. ACTION: 5-11-60 Two (2) weeks restriction. O. G. Blackwell, Assoc. Warden	

had also later found a bottle of Rem-Weld on top of the cellblock. Rem-Weld was a liquid plastic adhesive used in repairing books and was possibly used in the construction of the periscope and other gear. A later laboratory report ruled out Rem-Weld as the adhesive used on recovered life preservers and raft section. The most likely primary adhesive used for the raft and vests, was rubber bonding cement utilized abundantly in both the glove and cobbler shops in the Alcatraz industries. The prison purchased cement in single gallon canisters in large quantities, and these would have been accessible to the convicts. There was no detailed tracking of usage, and little suspicion would have been raised as the rubber cement was secreted into smaller containers.

On March 6, 1962, officers uncovered a "bar-spreader and file" during a routine shake down of the brush shop. With a small group of convicts working in this area, it's possible these items were concealed by Morris for use in the escape. Despite this finding, the prison administration didn't at all suspect that Morris was only months away from making the most historic break in American history. His progress report dated March 22, 1962, described in part:

> His supervisor officer reports he is a brush puller. He is a good steady worker who gets along well with both officers and inmates. The cellhouse officer reports he is a quiet, orderly inmate who seems to stay out of the pictures, does nothing to attract attention to himself. Doing his own time and seems to be excellently adjusted. In his leisure time he plays a custodial instrument. Upon interview this man was friendly and had a very good attitude. His only interest is having his good time restored. He claims that with the exception of one minor report for drinking coffee in his cell, which was almost two years ago, he has avoided any further disciplinary difficultly. He was commended on the fine job he is doing in the Brush Factory.

Earlier in July, Clarence had started working as an inmate barber. The barbershop was located in a fenced enclosure next to A Block, and almost directly across from their cells along Michigan Avenue. Clarence would have access to a critical item to help in constructing the dummy heads, he would covertly collect convict hair for the decoys. Using a shifty method to catch the hair, he cuffed the bottom hem of his pant legs and as he cut hair, and caught the strands inside the cuffs. He would empty the cuffs each time he'd returned to his cell. At least one officer, Lewis Meushaw noticed some amiss with Clarence. Meushaw had been working on Alcatraz since August of 1950 and was keen to the plots and schemes of the convicts. Like Miller had done months earlier, he reported to Blackwell that Clarence was up to something, but wasn't able to provide anything specific. Additionally, Carnes received information that he was being watched and decided it was best he abandon having an active role in the escape. He commended in a 1984 film documentary:

> About the time it came for me to move to where they were going to be working, we found out that I was being watched. A fellow named Vernon Kimbrough had got into the files where they'd moved them from somewhere up near the show booth (theatre above the prisoner visitation area). Vernon was one of those guys who could open locks as easily as if he'd had a key. He went into these files and found a special file on me and a couple of other guys that were being watched close... We had decided for the good of all, I should withdraw... I did, but I continued to help them. One of the reasons I continued to help them, aside from just being a good convict and help my friends, let somebody set foot in San Francisco, and I knew that place was gonna close. We knew it... That was one of my motives and others too... Everybody figured, let these guys make it, and they're gonna close this place. And I thought, boy, I've finally done something, or helped do it...

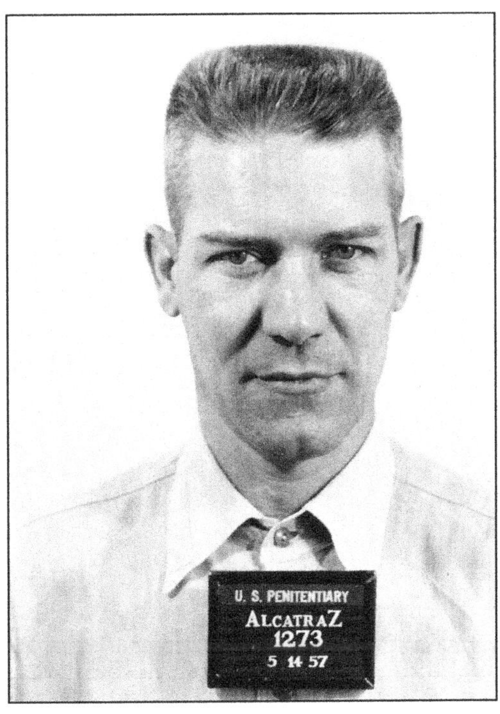

Vernon Kimbrough

June Stephens, Clarence Anglin's friend, had been working on a major plumbing project inside the utility corridors. Inmate plumbers had been working to install a secondary water

William "Billy" Boggs

spout into each cell providing prisoners for the first time, hot water in their cells. B Block was the first to undergo the plumbing upgrade, and once completed, they moved onto C Block to begin work. Stephens was working with William "Billy" Boggs (AZ-1415), who was serving a short sentence for importing narcotics and also a trusted associate of Mickey Cohen. In fact, when Cohen bonded out from Alcatraz, Boggs transferred into his old cell, B-226, located on the second tier of Michigan Avenue. Boggs would prove to be an important source for advice on the masonry and another set of eyes as having direct access into the utility corridors and cellblock rooftop areas. He was responsible for drilling the small holes into each cell that connected the hot water spout to the central water line located inside the utility corridor. He would be able to offer the men some of the best advice on drill methods.

Techniques for tunneling through the cell walls were to become a prime focus. After more than a half century of exposure to the harsh elements of the island's saltwater surroundings, the crumbling cement in both the main cellblock and other structures were apparent to both the administration and the prisoners. Numerous memorandums contained within the administration files stress concerns over the state of deterioration and costs of maintaining the structures to uphold a high security standard. The quality of the masonry and workmanship varied during the construction going back to 1909. The reinforced cement foundation was mixed and poured primarily by inmates and in some areas was crumbling and cracked, with rust from the corroding rebar support rods bleeding through.

Bureau Director James Bennett had been making a case in Washington that Alcatraz was no longer structurally sound, and as a result created both security and safety risks. A year prior to the escape, the Bureau of Prisons hired an engineering firm to perform structural survey studies. The focus of the survey was to determine whether Alcatraz was safe for operation and specify what steps would be necessary to correct any deficiencies. The report highlighted that the structural foundation of the cellhouse was deteriorating to the point where it could fail in the event of a significant earthquake and "soon" would be unable to safely support the main structure under normal conditions if no mitigation plan was implemented. The study also emphasized that the towers and catwalk structures were not safe for personnel, in addition to the powerhouse and entire electrical network was aged and ailing. The costs of repairs exceeded four million dollars and urged policy makers to reevaluate the effective use of Alcatraz. Bennett stated in part:

> The magnitude of the amount has caused us to reevaluate, with great care, the role which Alcatraz plays in our system. We continue to believe that we need an institution of this kind for the escape artists, the hostile, aggressive inmates who cannot or will not adjust in other institutions, and for big-time racketeers, gangsters, and hoodlums. We believe also that a maximum security institution of this kind, having a strict regime with minimum privileges, is a crime deterrent of importance. We do not, however, believe it would be an economically sound policy to invest over $4,000,000.00 in repairing Alcatraz.

The weaknesses provided the convicts the necessary edge in tunneling through the ailing structure. Rumors were making their rounds that Alcatraz was being considered for closure, with the convicts looking to be transferred to the new maximum security prison being built in Marion, Illinois, roughly 300 miles south of Chicago. The rumor had made its way to Clarence as he wrote in a letter home only months prior to the escape:

> "I don't know just how much chance there is of me and John getting any closer to home, but we have heard that they may close this place down and move us to a new place in Illinois. It sure would be closer to visit. I don't know this for sure, we will just have to wait and see…"

Benny Rayborn (AZ-1028) was a thirty-six-year-old prisoner serving a twenty year sentence for embezzlement of government property. On Alcatraz he was working as a clerk managing supply orders in the prison. Benny would secure one of the most critical tools to tunnel through the cement. He would secure two star drills that would prove the most effective in drilling the cement. He had concealed the drill set years earlier while processing routine orders as a supply clerk. Benny had noticed that one order included two additional items that were not on the original purchase order or packing slip. They were star drills and he secreted them, knowing that they could be valuable. The star drills would prove essential when boring holes around the ventilator grill. Joe Carnes remembered:

> I knew that Benny Rayborn had seven years before found a tool among some orders for the industry which he was processing as the inmate clerk. He found this one tool that was not part of that order, and he looked at it, and it was a star drill. He hid it, and it stayed hidden for seven years and now, it had to find its way into West's hands. I told him who to see, and he got the star drill. If you're not familiar with a star drill, it's a tool that is like a drill and it's got a hard / sharp point on it, and you can put the drill against a concrete wall and tap it, and you'll go right through

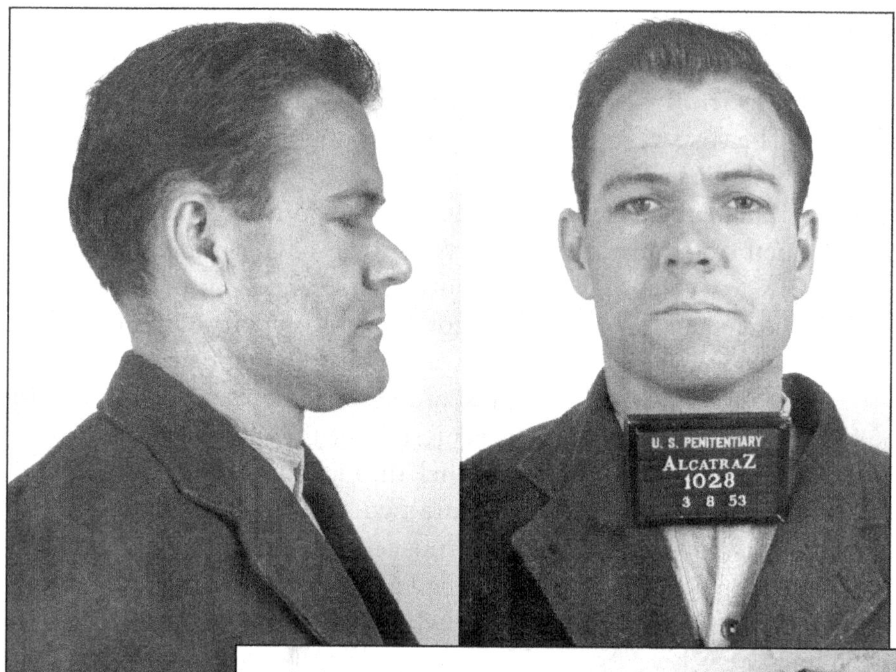

(Above) Benny Rayborn

(Right) Contraband items discovered in the prison library. Included in the hollowed out book were two star drills (pictured left).

that wall. They used this drill to drill holes, in a series, where they wanted to make the hole in the back of their cell, with the idea of going through the utility corridor and then through the ventilator.

Another tool they needed to get through the ventilator and the concrete wall were hacksaw blades. And to make that opening in the back, first the star drill of course and then the hacksaw blades since every concrete wall has reinforcement bars inside of them and you got to cut through that too. In the early 50s, a fellow came to my cell, and said I want you to do me a favor (he was the orderly), when you come out of your cell to take a shower (and I would be escorted by the guard) and when you start back, I'm going to stop this guard with some excuse, and when you come down to your cell, drop this string I'm going to give you into the little hole by the foot of your door, it's a door jam. There's a bar inside there that comes down and locks on a steel thing and deadlocks it. He said there are hacksaw blades down in there and those are the Doc Barker hacksaw blades. And he gave me a little string with lots of curls and little loops and I did that. I was able to pull them up on the first try and it was a little thing or a pouch with a hacksaw blade and it had wires and little hooks to catch on the string. They had dropped it in a bucket of paint before they dropped it down there and it had paint all over it. The blades were like brand new.

From the FBI:

West said that he had told them that he had cut out of cement before at other institutions and it could be done so long as they had plenty of time. He said that they could go out through the roof through the ventilator hole as he felt that he could get the lid off. It was then apparent that they had to get out of the back part of their cell into the utility corridor to get to the roof. The only possible escape area at the back of the cell was through a 6 inch by 9 inch iron ventilator grate. It was decided that this hole could be enlarged by taking out the cement to approximately a 10 inch by 13 inch hole. West volunteered that he had previously checked through library books while at various institutions and had ascertained that cement would start disintegrating at from 500 to 900 degrees. West obtained some element wires similar to those in a toaster. He does not recall the source of these wires; however, he recalls that this occurred in October of about 1961. West plugged this wire into the electrical outlet in his cell, but he could not get enough heat through it to deteriorate the cement. He had discussed this, as well as the escape with John Anglin and Clarence Anglin, brother of John. John Anglin had told West said that he had a spoon which he had sharpened and which somewhat resembled a screw driver. John Anglin started poking around the side of the ventilator in his cell and he made a little bit of headway into the cement. This was around December of 1961 and by this time West had discussed the plan with Frank Morris who was in #138 in "B" Block and who was to work with them. Clarence Anglin obtained a spoon and made a few dents in the cement next to his ventilator. The four of them got several spoons, the source of these spoons being not recalled, and by bending them similar to a screw driver, started making holes in the cement. It was decided to start the first hole a short distance from the top left hand corner of the ventilator grill. They started to work shortly after the 5:15 or 5:30 P.M. count in the evening and would work until 09:30 P.M. which is lights out.

The complex elements of the escape planning were in full force, and not obvious to the administration was that nearly every request or movement was a covert aid or ruse in the escape. Morris had requested magazine subscriptions to Popular Science, Popular

[F]rank L. Morris
#1441 (Date)
To Commissary Officer (Name) (Address)
Sir:
Would you please renew the subscriptions to the magazines listed below.

Popular Science 3.20
Popular Mechanics 3.15
Mechanics Illustrated 2.55
Science Digest 2.75
11.65

Also I would like to subscribe to the magazine—Chess Review— 5.50

Thank you
Frank L. Morris
#1441

6.35
4.00
1.30
11.65

A magazine subscription request by Frank Morris. The list included several technical magazines, including Popular Mechanics, from which he would extract useful information on crafting materials to aid in his escape plot.

Mechanics, Mechanics Illustrated and Science Digest. These were much more than general interest magazines to simply pass the time. By fortuitous luck, several editions included articles on water survival and other related subjects, including product reviews on life preservers. The May 1962 issue of Sports Illustrated included a series of articles providing information on inflatable products and how specific safety features worked, including inflation pumps and what styles were most durable and effective. As an example, one feature highlighted design concepts that incorporated redundancies in safety. It read in part:

> Most good inflatables now stress safety features such as dual air chambers that are completely independent of each other and which inflate and seal separately. If a stopper should pop off accidently or a puncture occur in one chamber, the other air chamber will support the float until safety is reached or repairs can be made. Valves on some of the better equipment are designed so that they allow air to enter freely but keep it from escaping. Caps are generally added to each valve as an extra precaution.

Another article on outdoor boating, provided very specific descriptions of essential boating equipment and each items use. Another article discussed in detail basic dock procedures and how best to keep mooring lines from getting fouled in the propeller blades along with ingress and egress procedures. Included were meticulous diagrams of the equipment and best practices for boat docking.

The March 1962 issue of Popular Mechanics included a five page

Owners Reports: Chevy II and Rambler

POPULAR MECHANICS

MAR. 1962
35 CENTS

WHOOSH! There Goes the PM JET

Be First to Build This Go-Anywhere Boat

LOST: Those enticing "extras" on old-time cars

"Guest Room" In a Table

Boaters vs. Anglers—*Here's Your Chance To Come Out Fighting!*

Power Tower Toting Tools

PLAYING DEAD, PM's vest tester demonstrates how buoyant vest holds unconscious man's head above water

WOULD YOUR "LIFESAVER" really save your life? That sounds like a senseless question, but the answer could be important if you ever have to go over the side with one.

Have you ever actually tested your life preserver? Don't feel guilty if the answer is no. PM's outdoors editor conducted a summer-long informal survey on the water last year, and of the hundreds of boaters, fishermen and water-sports buffs questioned, only a handful—less than five percent—had ever been in the water with the device they were staking their lives on.

NORMAL SWIMMER, below left, rides high and comfortable. Loose vest, right, slides up out of control

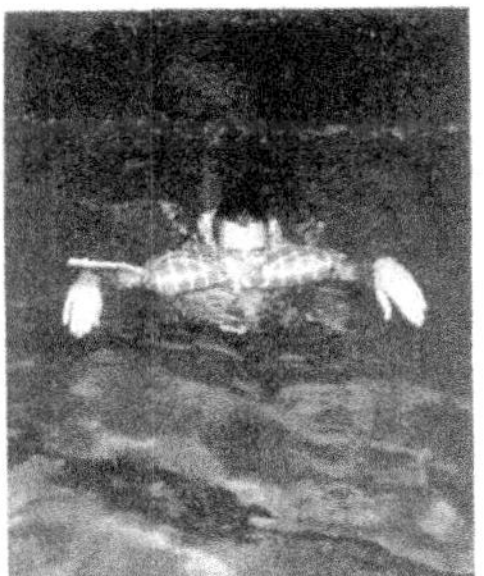

MARCH 1962 135

(Above left and right) This March 1962 issue of Popular Mechanics was found in Morris's cell, and was believed to have given him examples and ideas for fabricating the life vests used in the escape.

(Right) A November 1960 issue of Popular Mechanics was found in John Anglin's cell and depicted a method for vulcanizing rubber used in the fabrication of both the raft and life preservers.

Rubber Geese

Step one—cutting the pattern for half the neck and head section from an old rubber inner tube

Step two—seam edges are buffed and spread with solvent, then vulcanized with thin raw rubber strips

Rubber seam strips control the shape of the seam—if it's stretched before vulcanizing in place, it pulls the seam, and the rubber, into the desired curve

By Dan Brogan

J. C. SCHULTZ, of Aberdeen, So. Dak., tried a dozen types of field decoys for goose hunting without finding one he liked. They were either too heavy or too bulky—he couldn't carry enough decoys when he took along a carload of friends—or they weren't natural enough to fool the real geese. So like a lot of do-it-yourselfers faced with an unsatisfactory product, he decided to try making his own.

The ideal material seemed to be rubber—inflatable decoys are light, easy to carry and handle, and don't take up much room when they aren't in use. Schultz bought some new raw rubber and started to experiment, but the price of the material made the decoys impractically expensive, so he tried using cast-off inner tubes, which he could pick up free at any service station or garage. Even new tubes, condemned because of a flaw, were available at little or no cost.

To get a pattern, he laid a freshly-killed Canadian goose on a piece of paper and outlined a two-piece pattern, but when he put the two halves together, the outline wasn't right—it bulged where it should have been flat and was flat where it should have bulged. Finally he skinned his "model," tanned the skin, and laid it out, cutting off sections and laying them out until he had a nine-piece pattern. In later experiments with mallard duck decoys, he worked out an eight-piece pattern for that size.

The first decoys, assembled with a cold-patch method and painted with decoy paint, were not a success. The seams wilted in the sun, pulling the body out of shape, and the paint, intended for wood or plastic, reflected so brightly that it frightened the geese. But vulcanized seams and rubber-base paint solved those problems, and his current decoys are so lifelike that they have been endorsed by Ducks Unlimited, a waterfowl hunters' conservation group.

To make a decoy, Schultz first slits the tube down the center, lays it open on a flat surface, and cuts out the sections with a sharp scalpel. Then he joins the sections by vulcanizing a quarter-inch strip of raw rubber over the seams. When the decoy is assembled with the seam strips inside, the joints are all but invisible.

When all the seams are sealed, he inserts an inch-long piece of soft rubber tubing at the bottom, through which the decoy can be inflated by mouth. A cork is used to close the tube. On each side of the body he vulcanizes a one-inch length of stiff rubber tubing under a square of heavy sheet rubber, so it's open through the center. These fittings allow the decoys to be set up on shore or in shallow water by inserting foot-long sections of quarter-inch steel rod as legs, then planting the legs in the ground.

To get the different head and neck positions—feeding, resting and watching—nec-

154 POPULAR MECHANICS

NOVEMBER 1960 155

(This page and opposite page) A Sports Illustrated May 1962 issue included numerous reviews on design features of flotation watercraft and inflation devices. These articles support that the convicts at least considered an alternative escape option. The "tow theory" (supported by both former Alcatraz prisoner Darwin Coon and childhood friend Fred Brizzi; a pilot and convicted drug smuggler who was known to make runs between South America and Florida), alleged that rather than simply inflate a raft and make their way to land, they scaled the perimeter of the island circling around to the prison dock. Hiding carefully under the expansive wharf structure and out of sight of the officer manning the dock tower, they tied an electrical cord to the rudder post of the prison launch, then aligned the cable around the dock pillars to allow their concealment. They carefully strung the cable around with sufficient slack to allow the prison launch to move out of the slip without the cable or raft (hid under the western section of the dock) to be detected. Coon later stated that the "raft" was constructed more in the likeness of a "boat" and this alternate plan was "one of a few ideas" shared with him by John Anglin.

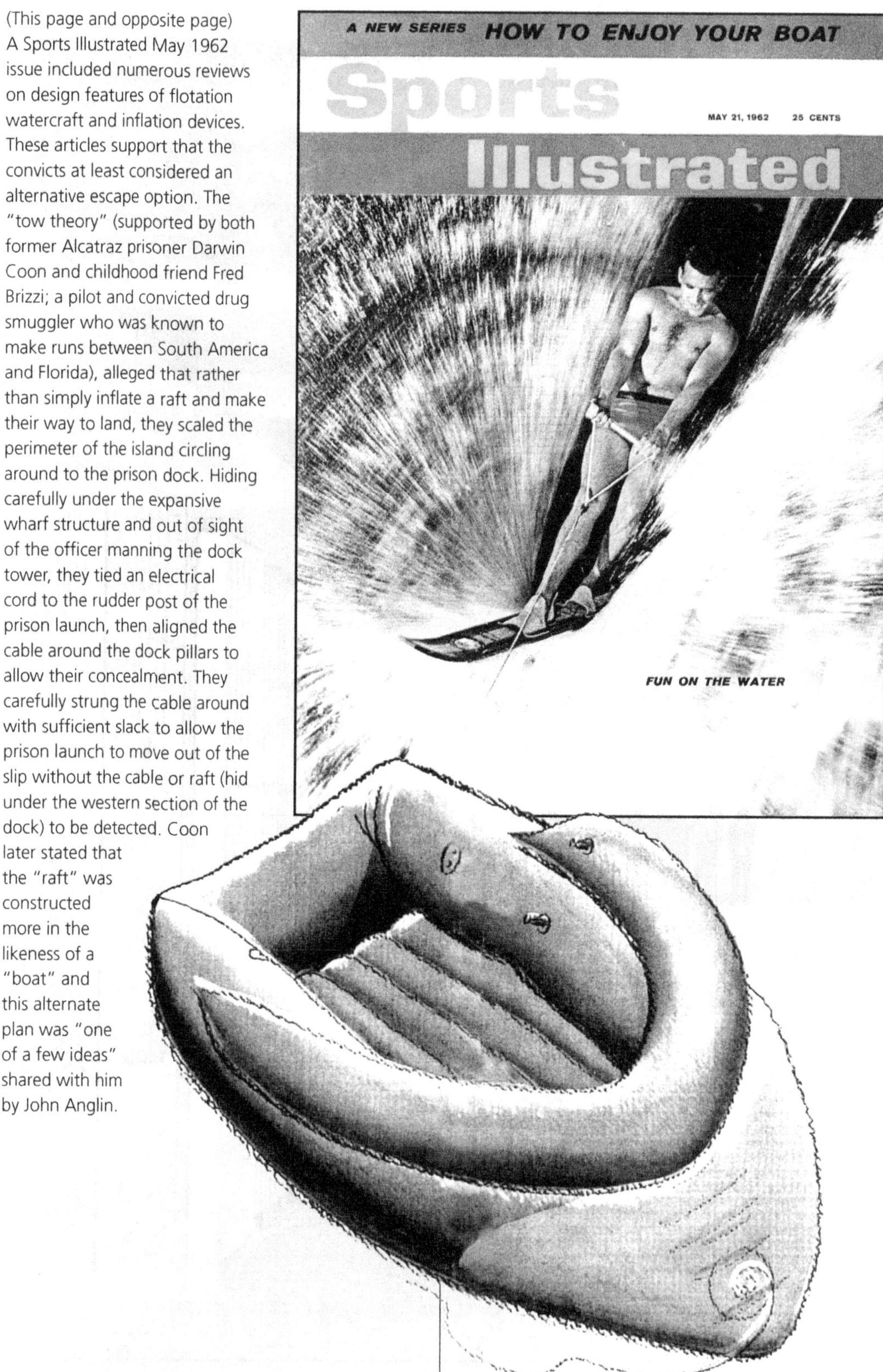

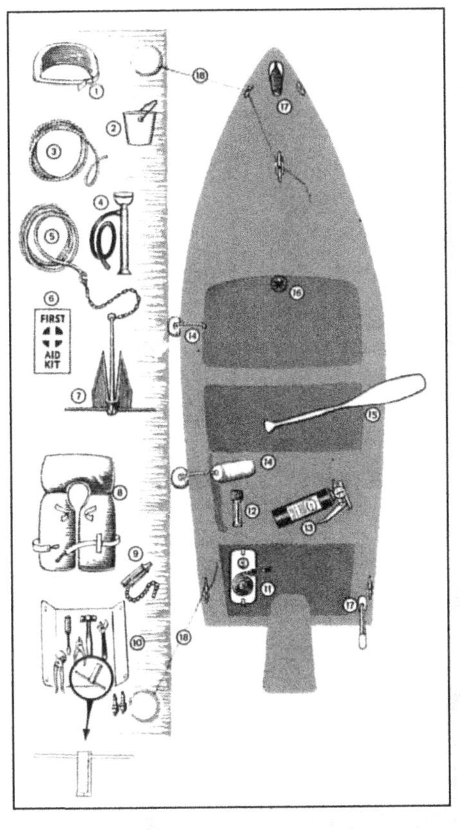

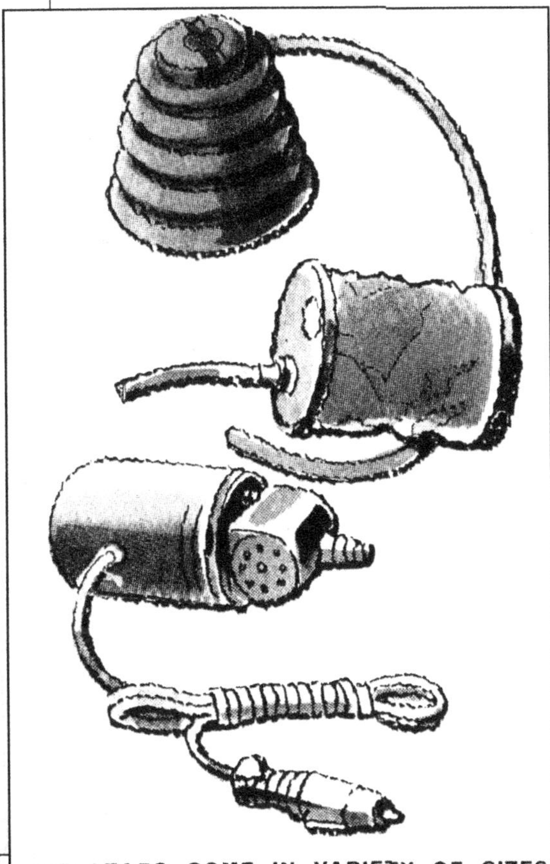

INFLATORS COME IN VARIETY OF SIZES

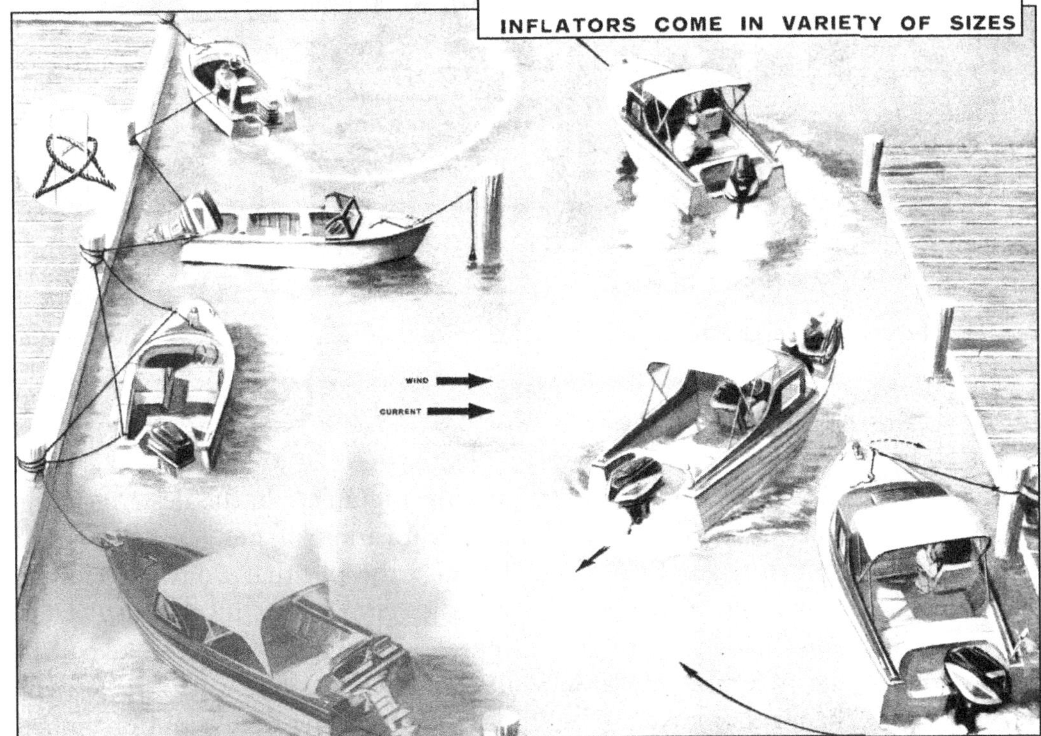

(Above) Several prisoners enjoyed painting as a favorite pastime. Many were excellent artists including John Paul Chase and Robert "Birdman of Alcatraz" Stroud.

comprehensive feature on life preservers and the strengths and weaknesses of various design elements. Another element of the article was providing coast guard specifications along with the descriptions of the two basic styles in buoyant vests. The feature proved to be a critical template in the design, fitting and fabrication of not only the vests, but also the raft that would be crafted by the convicts. Officers also later found a Popular Mechanics November 1960 issue in John's cell. The article described making decoys out of rubber

(Right) The Anglins were both excellent artists. The oil paints used to produce the flesh tones were also used to create the lifelike facial tones in the dummy heads. The two paintings are of John's girlfriend Helen and her sister Ruth (Clarence's girlfriend).

inner tubes, but more importantly, it discussed the vulcanizing process with detailed photographs. This would lend to their debate of the best design options for life preservers and the raft.

Another ruse used in the scheme was the convicts' interest in oil painting and music. Both John and Clarence had shown remarkable talents in painting portraits, and Clarence was considered an excellent guitarist and he practiced extensively while on Alcatraz. Acquiring painting supplies would not only prove critical in the actual escape, but also during the planning stages. On November 8, 1961, John purchased an assortment of artist supplies including a large spool of yarn (used to string between the back of the cells to alert the convicts when officers were approaching), and nine canvas 12 x 16 drawing boards. The brothers practiced oil painting, mixing colors which showed both fluency and flair. They spent hours creating striking sketches of their girlfriends. Behind the brush strokes were secrets known to only them. Tubes of flesh tone oils were amassed in large quantities and would be used to create dummy heads with lifelike features to fool the guards. It would not be realized until much later that the painting sent back to the family following the historic escape, was made of the same oils used to render the dummy heads. In later lab analysis of the materials, it was validated or at least firmly suggested that the differences in the paint

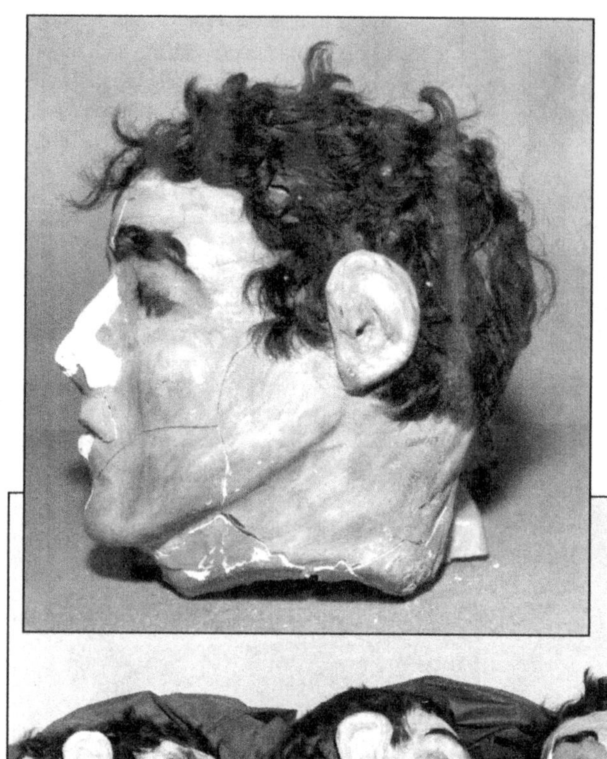

The convicts used clever decoys to fool the guards during the late-night counts. The amazingly detailed and lifelike dummy heads that were tucked under the blankets were fashioned primarily from scrap bits and pieces. The materials used included soap chips, concrete, wire, plaster, glue, paint, and hair that had been smuggled from the prison barbershop.

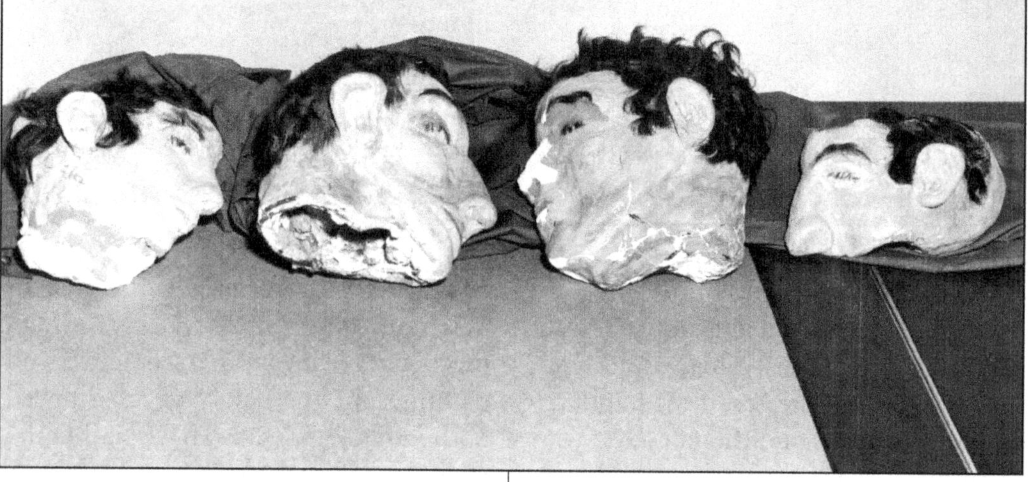

composites showed they had mixed paints to create unique shades in the convincingly real flesh tones. Earlier in September, Morris had also purchased art supplies which included a large 8 to 9 foot long canvas that many believed was used to strengthen the flooring of the raft. A second partially completed raft found on-top of the cellblock and hidden in the air duct had the dimensions of 6' x 2', making this theory plausible. West would later state that the raft was supposed to be constructed in a rectangular shape, but apparently the pontoon West was to furnish was left behind and the best indications are that the raft was more or less in a triangular shape. "This raft was supposed to have a bottom made of heavy denim cloth. A heavy denim type used to make laundry bags and trash bags."

In addition to painting, they would practice sculpting, using soap bars likely acquired by John in the shower room to mold facial features. Later examination of the dummy heads by FBI agents revealed that Clarence's dummy head was "primarily made of material resembling cotton rags or bed sheeting and taped together with exterior features molded with soap and painted to resemble flesh tones... Another head decoy has a concrete base, composed of Portland cement and sand. Over the concrete is a layer of white cement paint, while another looks to have been molded using what appears to be a form of paper mache." The official report reading:

> One side of the dummy head was covered with a heavy soap material which enabled the facial features of a human to be molded and this, in turn, was painted in general flesh tones. This head was complete even to the detail of an ear, which had a hole where it should be. This ear, however, had been either jarred loose or laid there by the prisoners or some other individual. The hair on this head appeared to be human hair and was dark in color.

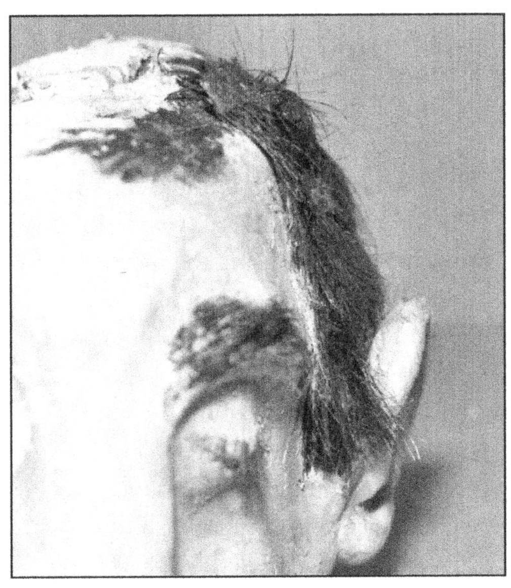

(Above and below) Period photographs showing the detail of the human hairs used for eyelashes, eyebrows and top of the head from Allen West's dummy head. Also shown is the underside of various objects that were utilized for bonding.

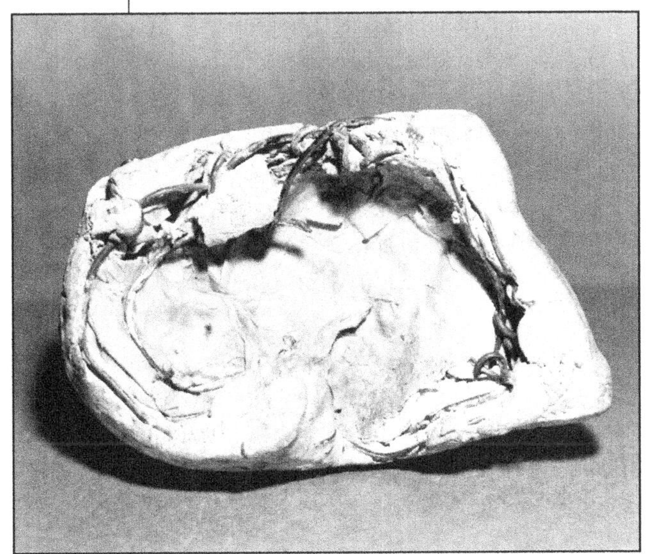

While the dummy heads were created using a variety of materials, the common ingredient in all four was bar soap. Mickey Cohen later wrote in his own memoir that working in the clothing issue gave him plentiful access to take showers two to three times a day, and likely made it easy to conceal soap that was abundantly supplied in the showers next to the clothing issue.

From the FBI:

> John and Clarence Anglin then made a small dummy face out of cement and gave it a flesh color. They put hair and eyebrows on it with glue and they named it "Oink." After

Clarence broke through his hole in the wall, they made a dummy back for the hole which can be removed. This was made out of cardboard and painted. One evening Clarence Anglin went up the utility corridor toward the roof, using the network of plumbing in the corridor as a ladder. He crawled on top of the cellblock. He used a screwdriver and tried to take the screws out of the 18½ inch diameter metal coupling which was between the roof ventilator and the roof. He couldn't accomplish this by himself and needed help. About this time West in connection with his work detail, had to paint one day in the utility corridor and above the cellblock area in the vicinity of this roof ventilator. While painting in that area that day, West took the screws out of the ventilator coupling. He had taken clasps from his bed and bolted them together, then used them as a clamp, thus succeeding in loosening the screws of the coupling. The coupling, although unscrewed, was still in place so no one would notice anything amiss.

About this time, Clarence Anglin made a second dummy head of cement which was stored on top of the cellblock next to the roof. This one was called "Oscar" and was to be given to Frank Morris. Then Clarence Anglin and Frank Morris went up to the utility corridor next to the roof on about three evenings and they took the coupling out of the roof hole and from the ventilator. They put grease around it so it would slide out easily and replaced it so that no one would notice anything amiss.

Another show of brilliance was the inflation tool created by Morris. On April 1, 1962, Morris used his earnings to purchase a concertina, an instrument similar in appearance to a small accordion type instrument, but substantially different in the interior mechanics and functionality. He purchased his instrument from the Columbia Music & Electronics mail catalog which was a local music retailer located on Market Street in San Francisco. The instrument was listed as catalog number 7132 with a retail price of $28.69, and described it as a "medium size Mahogany Concertina, solid wood frame, highly polished in Mahogany, nine bellows, twenty buttons, air release button, opens to 14 inches, 7 x 7, and weight of two and one-half pounds."

The bellows of the concertina would be used as an industrial air pump to rapidly inflate their flotation gear. Modifying the concertina proved to be ideal, and

The same model concertina purchased by Morris from the Columbia Music & Electronics mail catalog in April of 1962. He modified the instrument to use as an inflation device. They would use it to rapidly inflate the lifejackets and raft at the waters' edge. The concertina was never recovered.

UNITED STATES PENITENTIARY
ALCATRAZ, CALIFORNIA

JAN. 21 1960

Personal Property received in transfer of MORRIS - 1441-AZ
from ATLANTA.

ITEMS ISSUED TO INMATE
1 SPANISH DICTIONARY
1 LETTER
1 REM. MACH RECEIPT

ITEMS PLACED IN "A" BLOCK

ITEMS DESTROYED
1 CUP
1 PIPE
1 SOAP DISH & SOAP
1 PKG. PIPE TOBACCO.
1 COMB
1 TOOTHPASTE
4 MAGAZINES, "SELF REALIZATION"
1 SPOON
2 TOOTHBRUSHES

ITEMS PLACED IN PERSONAL PROPERTY ENVELOPE
1 SAFETY RAZOR & CASE

Morris purchased these self-teaching Spanish language guides. His personal item inventory from Atlanta when he transferred to Alcatraz included a Spanish dictionary and was a potential clue that he may have planned to cross the border into Mexico.

selecting this specific instrument represents the depth of research and planning. On an accordion instrument, there are piano style keys that are perpendicular to the bellows and the air travels past the reeds in a similar fashion. On a concertina, the main keys are pushed into the instrument and the resulting air flow travels in the same direction as the bellows. Morris was ever keen to the obvious, and leveraged the ease of simply removing one of the main circular note keys and inserting a custom spout to inflate their floatation devices. The FBI also indicated that Morris's cell contained an accordion "on loan from Alcatraz."

It was also clear that their preparation went well beyond the basic mechanics of the escape. Using income earned solely from the Alcatraz industries, on March 14, 1962, Morris purchased two books possibly revealing their intended direction of travel. For a total of $11.65 he ordered a copy of the "Berlitz Self

Teacher of Spanish" and "Spanish Made Simple." In the post escape cell inventories scribed by the FBI, a map with pages missing was located in West's cell and was described as: "Rand McNally Road Atlas of the United States, Canada and Mexico, pages eleven through sixteen inclusive, missing." Morris had admitted to officials in 1955 that following the Bank of Slidell heist that he had intended to flee to Mexico or South America to start over and settle down. Each night at lights out, his thoughts likely shifted to dreaming of a new life south of the border.

Working in Secret

By September of 1961, as the convicts were now acclimated to their cells along the cement flats of Michigan Ave, they had also solidified their plans for constructing their rafts, life vests and other essential equipment needed to make their break. The important work of finalizing the design and crafting of both the tools and flotation devices would come into play. Additionally, various plans in escape routes and final destinations would be considered and debated. The tides and environmental factors would also come into play as sorted through barriers and opportunities.

Bulger remembered their depth in planning:

> When it came down to the mechanics of the break, the trio planned it well and dealt with all of the points. They were disciplined... They exercised, they were young, strong, and in excellent physical shape. By degrees, they dealt with the issues of acclimating to the shock of cold water. They trained hard knowing full well the challenges they faced ahead. They exercised to build strength in their cells by running in place without socks on the cold cement floor. They draped cold wet towels across their neck and shoulders, and inside their clothing to adapt while doing strenuous activity in cold conditions. The water temperature in the showers was always kept real warm, so I had suggested get in an out fast to allow more exposure while standing wet on the cold cement. Morris was a natural athlete. I remember him playing handball, and also had a good arm when playing baseball and basketball on the Alcatraz rec yard.
>
> These guys were resourceful and wanted every advantage. I used to do skin diving with aqua lungs (double tanks) back in the 1950s, and used both wet and dry suits. Jack Twining and Frankie were close friends and offered to help. I as well as many others were all on Alcatraz because of our involvement with escape attempts or plots. I never approached the trio directly and everything I discussed was relayed through Twining.
>
> Paco had initiated the discussion of tides and equipment that I was familiar with by the way of Twining. So when Frankie was plotting the escape, I mentioned when using a wet suit how buoyant it was and it had to be overcome by use of a weight belt (canvas belt with lead weights attached) and how the suit helped ward off the cold. These were all important details and they were very interested in attempting to

TWINING Record Form No. 36 Rev. Oct. 1940 1362-AZ ASSOCIATE WARDEN'S RECORD CARD FPI—LK—5-5-58—47M—5517

Offense Robbery of FDIC Bank
Sentence 30 years Begins 12-5-56
Date Imp. 12-5-56 At N. Orleans, La.
Date Rec'd 7-11-58 fr Atlanta
Par. Elig. 12-4-66
C. R. 1-25-77 Max. 12-4-86
Comm. Fine G. T. 3600 days
PREVIOUS RECORD:
Jails 3 Ref.
Pens. Fed. 2 State 2
Detainers: Fed. State
Escapes: Fed. State 2
CUSTODY:
Crimes Involved: (Enumerate)

Auto Theft 4
Burglary 2
Attempted Armed Robbery 1

Aliases:

U.S. PENITENTIARY ALCATRAZ 1362 6 29 1958

Race White Age 9-11-35
Married no Deps. 0
Citizen USA Relig.
Physical Cond. Regular Duty
Mental Cond. High Average Intel
Education: S. A. T. 1.9 G. S.
PSYCHOLOGICAL & APTITUDE TESTS:
IQ 112
Occupational Skills:
Laborer
Avocational Interests:

History of Occupational Experience

Occupations	No. Yrs.	Verification of Performance Quality	Dependability

Name	Number	Residence	Occupations
TWINING, JACK WRIGHT	1362-AZ	N. Carolina	Laborer

Jack Twining arrived at Alcatraz in June of 1958. Twining was a close friend of both Bulger and Frank Morris. Twining had a violent past of bank robbery and murder. In February 1959, he stabbed to death fellow Alcatraz inmate Walter Mollett. Twining was cleared of all charges, since the stabbing was considered an act of self-defense. The FBI was aware of his close friendship with Morris. Following the escape, additional U.S. Marshal Agents were sent to escort him for a court appearance in New Orleans. The FBI had received a tip that Morris has planned to break Twining out of prison and the Marshal Service took no chances. Twining would later be involved in one of the violent and tragic murders of four California Highway Patrol officers in 1971 after being released from prison. He took his own life during the incident rather than be taken alive.

understand every detail, especially the suit design. I had explained how when I came out of the water and into the cold air, I'd pull the wristlet away from my wrist, and the trapped layer of water would hit my freezing cold hand and the water was very warm. The fitting of the suit was tight, and the tight seal around my wrists, neck and ankles was essential. There was discussion of available resources and how to create this. The trio had access to all kinds of glue, garments and other materials that could be made to be form fitting. I had also suggested that they fabricate caps that would be tight on their head but would help maintain body heat. I knew the head was a prime area of the body for heat loss, and a lot of effort was given to address these types of issues in the planning. I remember discussing the idea of using long sleeve wool shirts in two layers, then applying a thin layer of glue to both sides and then let harden. Also considered using raincoat material in the same fashion to duplicate a wet suit—the result was to trap air bubbles for buoyancy and warmth. It had to be a tight fit and

> the layer surface durable to withstand extended exposure to water.
>
> The tide tables were also very important and a concern of Paco. I remember discussing this matter with Jack Twining and explaining that you would need access to a newspaper that published the tables for the fisherman. They would need to acquire the tide table to help ensure their success, but that was a challenge considering cons were not allowed to read any newspapers on the Rock, only the Christian Science Monitor towards the end. I had discussed my experience in diving and if they were taken by the tide, not to fight by going hard left or right. I explained that it was better to use the tide to your benefit and let it carry you without exerting too much energy and move gradually towards land. Most important was not to panic... Distance looks greater when you're in the water. We even discussed swimming and flotation techniques. They had planned to jettison heavy footwear and create cloth type bags for dry clothing and using rubber gloves inside clothing material, similar to what was used in Scottie's (John Paul Scott) escape later in December of that same year.

Other convicts who could be trusted also offered advice. Richard Sunday (AZ-1431), a trusted friend of both Morris and Bulger also provided guidance acquired from his military training. Sunday recalled in a 2012 interview: "I told them that if their raft was to sink, their clothing could be used to help keep them alive until they reached the shore." It was important advice and both Morris and Clarence had taken special interest in understanding exactly how to use their clothing as flotation devices as a last resort in the event their raft and life preservers failed. In the military, Sunday stated he had been trained that clothing could be used not only to shield them from the environment, but as emergency flotation options. Prison issue denim pants were of exceptional use since they were tightly woven and the pant legs could be tied into large knots and then using shoe laces, fasten the upper sections into water-wing like devices. The objective was to squeeze as much water out of them as possible, and then hold the waist open while you wave the pant legs above the surface to fill them with as much air as possible. Sunday commented: "They wanted to have a Plan A, Plan B, Plan C, and even a Plan D for every scenario. They wanted to line up every duck and cover every base."

Robert Schibline would also offer his advice, and his job assignment would also give him access to vital information:

> One day the Captain pulled me out of the line going into the mess hall and he asked me if I'd ever operated any heavy equipment. I hadn't, but I think I just said yes to get the job. They wanted me to operate the crane on the dock and it sounded like a good assignment since I'd been working for months on a labor detail. When I worked the dock, I did a little of everything... Heavy equipment operator, handler, mechanic; you name it, I did it... I changed the

oil on the vehicles, emptied the garbage and did whatever needed to be done. I'd do my rounds and go into the office to empty the waste basket and clean up after the guards. There wasn't much conversation between the cons and guards. I didn't associate with any goddamn guard. I called them all "Boss" and conversations didn't happen except for things related to the job. We didn't even look each other in the eye, so these claims that maybe a guard had a role in the escape is bullshit. Guards and cons barely even spoke. There was one guard who always packed a newspaper in his lunchbox. Everyday he'd go into the office, open his lunchbox and read the paper while he ate. Not always, but most of the time, he'd read the paper and then throw it out into the waste basket. Sometimes he'd take it back to shore with him. I always made it a point when I emptied the waste basket to get that page of the paper with the tide tables. I couldn't get them every day, but usually a couple times a week.

PAGE 26 FHE ★★
Monday, June 11, 1962
San Francisco Chronicle

Sun, Moon, Tides

PACIFIC DAYLIGHT SAVING TIME

MONDAY, JUNE 11

Sun Rise .... 5:47 a.m.
Sun Set .... 8:32 p.m.
Moon Rise .... 2:26 p.m.
Moon Set .... 2:15 a.m.

MOON'S PHASES

Full Moon .. June 17 7:03 p.m.
Last Quarter . June 24 4:43 p.m.
New Moon .. July 1 4:53 p.m.

TIMES AND HEIGHTS OF TIDES AT GOLDEN GATE—JUNE 11 TO 15

	Low AM		High AM		Low PM		High PM	
11	2:04	2.0	7:33	3.5	1:16	1.1	8:22	5.1
12	2:55	1.4	8:43	3.6	2:03	1.4	8:37	5.3
13	3:39	0.9	9:44	3.7	2:49	1.7	9:29	5.4
14	4:18	0.4	10:38	3.9	3:13	1.9	10:00	5.6
15	4:55	-0.1	11:29	4.0	4:11	2.1	10:29	5.8

OTHER TIDAL TIMES

Hunters Point + 35 min.
Dumbarton Bridge .. + 1 hr. 10 min.
Oakland Harbor .... + 40 min.
Berkeley . ... + 25 min.
Point Richmond .... + 40 min.
Crockett .... + 2 hrs. 5 min.

Compiled by Marine Exchange from Coast and Geodetic Survey data.

The tide table from the day of the escape published in the San Francisco Chronicle.

During meals, since I sat close to the Anglins, I'd pass off the tide tables over to Clarence. They had asked some of the guys for help. They were asking for things like raincoats and extension cords. They'd ask for something and get it...I'd say listen, 'I don't want to know any of the details.' I thought for sure they'd be caught before they ever made it to the shore, and didn't want anyone to point the finger back at me. I remember one day Morris approaches me and says, "I understand you're giving the tide tables to Clarence?" Then he says, "I really appreciate it, but once we get on the roof and make it into the water, we've got to go then...The tables aren't going to make that much difference." I just explained that what you do with the tables is up to you, but at least you'll have an idea of what way the tides are flowing when you get into the water...

Morris and I didn't see eye to eye and on some things and we had a big clash one time talking about the escape. I tried to give him advice on how to make their own buoyancy compensator, since I had a lot of water survival training when I was in the navy. I later opened my own dive shop when I got out of prison, since I made more money owning my own business than I did robbing banks. I had extensive survival training and thought I could offer them some solid advice in this area. One of the things that was really easy to get your hands on was rubber surgical gloves. A guy I played Bridge with on the yard said he could get me as many as I needed and I told Morris that you could put them in your shirt and you'll float forever! Morris was stubborn though and he had a one way mindset. He'd read in a magazine about life vest designs and said he was going to make his own. That was his plan and he was going to stick to it.

In April of 1961, Thomas Bradley, was hired by Warden Madigan as Captain of the Guards and brought with him a casual style that some of the legacy staff didn't find favorable or conducive to the once security centered culture. While working as a correctional officer at USP Atlanta, Bradley earned a law degree from the John Marshall School of Law. In 1954, he received a promotional assignment to lieutenant at USP Leavenworth, and after nearly twenty years working in corrections, he accepted the captain assignment on Alcatraz. Several officers that worked under him didn't care for his "go easy" style and felt that he

Warden Blackwell with Captain Thomas Bradley (and two other unidentified men) at the wheel of the motorized cart he used to travel around the island.

shouldn't have ever been promoted as captain, especially never having had worked on Alcatraz. Correctional Officer Pat Mahoney, who had been working on Alcatraz since 1956, shared this opinion. He indicated that Bradley always carried himself in a way to let everyone know he had went to law school, and while easy going, he didn't seem to carry the competence of a seasoned officer that one would expect with that many years under his belt. Blackwell and Bradley hit it off well and by some accounts appeared to share a close friendship.

Arthur M. Dollison was appointed as the Associate Warden in 1961 by Blackwell.

After a long and prosperous career, in November of 1961, Paul J. Madigan retired from Alcatraz. Olin Blackwell, at only forty-six-years of age, became the final warden of Alcatraz. Arthur M. Dollison, who was working as the industries superintendent was promoted to the associate warden position. Dollison held a business degree from Ohio Weslyan University but as result of the Great Depression during the 1930s, and the need to support his family, he settled for employment working as a corrections officer at USP Leavenworth. After serving in the armed forces during World War II, he transferred to Alcatraz in 1953. Cliff Fish would later describe the styles of Blackwell and Dollison as night and day. Dollison was more an administrator type. He often wore a bow tie, was well spoken, and tackled issues with a more measured approach. Blackwell was less polished and almost always had a lit cigarette in his hand. A stream of smoke trailed behind him as he strolled the cellblocks holding court with his staff and officers. Fish remembered Blackwell as having a more hands off approach and was reserved to a fault. Having been reared under the early governance styles of Johnston, Swope and Madigan, Fish suggested that Blackwell didn't possess the leadership skills to operate close to the same level of his predecessors, and felt he'd never really transitioned from the associate warden role. Mahoney seemed to share a similar opinion stating: "He couldn't make a decision. He'd always have to consult with someone else. I didn't feel he was competent to be warden."

Even prior to Blackwell's appointment, there was a movement underway headed by the Bureau of Prisons to close Alcatraz, and Blackwell along with Bradley loosened security safeguards to an even lower level to align with the decreases in funding and staffing. In March of 1962, Blackwell and Bradley as a cost saving measure closed the road tower during the evening hours, and loosened policies that had been the foundation of security measures for Alcatraz. Even West would later reflect during an FBI interview that there was a full awareness among the conspirators that there was no sentry view from the cellhouse roof to the north shore.

In the weeks leading up to the escape, Darwin Coon indicated that John had started seeking help in acquiring raincoats from other convicts. The template for acquisition was the same from con to con. The inmate would wear the raincoat into the rec yard and then take it off while sitting and talking on the bleacher steps. John or one of the conspirators would put on the coat and then wear it back into the cellhouse. It wasn't at all uncommon for convicts to wear raincoats to work and in the yard year round. There was a running joke that the Seagulls had better aim than the officers and wearing the coats even during the springtime wouldn't have raised any suspicions.

From the FBI:

> West obtained a raincoat make of an olive drab rubberized material from one of the inmates who was transferred from this institution and over the next few days obtained a couple more such raincoats. Over the next few days, he would pick up another raincoat when it was placed down by another inmate and when this individual was not looking. In the evening he would take these raincoats and cut them up and paste them together with some glue which had possibly been obtained from the glove factory at the institution. He would also sew some of the material together. He made a yoke life preserver out of this. He made valves out of pieces of tubing which he could pick up at various times. At night the raincoats and the residue were hidden on top of the cellblock near the roof and the ventilator pipe. West made all four yoke life preservers. John Anglin was using the same type raincoat in making the raft they proposed to use. Upon occasions, bits of this material were handed into the back of West's cell so he could splice and glue the pieces together.

Duane Maness who worked with John Anglin and Mickey Cohen in the clothing issue, would be interviewed by the FBI just days following the escape. Their report also shed light on how the convicts secured raincoats in such abundance:

> Maness states that he was sentenced to the US Penitentiary Atlanta, Georgia, on January 17, 1958, about the same time as the Anglin brothers were sentenced to that institution. He was transferred to Alcatraz on March 29, 1958, for possession of hacksaw blades and the Anglin brothers had previously been transferred to Alcatraz. Since at Alcatraz Maness

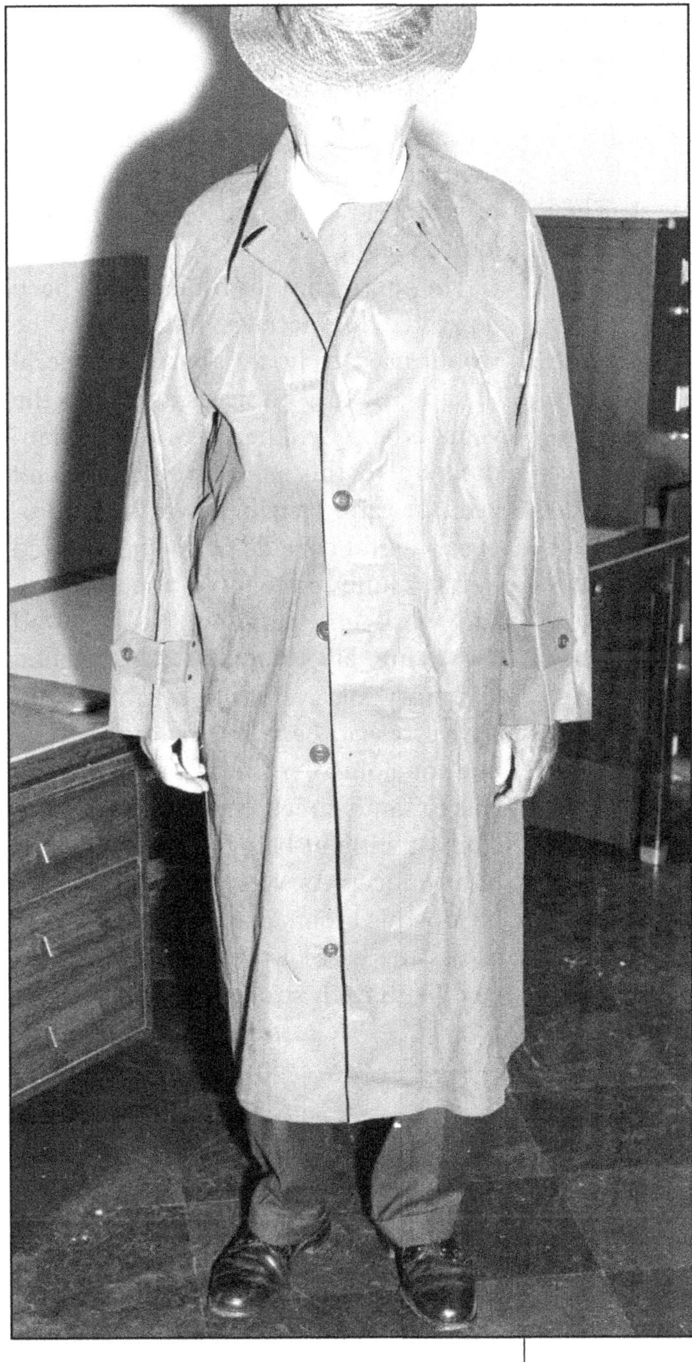

An FBI agent wearing one of the raincoats used by the convicts to fabricate their raft and lifejackets. The jackets were originally manufactured under contract with the U.S. Navy by the Marathon Rubber Products Company. They were composed of synthetic rubber and procured from surplus stock that had been produced in 1956, making the jackets just over six years old, but in excellent condition.

has been working as an inmate clerk keeping track of the inmate clothing records. John Anglin has been working with him for the past year.

Upon checking the inmate clothing he noticed that they were short of olive rubberized raincoats for inmates and he made out a requisition for three dozen of these to be obtained from the prison warehouse. He said that each of the inmates is issued a raincoat when he arrives. If an inmate turns in one which is old or torn this inmate is issued a new one. He said that he had not ordered raincoats for inmates for about a year and at that time he had ordered three dozen.

Upon many occasions he had discussions with John Anglin while in the clothing room relative to the tides and heavy currents surrounding the island. Upon occasion, John Anglin asked him if he had any friends around San Francisco. Maness stated he had some acquaintances but that he had not furnished this information to anybody at Alcatraz.

By April of 1962, the convicts had completed tunneling through the ventilator sections in the back of their cells. Perhaps the biggest and most significant breach in security fell into the officers placing too much trust in West. They needed greater access not only to secure a way out, but also a safe area to conceal their growing inventory of materials.

John D. Herring was the day watch officer in charge of the cellhouse, and had overall responsibility of the convicts assigned to the orderly and maintenance, but also was in charge of all movements of convicts to and from their work assignments, meal and recreation periods. Herring had been on the Rock for approximately five years and though only in his late twenties, was considered a good and competent officer. Though not solely responsible for the breaches in security, he tipped one of the first dominos and set in motion one of the greatest prison breaks in history.

During his normal duties, and after the digging and fake vent covers had been completed, West volunteered to tackle a major cleaning and paint project on the top of B Block. It was a ploy for access, but the most critical part of their plan since it was the best way out of the cellhouse undetected and the dark of night.

The top section of B Block had been neglected for decades. West knew he would need to figure a way to conceal their work to gain access through the vent, otherwise, their work and planning up to this point would have all been in vain. Herring gave West's proposal careful consideration and allowed him to climb to the top of the cellblock and work unsupervised. He surveyed the entire layout and took a mental inventory of everything within plain sight. He had been in this area before, but not alone. For the first time, he was able to stand directly under the vent and study it without being under the watch of an officer. As West started to clean, he took his broom and vigorously swept across the base of the roof cage perimeter. With each stroke a dense cloud of dirt, dust and nicotine stained paint chips drifted gradually downward and settled onto the tiers below. The long-established shine of the cement flats was now dimmed with dirt, and the convicts quickly started

The fake ventilator cover that was used by John Anglin.

The encaged rooftop area located above the cells of B Block.

protesting in anger as their pillows and bedding became fouled. Many started moving their beds away from cell fronts and this sparked a tug of war between the inmates and officers.

Alcatraz was a model of cleanliness, and the officers needed to uphold their directive to keep the environment "spotless, orderly and secure." Perhaps one of the greatest controversies relating to the escape centered on West's proposal to request blankets and use them to conceal the entire area for a thorough cleaning and paint. Despite protests from several officers, West was provided dozens of blankets to hang over the barred-cage encloses and fully conceal his activities. Jim Albright, who worked four years on Alcatraz as a guard later wrote:

When West suggested to the lieutenant the blankets could be hung up to stop the dirt and dust from falling and to prevent any paint from falling on the floor when the painting started, the lieutenant, then the acting captain, approved the hanging of the blankets. The other part of the breach of security and probably the major blunder was the fact these blankets were allowed to remain up for months. It really ticked me off that nobody would listen, and I got frustrated every time I saw them. I got to the point where I would go in and say "These goddamn blankets are still up there" but that didn't really help. Everyone knew the blankets were there, including the warden. I strongly voiced my opinion as

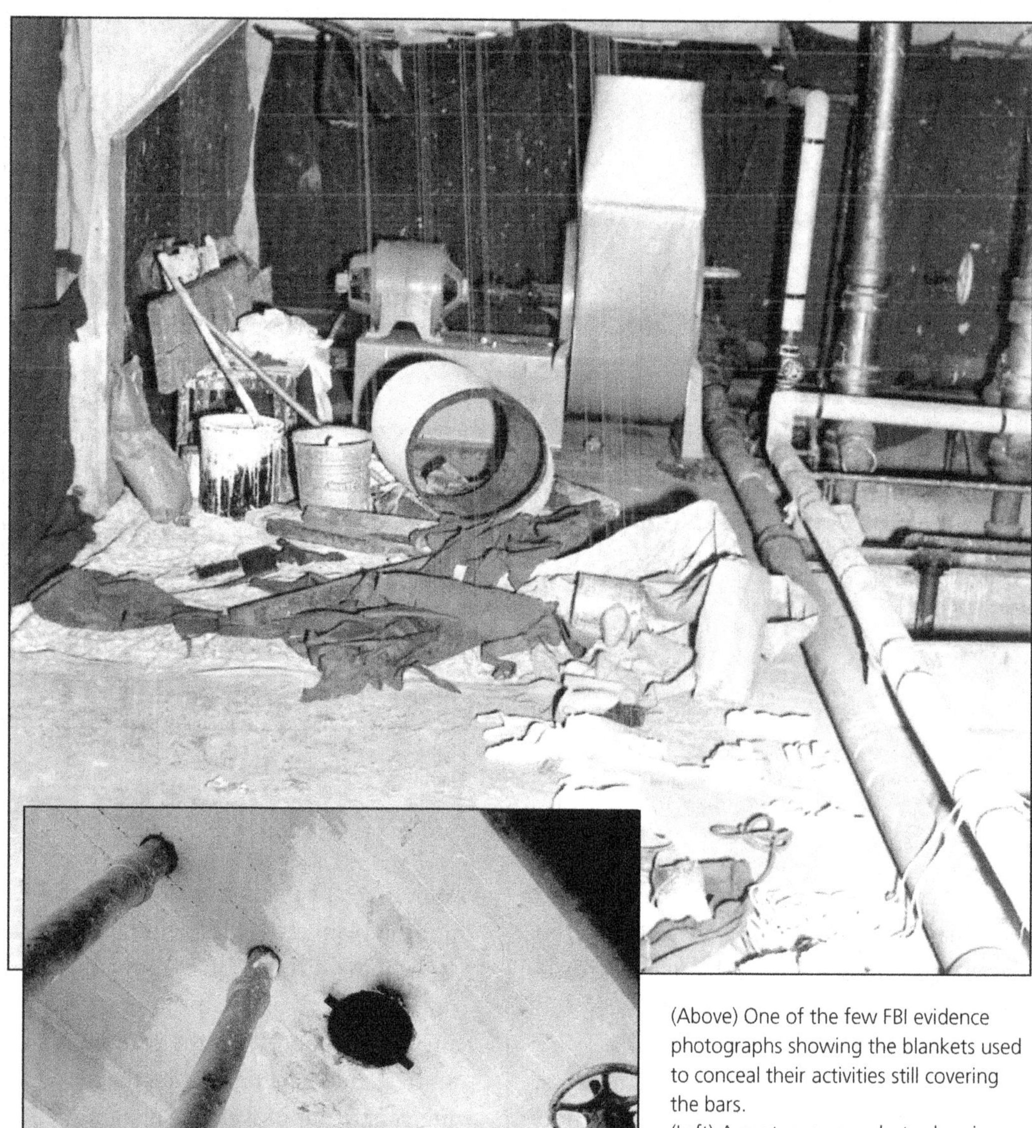

(Above) One of the few FBI evidence photographs showing the blankets used to conceal their activities still covering the bars.
(Left) A contemporary photo showing the rooftop ventilator access area used by the escapees. Note that if you examine the photo carefully, West's unfinished paint job is still visible over half a century later.

did other guards saying that they shouldn't be there and should be removed.

The blankets completely insulated the views of the top area of the cellblock from the gun galleries and upper tiers of Broadway. While the east gallery was no longer staffed, officers walking along the upper tier of C Block on the Broadway side (mostly along the cell fronts of C-329 through C-353) would've had a reasonable view during daylight hours up into that section of cellblock. Regardless, it's not surprising that over the course of several months that West was not routinely supervised while working in that area. There was no easy access for entry or viewing. Inspections were likely cursory at best. In a later review of the contributing factors leading to the escape, Herring testified that he'd felt West had been "adequately supervised since he was either in sight of the officer or his paint brush slapping against the ceiling could be heard."

The most significant and intentional omission of evidence was made by government officials most likely to avoid personal responsibility in the escape. While the official photographs clearly show the blankets still in-place, not one report by the warden, associate warden, Bureau of Prisons or the FBI made any mention of this major security breach. The blankets were never mentioned in any official government report other than in photo captions. It was a defining factor in the escape.

From the FBI:

> While working around the cellblock area painting, West noticed that bolts in certain instances were screwed in a tap pin and were not braided. He thus believed that this type of bolt could be loosened and therefore, since this was a type on a lid

(Above) A custom crafted wrench found on top of the cellblock which was used to unscrew the ventilator assembly.

(Right) A photograph of the security grate that the convicts removed from inside the vent opening. The official caption from the FBI read: "The pen is used to point out the bolt head made of soap and camouflaged with paint which is one of two."

covering the ventilator hole to the roof, they would be able to remove that lid. When West was painting near the barbershop he grabbed some electric barber clips, placed them in a plastic bag and dropped them into his paint bucket. He removed them later the same day and secreted them in his cell. About that time, one of them was able to obtain about a dozen drill bits, the source of which was unknown to West. West then set up the motor of the barber clippers so that it could be used with the aid of the drill bits as a drill. Morris and one of the Anglin brothers try to use this as a drill and removing the bolts of the lid covering the ventilator to the roof. They said the motor was too small and wouldn't do the job. About that time the vacuum cleaner in the cell area broke down and West had a chance to examine it to see if it could be repaired. West noted that it had two motors in it. He took out and then he wired the other one up so that it would run the vacuum cleaner on its own.

On the day he obtained the motor from the vacuum cleaner, one of the inmates was hit over the head by another con in the kitchen area and during the confusion he was able to smuggle the motor to his cell without anyone noticing him. This motor was given to Morris and the Anglin's, and they took it to the roof to use as a drill. They said that it made too much noise and they could not use it much. They were finally able to loosen the screws to the lid that secured the ventilator to the roofing. After getting them out, they replaced them so they could easily be removed. Sometime before this, Clarence Anglin made a dummy head out of cement which was to be used by West when and before he left his cell and which was to be stored on top of the cellblock near the roof.

The Great Escape

The morning of the escape was one of the happiest moments of my life. I can still remember it as if it were yesterday. When the frantic guards realized that Morris and the brothers had escaped, the cheers were so loud that it could be heard for miles! I think I can speak for everyone in the cellhouse that morning, it remains one of the greatest moments of my life... It was a moment of freedom for all of us ...

—JAMES "WHITEY" BULGER, AZ-1428

Bulger remembers:

THE NIGHT OF THE ESCAPE was exciting, but it was also unusually quiet at times. There were the typical counts at 5:00, 8:00 and 9:30 P.M. at lights out. Many of us knew what was in the works. There wasn't much talking between the cells of those of us in the know. Once we were locked in at 4:50 for the 5:00 P.M. count, the place would

always change. You would not hear cell doors open or shut, only the gates when guards were entering the cellhouse. If you heard a cell door racked open, the whole place would be buzzing concerned that someone was sick, being locked up in segregation, or even dead! It would have had to have been real serious if a cell door was opened after the 5:00 P.M. count. Any noise out of the usual would cause a reaction if you were reading, listening to the radio with the earphones or writing a letter. It would grab you like a physical thing and you couldn't ignore it. On B Block, during music hour when guys were allowed to play their musical instruments, once in a while someone with a trumpet would sound "CHARGE!", and guys would bang the bed frames hollering and laugh like mad. It would distract the guards—but they heard such things often and would write it off as nuisance behavior—and many would be white guys joking with the Hispanics—because there was much of that at times. It was always good natured and it would go back and forth. It provided lots of background noise for months of escape work.

Shortly after 9:30 P.M.—Lights Out—it was quiet and then we heard a loud thud on the roof, followed by the loud squawking of seagulls who lived on the cellhouse roof. They were startled by the sudden loud noise of the ventilator cover falling over and crashing down as the trio emerged. All of us acted out by guys hollering and creating a deafening noise that had to rattle the guards and fortunately proved to distract them. There was a real short interval between the "thump" and seagulls reaction, and it worried me that guards would react to it, because never in the history of the Rock had there been such a thing heard, or ever again. Also, after years of routine counts while walking the flats and tiers, the guards never dreamed of anyone being out of their cells and probably didn't process a noise coming from outside the building. If they lived on the island, the noise of the seagulls may have been routine to them. There were gulls nests all over the island (the grounds, sides of the cliffs, building roofs, etc...). Well after we made lots of noise to help divert attention, the sounds just fizzled out and the cellhouse came to a normal quiet. Then a long night of visualizing what it was like for the guys and sweating it out. No alarms and the "quiet" meant hope. I was so excited I couldn't sleep the entire night. Every minute undetected meant one more minute ahead of the authorities.

At night, guards making their rounds were very quiet. They would put felt covers on their shoes—sort of like slippers—to mask the noise of the rubber soles of their shoes. I could smell the guards when they started to count on the flats. As an example, Lewis always smelled of pipe tobacco. Others smelled of powder or aftershave or cigarettes. My sense of smell was powerful back then. The absence of motor vehicles and the fresh ocean air seemed to remove the smoke from the convicts in the cellhouse. Anxiety would rise as the guards soft steps could be heard walking towards the B Block corridor.

In the Alcatraz officer reports, everything was quiet and seemed normal, however, there were some indicators that in hindsight would suggest something was in the works. In Captain Bradley's report, he indicated that officers were certain the Anglins were both in their cells because they had complained that the lights in A Block, directly across from their cells was "too bright and they were unable to sleep." In a memo to Captain Bradley dated June 12, 1962 (the name was redacted by the FBI), the report stated in part:

> On Tuesday night after the 5:30 count, I passed out medicine and mail. It was mentioned at that time about a light being left on in "A" Block across from the Anglin brothers' cell and I said I'd see what I could do. There was excessive playing of instruments in the cellhouse. Young on the third tier and Banks on the "B" side were both warned to play more quietly or their instruments would be taken away from them. The Lieutenant walked with me to the east end, I got the key from Mr. Gronzo and shut off the light across from their cell. I feel I made a complete count and they were there when I made my 9:30 P.M. count which was started at about 9:05. In the past two weeks since I have been in the cellhouse, every time I make my count, the two Anglins are always whispering, also two other inmates on "C" 1, are always whispering when I make my rounds; that is the way it was last night.

Other officers even in hindsight were completely unaware of what was about to transpire. Correctional Officer Charles H. Herman Jr. worked the 4:00 P.M. to 12:00 A.M. shift and was relieved by Lawrence T. Bartlett who worked the midnight to 8:00 A.M. watch. Herman later stated that his last count was at 9:30 P.M. and that he made no other counts during his shift. Bartlett signed the count slip at shift change and turned it into the Control Center. Both men would later be subject to scrutiny for their complacency as later determined by prison officials.

From Allen West's Official FBI Statement:

> Monday night, June 11, 1962, Morris had told me that we still had to complete taking the top off of the ventilator to the roof and to separate the bars. In addition, he indicated that there was little work left to complete the raft. Frank Morris said that the Anglin's were talking about completing the work and breaking out that night. Clarence Anglin and Frank Morris left their cells and went up the utility corridor to the roof about 7:00 P.M. on June 11, 1962. Morris came down at about 8:45 P.M. that evening and said the bars were out of the hole on the roof and I gave him some water as he was thirsty. My vent to the utility corridor was not quite

(Above and below) On August of 1961, a state of the art control center was built to enhance prison security. All of the prisoner counts would be called into this location.

completed since my job was making the life preservers, and this did not call for me to leave my cell. Also, if I had completed mine, it would have been necessary to make the false rear to prevent detection. John Anglin had cemented up a portion of mine to the rear where I had cracked the side of the cement to the utility corridor so no one would notice it. In addition, while working in my cell, I helped make the paddles we intended to use. I made four paddles, they were plywood, 12" x 8" and with a wooden handle. I put about two or three bolts through the paddle and handle to hold them together. These paddles were stored up on top of the cellblock and inside the ventilator pipe.

Morris indicated that we could go that evening if we got the lid off of the top of the ventilator. He said that the bars below it were out of the way and he felt they would get that off by 9:30 P.M. he left and went up to the roof. Shortly thereafter I heard some noises and I started making noise to cover it up so no one would notice it. At 9:22 P.M. that date, Clarence Anglin tapped on my ventilator and said that they could see the moon. I tried to kick the rest of the cement out of the hole at the back of my cell. I could not do it. He tried to help for a minute or so but couldn't do

(Right, top and bottom) The B Block utility corridor. The corridor was a narrow service passage with a mass network of plumbing and electrical conduits.

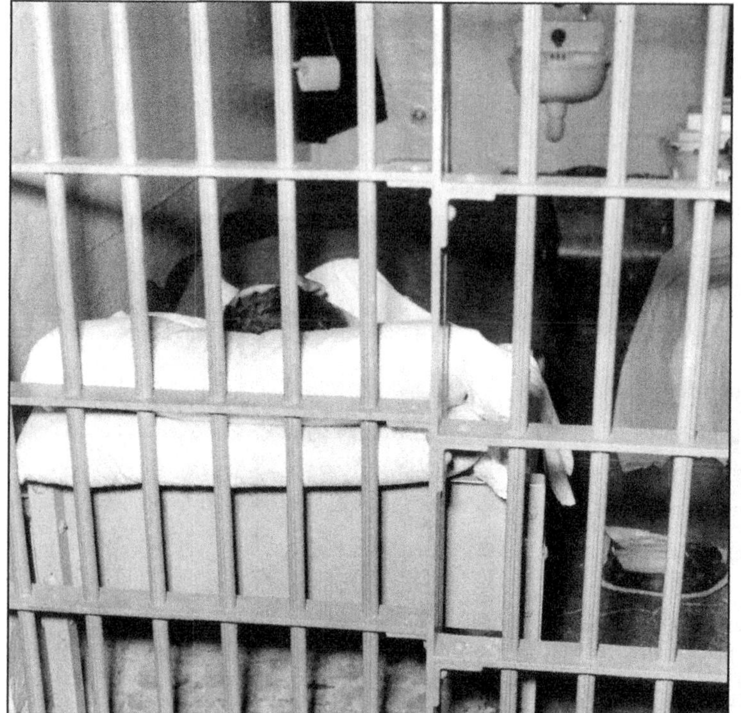

(Left and below) Photographs of Frank Morris's and Clarence Anglin's cells taken on June 12, 1962. These views show how the cell appeared as the officers conducted their counts on the night and morning of the escape. After lights out at 9:30 P.M., the cellhouse was considerably darker, and the heavy blanketing likely made it difficult to discern that the heads were dummies rather than human.

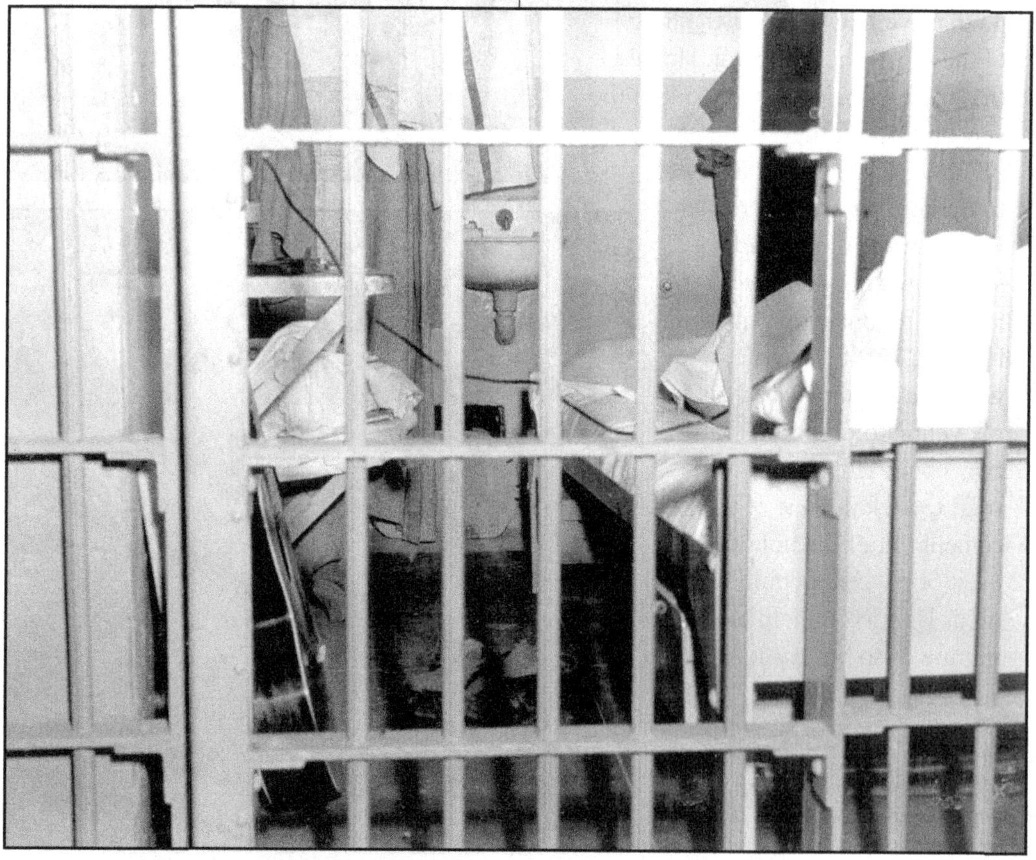

anything. He then went up and got Morris. Morris came down and put the dummy in his bed. The lights were out at 9:30 P.M. and Morris went up to the roof and got a two inch piece of pipe and handed it to me. I tried to push it out but couldn't do it without making too much noise. Morris left to go get Clarence Anglin to help clear out my hole. This happened at 9:37 P.M. that evening. This is the last I heard or saw of them. As there was no dummy head for my bed, I was afraid at that time to break through and leave my cell until after the 3:00 A.M. count.

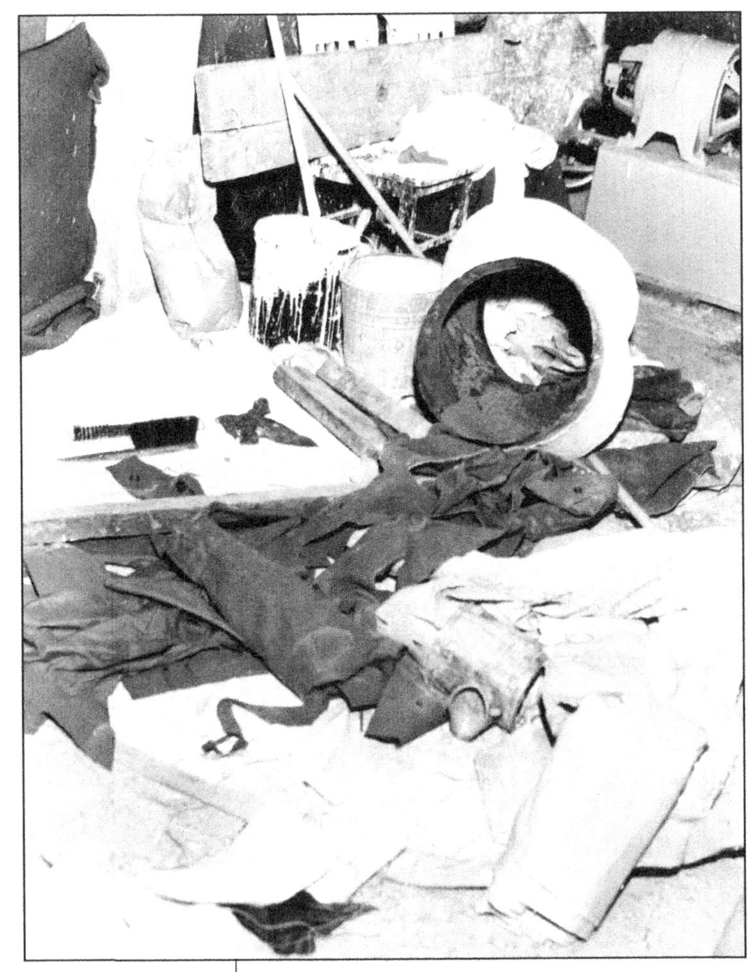

Sections of a raft and materials from raincoats and other items used in the escape were found hidden inside the large blower ducting on top of the cellblock.

At about 1:45 A.M. of June 12, 1962, after waiting for some time for them to come back I became anxious, I broke through my hole and went to the roof by way of utility corridor. There was no dummy for my bed when I got into the utility corridor I noticed that they had left "Oink" lying there and I use this dummy head in my bed. I took my blue dungarees, undershirt and blue pea jacket to the roof with me. I can see that they had gone since a lot of the items we had fabricated were gone.

In addition, there had been some 100 feet of a heavy electrical cord which had been lying on the floor of the utility corridor and I had noticed upon leaving my cell that it had disappeared. This cord was to be used in lowering our material down from the roof of the cellhouse and possibly in assisting in lowering one of us down.

I put my life preserver on, and my pants, and started to go through the hole in the roof. I had to remove my clothing before I could get through

(This page and opposite page) The roof of the cellhouse where the convicts removed the ventilator and made their escape.

the hole. When I got on the roof I put my clothing on again and went to the edge of the roof near the cage where the large black pipe leads to the ground. We had contemplated going down this pipe to the ground. I looked around and could not see them and figured it was too late for me to go. Also they had taken the raft which was to be our means of escape. It is my belief that they would have been able to leave the island by 10:30 P.M. that night or possibly no later than 11:00 P.M. that evening.

They had planned to go through the ventilator hole, on the roof and then down a large black pipe by the bakery. They had located about 125 feet of electrical cord about one half inch thick in the utility corridor and that was to be taken with them to assist in getting down from the roof and to lower their material. They would go over by the water tank and then down by the machine shop next to the water. They would pump the 14 x 6 feet raft, made of raincoats which had 15 inch pontoons, with the concertina that Morris had purchased. We had talked about going to Angel Island and then stick a knife in the raft so it would sink. It was believed that there would be less chance of detection if we proceeded in that direction.

Upon getting to the mainland we had decided that we would commit a burglary so we could obtain guns and clothes, and then steal a car. It was our desire to go as far from this area as we could, although we had no plan as to where we would go. Just the four of us were involved in the escape. To assist in this effort, I had made a periscope out of paper and mirrors which we could stick out of the hole on the roof to see if there were any guards in that area. I had given this periscope to Morris for one of the Anglin's and it was stored next to the roof. The only weapons which they would possibly have is a kitchen knife or some similar type objects which they might have sharpened.

When we were working attempting to get out of our cells, we would work between 5:30 P.M. and 9:30 P.M. at night. Generally, Morris was with one of the Anglin's when they went to the roof. I didn't desire that the two Anglin's go there together as I didn't trust them. If we were successful in escaping, Morris and I had planned that sooner or later we would go in one direction and let the Anglin brothers go in another.

Officer Freeman "Pep" Pepper who had been working on Alcatraz since the 1930s, overheard West telling fellow prisoners about the escape after he had been placed in a closed front isolation cell. Freeman wrote that he had overheard the conversation from "inside the treatment unit cutoff." West had been placed in closed cell #13 and it's possible that West emptied the water from the toilet and others were listening using the same method via the plumbing network. Freeman overheard West say: "Everybody better listen cause I'm only going to tell you once and that'll be it... Is everybody on the telephone?" Pepper documented what he'd overheard. He wrote in part:

I started planning this when I first came out of T.U., I got to looking over this vent and figured that's a good place to go out (West was in C Block at this time). I talked to the Anglins first about it and they thought it'd be a good idea. Then I moved over to B Block by then, but I couldn't get right next to them so we had to have another man in on it. The man we talked to backed out so we got Morris in on it. We drilled in the cement for five months and I was the first on finishing drilling. Fifty raincoats were used, except for the sleeves, to make the life rafts and lifejackets. If this didn't do anything else, it ruined Alcatraz's thirty year reputation.

I went to the top of the cellblock to see if I might be able to go [responding to a question as to why he didn't leave with the others], but didn't find any rope or cord to go down with and I wasn't going into the water with just a lifejacket. Morris was the first one out last night. He came by my cell, but he couldn't get me out. He said he'd get Clarence to help, but that I'd have to get it from the inside and he passed me the pipe, but never came back. That was the last I saw him. They used my accordion to pump up the raft and I figured it'd take about an hour to pump it up.

I finished the 25th of April. Morris was second, he finished May 11th. Clarence and Frank were feuding Sunday night on top of the block, I thought they'd get busted then with all of the noise they were making. They started out last night at 8:15 and everybody was out by 9:30, but me. I got out at 1:00 A.M. and they

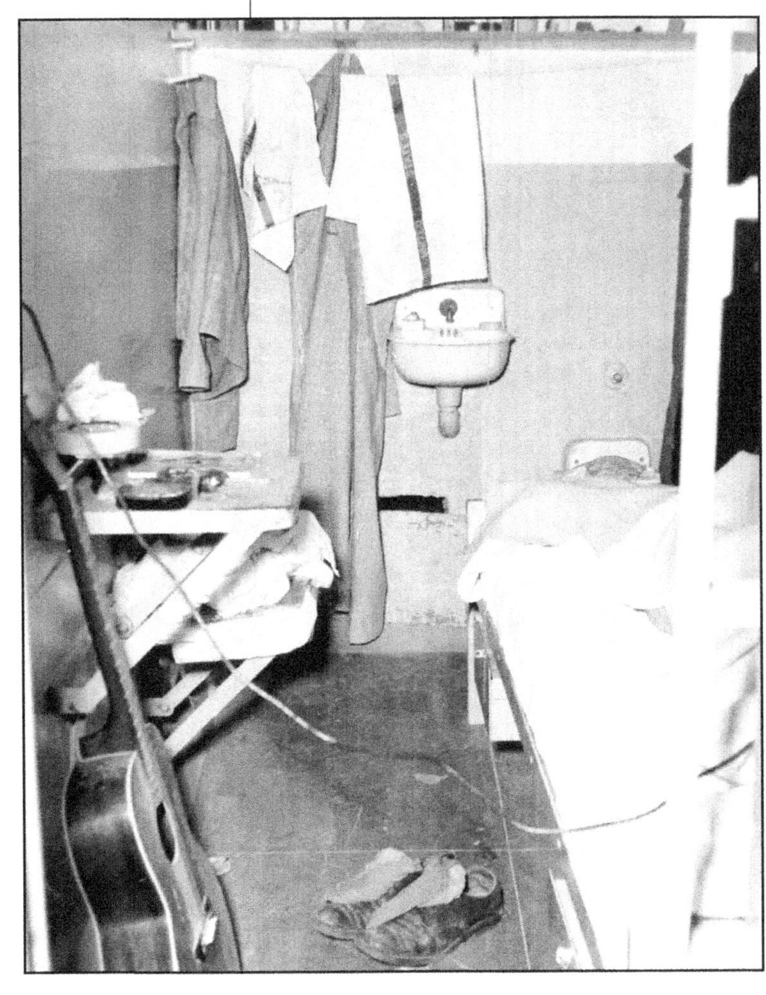

Clarence Anglin's cell photographed on June 12, 1962.

were gone. I went up on the roof at 1 o'clock and ran around trying to figure out what to do. I finally gave up and went back to my cell.

From the FBI:

Albert V. Young, Correctional Officer, advised that on June 11, 1962, he worked the 4 P.M. to midnight shift in the west gallery. Young said the west gallery is the enclosed catwalk located at the western end of the cellblock.

Young advised that at about 10:30 P.M. on June 11, 1962, he heard a noise which sounded to him like a person hitting the end of an empty 50 gallon oil drum with the heal of his hand. He said the noise sounded like it came from the prison hospital. Young said he immediately reported the noise telephonically to Lt. Robert Weir. Young said he heard the same noise approximately two minutes later and then heard it a third time approximately five minutes after that. During this time he was on the telephone with Lt. Weir. The last time he heard this noise it sounded like it came from the "dining room cage" which is a guard post located outside

Contemporary photographs of Clarence's ventilator grill that still show where he sawed through the metal framing and the thickness and textures of the cement.

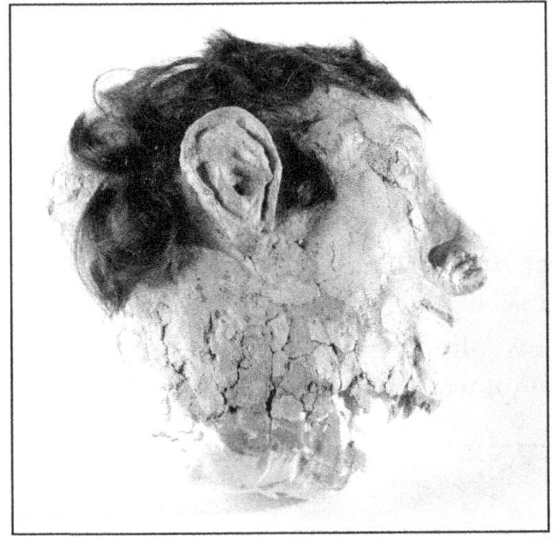

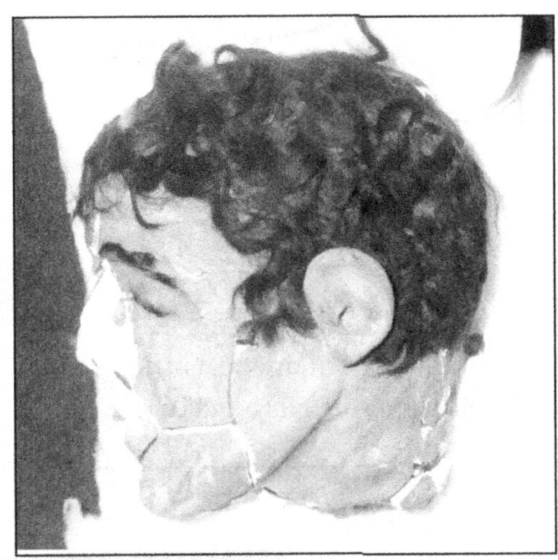

(Above left) A modern photo of the dummy head from Clarence's cell. The writing on the decoy indicates the cell number and date it was recovered and entered into evidence.

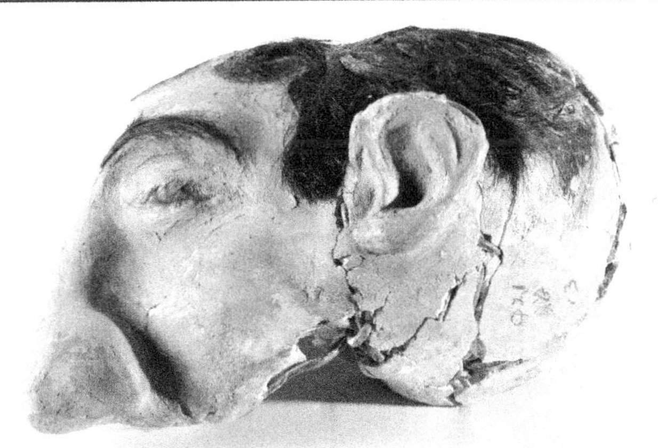

(Above right) The dummy head used as a decoy by John.

(Left) West's dummy head.

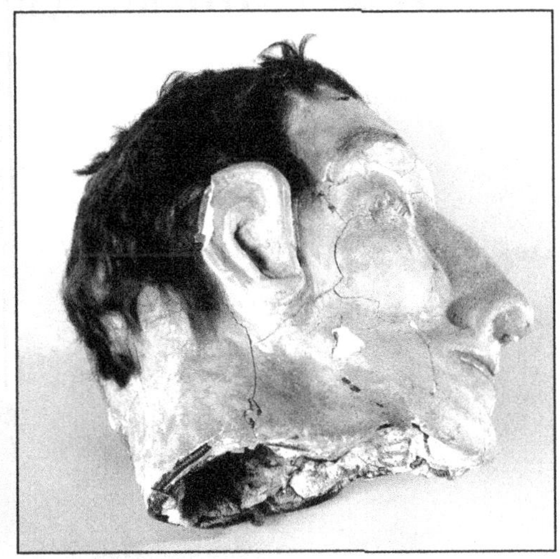

(Above, left and right) The dummy head used by Frank Morris.

the dining room wall over an alley way leading from the cellblock to the recreation yard. Young advised after reporting these incidents to Lt. Weir, he assumed that Lt. Weir checked them out.

On the morning of June 12th, there was an air of excitement as the sounds of the officers started to make their final morning counts and prepare for the oncoming staff. It was a Monday morning and the start of a new work week for the convicts. William "Bill" Long was a lieutenant on-duty the night of the escape. A native of Mifflinburg, Pennsylvania, he had arrived on Alcatraz in 1953, and was well respected by many fellow officers. His wife, Jean, was also employed on the Rock as its Postmaster.

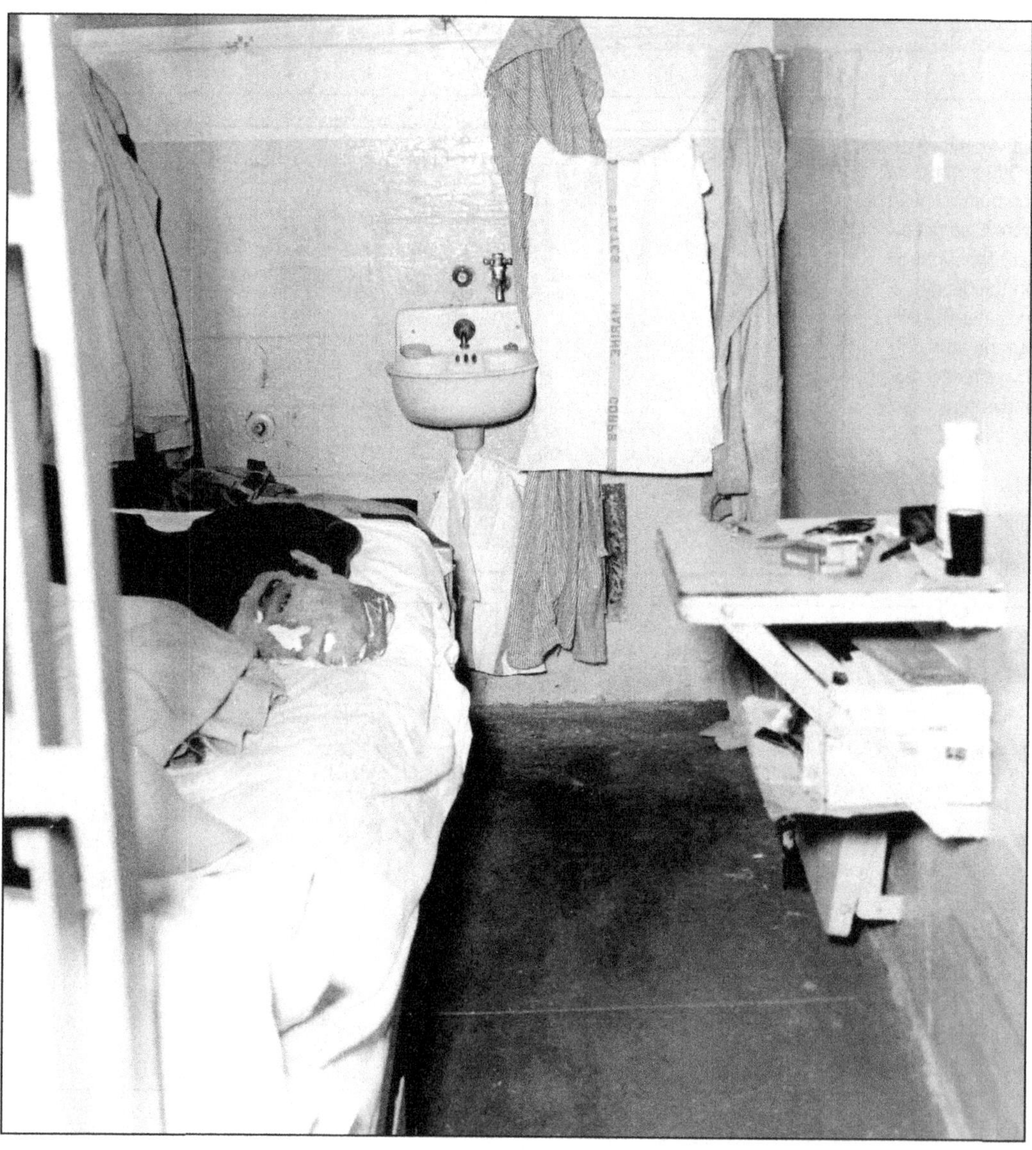

John Anglin's cell.

Long vividly remembered the morning that they had discovered the prisoners missing:

> I was a little late to work that night . . . Weir was in a hurry to get off work. There was almost no briefing from him and he left just saying it was a "routine watch." One of our regular duties before going off shift was holding a standing count. The watch going off puts in a count and the new watch coming on puts in a count. Our counts had to correspond. I knew nothing about the big noise that was reported on the roof the night before. The hospital officer, Levinson, called in that he had heard footsteps on the roof and also a rumbling like noise. He called back

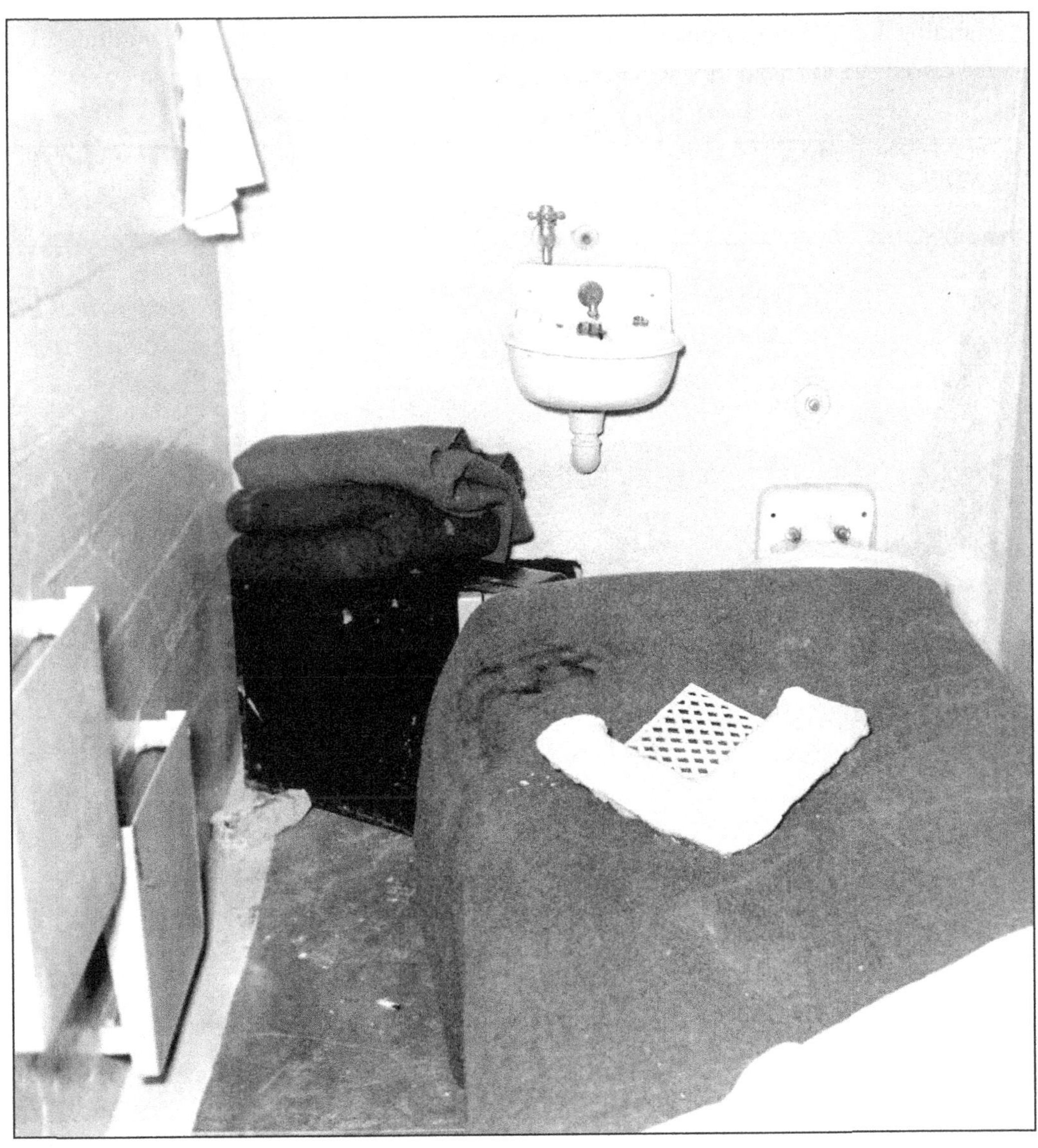

Allen West's cell.

a second time and told Weir that he heard them again. Weir looked around the hospital but never went to the roof. The noise was described as a hub cap from an automobile that was tumbling around, so this certainly was no routine watch. We had a stairwell inside the cellhouse that gave us easy access to the rooftop. The top area was enclosed, so he could have investigated the noise by standing at the doorway and would have seen the vent cap push over. You didn't have to go up a ladder or anything like that, so it would've been real easy for him to go up and investigate that noise. He didn't though and just wrote it off to the wind...

Ordinarily, when they count at night, the officer using a five cell flashlight wouldn't shine the light down on the face of the inmate. You have very volatile men and if you shined the flashlight on them during every count, they're going to be a

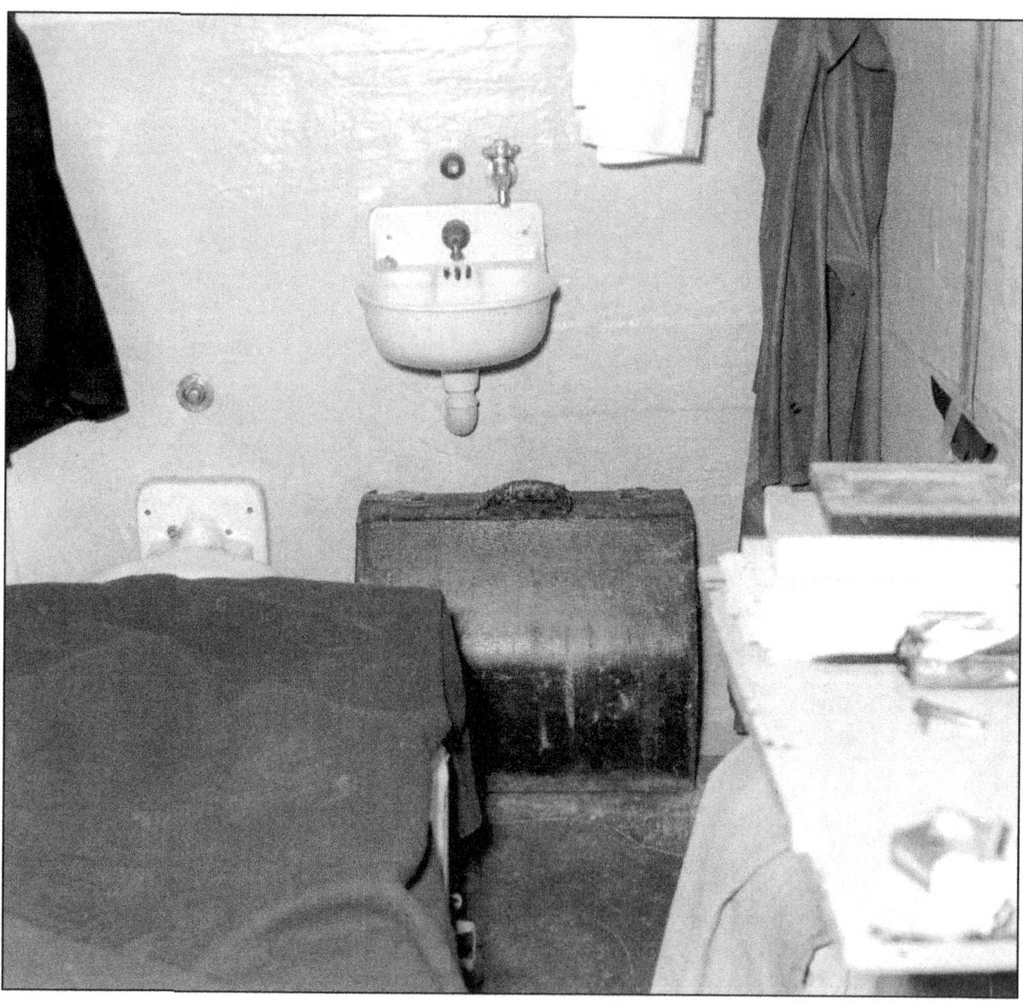

An evidence photo of Frank Morris's cell prior to being to being formally examined and inventoried by prison and FBI officials.

little upset the next morning. Some of them would put the covers over their heads and you'd take the butt of the flashlight to move the covers off. The officer doing the count would point the beam of light on the ceiling and visualize the inmate from the reflective light. One of the things they did at night, was on the cellhouse ceiling, there were a series of 25-watt light bulbs (basically night lights) and sometimes inmates using rubber bands as slingshots would shoot pebbles at them to bust them out for a little extra darkness.

There was a count a little before midnight and then around 3:00 A.M., 6:00 A.M. and then at 7:00 is when the day watch came in. During the night one of the duties of the evening watch officer was to make a fire patrol. I went down into the family living area, then on to the dock, to the Industries building and then back up. If these guys would have escaped along the same path and same time

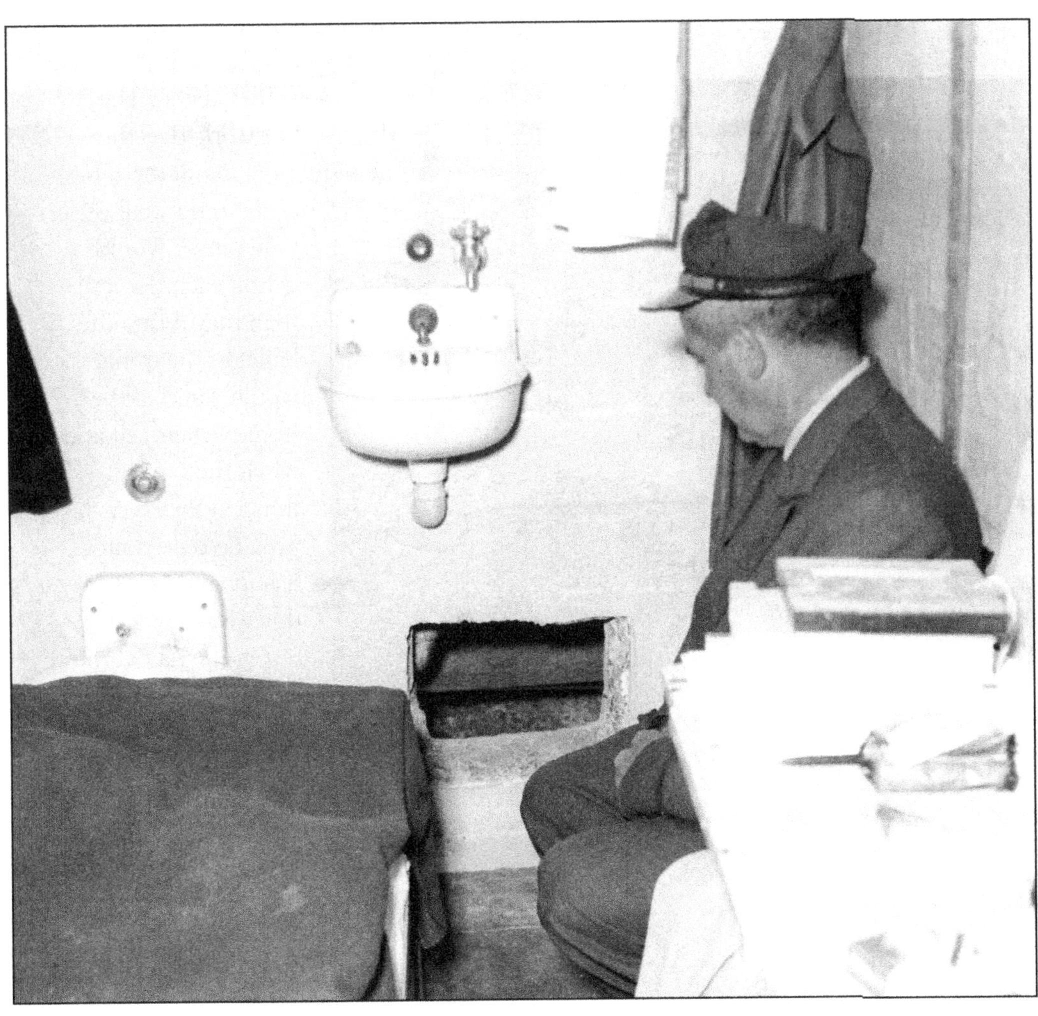

Senior Officer Howard Waldron examining Morris' cell and the opening where the ventilation grill was originally located.

(Left) While the evidence photos do not lend to this rumor, it was claimed that this page from the Sports Illustrated magazine was left open in Morris's cell to taunt prison officials.

(Below) An officer examines one of the cell openings from the utility corridor.

I made my walk, they might have been real hard on me because there was three of them and only one of me. They could have over powered me.

The new watch came in and there was about seven or eight officers. The officer in charge always sat at the desk that was right near the kitchen. The desk sort of worked as the headquarters for all the officers working in the cellhouse. One officer would get on each tier and then they'd ring the bell and the inmates would stand at the front of their cell and when the officers finished they'd each provide their count. It happened everyday this way...

On the day of the escape, the first five guys came down with their counts; three from C Block and two from the upper tiers of B Block. Lawrence Bartlett, the guy who was covering B-1 didn't come around with the rest of them. I walked over to the

> edge of where I could see down the flats of the A-B corridor and Sarge Bartlett was coming in my direction hot-foot'n it, and he's about 20 feet away and he starts yelling Bill, Bill, Bill!!!! I got a guy here who won't get up for the count! So I went up to B-150 which was John Anglin's cell. I went up to the bars, knelt down, I reached in with my left hand to tap him on the head and it felt like it crumbled and the head flopped off onto the floor. People who were observing me said that I jumped back about 4 feet. That's when all hell broke loose and the captain started ringing the bell. All of the officers came running up to the cellhouse.

Long's official report filed to the Captain on June 14, 1962, read in part:

> The count started routinely, but Bartlett who was counting B Block rapidly came around the corner and I could see he was excited. He said, "Bill, I can't wake these two guys up, they are either dead men or dummies." I immediately accompanied him to Cell B-150 and I reached into the cell and with my left hand and tapped on the pillow. Things did not seem exactly normal but until I tapped the back of the head with almost the same motion and the head fell onto the floor. I then threw off the blanket covering the supposed body and then I reached into the next cell B-152 where the other dummy was and threw off the blanket. I remember at that time seeing another "man" in bed and went and checked the cell. It was Morris's cell B-138. I told the officer not to touch it because on examination I could see that it was a dummy like the other two.

Bill Long in 2009 on Alcatraz reminiscing about the escape.

I went to the phone to call the control center and dialed the Captain's office. I informed Officer Martin of the dummies and was told that Lieutenant Severson was in the Officer's mess. I looked into the Main Gate and Lt. Severson was coming down the stairs. I informed him that there was dummies in the beds and told the Control Center to call the Associate and the Captain. Lt. Severson told him to sound the alarm.

We went into the cellhouse and opened the plumbing corridor. I immediately saw that the rear of the Anglin brothers' cells were tampered with and then I went on to the rear of the corridor and in the checking to see if Morris's cell was the same way, I discovered that the cell next to Morris's cell was opened too. This was cell #140. I immediately came out and reported that there was another cell opened and went to check who was in that cell next to Morris. When I came to the cell, West AZ-1335 was talking to Officer Howard Waldron. West had called him over and said: "You might as well look me up too, I planned the entire escape." He was telling him how he was involved and explaining how the plan was to have worked. "No shakedown could ever discover this!!!" West was holding up a fake cardboard duplicate of the air vent and was beating it with his fist...

Bulger remembered the morning the convicts were discovered missing:

The night seemed to linger on forever... It felt like a year until sunrise and count time. This was the big moment and my heart was racing with excitement... Bartlett, a guard we all called "Sarge" who had retired from the U.S. Army—got to Morris's cell and because he wasn't standing up for the count yelled "Morris... Get-up!" Sarge then reached into his cell and forcefully jabbed his head. Imagine his shock when it rolled off the bed and onto the floor. He leaped backwards in horror and was speechless and pointing into the cell as he tried to get words out. A guard in the gun gallery tried to get an answer as to "who" was missing and Sarge yells out at the top of his lungs "MORRIS... MORRIS IS GONE!" Well, the cellhouse exploded into cheers and all hell breaks loose. One by one, they find the others missing... There were cheers of pure elation, joy, laughter and jokes as the guards scrambled frantically.

Woodrow Wilson Gainey (AZ-1520) was another convict who was later identified as a conspirator in the escape. During a mass search of cells in the days following, holes and the same methods for tunneling through the cement was found in the back of both his and June Stephen's cells. Gainey spoke with officials and admitted that both he and Stephens had originally been part of the plot. Gainey had become acquainted with John Anglin in 1958 when both of them were in the US Penitentiary, Lewisburg, Pennsylvania. After arriving at Alcatraz on September 7, 1961, Gainey was introduced to Clarence Anglin, Morris, West and Stephens. He

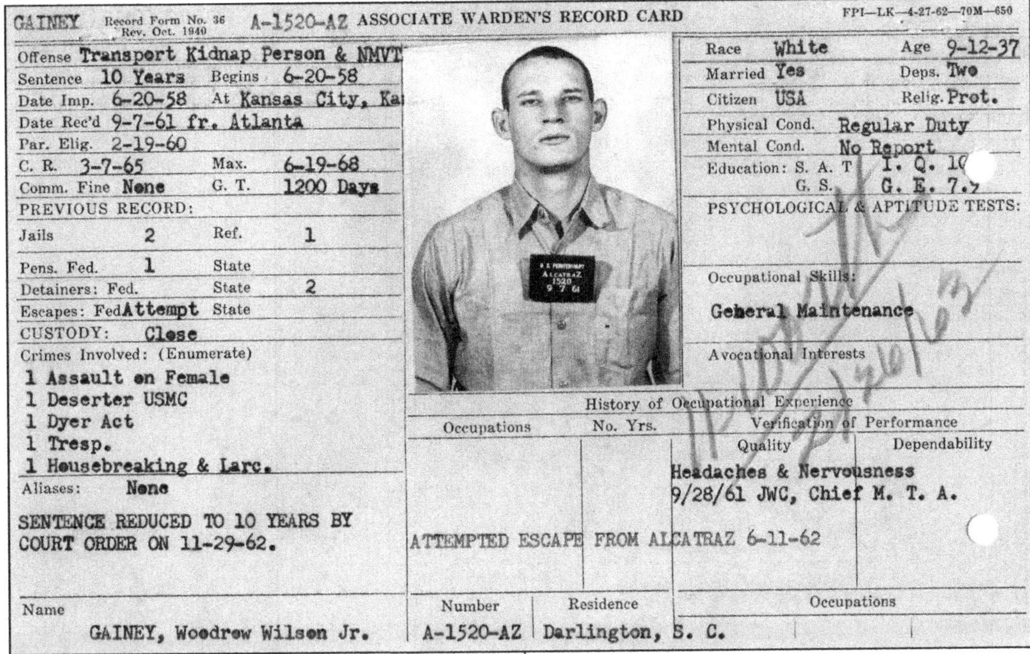

GAINEY Record Form No. 36 Rev. Oct. 1940 A-1520-AZ ASSOCIATE WARDEN'S RECORD CARD FPI—LK—4-27-62—70M—650

Offense Transport Kidnap Person & NMVT
Sentence 10 Years Begins 6-20-58
Date Imp. 6-20-58 At Kansas City, Ka
Date Rec'd 9-7-61 fr. Atlanta
Par. Elig. 2-19-60
C. R. 3-7-65 Max. 6-19-68
Comm. Fine None G. T. 1200 Days
PREVIOUS RECORD:
Jails 2 Ref. 1
Pens. Fed. 1 State
Detainers: Fed. State 2
Escapes: Fed Attempt State
CUSTODY: Close
Crimes Involved: (Enumerate)
1 Assault on Female
1 Deserter USMC
1 Dyer Act
1 Tresp.
1 Housebreaking & Larc.
Aliases: None

SENTENCE REDUCED TO 10 YEARS BY COURT ORDER ON 11-29-62.

Race White Age 9-12-37
Married Yes Deps. Two
Citizen USA Relig. Prot.
Physical Cond. Regular Duty
Mental Cond. No Report
Education: S. A. T I. Q. 10
G. S. G. E. 7.
PSYCHOLOGICAL & APTITUDE TESTS:
Occupational Skills:
Geberal Maintenance
Avocational Interests

History of Occupational Experience

Occupations	No. Yrs.	Verification of Performance: Quality	Dependability
		Headaches & Nervousness 9/28/61 JWC, Chief M. T. A.	

ATTEMPTED ESCAPE FROM ALCATRAZ 6-11-62

Name	Number	Residence	Occupations
GAINEY, Woodrow Wilson Jr.	A-1520-AZ	Darlington, S. C.	

Woodrow Wilson Gainey

revealed to the FBI some of the early dynamics of the escape plan. An FBI report included Gainey's account along with other details constructed from various prisoner interviews:

> Inmate Gainey stated that he and June Heyward Stephens Jr., were initially in on the escape plot. Gainey claims he quit after digging a few holes in his cell wall (B-348). He stated Stephens dug several holes in his cell but stopped along with the escapees to avoid detection while the plumbing was installed, and told not to start digging again by the escapees. Eight holes were uncovered in Gainey's cell and some 36 holes were uncovered in Stephens' cell, all carefully camouflaged. Gainey states Harold Pitts Roe, FBI No. 519052A, and Harold Wayne Davis, FBI No. 394760A, both inmates acted as Stephens' lookout for about one week and then quit. He said that John Anglin in February 1962, showed him two files which Anglin claimed he had obtained from an inmate, suspect Wilbur Marcum, FBI No. 3985310.
>
> At the first part of February 1962, June Heyward Stephens, Jr., an inmate of Alcatraz having cell B-346, asked Gainey if he was interested in escaping. Stephens advised him that the Anglin brothers, Frank Morris, and Allen West, all inmates residing on the first tier of B Block, were obtaining spoons and digging at the back of their cells under the sink around the ventilator. They were taking the cupped portion of the spoon off and sharpening that end of the spoon in the fashion of a screw driver which was then utilized in the digging.

(Above and left) Eight holes were found around Gainey's ventilator grill (B-348) and he would later admit to being a part of the escape in the early stages but was later asked to back out.

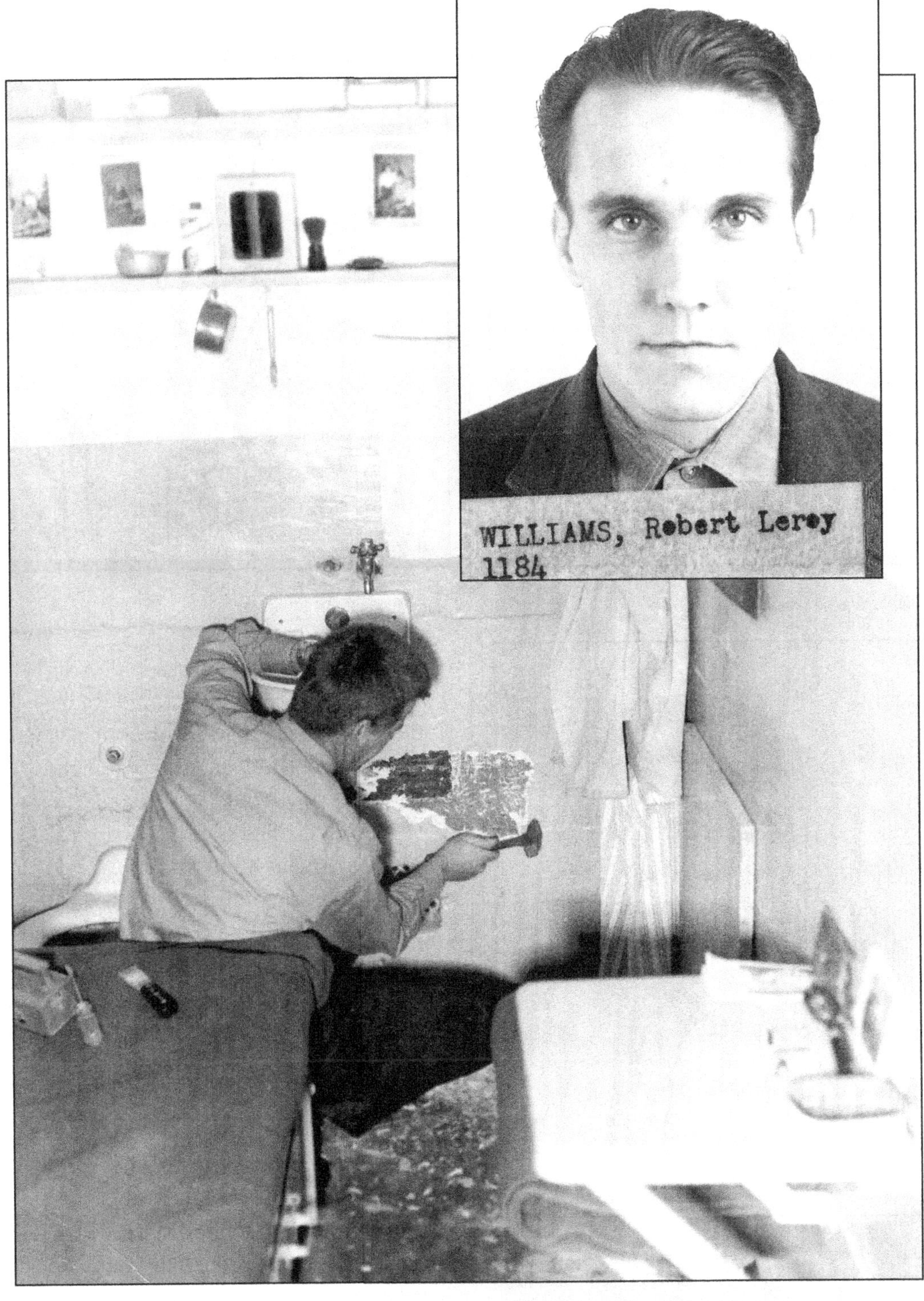

In the aftermath of the escape, correctional officers swarmed through the cellhouse, painstaking inspections of every cell in B Block. Senior Officer James Lewis is seen chipping away paint and soap around the vent grill in cell B-134, where Robbie Williams (AZ-1134) resided. Williams denied having any knowledge of the escape and claimed the holes were not made by him.

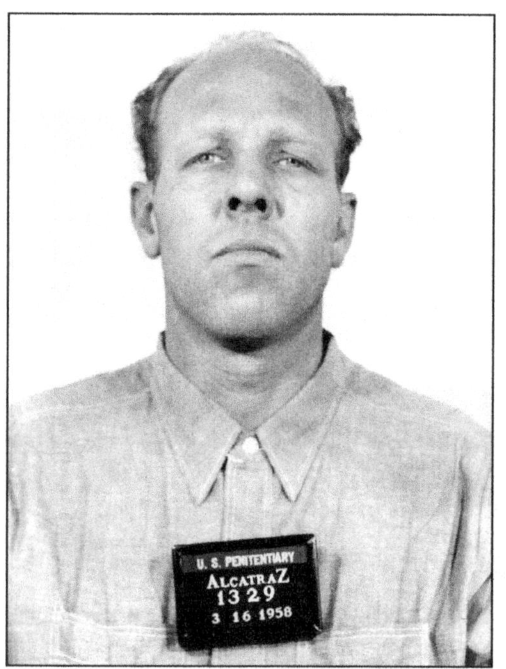

Harold Wayne Davis

Harold Pitts Roe

Charles "Jeep" Wilbur Marcum. Jeep was a close associate of James Bulger and John Paul Scott, and had been part of their escape plot in Atlanta.

Gainey and Stephens started to dig holes in their cells. One would watch during the evening while the other one dug in his cell and the next night the procedure would be reversed. Gainey had talked over the escape with the Anglin brothers and West while at recreation periods in the prison rec yard. They would start digging about 6:15 P.M. and would work until 9:30 P.M. when the lights were turned off. Stephens told Gainey that West worked around the cellblock doing painting and West was of the opinion that once they got through the cell walls and into the utility corridor, immediately behind it they could proceed to the top of the cellblock and break through the ventilator area and onto the roof.

About the first of April, 1962, the Anglin brothers indicated they had completed making the holes in their cells near the ventilator area. They indicated that they had proceeded to the roof and checked the ventilator area and they believed they could break through the lid and onto the roof. Gainey stated he dug approximately six holes in his cell in the vicinity of the ventilator. This was accomplished in about seven days of digging over a two week period. He decided against trying to break out and told the others of his decision. As he dug out each hole he would fill it with soap and then paint over it with cement paint so that they would be well camouflaged.

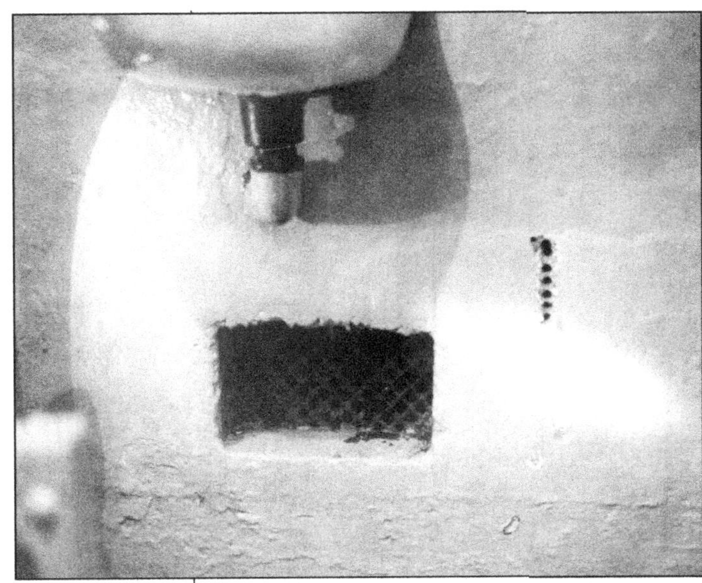

(Above and below) Officers photographed the removal of soap and paint covering the holes found in June Stephen's cell B-346 on the top tier of B Block.

When Gainey decided to quit, Stephens continued digging for about three or four weeks and Gainey watched for him. Gainey then told Stephens he wanted nothing to do with it. Stephens then got Harold Wayne Davis, an inmate in cell B-344 to watch for him. Davis watched Stephens for about one week and then Davis quit. Davis did not try to dig out of his cell to get out. Stephens then got Harold P. Roe, an inmate in cell B-350, to watch for him. Roe then watched for Stephens for about one week and then Roe quit. Roe also did not try to dig any holes in his cell.

After breaking through the cell walls they had planned to put a fake cell wall and ventilator in the area which they had broken out of. They

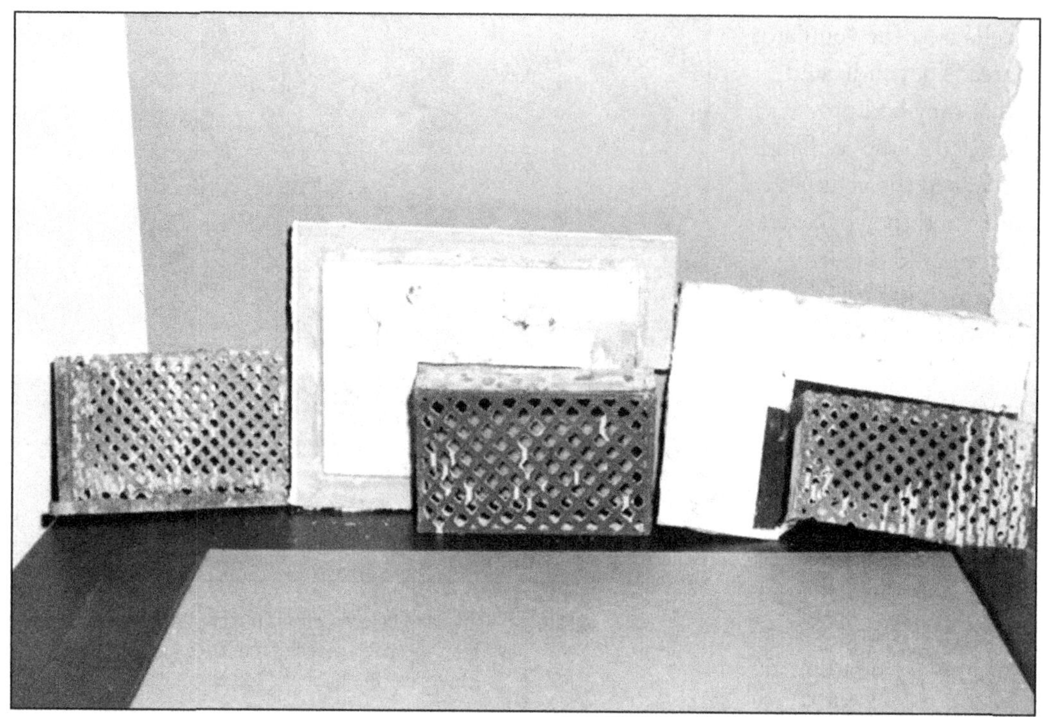

The fake grills recovered from Morris and the Anglin brothers' cells.

had received some instruction from the Anglin brothers on how to construct the fake cover. About March of 1962, the Anglin brothers and West said that they were going to build two rafts out of olive green rubberized rain coats issued to prisoners. From their conversation Gainey believed that they were obtaining tape and paste from the tailor shop to assist in making the rafts. After the rafts were completed, it was planned to place them in the ventilator pipe on top of B Block, and just under the roof. The Anglin brothers told him that Morris had made a hand pump out of steel pipe, a leather type of plunger and wood which would be used to inflate the rafts. They talked of wearing long underwear which they might dye or paint black and sweatshirts similarly dyed or painted. This would be under their regular prison clothing, which they would discard on the beach when they were ready to leave the island. They had talked about paddles out of some wood, 1x8 inch board and each was to make his own.

After Stephens had dug for a few weeks, the Anglin brothers, Morris and West had told Stephens that all of them had stopped digging since there was to be some new plumbing installed in the utility corridor of B Block. Stephens told this to Gainey and said that they were to camouflage their holes so he dug six holes in the vicinity of the ventilator. This was accomplished in about seven days of digging over a two week period. He decide against trying to break out

Gainey would later state in his interview with the FBI that they had considered leaving from the Alcatraz dock area.

and told the others of his decision. As he dug out each hole he would fill it with soap and then paint over it with cement paint that was given to him by Stephens so that they would be well camouflaged.

Stephens worked in the utility corridor upon various occasions since he was an inmate plumber and West who painted around the cellblock area were the ones who did the main scheming and working on breaking through the ventilator lid on the roof. During their conversations John Anglin had indicated that it was a shorter route to go from the island to the mainland of San Francisco rather than toward Angel Island. At that time they were considering building the rafts and going with them to the docks near where the Alcatraz prison boat docked. They would consider hiding the raft, try to locate an armory where they might steal firearms.

Later the Anglins mentioned that they might try to steal a helicopter as Morris had read considerably in the prison library about flying and Morris thought he would be able to pilot the aircraft. They would also steal food and clothing. If they obtained a helicopter they would fly a considerable distance from here and thought somewhere in the California desert where they would stay for a number of months until the "heat" was off. If they had arrived in the desert, they had discussed stealing a big trailer truck body, digging a hole in the ground of the desert and putting the trailer truck body down in the hole

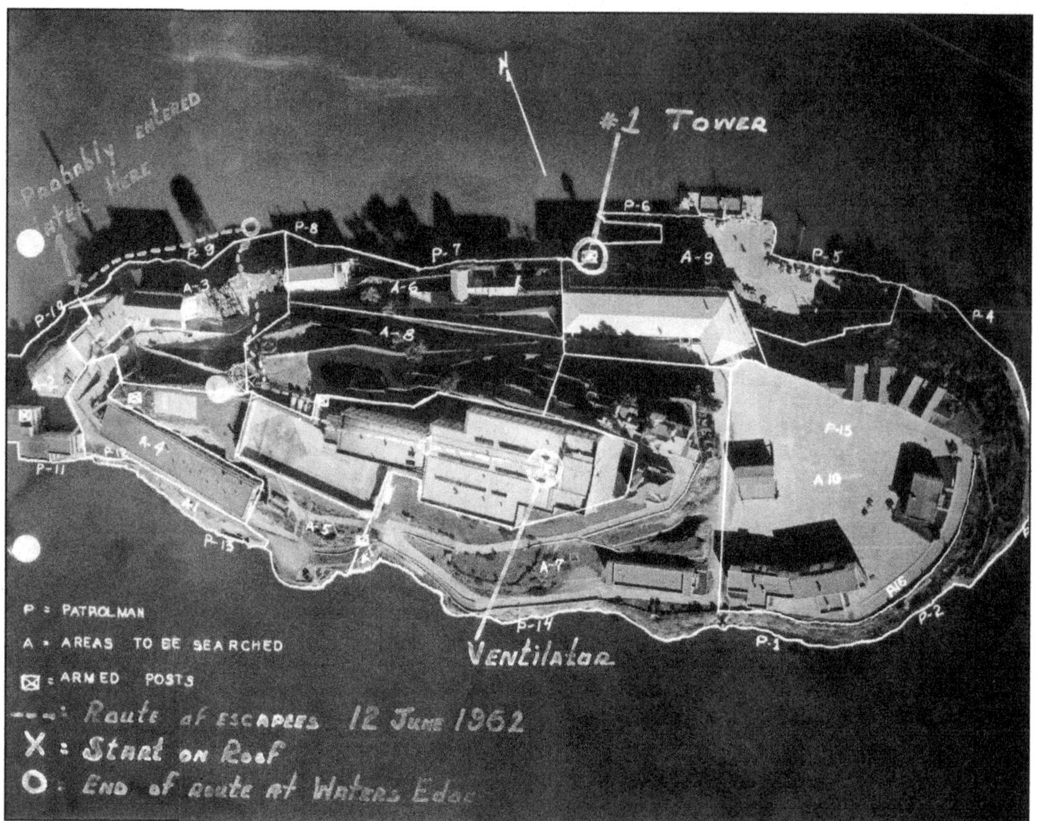

The perimeter search map used by prison officials and the FBI. Investigators plotted the presumed path of the escapees to the water's edge.

and camouflage it so that nobody could see it. They would leave it and then out when no one was in the vicinity.

They talked about later on getting together and robbing banks. They mentioned they would like to get their brother Al, out of the Atlanta Penitentiary. None of the individuals mentioned anyone that they could contact on the outside nor did they ever ask Gainey for his acquaintances or friends, nor did he volunteer the same.

Gainey indicated that since he "backed out" of trying to escape, after initially being in on the plot, he was not in their recent escape plans and probably Stephens was not since they had not told him to start digging at his cell hole again. John Anglin showed Gainey two files. Anglin told Gainey that one of the inmates called "Jeep" who Gainey identified as Charles Wilbur Marcum (AZ-1407), stole these files from the tailor shop and gave them to John Anglin. Gainey said Marcum resided on the first floor of C Block and he still works in the tailor shop on Alcatraz. Gainey advised that Marcum was not in on the plans to escape from the cells as far as he knew.

An aerial view Alcatraz showing the entire roof area in 1962.

Gainey stated that he did not desire to testify in court against anyone of the above individuals so long as he was at Alcatraz. To do so would mean his life since the inmates would take care of that. He did not desire to furnish a signed statement. Stephens, Davis and Marcum all deny any knowledge or participation in the escape.

Stephens was interviewed on June 19, 1962, regarding his potential role and denies all knowledge despite the evidence proving otherwise. Stephens volunteered that he was serving a twenty-five year sentence imposed

(This page and opposite page) A series of photographs taken by the FBI of the roof and bakery duct pipe that the escapees used to scale down the side of the cellhouse. The footprints of escapees are visible leading away and around the enclosure.

in September 1953 for bank robbery. He stated that he had been incarcerated in cell B-346 since late fall of 1961 and at Alcatraz since 1956. He stated he never dug any holes in his cell which includes the vicinity of the ventilator grill, nor had he tried to escape since at Alcatraz. He said if there were any holes in his cell in the vicinity of the ventilator grill they must have been put there by a prior occupant. He said he was not acquainted closely with the Anglin brothers, West or Morris. He only knows Clarence by sight. He never assisted them to escape nor has he been asked to do so. He has never heard anything relative to any of the inmates planning to escape. He is an inmate plumber and works around the cellblock, however, no one has asked him for any materials which could be used in escaping. He volunteered that he heard no digging noises in the cells, nor had he heard any unusual noises on the evening of June 11, 1962. He said he had never given names of any friends, relatives or acquaintances to the Anglin brothers, West or Morris nor had he been asked to do so.

From the FBI:

Training Officer L.R. Howell advised he was notified of the escape at 7:30 A.M. by the paging speaker system. He and Lieutenant Robert Weir, after being advised of the basic details of the escape, proceeded to the north end of the cellblock to the bakery smoke stack. He advised that they

(Left) After scaling the fence outside the kitchen basement area, the convicts entering the officer recreation yard catwalk, cut barbwire and dropped next to the old morgue below.

(Below) A photograph taken fifty years after the escape shows the catwalk where the convicts quietly crept and escaped.

(Below, left and right) Officers examined and charted the pathway down to the waters' edge.

(Above and below) The area near the powerhouse where the convicts inflated their flotation devices and entered the water.

(Left and below) An officer standing at the location the escapees entered the water. The electrical extension cord is seen rolled up where it was left by the convicts. Numerous starfish can also been seen in the area showing the rise and fall of the tide.

noted barbed wire sagging on top of a cyclone fence located approximately 10 feet from the base of the smoke stack. They then noted a strand of cut barbed wire on the catwalk outside the yard wall 50 feet from the first fence. It is in the north east corner of the island. From this spot he noted grass bent down near the water tower. This is about 100 feet from the last fence crossing. This bent grass area is towards the beach and there is a 45 foot downward slope to the road level. He believed that the inmates then apparently crossed the road to the lumber and debris area to the edge of the slope leading to the beach seawall. The seawall is about 4 to 6 feet high down to the water's edge and rocks. He advised they found a one-half inch diameter black electrical extension cord about 100 feet long rolled up in a coil near the rocks below the seawall.

The Search At The Water's Edge

AT THE WATER'S EDGE of Alcatraz, one of the greatest crime mysteries of the 20th Century was born. Once the trio entered the water and sailed into the dark of night, it would launch one of the largest manhunts in American history. It is a mystery that is still debated by investigators and historians over a half century later.

There remains no definitive proof as to what happened to the men after they made it into the frigid waters of the San Francisco Bay. For every piece of evidence or compelling theory that suggests they perished battling the fierce tides, another emerges that is equally persuasive and hints that the escapees may have survived. The FBI files show no firm conclusions and all theories were based on limited evidence as to determine the ultimate fate of the escaped convicts. Convincing leads that turn cold and empty theories that ripen with promise mold a complex case which has foiled investigators for decades. What is conclusive is that the trio successfully escaped from Alcatraz Island. They broke from the cellblock, made it past patrolling guards undetected, inflated their raft and set sail into a foggy history...

As the wailing escape siren resonated to the shores of San Francisco, the officers hurriedly retraced the footsteps of the escapees looking for any piece of evidence that might indicate their fate. Prison officials and the FBI fiercely interrogated Allen West and other inmates, attempting to extract any clues as to the trios' whereabouts. Every theory was mulled and considered by investigators. Warden Blackwell had been away on a weekend fishing trip at Lake Berryessa (located approximately 80 miles north of San Francisco) with his wife and son, and became aware of the escape from a radio news bulletin. During Blackwell's absence, Dollison had been left in charge, and knew when his phone rang so early in the morning it would be grave news. Officers initiated their escape procedures and systematically searched every inch of the island, looking for any potential clues left behind by the convicts. Blood hounds were brought to the island to search the caves and any scent giving clues, but their trail went cold at the water's edge.

At the base of the bakery smokestack, footprints made from the soot residues showed the location were the convicts descended the pipe and then quietly walked around the caged perimeter

I.O.
No. 3584
6-18-62

ESCAPED FEDERAL PRISONER

WANTED BY FBI

FRANK LEE MORRIS

FBI No. 2,157,606

22 M 9 U 100 12
L 1 U 000

ALIASES: Carl Cecil Clark, Frank Laine, Frank Lane, Frank William Lyons, Frankie Lyons, Stanley O'Neal Singletary, and others

Photographs taken 1960

Frank Lee Morris

DESCRIPTION

AGE: 35, born September 1, 1926, Washington, D. C.
HEIGHT: 5' 7½"
WEIGHT: 135 pounds
BUILD: medium
HAIR: brown
EYES: hazel
COMPLEXION: ruddy
RACE: white
NATIONALITY: American
OCCUPATIONS: car salesman, draftsman, painter
SCARS AND MARKS: numerous tattoos including devil's head upper right arm, star base of left thumb, "13" base of left index finger

CRIMINAL RECORD

Morris has been convicted of burglary, larceny of an automobile, grand larceny, possession of narcotics, bank burglary, armed robbery and escape.

CAUTION

MORRIS HAS BEEN REPORTED TO BE ARMED IN THE PAST AND HAS A PREVIOUS RECORD OF ATTEMPTED ESCAPE. CONSIDER EXTREMELY DANGEROUS.

A Federal warrant was issued on June 13, 1962, at San Francisco, California, charging Morris with escaping from the Federal Penitentiary at Alcatraz in violation of Title 18, U.S. Code, Section 751.

IF YOU HAVE INFORMATION CONCERNING THIS PERSON, PLEASE CONTACT YOUR LOCAL FBI OFFICE. PHONE NUMBER LISTED BELOW. OTHER OFFICES LISTED ON BACK.

Identification Order No. 3584

J. Edgar Hoover
Director
Federal Bureau of Investigation
Washington 25, D. C.

I.O.
No. 3583
6-18-62

ESCAPED FEDERAL PRISONER – BANK ROBBER

WANTED BY FBI

JOHN WILLIAM ANGLIN

FBI No. 4,745,119

20 L 29 W 100 18
I 12 W 001

Photographs taken 1960

John William Anglin

DESCRIPTION

AGE: 32, born May 2, 1930, Donalsonville, Georgia (not supported by birth records)
HEIGHT: 5' 10"
WEIGHT: 140 pounds
BUILD: medium
EYES: blue
HAIR: blond
COMPLEXION: ruddy
RACE: white
NATIONALITY: American
OCCUPATIONS: farmer, laborer
SCARS AND MARKS: scar left side of forehead, scar on left forearm near wrist, scar left side of abdomen, small scar left cheek

CRIMINAL RECORD

Anglin has been convicted of grand larceny and bank robbery.

CAUTION

ANGLIN HAS BEEN CONVICTED OF BANK ROBBERY AND WAS IN POSSESSION OF FIREARMS WHEN LAST ARRESTED. HE HAS A PREVIOUS HISTORY OF ATTEMPTED ESCAPE. CONSIDER EXTREMELY DANGEROUS.

A Federal warrant was issued on June 13, 1962, at San Francisco, California, charging Anglin with escaping from the Federal Penitentiary at Alcatraz in violation of Title 18, U.S. Code, Section 751).

IF YOU HAVE INFORMATION CONCERNING THIS PERSON, PLEASE CONTACT YOUR LOCAL FBI OFFICE. PHONE NUMBER LISTED BELOW. OTHER OFFICES LISTED ON BACK.

Identification Order No. 3583
June 18, 1962

J. Edgar Hoover
Director
Federal Bureau of Investigation
Washington 25, D. C.

searching for the best pathway. They scaled a 12-foot barbed-wire fence onto a catwalk that was typically occupied by an armed officer when convicts were present in the recreation yard, cut a section of barbed-wire and dropped down next to the old prison morgue and water tower, then scrambled across a narrow road and entered the area where lumber was stored next to the base of the powerhouse along the northeast shore. The only piece of physical evidence left were footprints leading away from the prison, and a 125 foot section of an industrial electrical cord found abandoned on the cement sea wall. It's guesswork as to how long they waited before entering the water. While some reports suggest they entered in quick fashion, others predict it would have taken approximately an hour to inflate their life preservers and raft. It's also possible they might have taken some of the lumber from the surplus area to supplement their floatation devices. From here, it is all speculation.

There are two prominent theories as to what time and what path the trio took once they entered the water near the powerhouse. The most popular and widely accepted theory is that the men inflated their raft and life vests and then paddled under the cover of night and into the abyss, likely setting their course towards either Angel Island or Horseshoe Bay, located at the base of the Golden Gate Bridge on the north side of the Bay. Many theorize that the men just entered the water and unable to navigate the turbulent conditions, perished either as a result of the floatation devices failing, or were simply carried out to sea unable fight against the powerful forces of a flooding tide that took over 325 square miles of bay water and creating an intense band of current, forced it through the narrow but deep section of the Golden Gate (a rough span of 1,700 yards). There is also no conclusive evidence that the men utilized the tide tables provided by Schibline or factored some of the potentially fierce conditions of the San Francisco Bay. The traditional theories are all reasonable based on some of the physical evidence

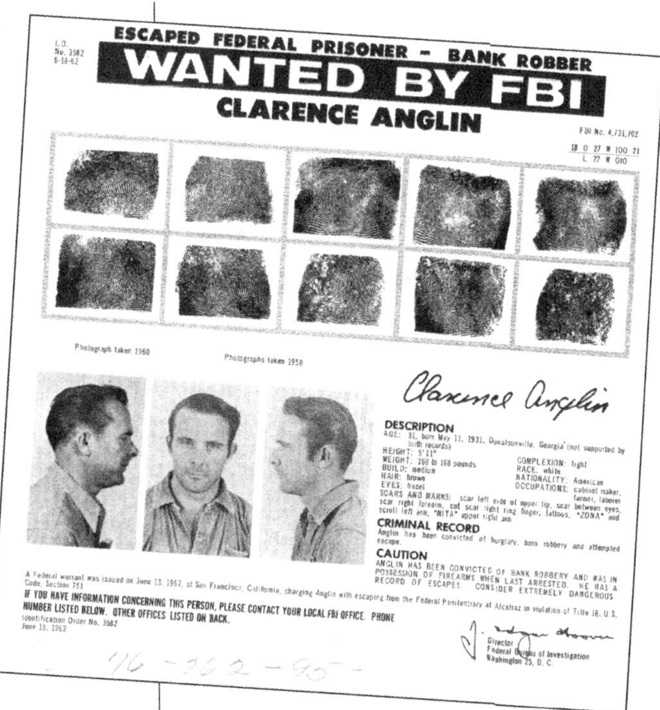

I.O. No. 3582
6-18-62

ESCAPED FEDERAL PRISONER – BANK ROBBER

WANTED BY FBI

CLARENCE ANGLIN

FBI No. 4,731,702

18 O 27 W IOO 21
L 27 W OIO

Photograph taken 1960

Photographs taken 1958

Clarence Anglin

DESCRIPTION

AGE: 31, born May 11, 1931, Donalsonville, Georgia (not supported by birth records)
HEIGHT: 5'11"
WEIGHT: 160 to 168 pounds
BUILD: medium
HAIR: brown
EYES: hazel
COMPLEXION: light
RACE: white
NATIONALITY: American
OCCUPATIONS: cabinet maker, farmer, laborer
SCARS AND MARKS: scar left side of upper lip, scar between eyes, scar right forearm, cut scar right ring finger; tattoos, "ZONA" and scroll left arm, "NITA" upper right arm

CRIMINAL RECORD

Anglin has been convicted of burglary, bank robbery and attempted escape.

CAUTION

ANGLIN HAS BEEN CONVICTED OF BANK ROBBERY AND WAS IN POSSESSION OF FIREARMS WHEN LAST ARRESTED. HE HAS A RECORD OF ESCAPES. CONSIDER EXTREMELY DANGEROUS.

A Federal warrant was issued on June 13, 1962, at San Francisco, California, charging Anglin with escaping from the Federal Penitentiary at Alcatraz in violation of Title 18, U.S. Code, Section 751

IF YOU HAVE INFORMATION CONCERNING THIS PERSON, PLEASE CONTACT YOUR LOCAL FBI OFFICE. PHONE NUMBER LISTED BELOW. OTHER OFFICES LISTED ON BACK.

Identification Order No. 3582
June 18, 1962

J. Edgar Hoover
Director
Federal Bureau of Investigation
Washington 25, D. C.

76-262-95

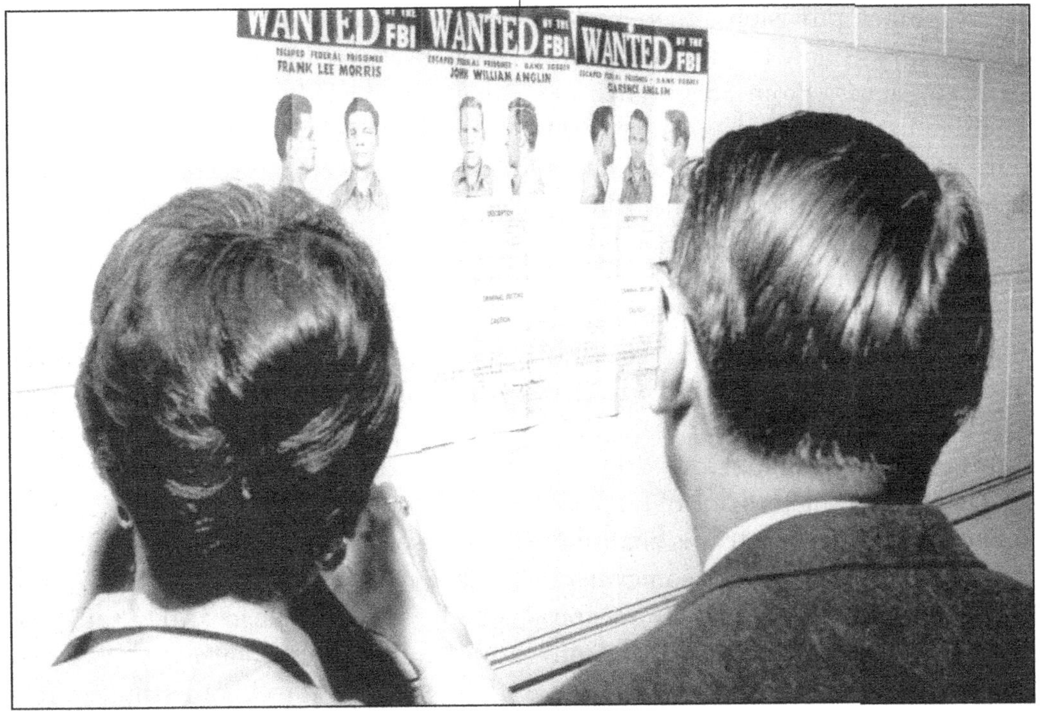

recovered in the surrounding waters, however, the truth remains elusive.

Allen West had described to FBI agents that their original plan had been to inflate their raft and life vests at the water's edge. After entering the water, they would paddle due north and make their way to Angel Island. Once landing, they would briefly rest; hike to the west side of the island; re-enter the water and then swim through a waterway called Raccoon Strait and on into Marin. From there they had planned to steal a car, burglarize a clothing store, and then venture off in their own direction. Darwin Coon later stated that John mentioned they were considering to stay in hiding during daylight on the first day, then later in the evening, find a "Sears" somewhere in Marin, sneak inside at closing time and attempt to hide inside a large apparel carousel (round style clothing rack) until the store was closed. They'd steal clothing and other provisions, then find a car and drive south to Mexico during the night hours. From San Francisco, the drive to the border is just over 500 miles and could've been made in less than eight hours using the main highways. Other convicts believed their plan was simply to make an immediate run for Mexico right after landing in Marin. In concept, they could sneak across the border before the first morning prisoner count. Benny Rayborn later said he'd once heard they'd planned to drive to San Diego, then slip into one of the boat harbors late at night, steal a boat and then cross the border down somewhere along the Baja peninsula. There was no shortage on theories from the prison population.

The convicts left behind few clues apart from the fake grills and dummy heads. In Morris's cell, there were only fingernail clippers, assorted nuts and bolts, three hacksaw blades (found under the foot of his bed), the March issue of Popular Mechanics illustrating life vest designs along with water survival techniques, and a May issue describing boating and docking methods. These articles and the testimony of Gainey that decades later would spark speculation to a second theory that they had entered the water, but rather than paddle out north towards Angel Island, they circled the perimeter and came up under the dock structure; hiding and then tethering a long line to the prison launch where they caught a ride towards Fort Mason on one of the last excursions.

In John's cell, they located a November 1960 issue illustrating vulcanizing methods in constructing rubber geese, as well as art supplies and a six-inch hacksaw blade. Clarence left the majority of residual clues, but only specific to the escape scheme itself. Under the sheets were army blankets rolled up to create a façade of a human body. The paints used to conceal the fake grills were located under his bed, along with the brown twine strung between his and John's cell that they used as a signaling device. Also hidden away in prison envelopes and bundles of handkerchiefs, were strands of hair tied into small pony tails that he'd secured from the prison barbershop.

The missing pages from Allen West's Rand McNally Road Atlas initially offered the most promising clues as to their possible travel route, but as the missing pages covered most of the northern and southern regions of California all the way down to Mexico (equaling thousands of square miles in geography), investigators had no conclusive information as to both their intended destination and route of travel. A rumor among the prisoners was that Morris had left open the Sports Illustrated magazine showing a beer advertisement page in jest. The ad depicted a couple sitting against an overturned wooden boat on a sandy beach, barbequing and enjoying an idyllic evening. It was a taunting image left for officials to ponder.

The first FBI bulletins provided physical descriptions of the escapees and leads from all over started to pour into the FBI offices. Captain Bradley reported that right after the prisoners were discovered missing and officers began arriving, he put the escape plan into operation and set up a perimeter guard around the island. The extra boat was launched and sent to search the waters around the island along with officers combing every inch on foot looking for evidence. The Coast Guard dispatched a helicopter and four patrol boats and searched the waters and shores for any leads or evidence. One hundred Army troops from the 561st engineering battalion were transported by landing barges to join thirty-five military police that had already landed and were searching Angel Island. Officers prowled the rocky caves of Alcatraz looking for any evidence of the escapees. Marie Anglin Widner, the younger sister of John and Clarence was at home and heard over

Assistant Director of the Federal Bureau of Prisons and Warden Olin Blackwell held a press conference offering insight to the escape.

(This page and opposite page) Coast Guard, San Francisco Police and the prison vessels were all engaged in an aggressive search for the convicts. The caves and rocky cliffs of Alcatraz were investigated looking any traces of the escapees.

the radio that there had been an escape from Alcatraz. She would later state that before the radio host was able to announce the names of the escapees, she knew immediately it was her brothers. By midmorning, state, federal and local law enforcement were engaged in the largest manhunt since the Lindbergh baby kidnapping in 1932. James "Whitey" Bulger remembered:

> All day we were put on "Dead Lock" as the guards searched the Island, cursing at the seagulls as they raced around hills, cliffs and nesting areas, and the gulls were flying up squawking and messing down on the officers during their search. You could hear the distant sounds of the commotion happening outside. The story we heard was that "Double Tough" Ordway was swinging his blackjack at the gulls. Easy for us to picture and to believe. We heard they threw grenades into the caves at water level—as the FBI, U.S. Marshals, S.F. Police and Coast Guard all searched in vain for the trio. A short time later, we heard about the footprints on Angel Island and talk of an inflatable lifejacket being found. Things were tense between the guards and convicts for a period after the break. The trio made history and the guards & warden felt it a personal affront—like they did this to us!

Only two days after the escape, Fred T. Wilkinson, now the Assistant Director of the Bureau of Prisons, held a press conference on Alcatraz to provide details of how the convicts made their break from the Rock. The conference was held in the administration area location in the front section of the prison and the press voiced their frustration that they were not allowed to photograph the cells or other areas. Prison officials provided hand-out photos of the actual cells, and then laid out in the visitation area, behind the barred entrance and restricted from any close examination was Frank Morris's dummy head and fake ventilation grill cover. Both Wilkinson and Blackwell provided limited info and remained evasive in answering too many specific questions, reemphasizing that it was an active investigation and the Bureau of Prisons was working closely with the FBI. One disgruntled headline read in bold print: "Alcatraz Safe -- We Can't Get In." Wilkinson had known all of the convicts personally from his years at USP Atlanta and was quoted:

> Information so far leads me to believe definitely that these three men, each of whom I know well from the Atlanta Penitentiary, made it off the island but never made it to shore. The tides that night were strong, these convicts were not the athletic type. Only a trained athlete could make such a swim. These men have neither friends nor relatives with resources to come to San Francisco and spend time and money necessary to help in an escape. It would cost thousands of dollars to put a boat in the Bay every night, say for a month, waiting for the right night. It is a matter of long prison experience that in temporarily successful escapes, the fugitives begin to leave a closely marked trail

> within a few days. They'd have to get clothing or food or do something to get money. There has been none of that in this case. It would take an athlete to successfully make a swim. The only swimming these fellows were accustomed to was in little old creeks or in the swamps of Florida and Louisiana.

J. Edgar Hoover, Director of the FBI, along with several other heads from other district offices communicated their frustration with the BOP talking with members of the press. Reporters had already heard news of items being recovered by the US Coast Guard conducting searches of the San Francisco Bay. Numerous memorandums were fired back and forth between the San Francisco, D.C. and Tampa offices strongly protesting any further public comments, with one memo taking aim by stating the "the talking done by Bennett and Wilkinson has already impeded the investigation." A hand written note from Hoover on a news clipping in the file read: "We may be in charge of the search but we are certainly not in charge of the publicity!" When the Washington Post published a feature in their June 13th edition, Hoover commented to one of the San Francisco bureau officials: "I trust our S.F. Office isn't giving a 'blow-by-blow' account to the press nor anyone else. Our job is to find these thugs, not keep them advised of our progress." Hoover's frustration finally came to a head when the San Francisco Chronicle started to provide details of items that were later recovered in the Bay. Hoover responded with a firm directive to his staff:

> It is expected that you will assert the necessary leadership and direction to insure matters pertinent to the investigation are promptly reported to your office. Items found during the course of the investigation should be channeled through your office and premature disclosure of information can, of course, seriously jeopardize the investigative activities. There should be no question as to the fact that the FBI is in charge of the over-all search to locate these subjects and all aspects must be fully explored.

The press not only remained relentless, but harshly criticized the administration for its handling of the day to day operations:

> "The apparent ease with which a trio of bank robbers escaped from the reputedly escape-proof Alcatraz Prison in San Francisco suggests that there is something very wrong with the operation of that institution... The "maximum security" with which the prison was supposed to operate is more fictional than real."

Famed columnist Drew Pearson was so persistent that following numerous telegrams and phone calls to government officials, Blackwell finally conceded to a special tour and walked him through the main cellblock. They had not allowed him to walk along the Michigan Ave / B Block corridor to inspect the escape cells, and he made his opinions no secret as he openly criticized both the operations and physical state of the prison. Hoover continued

(Left and below) The unfinished raft located on the top of the roof of the cellblock provided insight to the complex design and fabrication of the air valve. The stitching of the raincoat material is also easily discernable.

to blast the BOP for their poor handling of the media and was rumored to have personally called Bennett and demand a lockdown of access to the press.

On the morning after the escape, the US Coast Guard along the prison launch officers combed the waters searching for clues of the escapees. The FBI recovered two rafts; one on Angel Island and another near Point Richmond, California. In both cases, officials determined that the rafts were "not likely" used during the escape or had belonged to any of the conspirators. The official investigative reports provided insight to the recovered items during the intensive search efforts:

> On June 12, 1962, 10:15 P.M., Roy Eastman working aboard the Coast Guards' Cutter #40383 observed an object floating in the water approximately 100 to 200 yards off shore between Point Stuart and Point Knox on Angel Island (located on the northwest side). He and the crew were patrolling the area surrounding Angel Island and had just completed a west bound pass through Raccoon Straights, and had turned south off Point Stuart and Point Knox, at a distance of 100 to 200 yards off shore, an object was sighted floating in the water as a result of directing the cutter's spotlight along the shoreline. The depth of the water was about 30 feet (5 fathoms). The object was retrieved

by him and identified as a homemade paddle about 4 feet long. The paddle was bolted onto the handle. The paddle was delivered to authorities at Alcatraz.

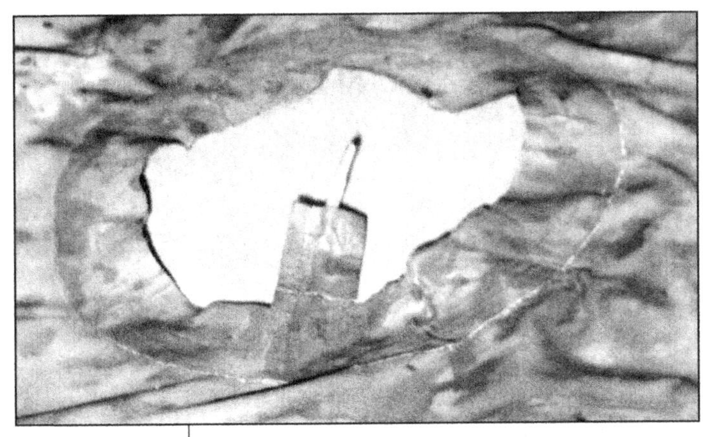

On the afternoon of June 15th, Robert Peterson, a self-employed feature writer, on a walk with his wife and four year old daughter at Fort Chronkhite Beach, north of San Francisco on the Marin Coast, spotted something floating about 50 feet offshore. He kept watching it until it finally washed-up close enough for him to grab it out of the water. It was olive drab in color, and as he examined it more closely, he realized it appeared to be a homemade life preserver. His wife Britta had read the newspaper articles about the escape and realized what they'd found "might have something to do with the Alcatraz escapees." They searched up and down the beach area for other objects but didn't see anything. They drove to the Sausalito Police Department and turned the vest over to authorities. The item was described in the FBI summary report:

(Above and below) A lifejacket found just fifty yards east of the Alcatraz dock. The vest was saturated with stains (originally thought to have been blood but later defined as grease), and visible teeth marks around the air tube. Based on this evidence, it was believed that the inmate who wore it was desperately attempting to maintain enough air pressure to keep afloat. The prisoners used binder claps to seal the air inside the vests, and these were probably unable to sustain adequate air pressure.

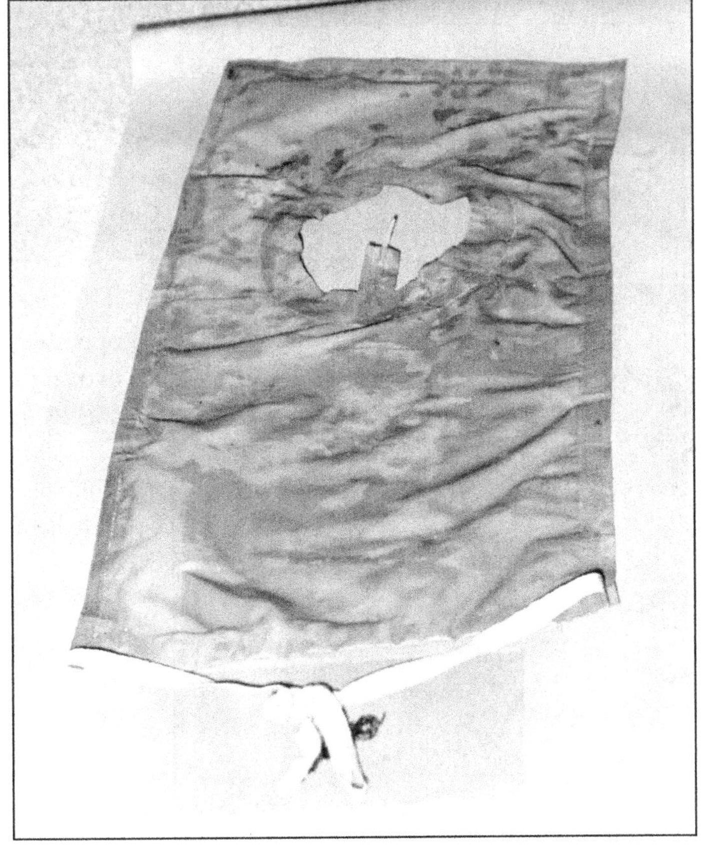

One side is about 30-inches long. The

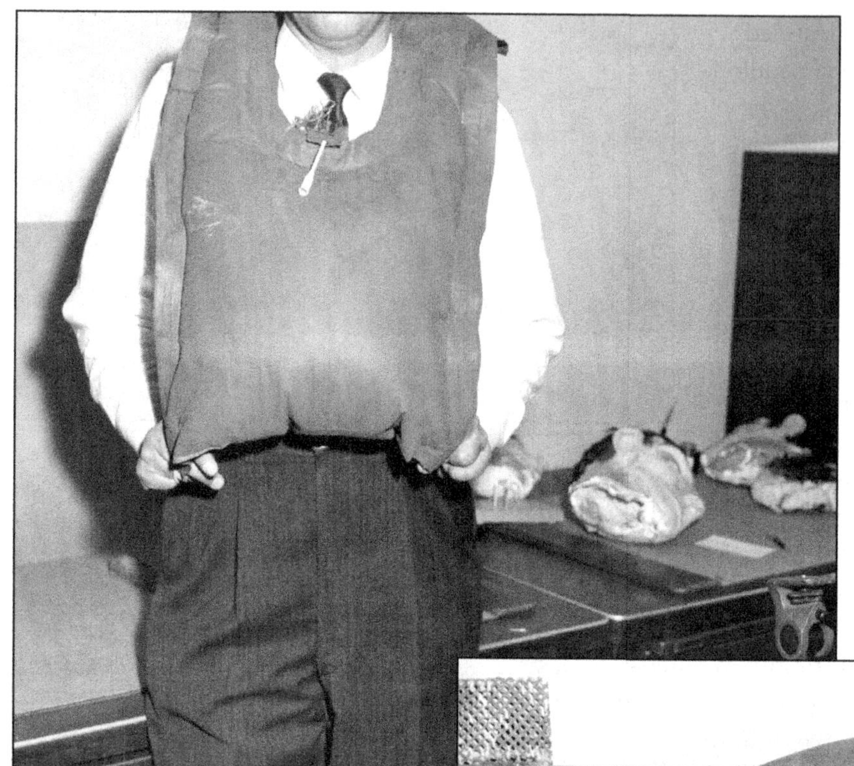

(Left, and below left and right) An FBI agent testing and demonstrating Allen West's fully inflated lifejacket.

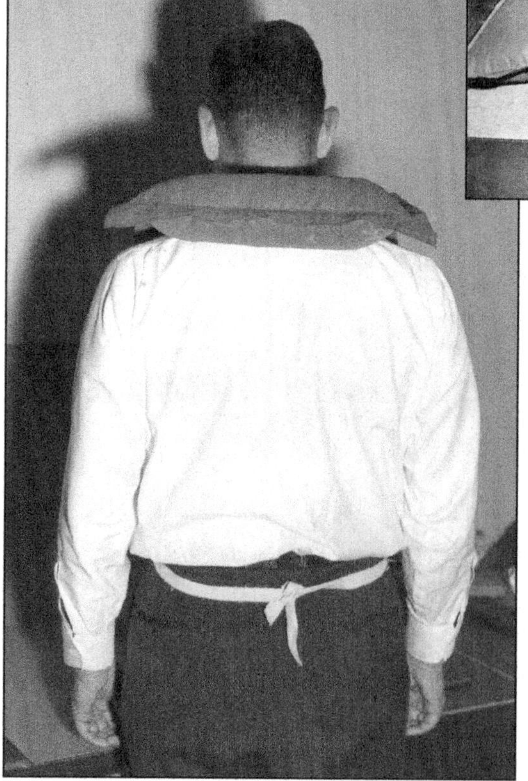

opposite side is 34-inches long. The two ends measure approximately 17 and 18 inches. Attached to the corners of the preserver are two long, white tie strings which appear to possibly be made of canvas. These were measured and the white portion of the strings was determined to be 22 inches and 21 inches, respectively. A hole apparently cut for the head is in the middle of the preserver and has the diameter of 6 ½ to 7 inches. The preserver is olive drab and appears to be homemade.

Warden Olin G. Blackwell, United States Penitentiary, Alcatraz, California, was shown the life preserver located on Fort Chronkhite Beach, California. He noted it was olive green in color and evidently made from parts of rubberized raincoats similar to the raincoats issued to inmates at Alcatraz. He advised that this life preserver was almost identical to the one located on the top of Cell Block B on the morning of June 12, 1962, and that this life preserver was evidently one which the escapees had utilized.

The U.S. Army Debris Boat Coyote, midway between Angel Island and Alcatraz Island recovered items related to the escape. The boat is equipped with a net which rides between two forward pontoons scooping up debris from the Bay. The net extends to approximately 2 to 3 feet beneath the surface of the water and the debris are trapped between the two pontoons.

At 1:15 P.M., that date, while collecting debris in a tiderip in the area between Point Blunt, Angel Island, and Alcatraz, he noted an apparently waterproof package in the debris net. Stephens stated he cut open the package to determine its contents and noted that it contained numerous pictures and slips of paper with addresses, as well as a second similar package which was likewise cut open and found to contain the same type items. The package appeared to be a rubberized material, olive green in color, approximately 8x10 inches in size. The inner package was the same material and color, approximately 6x8 inches in size. Stephens stated that he noted there was a considerable amount of water in the package when he cut it open, indicating a leak. The items were spread out on the galley table to dry and turned over to the interviewing agent. It was noted that the property included a Department of Justice receipt for $10.00 to be deposited to the account of Clarence Anglin dated December 5, 1961, received from Rachel Anglin. Stephens described the contents, "There were about fifteen pictures of an attractive brunette, all of the same girl. I suppose she was the girlfriend of one of these fellows. The rest looked like they came out of a family album—children, grownups, ordinary people."

The pouch was to become a prime point of focus for investigators since it offered a wealth of clues. It appeared to have been constructed using the sleeves of the raincoats and fashioned to be waterproof. On June 18, 1962, investigators carefully began to inventory and examine the contents of the pouch looking for clues and contacts of the escapees. Handwritten in blue ink, the first slip of paper included the name "Mr. Jack Burnam," along with his Market Street office address. Burnam was identified as a prominent trial lawyer who had represented numerous Alcatraz convicts in various appeals, as well as what he described as human rights violations by the Bureau of Prisons. He was a prominent public figure, and in the 1950s, had sat on the city council in Piedmont, California, but more notably was well known for being close with

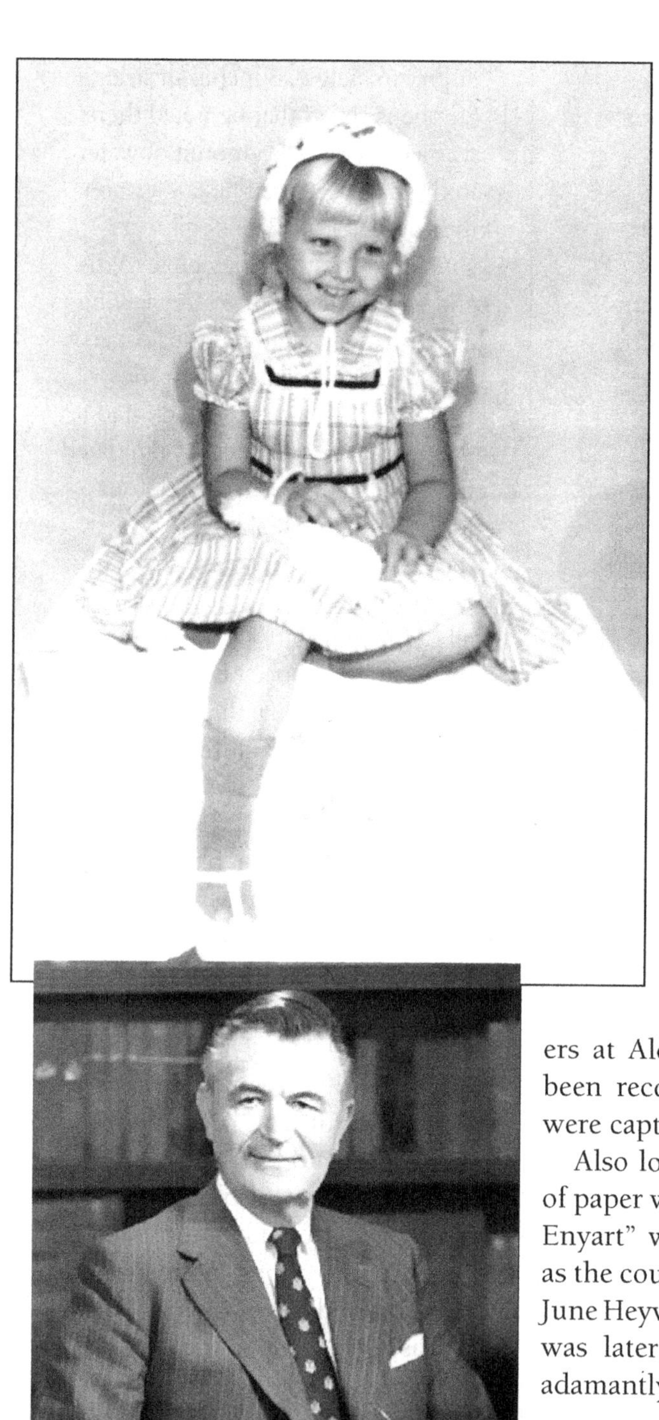

the Kennedy family. Before John F. Kennedy had been elected President for the US, the two served together on the formation host committee of the United Nations in San Francisco. Burnam was later asked by the President to serve as the Assistant Attorney General, supporting his younger brother Robert Kennedy who later closed Alcatraz. He turned down the invitation as he wanted to continue practicing law and as well as remain close to home. The FBI immediately made contact with Burnam who indicated that he was surprised that his name was located in the pouch as he didn't know or had ever heard the names of any of the escapees. He could only presume that as he'd represented so many prisoners at Alcatraz over the years, he had been recommended in the event they were captured and needed legal help.

Also located in the pouch was a slip of paper written in pencil the name "T.J. Enyart" who was identified by the FBI as the cousin of fellow Alcatraz prisoner June Heyward Stephens. When Stephens was later interviewed by the FBI, he adamantly denied any knowledge of

(Above and left) This photo of Sue Widner, the niece of John and Clarence was included in the pouch located off Angel island. Also included was the name and address of prominent San Francisco Attorney Jack Burnam.

The inmates concealed their discarded tools and equipment inside a five-gallon container, and then filled it with plaster. Investigators found wire, spoon handles, steel bars, a vacuum cleaner motor, staples, a homemade flashlight, ladle handles, and other bits of contraband embedded in the hardened plaster.

the escape or providing any assistance or outside contacts to the trio. Despite finding holes around the ventilator grill in his own cell, he continued to deny any involvement.

Another slip of paper written in pencil included the name and address for fellow prisoner William "Billy" Boggs' father. Boggs was the close associate of Mickey Cohen, and the FBI surveilled these residents in hopes that the convicts would seek them out for refuge. For the officials, two addresses located in San Diego seemed to indicate their intended route of travel. Some of the other contents appeared to be more random and the reason for being included was left unclear. A deposit receipt for

$10.00 from a money order that was provided by Clarence's mother into his trust fund account along with other slips of paper that appeared to have no significance. The contents seem to perplex investigators as they'd felt that the escapees would have chosen what to take carefully and travel as light as possible.

The majority of items that had been sealed in the pouch were seventy-nine photographs of family members, girlfriends, and in at least one case, a photo of Clarence during his youth. Some have speculated that leaving behind the pouch was a ruse for investigators to suggest they'd drowned, while others remained convinced that it was proof of an intense struggle for survival and though not conclusive, a sign that the escape had likely ended in failure. Another report described the recovery of a second lifejacket spotted floating in the Bay nearly two weeks following the escape:

> Alcatraz Officer Wilson McCracken who was assigned to the boat detail, which operates between Alcatraz and Fort Mason, said that approximately 12:10 P.M. on June 22, 1962, he retrieved a lifejacket from the San Francisco Bay, located about 50 yards east of Alcatraz Island. Mr. McCracken advised that he initialed and dated the lifejacket. He further advised that Mr. U.S. Johnson was the Alcatraz boat operator at the time the lifejacket was retrieved. The lifejacket appears to be handmade of a green or olive drab rubberized material similar to the raincoats issued to inmates at the US Penitentiary, Alcatraz.

The FBI examined both of the lifejackets along with performing analysis in their laboratory to determine the composites of the stains which initially were believed to have been blood. The later results concluded that the stains in both samples were not blood, but rather a grease compound. Both lifejackets were identified as having been fabricated from the same materials as the one found on top the cellblock. The air stem which appeared to been taken from of a "plastic type spray bottle," had teeth marks which were believed to have been the result of the convict biting down with excessive force to prevent air leakage. Since West had indicated they were using binder clamps and paperclips to seal the air stem, this tended to support a theory by investigators that the clip may have come off in the water, and thus contributing to exhaustion and eventual drowning. The FBI laboratory provided information on the stability and composites of their floatation gear:

> The FBI Laboratory advises the life preservers recovered from B Cell Block, on Fort Cronkhite Beach and from San Francisco Bay; the partially completed pontoon recovered from B Cell Block and the Alcatraz inmate raincoat are all composed of the same type material, mainly rubber coated cotton fabric. The life preservers are all yoke type, placing flotation behind the head as well as in front of the body. "Popular Mechanics" March 1962 issue located in cell of West contains article discussing the various types of life preservers. However, the article states that the yoke-type

(Above, right, and below) Evidence items recovered by prison staff and FBI agents.

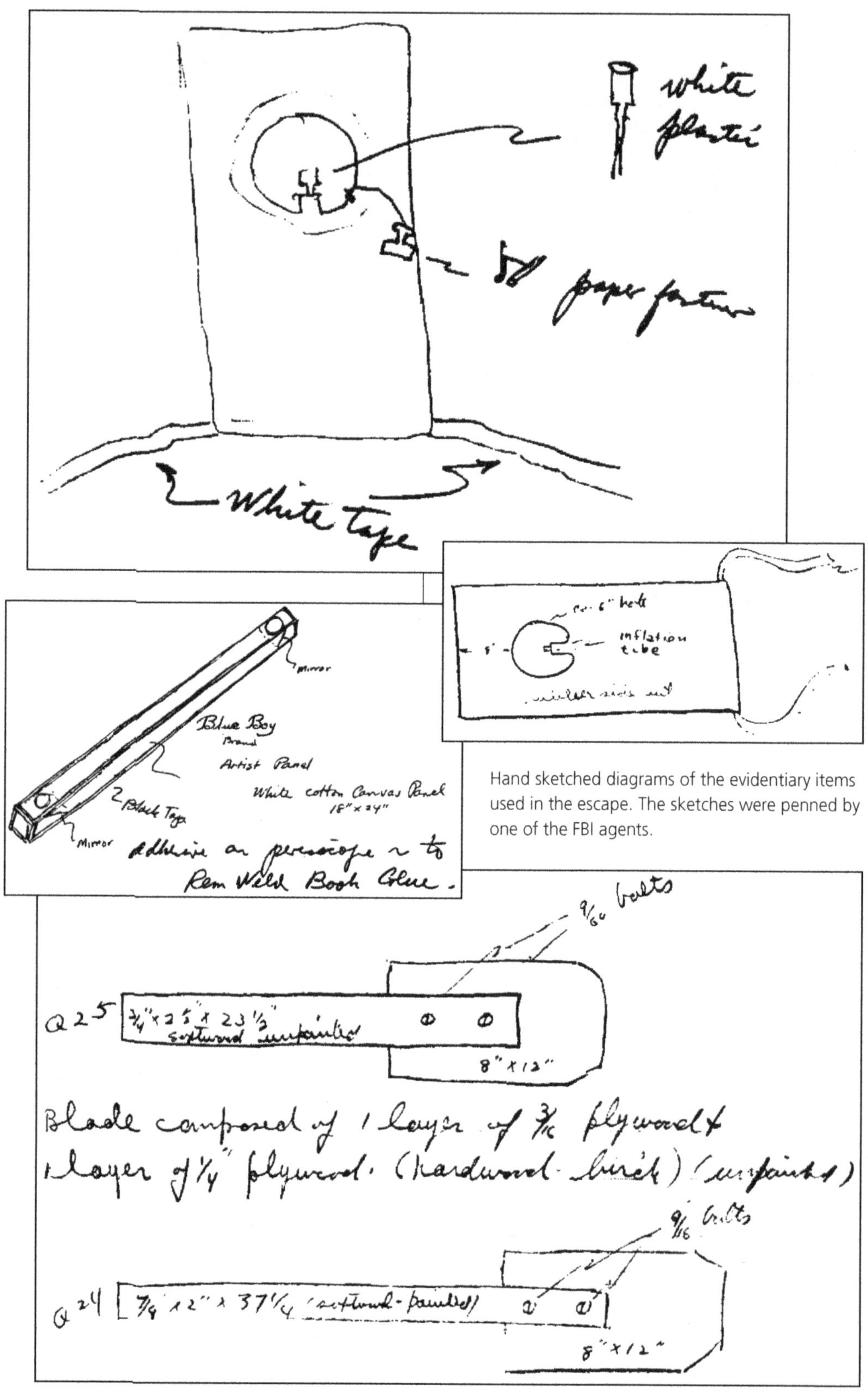

Hand sketched diagrams of the evidentiary items used in the escape. The sketches were penned by one of the FBI agents.

> preserver make swimming difficult. "Sports Illustrated" March 21, 1962, issue located in the cell of Morris contains article discussing various inflatables as vinyl plastic or rubberized fabric, the latter being durable and more difficult to puncture.
>
> The FBI Laboratory inflated life preservers and placed weights on them. The Life preserver recovered from the top of B Cell Block was discovered to be completely air tight, remaining firm for several hours. Other two life preservers lost most of their air about an hour by slow rate of deflation, but pressure could be maintained by mouth.

Investigators also explored theories as to whether they could have survived the exposure of the chilling cold water that was estimated to be between 52 and 55 degrees on the night of the escape, and a variety of external factors. The FBI spent time at the U.S. Army Corps of Engineers office in Sausalito, which operated a working hydraulic model of the San Francisco Bay. The model determined at 10:00 P.M., Pacific Daylight Time, there was a slack tide which meant that the water became stagnant and was not moving any direction, and then shortly after, began flowing out the Bay with a peak velocity at around midnight. The tide would then taper off to a slack tide at around 5:00 A.M. Suicides and the number of bodies that were never recovered from the Golden Gate Bridge were also examined. It was complicated for officials to determine accurate statistics as the official listing of suicide deaths were typically limited to those individuals who were recovered or witnessed by more than two people.

On July 9, 1962, a report to J. Edgar Hoover from the San Francisco Bureau office indicated from 1960 to 1962, there were thirty-five confirmed suicides that had been recorded as jumping from the Golden Gate Bridge and into the San Francisco Bay. In the report, it was identified that five of those bodies had either hit the rocks near the columns, or at the extreme ends of the bridge where they struck ground. Of the remaining thirty, thirteen were never recovered. It was further noted that whenever an individual jumped near the center of the bridge, and there was an outgoing tide, the body was rarely recovered. This had been the case relating to Seymour Webb who took his own life on the same night of the escape. At thirty-three years of age, Webb was reportedly despondent over a failed relationship and in front of sixty-two horrified witnesses, Webb abandoned his car mid-span and jumped to his death off the bridge. Despite a quick response from the Coast Guard and deploying a marker of where he struck the water surface, his body was never recovered. The FBI cited Webb's death along with the other report as significant factors stating:

> The above is submitted as significant, since at the probable time the escapees would have entered the water near Alcatraz, it would have been at the beginning of an outgoing tide, which offers the distinct possibility that they could have been taken out to sea in a short period of time under the Golden Gate Bridge. In this regard, from the life preservers

The S.S. Norefjell

recovered in this case, their exit through this means the ocean could have been facilitated by the additional buoyancy of the preservers.

This office has discreetly consulted San Francisco Bay experts for opinions regarding floating to the surface of bodies of drowned persons. These authorities state that the period of time before a body surfaces varies in each case and is influenced by the following factors: 1. Temperature of Water 2. Air Temperature and Weather Conditions 3. Season of the Year 4. Wind Conditions 5. Tide Conditions 6. Weight and Body Structure of the Deceased 7. Sex of the Deceased 8. Quantity and Nature of the Food Consumed by the Deceased.

One individual from the San Francisco Coroner's Office said in his experience, bodies have been recovered in the water anywhere from one to fourteen days and recalled occasions where bodies were recovered up to three weeks later. He stated that of all contributing factors, that in his opinion, water temperature and state of the internal body gasses were most influential. Cold water retards formation of body gases and inhibits buoyancy. He further stated if the body cavity was ruptured by marine life, gasses escape and the body may not rise to the surface. The San Mateo County Coroner indicated: "Bodies disappearing in the San Francisco Bay have been known to wash out to the ocean where they generally float south along the shore of San Mateo County."

On August 8, 1962, two crew members from the S.S. Norefjell, a Norwegian freighter, mentioned to the Bar Pilot who was navigating the vessel into the San Francisco harbor that they had seen a body floating in the Pacific Ocean some twenty miles north-west of the Golden Gate Bridge on July 17th. At the time the body was observed, they were proceeding to Canada and then onto New Zealand. They indicated that they did not have radio communications on the United States marine band and in the absence of any boat in the area, they continued their journey without reporting it to police and noted their observation in the ship's log book.

One of the crew members stated that between 5:45 P.M. and 6:00 P.M., on July 17, 1962, the S.S. Norefjell was proceeding away from the United States, and at about twenty miles west by north-west of the San Francisco Golden Gate Bridge, the crewman noticed something bobbing in the water. He took the ship's binoculars and observed that it was a body, evidently floating face down, with the hands and feet apparently intact and dangling in motion with the water. He could see the buttocks clearly, however, from his angle, he could not see the upper portion of the body. He stated that the body was clothed in "dirty white, full length trousers." He immediately gave the binoculars to another crew member standing on the deck who also confirmed that it was a body.

FBI agents brought samples of the prison issued clothing to see if the two crew members felt it matched. The agents also suggested that the clothing could have been bleached after weeks of exposure against the sun and sea. Both men, stated that the body "could have" been wearing denim type prison trousers, however, they could not make a close enough inspection to make any positive determination. Several coroners examined the testimony and indicated that while not likely, it was possible for a body to still float after five weeks from time of death. The Coast Guard and California Highway Patrol advised that no missing bodies of known death or suicide from the Golden Gate Bridge were clothed in the white or similar type trousers during the pertinent period and therefore conceivably was one of the convicts. Also referenced in the report was the delayed recovery of the body of Robert Panis, an eighteen year old Filipino male who had drowned while swimming at St. Francis Beach in Half Moon Bay, California, located approximately 25 miles south of San Francisco. Panis' badly decomposed body was recovered on June 30th, eleven days after he had drowned.

Despite many officials believing this was overwhelming evidence as to the fate of the convicts, San Francisco County Coroner Henry Turkel did not share the same opinion. He cast serious doubt as to whether the body seen by the Norwegian freighter crew was one of the escapees. He'd felt the bodies would have revealed themselves much earlier and it was "extremely unlikely" that a body would remain intact and float, even while clothed, for more than five weeks in the open ocean. He was also skeptical that the escapees had died by drowning stating: "It is barely possible, but highly improbable, that three bodies could remain submerged more than three weeks... This goes against my personal experience. I am not convinced they drowned or the body observed over one month after the escape is one of the prison inmates...It's not impossible, but it is highly and extremely improbable."

Tips poured in from all over the United States and every lead was examined to help determine the fate of the escapees. Additionally, the tides, wind and water conditions also became a point of focus as to whether it would have been possible to survive the currents using traditional escape theories.

On February 15, 1963, one of the most prominent leads in the case surfaced when a woman walking along the beach near the Point Reyes Coast Guard light station found a partial skeleton that had washed to shore. The discovery created a flurry among investigators as many were convinced that they were likely the remains of one of the escapees and a possible answer to their fate. The bones consisted of a pelvis with both femurs attached, and four spinal vertebra. There was also seven short ribs attached to the spinal section. Marin County Deputy Coroner William Bradley indicated to the press that a pathologist had examined the partial skeleton, but no positive identification could be made. The femurs measured at 18 ½ inches and would place the height of the subject at 5 feet 7 ½ inches, which matched the height and frame of Frank Morris, but as forensic science was still in its youth, DNA testing wasn't available to make a positive identification. For decades, investigators and experts pointed to these bones and many held to the belief that these were in all probability the remains of one of the convicts.

As time passed, leads and any solid sightings or indicators as to the fate of the escapees began to fade. The FBI investigated more than a hundred leads from across the United States. The alleged sightings were voluminous and agents chased leads from sightings in everything from hotels, bars and banks, to more random sightings of "three suspicious looking men" in various automobiles across the nation. Warden Blackwell received a postcard that simply read: "Ha Ha We Made It..." Signed Frank, John and Clarence. The handwriting was not able to be matched to any of the escapees by an FBI graphologist. Clarence "Joe" Carnes claimed more than a decade later he'd received a postcard that had the code words confirming their success: "Gone Fishing." A well-known San Francisco attorney also claimed she had received a call from a man who had identified himself as one of the escapees. She would later be named in a prominent conspiracy plot that surfaced in February of 2002 when it was handed over to the U.S. Marshal Service. San Francisco Attorney Eugenia MacGowan, who along with her husband Leslie owned their own law firm, received a phone call from a man who claimed to be John Anglin. He called the firm asking to speak with Leslie, who had represented several convicts on Alcatraz, but as he was in court, the receptionist put him through to Eugenia. She remembered during a 1989 interview on the television program Unsolved Mysteries:

> The person called and the receptionist put him through to me, and he said, "I'm John Anglin, and I want you to contact the U.S. Marshal's office to set up a meeting." I said, for what purpose? He said something

A postcard sent to Warden Blackwell, allegedly signed by the three escapees. Analysis of the handwriting samples by the FBI were inconclusive and therefore never established as being legitimate.

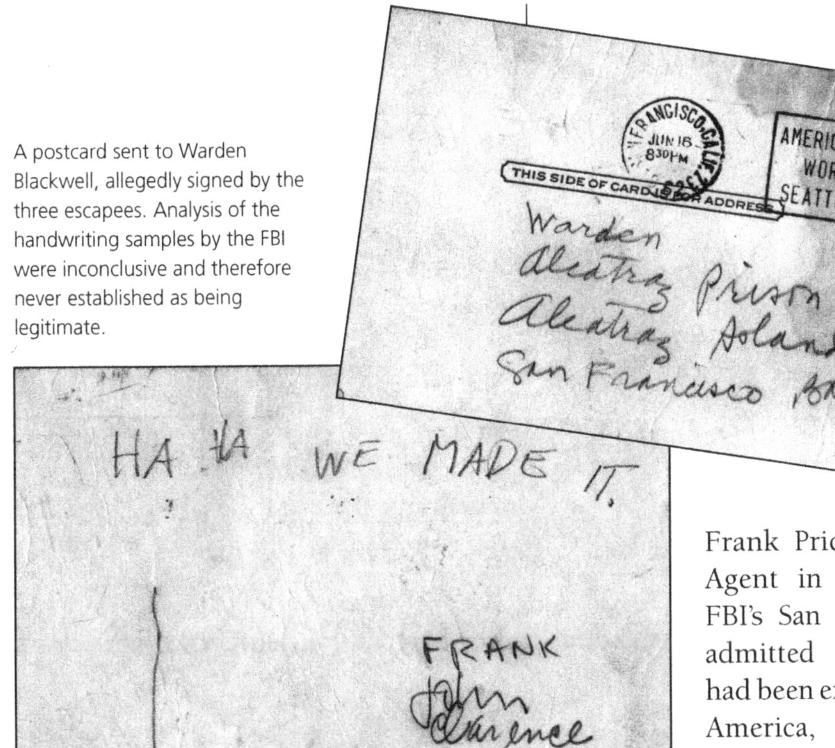

> to the effect, "Don't ask questions, just do as I tell you... Call the U.S. Marshal's office to set up a meeting..." I said, well I'm not going to do that unless I know why? He's says, "Do you know who I am?" I said no... "Read the newspaper" and he hung up.

The FBI set up a wiretap in her office, but he never called again. On July 2, 1962, the FBI wrote in an internal memorandum to satellite offices: "In view of the findings to date and absence of any evidence that subjects survived the escape attempt, SAC, San Francisco has been instructed to limit future investigation accordingly. He has been instructed that there should be no indication given of any lessening of our investigative interest in this matter." Two days later, Frank Price, SAC (Special Agent in Charge) of the FBI's San Francisco office, admitted that the search had been expanded to South America, he commented: "all US legal attaches in Central and South America have been alerted to be on watch" as they believed "if they survived, which remains to be proven, they could now be somewhere in South America." As one of many leads investigators pursued, on January 20, 1965, J. Edgar Hoover received a confidential memorandum that provided information that Clarence Anglin was living under an assumed name in Rio de Janeiro. The fugitives were never located and no substantial traces ever came of the South America rumors, but the claims would surface again decades later.

Security measures following the escape seemed to tighten as cell searches intensified and as did the tone of the officers towards the convicts. Officers Charles Herman and Lawrence Bartlett both received harsh reprimands for "breach of duty" during their respective shifts. Each received thirty day suspensions without pay. Bulger remembered:

> Later on when things started to turn back to normal, a young guard we called 'Herman the German' came over to the corner on the rec yard where we were lifting weights—sick and miserable he said: "They're blaming me..." Herman was a little overweight, always nervous and became one of the scapegoats for the breakout. I jokingly said, "Well, you will never make Acting Lieutenant!" This was a common joke among the cons. Every so often they would make a regular guard "Acting Lieutenant," but there was no change of uniform, no raise in pay, and the title would only be for a short period of time. Certain guards would get real serious, walk more erect and with more of a purpose. They would exercise their new found power over the guys they worked with. They'd shout loud orders of such things as "Hey so & so... Check out the library areas" or "Go inspect the cut off by the barber chair." The older guards would roll their eyes and try to keep a straight face in front of the convicts, and 'Herman the German' would have made a typical Acting Lieutenant. I remember Herman and this talk real well. It was one of the rare occasions where a guard mingled among the convicts in conversation.
>
> The guards monitored the radio and whenever there was mention of the escape, the guards would scurry to cut it off. The guys would cheer and raise hell. Sonny James wrote a song about the break. It was a hillbilly western song titled 'A Mile and a Quarter.' You'd hear the opening lyrics " A mile and a quarter of treacherous water keeps men in Alcatraz... " and then click! OFF! It would illicit the usual response of cons slamming the bed frames on the floor and loud cursing... The cons went wild every time it came on... It really was one of the happiest moments of my life. Those guys were heroes to all of us back then.

In what would become one of the greatest ironies of Alcatraz was that its location in the middle of San Francisco Bay, which had been credited as the ultimate deterrent to escape for nearly three decades, proved to be one of the primary contributors to its downfall. The crumbling cement structure resulting from decades of exposure to the harsh sea and wind conditions, paired against budget cuts that forced diminished security measures finally set into motion formal plans for closure. The Associated Press broke the news in a July 4, 1962, article that the remaining 269 prisoners would soon start being transferred to other facilities as they prepared for the opening of the BOP's new state of the art facility being built in Marion, Illinois. Director James Bennett later wrote in his personal memoir:

> During the 1960's, financial considerations determined the issue and freed me from my dilemma. Alcatraz's buildings and steel towers were gradually being eroded by the salt spray, and would cost several million dollars to restore. The cost of supplying the island prison was exorbitant since food and water had to be brought across the bay. Alcatraz was also expensive to run, because it was located far from the continental center of the population, far from most of the other prisons, and men had to be transported long distances from and back to the East and Middle West. The daily per-prisoner operating costs at Alcatraz were far higher than at any other federal institution. So we drew up plans for a new maximum-security prison to be built in the heart of the continent at Marion, Illinois, which could be built and operated at a lower cost. When the federal funds were made available for the new prison, we could close Alcatraz down.

After years of investigating the escape, every promising lead pursed by the FBI eventually went cold. On December 31, 1979, the FBI turned over investigative authority to the U.S. Marshal Service as part of an order by the Attorney General as they held responsibility for the location and apprehension of federal fugitives. It would be decades before the cold case file would reopen with new leads and theories.

John Paul Scott and Darl Dee Parker being led to court following their break from Alcatraz in December of 1962.

The Last Escape

FOR THE WEEKS AND MONTHS following the great escape, the feat of Morris and the Anglins dominated conversations among the prison population. "It's the only thing we talked about..." Tom Kent recounted in a later interview. The hope that they'd beat the system and were living prosperously in freedom seemed to brighten the spirits of fellow cons. By December of 1962, with the closure of Alcatraz now clearly on the horizon, only 206 prisoners remained. The final break would not only provide the first confirmed case of an escapee making it to shore alive, but forever shatter the myth that cold tool proof steel and rushing tides protected the public from its enemies.

John Paul Scott's spectacular break proved that with properly constructed floats and a favorable current, it was technically possible for an inmate to enter the Bay with little to no gear and make it to the mainland alive. Thirty-five year old John Paul Scott (AZ-1403) had been transferred to Alcatraz following a failed escape attempt at USP Atlanta that he tried to pull off with the help of James "Whitey" Bulger. While prisoners at Atlanta, Scott and Bulger, along with other associates, Charlie Catalano (AZ-1381), Louis Arquilla (AZ-1386) and Charles Wilbur "Jeep" Marcum (AZ-1407), plotted to escape from the prison hospital. Bulger remembered:

> Charlie, Louie, Scotty, and Jeep were able to cut the bars of the ward hospital window. Using a ladder made from pipe, they attempted to scale a 45-foot wall. At the weakest spot the ladder collapsed, and they had nowhere else to go. Warden Wilkinson was out there with a shotgun. There were other guards out there, and all of them were demanding that the convicts surrender or they would be shot. The cons told the guards, "After we have this last cigarette we will come down. We know that this will be our last cigarette for a long time." We were so close...

Scott was a university-educated bank robber of the modern era. His inmate file details a multitude of bank heists, dramatic prison breaks, and spectacular shootouts with police. His partner in the escape, thirty-one year old Darl Dee Parker, also has a vast and lifelong diary of crime. The escape of Scott and Parker was detailed in

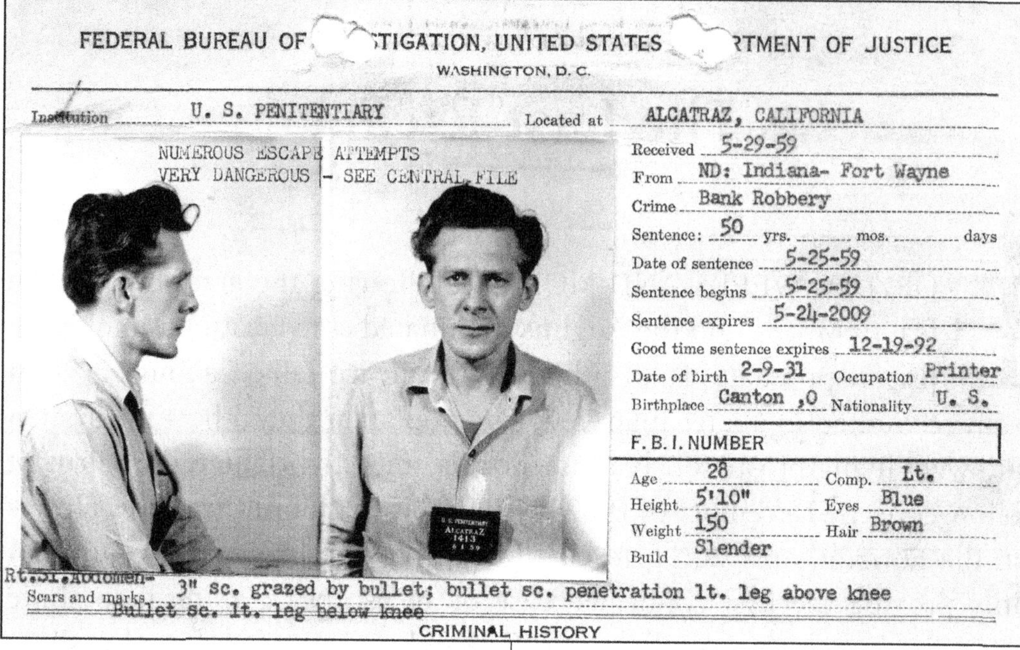
FEDERAL BUREAU OF [illegible]TIGATION, UNITED STATES [illegible]RTMENT OF JUSTICE
WASHINGTON, D. C.

Institution U. S. PENITENTIARY Located at ALCATRAZ, CALIFORNIA

NUMEROUS ESCAPE ATTEMPTS
VERY DANGEROUS - SEE CENTRAL FILE

Received 5-29-59
From ND: Indiana- Fort Wayne
Crime Bank Robbery
Sentence: 50 yrs. mos. days
Date of sentence 5-25-59
Sentence begins 5-25-59
Sentence expires 5-24-2009
Good time sentence expires 12-19-92
Date of birth 2-9-31 Occupation Printer
Birthplace Canton ,O Nationality U. S.

F. B. I. NUMBER

Age 28 Comp. Lt.
Height 5'10" Eyes Blue
Weight 150 Hair Brown
Build Slender

Scars and marks Rt. Sl. Abdomen- 3" sc. grazed by bullet; bullet sc. penetration lt. leg above knee
Bullet sc. lt. leg below knee

CRIMINAL HISTORY

Darl Dee Parker

an investigative summary written by Warden Blackwell:

On Sunday, December 16, 1962, the two above inmates were missed from their detail in the culinary unit, at 5:47 P.M. We have definitely established that both of those individuals were accounted for on the official 5:20 P.M. count and again counted by the lieutenant on duty, Mr. Harold Robbins, at 5:30 P.M.

The alarm was sounded, immediate search of the area was instituted, and the entire escape procedure was placed into effect. At 6:10 P.M., our boat officer spotted Parker clinging to a rock some 100 yards off the northwest end of the island, known as "Little Alcatraz." At approximately 7:20 P.M., inmate Scott was spotted clinging to a rock off Fort Point, which is located almost directly under the south end of the Golden Gate Bridge. Scott was spotted by two teenagers who reported the sighting to Presidio MPs. A fire department emergency response team rescued Scott from this rock, and took him immediately to Letterman Hospital for treatment. For the first thirty minutes, several doctors worked with Scott and stated that they were very much uncertain as to whether he would live or die. He was suffering from numerous cuts and bruises and severe shock that resulted from extreme lowering of his body temperature, caused by a prolonged exposure to the cold water of the Bay, which normally runs from 52 to 54 degrees the year around. Parker, of course, was returned to the institution, examined by the medical staff and locked up immediately after he was found. Scott was returned to the

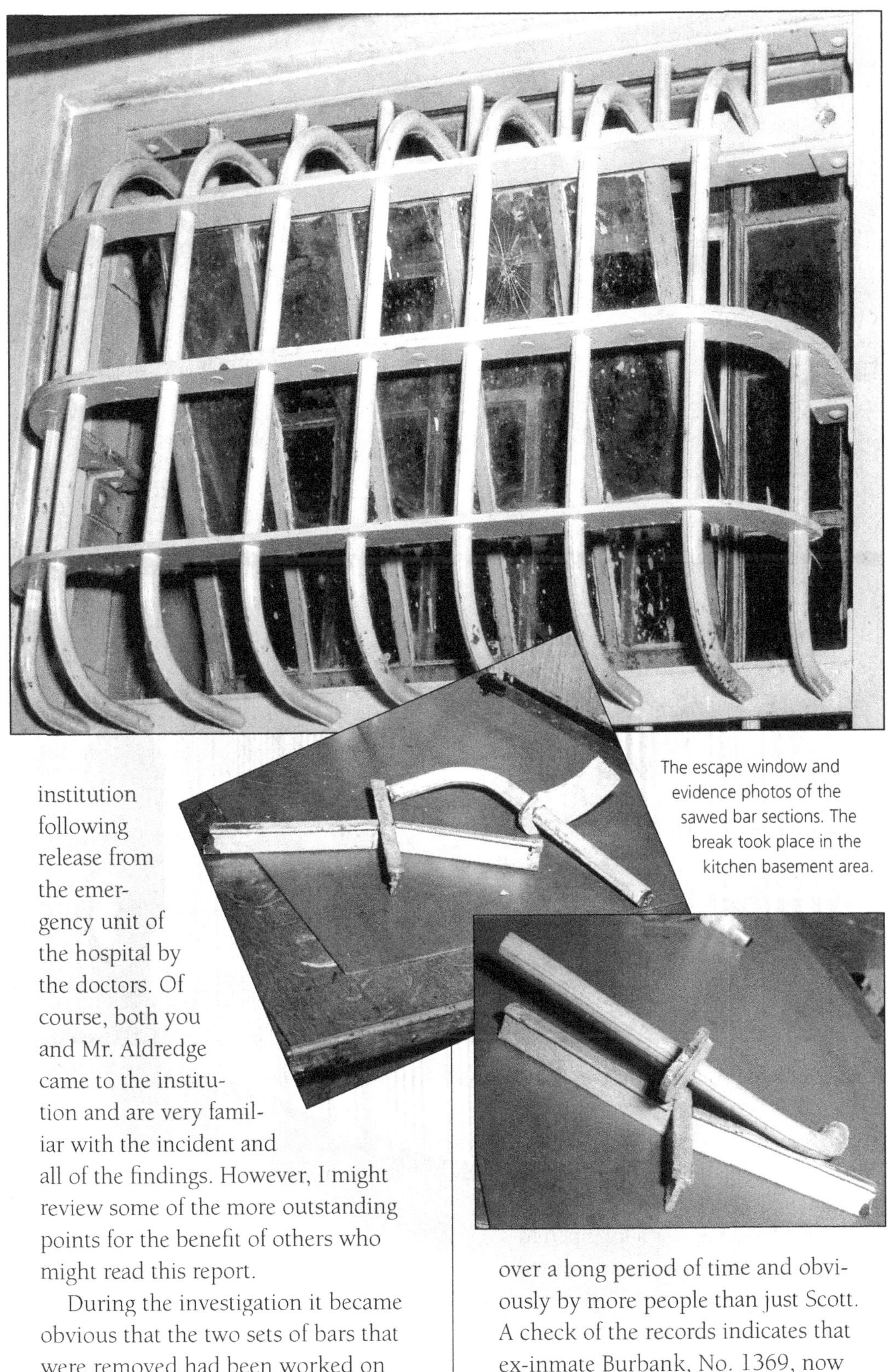

The escape window and evidence photos of the sawed bar sections. The break took place in the kitchen basement area.

institution following release from the emergency unit of the hospital by the doctors. Of course, both you and Mr. Aldredge came to the institution and are very familiar with the incident and all of the findings. However, I might review some of the more outstanding points for the benefit of others who might read this report.

During the investigation it became obvious that the two sets of bars that were removed had been worked on over a long period of time and obviously by more people than just Scott. A check of the records indicates that ex-inmate Burbank, No. 1369, now

The area behind the library where they descended and then made their path to the water. The cord they used to scale down the side of the wall is seen in the center area.

in custody by the Missouri State Penitentiary, was assigned to the kitchen basement for a long period of time and could well have started the removal of the bars. Following his assignment, inmate Leonard Williams, No. 1045, was assigned to the basement area and he too could have contributed to these cuts. It is noted by the record that Williams was involved in several escape attempts, including an effort to escape while being transported to Alcatraz.

We are not quite sure of all instruments used to sever these bars; however, we are rather positive that a spatula, with serrated edges; a grease scraper used by fry-cooks in scraping down grills; string, which had been impregnated with floor wax and institution scouring powder were at least three items that were used to sever these bars. One set of these bars, incidentally, is commonly referred to as "tool-proof-steel."

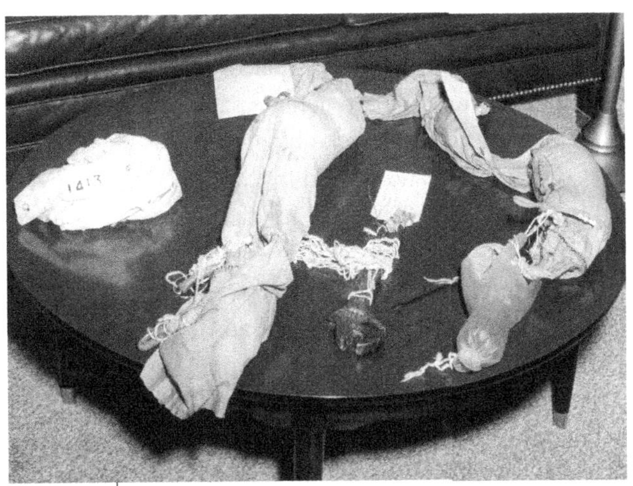

(Top, middle, and bottom) The shirtsleeves and inflated surgical gloves that were used to create floatation devices, similar to water wings used by military pilots when ditching their aircraft into the ocean.

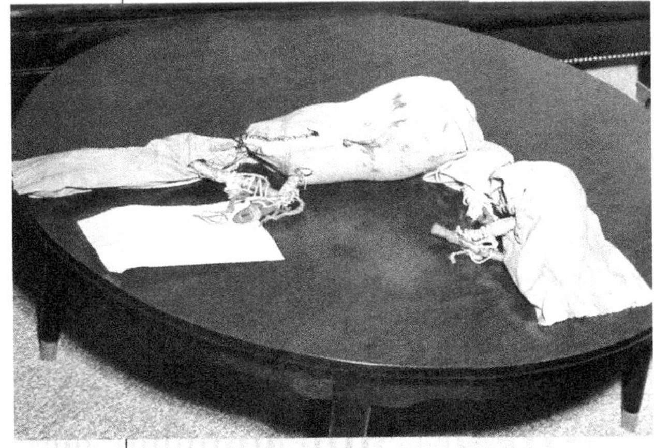

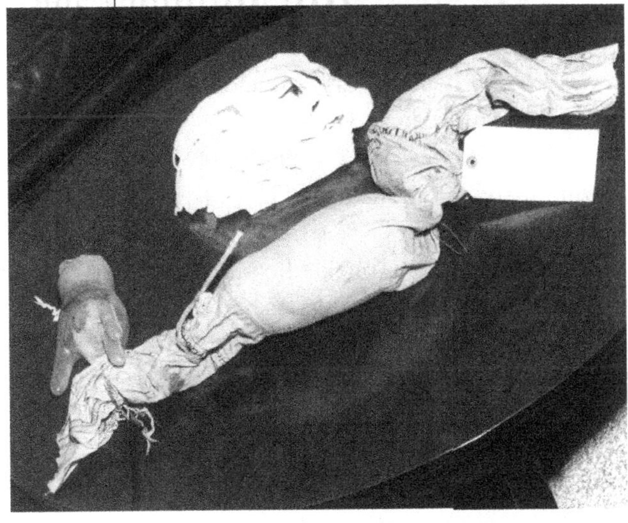

As we see the picture, and as admitted now by Scott and Parker, when Scott almost completed severing the bars, he alerted Parker that he expected to try to escape that evening and invited him then to go along. Immediately after the 5:30 P.M. count, under the guise of taking the garbage to the basement, Scott got on the elevator, took the elevator half-way down, jumped off and completed severing the bars, which he states took approximately five minutes. He then dashed to the elevator shaft and signaled for Parker, who jumped down the shaft, landing on the elevator halfway down, then jumped off to the floor and they both went out through the window.

This window is the last window on the south side of the kitchen basement and is partially hidden by two butane tanks that service burner units in the hospital. They evaded the officer who was patrolling the back of the kitchen area and seeing that he had checked that side of the building and started in the other direction. They then hurriedly climbed two pipes at the corner of the building, gaining access to the roof. They crossed the roof and lowered themselves to the ground directly behind the Library on a length of extension cord that they had tied knots in, approximately 3 feet apart. This cord was removed from the buffing machine that is used to polish the basement floor. They then slid and fell down the steep hill directly behind Apartment Building "A." During this fall Parker apparently broke his foot and received several cuts and bruises. They then went down the rather high bluff to the water's edge by sliding down a sewer pipe. At this point they inflated rubber gloves that they had inserted in shirtsleeves, and pieces of shirt that had been crudely stitched together, making a set of so called "water-wings" to be used as flotation equipment.

It was dark and rainy. Visibility was extremely poor. Parker stated that Scott moved out first and he followed after checking his flotation equipment and immediately lost Scott, but thought he saw him. As it turned out, it was a bucket floating in the bay. He fought the tides as hard as he could but could make no headway and it washed him back in to the rock known as "Little Alcatraz," and he hung on to this rock until found by our boat. He received further cuts and bruises attempting to stay on the rock. Scott claims that he almost drowned when he hit the rock at Fort Point because the waves were coming over his head, and he could not find any protection on this rock at all.

In searching the basement area several times, we found items which included the impregnated string, and a 12 inch crescent wrench that had been missed over two years ago from the old Furniture Factory and apparently had been secreted in the kitchen basement behind one of the huge refrigerators. The rubber gloves obviously had been stolen from the hospital unit and Scott claims they had been there for a long time. The crescent wrench was used to twist out the last section of the outside detention sash, which was extremely eroded from the elements and of course, was never designed to be first-rate security material.

As attached reports will indicate, searches of the basement area had been ordered and apparently completed. The bars had been tapped by officers on both Saturday and Sunday, the day of the escape. At first glance it seemed strongly indicated that disciplinary action should be instituted against those who were ordered to knock the bars in this unit. However, after careful examination of all of the facts it became highly conceivable, from a technical or mechanical standpoint, that the officers hammering these bars with rubber hammers could very well have struck them a heavy blow (and they insist they did) without noticing any particular difference from any other bar. It is obvious,

Scott and Parker entered the water near the family residences.

of course, that their visual inspection was not effective. However, since the cuts were on the back side of the main bar, and the duty of hammering bars is rather monotonous, it is highly possible that they could have overlooked the carefully concealed cut, thinking that they were doing a good job. With all of this in mind, and after careful consideration of all of the facts by the captain, associate warden, Mr. Aldredge, and myself, at this point we do not feel that disciplinary action against the officers is indicated.

To further explain the reasoning, the top of the upright bar was not cut, but was eventually removed by

(Above) Using his home fashioned water wings, Scott floated to Fort Point near the base section of the Golden Gate Bridge. He was hypothermic and lethargic when found and nearly died in his attempt.

(Below) Staff members at Letterman Hospital provides details on Scott's condition.

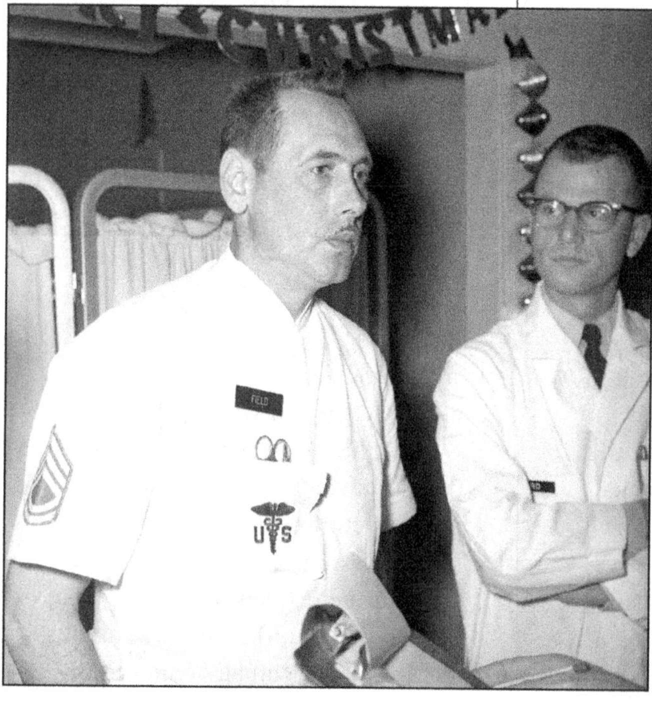

Scott through the use of a 3 x 2 foot piece of oak, and it required considerable leverage to break loose the welds at that end. Scott claims that enough of the lower section of the bar was left solid that it took him five minutes to remove it, which would have fastened that end, making both ends rather solid and quite capable of receiving a heavy blow with a rubber hammer without showing any appreciable movement.

Investigators and reporters quickly drew comparisons at Scott's attempt to that of Morris and the Anglins. When Scott had been reported missing, the Coast Guard dispatched three 40-foot cutters, an 82-foot patrol boat and a

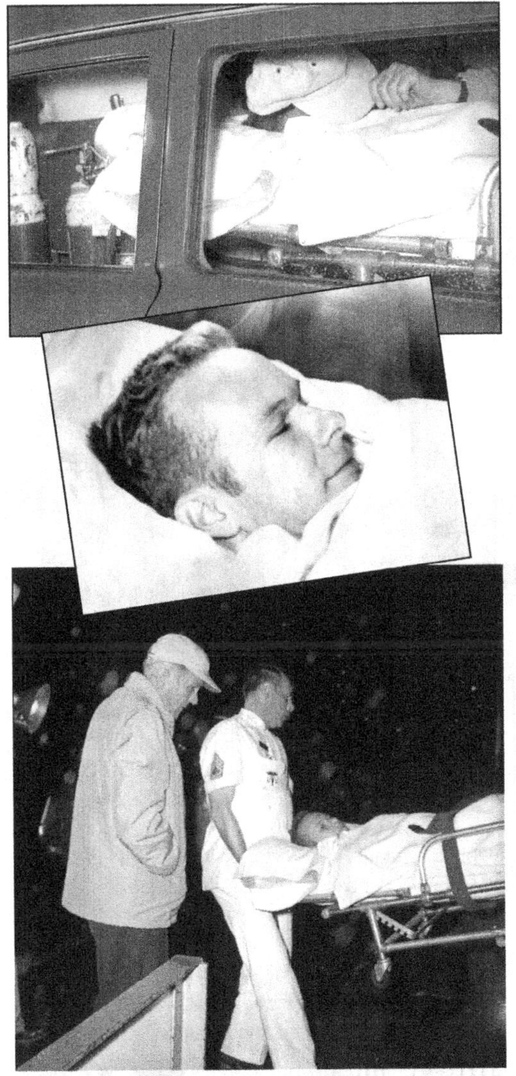

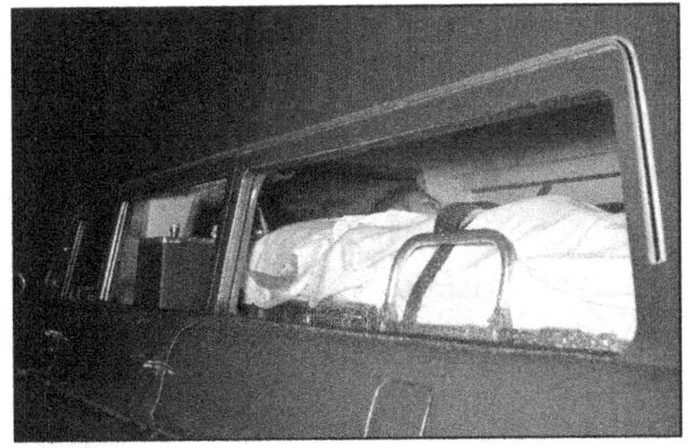

Following treatment for hypothermia, Scott was transported back to the island launch by ambulance and returned to Alcatraz. He stated during his interview with officials that he became seriously disoriented in the water and was unable to identify the mainland. His hands and legs became numb from the freezing water and he acknowledged that he thought he might drown.

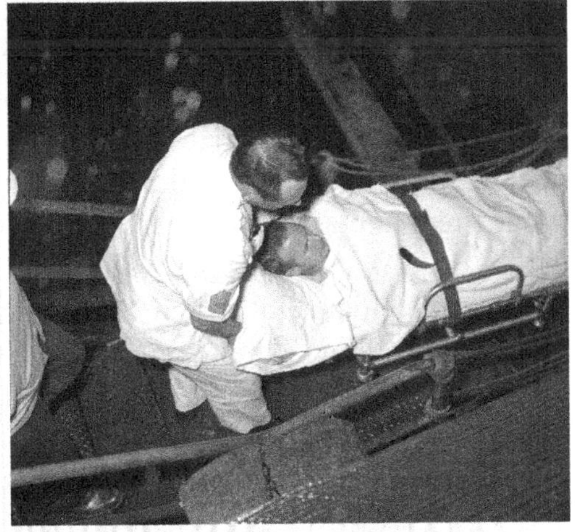

harbor that tug crisscrossed the area between Alcatraz and the Golden Gate. Scott had successfully drifted through their search grid without being detected. After being admitted to the emergency room, it was discovered that his body temperature had dropped to 94 degrees, 4.6 degrees below normal, which a doctor called "not dangerous, but not healthy." After being stabilized, he was immediately transported back to Alcatraz. Scott was examined and allowed to spend the night under observation in the prison hospital, but the following morning he was placed into solitary confinement in D Block. Correctional Officer Levinson would later confide that it was the only time he remembered ever losing his composure towards a convict. He said the following morning he escorted Scott down from the hospital to a closed front isolation cell. As soon as they walked out into Times Square along their walk to D Block, the cellhouse broke out in cheers chanting Scott's name. As he slammed the heavy steel to the dark cold isolation cell, he opened the port window and said to Scott in sarcastic tone: "OK sailor... Let's see you escape this..."

The day following the escape, BOP Director James Bennett held a press conference on the mainland. The administration took harsh criticism not only from the press, but also from the San Francisco Police Department. They voiced their frustration for not been notified of the escape until Scott had already been rescued. Blackwell took most of the blame, and by many accounts he looked exhausted, embarrassed and defeated. With two escapes happening under his watch, Blackwell, stood silent during most of the press conference, only nodding and answering questions tersely when prompted by Bennett. One reporter later described the scene: "Alcatraz Warden Olin B. Blackwell stood silently nearby—chain-smoking nervously—as Bennett coped with a barrage of often pointed questions." When asked if the gradual transfer of men to other facilities will continue at the same pace in

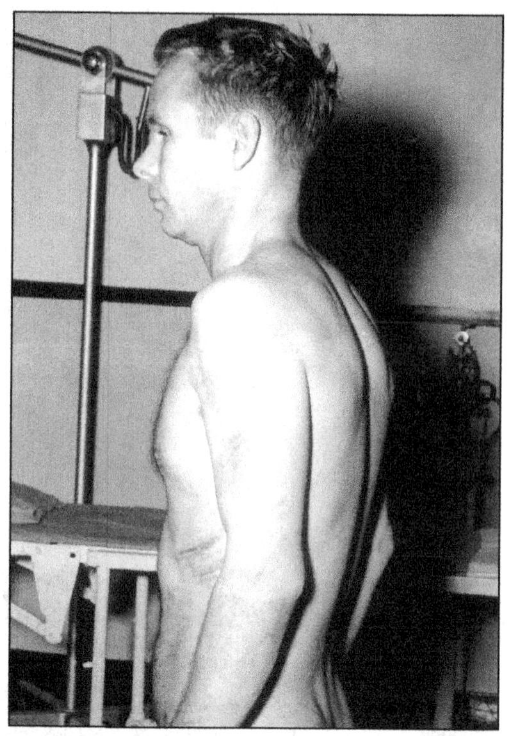

(Above) Scott suffered several cuts and bruises when he washed up on the rocks near Fort Point.

(Opposite page) The Director of the Federal Bureau of Prisons and Warden Blackwell held a press conference to provide information on Scott and Parkers' escape just six months after the Morris and Anglin break. They took harsh criticism for the serious breaches in security and one reporter indicated that Blackwell looked "Exhausted, embarrassed and defeated" as a result of the second escape occurring under his tenure at warden.

Frank Weatherman

anticipation of the opening of the new super-max prison being built in Marion, Illinois, Blackwell commented sarcastically: "Apparently, we weren't phasing out fast enough."

On March 21, 1963, Alcatraz closed its gates for the last time. Assistant Director Fred Wilkinson and Warden Blackwell invited the press to witness the last group of inmates to leave the Rock. After breakfast, the inmates had filed back to their cells, each was met by an officer and then handcuffed, shackled, and prepared for final departure. The inmates stood quietly until the cellhouse officer gave the signal to march single-file down Broadway. The quiet procession was broken only by the clank of the inmates' shackles and the snapping shutters and flashbulb pops of the press-pool cameras capturing the exodus. Several men covered their faces. Following the "last in, last out" rule, Frank C. Weatherman (AZ-1576), was the final inmate to board the prison launch. When the press asked him how he felt about the closure, he uttered what would become the prison's eulogy: "Alcatraz was never good for anybody."

The closure of Alcatraz marked the end of an era. While several men tested their fate and plotted to escape the Rock, most convicts served their sentences uneventfully. They lived their days on Alcatraz, enduring the prison's iron rule, all set against the painfully enticing landscape of the San Francisco shoreline. Although Alcatraz closed, it never loosened its grip on public intrigue.

The last group of prisoners being marched down Broadway on the day of the prison's closure. The convict leading the prisoners is Harold Wayne Davis. He had been identified as a lookout for the convicts on the third tier of B Block during the 1962 escape.

The Mysterious Death and Final Escape of Alfred Ray Anglin

"Prison is tearing me up inside. It hurts every day . . . Every day it takes me further from my life . . . "

—JACK HENRY ABBOTT

THE UNEXPLAINED DEATH of Alfred Anglin formed another complex layer in the saga of the great escape. The mystery of Alfred's desperate break so close to potentially being paroled has baffled investigators for decades. In June of 1962, Alfred Anglin closely followed the news reports of his brothers' famed escape trying desperately to learn of their fate. One family member would later comment that Alfred's time at Atlanta following the break was "low and lonely" and the news reports speculating the deaths of both brothers were heartbreaking for him to read.

By all accounts, Alfred was a model prisoner who quietly served his time. He was respectful towards staff and fellow prisoners, and made strident efforts at keeping a clean record. He continued his earlier fights seeking an appeal on their double jeopardy case and gained strong support from the American Civil Liberties Union. He never lost faith that they would eventually have the state trial overturned. Alfred found a friend in David Shapiro, a Washington D.C. based attorney along with the National ACLU Director Lawrence Speiser who both helped file lengthy appeals challenging legality of the State of Alabama trial. Both Sharpio and Speiser aggressively fought on behalf of the Anglins to have the detainers withdrawn. Each motion for an appeal was rejected, including one brought before Federal Judge Frank M. Johnson, who ironically was the same judge that sentenced the brothers during their first trial. While Alfred's letters to family members show frustration, they never suggest losing hope or submitting to defeat.

Desperate to find any means to lessen his prison term, Alfred's inmate case file reflects that from December 1958 to February 1960, he agreed to be a test subject in the LSD test program led by

Dr. Carl Pfeiffer and Emory University. Pfeiffer's program was alleged to have been part of the MK-Ultra study, the code name of a covert research operation experimenting in the behavioral engineering of humans through the CIA's Scientific Intelligence Division. The program began in the early 1950s, and employed many illegal activities; including the use of unwitting prisoners as its test subjects. While Pfeiffer's official profiles are silent as to any association to these studies, it is alleged that he led much of the principle research using prisoners as the main subjects. Numerous convicts were subjected to these trials including James "Whitey" Bulger who recalled: "I was on this project for one year, and it was the worst year of my life...Since then, I have never had a good night's sleep; my sleep is filled with violent nightmares and restless nights."

Prisoners earned good time credits for their participation in these medical experiment and research trials. As there was significant health risks involved, in most cases they received accelerated reductions to their sentence. Alfred was legally eligible for parole on February 9, 1963. He remained optimistic that if he could successfully challenge the detainers held by the State of Alabama, he could be out of prison in less than a year.

During the phase that Alcatraz worked to reduce its population as result of the pending closure, several prisoners, including Mickey Cohen were transferred to Atlanta to complete their terms. It is with reasonable certainty that Alfred would have sought them out for inside chatter on the escape, especially as Cohen and John worked side by side in the clothing issue. Though Cohen later denied knowing any of the details behind the planning, some still theorize that when he bonded out of Alcatraz, only to return a few months later, he helped make outside arrangements for the trio.

In a confidential report later filed by the FBI, it showed they had interviewed a former cellmate of Alfred's who agreed to provide information under the condition of anonymity. The informant indicated that he had occupied a cell with Alfred from December 12, 1962, up until his transfer in September of 1963. He also allegedly knew all three escapees, Frank, John and Clarence, as they had all "built time" together at one time or another over the course of fifteen years at various institutions. He claimed that Alfred confided to him just two months prior to the June '62 escape that his brothers were planning to make a break from Alcatraz. Alfred was apparently skeptical and concerned as to whether it could be pulled off until news broke confirming his brothers were again fugitives.

Following the break, several news reports predicted the convicts had perished and Alfred was described as being "morose and gloomy" until his older brother Robert visited. The source indicated that from that point forward Alfred "was his normal, cheery self again." Alfred commented that on several occasions he had confirmation that his brothers John and Clarence were alive and well. It was "his own impression, based on his own knowledge of the subjects that they are probably in Mexico."

There were also other key clues pertaining to their planning. The source indicated that Alfred had knowledge that a fellow prisoner at Alcatraz had "fixed the subjects up with a 'contract' in California," and that this 'contract' had a small boat. He further advised that if he was to start looking for the subjects, he would "start looking in the vicinity of Guadalajara, Mexico," in that subject Morris, who speaks fluent Spanish, spent a great deal of time in that area from 1953 to 1957. He stated Morris has a lot of contacts there, and that if the subjects were alive, as he believes, Morris would be 'calling the shots,' and in all probability would be 'holed up' in that area. He explained that the subjects were all excellent woodsmen and would think nothing of 'holing up' in the Guadalajara mountain range for years."

More than a year following the escape of his brothers, on September 10, 1963, Alfred Anglin was transferred to Kilby Prison, the State Penitentiary located in Montgomery County, Alabama. In October of 1963, Alfred's older brother Robert, along with other family members made the 500 mile drive to visit. Robert would later recount a story that during the long visit, both men took a quick break and entered the restroom together. In secrecy, Alfred explained that he had received a package that included a leather style hand embroidered pouch that he knew was from Clarence. The leather pouch was hand embroidered with the image of a brown stallion horse, and was stitched around the edges which appeared to have been cut open by prison staff. It was meaningful to Alfred as he was not only convinced that it was the leather embroidery work of Clarence, but even more significant was that the horse was a cryptic symbol of where they were in hiding, a clue only known to the brothers.

On Sunday, December 22, 1963, just days before Christmas, Marie Anglin Widner, her husband Frank, and children Kenneth and Betty Sue visited Alfred. She brought with her a cake she had baked (later stating prison staff cut it apart before Alfred could see it) and they enjoyed the entire afternoon together. He was openly optimistic regarding parole eligibility and his spirits seemed unusually high. Alfred was fully confident that he would see parole years before his originally scheduled release date, and the parole office in Florida had already contacted the family discussing his eligibility for release. For these reasons, when Alfred attempted to escape from Kilby less than a month later, everyone was left in disbelief. From an FBI report detailing Alfred's death:

> The family stated they had been contacted by a parole officer of the State of Florida concerning the possible parole of Alfred Anglin, who had been transferred from the Federal Penitentiary at Atlanta, Georgia, to Kilby Prison on September 18, 1963, to serve his state prison sentence of twenty-five years, while still serving the remainder of his federal sentence for bank robbery concurrently. His mandatory release date was October 5, 1967, but he was to be under federal supervision until August 13, 1972.
>
> A family member advised that the last contact they had with Alfred Anglin was a letter written December 25, 1963, in which he was cheerful and gave no indication of being

(Above, right, and below right) Kilby Prison, the State Penitentiary located in Montgomery, Alabama. Alfred Anglin was transferred to this facility in September of 1963.

(Below left) The brown leather pouch that Alfred received while at Kilby. The tear on the right shows where officials cut open and examined the fold section. He was convinced it was made and sent to him by Clarence and later told his brother Robert that the embroidered image of brown stallion horse was a cryptic clue as to the brothers' whereabouts.

Alfred with his sister Marie Widner during a family visit at Kilby only a few days before Christmas. He is seen holding his nephew Kenneth Widner, with his niece Sue in the foreground, along with their father, Frank.

restless. They said he was visited by other relatives, the last time being the Sunday before Christmas, and Alfred indicated to them he would be eligible for parole soon, and that he liked Kilby Prison, as he felt "free" after Atlanta Penitentiary. They stated that he wrote another letter to a sister, which was on blue paper, and was received January 1, 1964, and they indicated they believed that this blue paper could mean he was in solitary confinement, as another family member who had been incarcerated had written on different colored paper when being punished in prison.

The circumstances of the escape are as follows. On the night of January 11, 1964, at approximately 6:30 P.M., Anglin, along with inmate Othis Senn gained entrance to and secluded themselves in the institution's clothing room on the second floor at Kilby Prison. At approximately 8:00 P.M. that date, the indicator [electrical panel status light] in the lobby at the prison indicated a ground on the high tension security wires surrounding the compound. Investigation revealed inmate Senn attempting to attract the attention of a guard on that floor. When the guard approached, Senn told him that Anglin had come into contact with the electric wire outside the window. Examination revealed that two window bars had been sawed at the bottom and were bent upward, which had been done by a piece of 1½ inch water pipe as a bender. A protective screen on the outside of the bars was also sawed through. Anglin was completely through the window with the exception of his feet. The inmate's face and body were lying on the flat roof of the Administration Offices, and his feet were still in the hole in the window when he came in contact with the high voltage security wire, thereby electrocuting himself.

A search of Senn and Anglin was made and the area surrounding the scene. A hacksaw in a crudely made frame, a pair of wire pliers, two sets of jumper wires designed for jumping the ignition of automobiles, a forged Alabama Driver's License, and approximately $16.00 in currency was found. Personal photographs were packed in a waterproof container and a list of addresses also starting locally and covering several states.

It appeared that Anglin's clothing had become entangled on a portion of the window. In bending and twisting in an attempt to release his clothing, he had raised up too high coming in contact with the wire at a point about the middle of his back, thus causing his death. State Commissioner of Corrections Frank Lee indicated that Alfred had wrapped an automobile inner tube around the electric wires, then sawed through the window. He stated the insulation wasn't heavy enough as Alfred was still electrocuted when he brushed up against the wires.

Following his death, the coroner at Montgomery, Alabama, was immediately notified of it. An examination was made by the coroner and a death certificate was filled out at the hospital, Kilby Prison, which was sent to the coroner for his signature. As it is normally the case, the death certificate was forwarded by the coroner to the Alabama Bureau of Vital Statistics, Montgomery, Alabama. A record of

Alfred Anglin Electrocuted Trying To Flee From Kilby

death was filed and is currently on record.

The family was notified at 11:30 P.M., Saturday night, January 11, 1964, that Alfred had been accidently electrocuted at 8:30 P.M. that day while trying to escape, and the family paid $283.00 to have the body returned to Ruskin for funeral services and they stated they were further upset because no death certificate was received with the body although several attempts were made by the funeral director to obtain it. They also stated that the body was in bad shape and had "stripes" across his back and caused them to wonder how Alfred died. A staff member of Lewers and Shannon Funeral Home Ruskin stated the body showed no indication of mistreatment but had two small burned areas on the upper back, and burned areas above each eye and bridge of his nose, possibly from electric current going through his eyeglasses. He stated that although glasses were not sent to him with the body, Alfred Anglin allegedly wore glasses all the time. He said that Alfred had an abrasion on the right cheek and the right lower abdomen, possibly caused by a scrape against concrete and the only complaint he had concerning the condition of the body was a compliant over inferior embalming and restorative work by the funeral parlor in Montgomery, Alabama, which he mentioned to relatives and made no open complaint.

(Above) A photograph taken in February of 1964 of a window from the industries at Kilby with powerlines visible in background.

(Below) High voltage security wires marking the perimeter of Kilby.

THIS IS A LEGAL RECORD AND WILL BE PERMANENTLY FILED

SEE OTHER SIDE

FILL IN WITH A TYPEWRITER OR WRITE PLAINLY WITH DARK INK. DO NOT USE GREEN NOR RED INK. LEGAL COPIES CANNOT BE MADE IF ENTRIES ARE DIM

ALL ITEMS MUST BE COMPLETE AND ACCURATE

IF NO DOCTOR WAS IN ATTENDANCE MEDICAL CERTIFICATION SHOULD BE COMPLETED BY THE LOCAL HEALTH OFFICER, OR CORONER IF HE IS A PHYSICIAN OR IF INQUEST WAS HELD

VS-2—

CERTIFICATE OF DEATH
STATE OF ALABAMA

1861

1. PLACE OF DEATH a. COUNTY Montgomery 5/XX7 BEAT NO.

2. USUAL RESIDENCE (Where deceased lived. If institution: Residence before admission) a. STATE Georgia b. COUNTY

b. CITY, TOWN, OR LOCATION Montgomery, Alabama c. IS PLACE OF DEATH INSIDE CITY LIMITS? YES ☐ NO ☐

c. CITY, TOWN, OR LOCATION 5/XX7 Donaldsonville, Georgia e. IS RESIDENCE INSIDE CITY LIMITS? YES ☐ NO ☐ ON A FARM? YES ☐ NO ☐

d. NAME OF HOSPITAL OR INSTITUTION (If not in hospital, give street address) Kilby Prison e. LENGTH OF STAY IN 1b

d. STREET ADDRESS General Delivery

3. NAME OF DECEASED (Type or print) First ALFRED Middle RAY Last ANGLIN 524

4. DATE OF DEATH Month 1 Day 11 Year 64

5. SEX Male 6. COLOR OR RACE White 7. MARRIED ☐ NEVER MARRIED ☐ WIDOWED ☐ DIVORCED ☒ 3

8. DATE OF BIRTH 10-11-29 9. AGE (In years last birthday) 34 IF UNDER 1 YEAR Months Days IF UNDER 24 HRS. Hours Min.

10a. USUAL OCCUPATION (Give kind of work done during most of working life) Farmer &Textile Worker 10b. KIND OF BUSINESS OR INDUSTRY

11. BIRTHPLACE (State or foreign country) Georgia 2 12. CITIZEN OF WHAT COUNTRY? U S A

13. FATHER'S NAME George Robert Anglin 14. MOTHER'S MAIDEN NAME Rachell Miller 14a. NAME OF SURVIVING SPOUSE (ex-wife) Jeanette Anderson

15. WAS DECEASED EVER IN U. S. ARMED FORCES? (Yes, no, or unknown) (If yes, give war or dates of service) Unknown X

16. SOCIAL SECURITY NO. Unknown 17. INFORMANT'S NAME Address Institutional Record

MEDICAL CERTIFICATION

18. CAUSE OF DEATH Enter only one cause per line for (a), (b), and (c).
PART I. DEATH WAS CAUSED BY: IMMEDIATE CAUSE (a) Electrocution
INTERVAL BETWEEN ONSET AND DEATH immediately

Conditions, if any, which gave rise to above cause (a), stating the underlying cause last. DUE TO (b) DUE TO (c) 9147

PART II. OTHER SIGNIFICANT CONDITIONS CONTRIBUTING TO DEATH BUT NOT RELATED TO THE TERMINAL DISEASE CONDITION GIVEN IN PART I(a)

19. WAS AUTOPSY PERFORMED? YES ☐ NO ☒

20a. (Probably) ACCIDENT SUICIDE HOMICIDE ☒ ☐ ☐

20b. DESCRIBE HOW INJURY OCCURRED. (Enter nature of injury in Part I or Part II of item 18.) Accidentally electrocuted while attempting to escape Prison trapped in security wire -

20c. TIME OF INJURY Hour 8:30 a.m. p.m. Month, Day, Year 1-11-64

20d. INJURY OCCURRED WHILE AT WORK ☐ NOT WHILE AT WORK ☒

20e. PLACE OF INJURY (e.g., in or about home, farm, factory, street, office) Kilby Prison

20f. CITY, TOWN, OR LOCATION Montgomery, (Kilby Prison) COUNTY Montgy, STATE Alabama

21. I attended the deceased from ..., to ..., and last saw him alive on ... Death occurred at ... on the date stated above; and to the best of my knowledge, from the causes stated.

22a. SIGNATURE (Degree or title) [signature] Coroner 22b. ADDRESS Montgomery Ala 22c. DATE SIGNED 1-23-64

23a. BURIAL, CREMATION, REMOVAL (Specify) Removal 23b. DATE 23c. NAME OF CEMETERY OR CREMATORY 23d. LOCATION (City, town, or county) (State) Donaldsonville, Ga

24. FUNERAL DIRECTOR ADDRESS White Chapel Funeral Home;Montgy.Ala. 25. DATE RECD. BY LOCAL REG. 24 Jan 64 26. REGISTRAR'S SIGNATURE O. L. Burton, M.D.

Alfred Anglin's death certificate.

On January 15, 1964, Federal Bureau of Prisons Director James Bennett inquired with the acting Warden William C. Holman, seeking details on the escape. Holman provided the above account, and in the cover letter penned by Holman's secretary to Bennett stated: "We fail to find any disciplinary actions lodged against Anglin." In the margin written in Bennett's own hand was a note: "They apparently don't like to fool with simple alarms."

Alfred's sister Marie also received a letter from Associate Warden Oscar Wells who commented: "I was surprised as you were as Alfred Ray was not giving us any trouble whatsoever." As the family sought answers to determine the motivations behind his escape, there were suspicions of a conspiracy and some felt Alfred had been murdered. Everyone was puzzled as to why Alfred would escape with so little time left to serve. Many believed he had been tortured by officials demanding answers as to the whereabouts of his fugitive brothers. Although the funeral director later made differing statements to the FBI, several family members stated he told them that Alfred's body looked as if it had been beaten rather than electrocuted. When Marie wrote the prison asking if she could write to Othis Senn, Associate Warden Mills replied: "As to you writing to inmate Senn, that would be out of the question, as the inmates

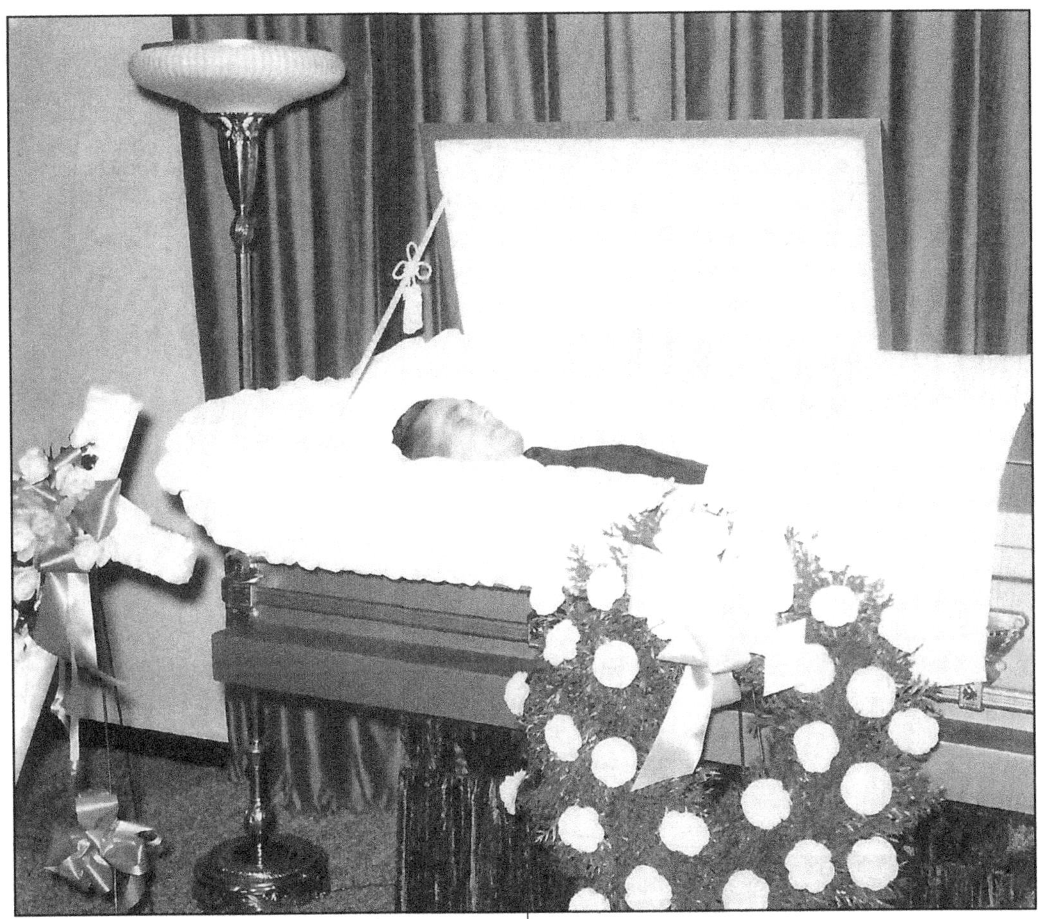

Alfred Anglin at the funeral parlor in Ruskin, Florida.

here are only permitted to receive mail from their close relatives that are listed on their correspondence list." Senn who was serving a 50-year sentence for a the robbery of a Clio, Alabama bank, passed away in July of 1975, and possibly took with him the secrets surrounding Alfred's motivation to escape.

On January 16, 1964, at the Fellowship Cemetery in Hillsborough County, Florida, Alfred was laid to rest in the family plot. Next to his modest headstone was a photo of Alfred and Jeanette announcing they had married. A painful memorial as he was still a fugitive when they slipped across state lines to marry. A future lost, now only loving memories of their past...

His father would exhaust his savings as he insisted his son be buried in an expensive bronze style casket and then sealed in a cement vault for burial. It proved to be a gesture that would later help not only give the family answers to a mystery that was now over a half century old, but also provide investigators a pure DNA source to validate whether the bones that washed up on the shore at Point Reyes, California, was the remains of one of the Anglins.

Overcast
BAY WEATHER—Overcast night and morning, fair afternoons through tomorrow. Highs today San Francisco 63, Oakland 66, San Mateo 68, San Rafael 70. Westerly winds 8-15 mph.

News Call Bulletin

San Francisco's Evening Newspaper

FILE AUG 9 1962

Vol. 3, No. 266 · Phone EX 7-5700 · FRIDAY, JUNE 15, 1962 · Price 10c

9 STAR FINAL · SPORTS PICTORIAL · COMPLETE N. Y. STOCKS

THE BIG ALCATRAZ MYSTERY ---DID 3 SWIM OR DROWN?

By ANDREW CURTIN

Did the three Dixie desperadoes of Alcatraz swim to freedom?

No, said one of the top officials of the U. S. Bureau of Prisons. "They must have drowned."

Yes, said a well known San Francisco swimming coach. "It would have been easy."

Controversy mounted over whether Frank Morris, 35, John Anglin, 32, and his brother Clarence, 31, successfully escaped from Alcatraz.

Did they swim to shore?

Did they have outside help?

The answers to the questions remained a mystery.

Old-timers recalled that Grace Anastasia (Babe) Scott, a year before Alcatraz became a federal prison in 1934, easily swam from Alcatraz to the Dolphin Club at the foot of Polk st. in 47 minutes.

SHE WAS A girl of 17 at the time, a student at Galileo High School and daughter of an Army sergeant stationed on Alcatraz.

"I just jumped off a rock and swam for San Francisco. It wasn't hard at all."

She already had a reputation as a fine swimmer, however.

Associate Director Fred T. Wilkinson of the U. S. Bureau of Prisons said it would take a "trained athlete" to make the swim.

"The only swimming these fellows were accustomed to was in the little old creeks and swamps of Florida and Louisiana. The three men definitely made it off the island. But they never made it to shore."

FRED T. WILKINSON
Believes convicts drowned
—News Call Bulletin Photograph

GRACE SCOTT QUITTING ALCATRAZ IN 1933
"I jumped off a rock and swam for San Francisco"
—News Call Bulletin Photograph

"The tides and the winds that night were strong," Wilkinson said. "The convicts were not the athletic type. Only a trained athlete could make such a swim.

"Unless the tide carried them to the mainland, they never could have made it."

THERE REMAINED A possibility that the three escapees could have received information and arranged a rendezvous on the outside through a still undetected prison "grapevine."

But Wilkinson, who has been on Alcatraz directing an investigation of the break, declared flatly:

"I dismiss absolutely the possibility of any outside help. I would wager my life's savings that they did not have the kind of friends, relatives, or resources which they could have used."

Wilkinson said a check of records revealed that none of the three has had a visitor on the Rock. Morris had been there since Jan. 18, 1960; John Anglin since Oct. 24, 1960, and Clarence since Jan. 16, 1961.

Wilkinson said that when he was warden at the federal prison at Atlanta, Ga., and the three were there they had no visitors—although the Anglin family lived only a day's drive away near Tampa, Fla.

"It is my personal feeling that they have drowned," Wilkinson said.

"I base this on my experience that when a prisoner makes a good escape, within a period of time you start getting legitimate tips or leads which indicate a burglary to get clothing.

"These men had absolutely nothing—neither clothing, money, nor a car—and if they reached the mainland they certainly would have had to break in somewhere, and we would have gotten a tip.

"We've had absolutely nothing yet."

WILKINSON SAID THAT Allen West, who occupied the cell next to Morris and who apparently had

Continued on Page 4, Col. 1

EARL GENECK
"Would have been easy"

Robert "Man" Anglin

Exploring the Evidence and Theories of Conspiracy

"We had to operate under the assumption that they lived as there's never been any proof otherwise. If they lived and made it through the escape, they probably would've had to have gone to another country... I've seen some information that leads me to believe that the raft did land on Angel Island, and there were footprints near the raft. I've gotten leads from places all around the world, but leads that make me feel like there's a possibility that at least the brothers probably lived..."

—MICHAEL DYKE

Supervisory Deputy, United States Marshal Service

IN OCTOBER OF 2010, Robert "Man" Anglin, the eldest of brothers John, Clarence and Alfred was on his deathbed. Now eighty-four years of age, he was spending his final hours in a Florida hospital with family close beside him. In his own right, "Man" had been somewhat of enigmatic figure. He shared a deep bond with his kid brothers growing up, and later in life was guarded about his own theories on the escape. During one period of his life, he left Florida to reside in Texas without any logical explanation. It made everyone suspicious and some believed his move was connected with the escape of his brothers. In his last breath, he confessed in a whispered voice, "I've been with the boys...I know they made it..."

Man's admission was a shock to some, but not those close to him. It simply reaffirmed what they had believed all along...Even the younger Anglin generation who grew up with the stories of their uncles, overheard the murmurs of family members talking behind closed doors. There were many stories within the family circle that could only be attributed to the survival of the brothers. Some siblings stated that their mother Rachel received two dozen red roses on her birthday each year and were always accompanied with two unsigned cards up until her death in 1973. There was also Christmas cards that were signed by

Fred Brizzi

family received a visit from a childhood friend who brought with him compelling evidence that the brothers may have made it to freedom. His "proof" also gave some credibility to the 1989 lead.

Fred Brizzi grew up with the Anglin brothers in Ruskin, and they'd remained good friends throughout their childhood. Close in age, they were mischievous in youth and spent many summers together lounging on the beaches and waterways around the Tampa Bay. In line with the brothers, Brizzi had a lengthy criminal history with his first felony arrest occurring at only fourteen years of age for grand larceny. His criminal case file was a tome of various arrests and convictions. His crimes ranged from robbery and assault in his youthful years, then years later escalating to more serious offenses involving drugs and weapons. After turning eighteen, he had a brief enlistment in the military where he completed pilot training and earned his multi-engine rating. He would later use his aviation skills in a major drug smuggling ring running cocaine, marijuana and hashish from the Caribbean and South America into Central Florida. Using a waterbed mattress on the floor of the cabin as an additional fuel tank, he conducted a series of long range flights in his twin-engine aircraft that typically involved transporting more

the brothers without postmarks or hints of origin, and the well-publicized claim that two unidentified "women" showed up at their mother's funeral, and though they kept a distance, several who were in attendance believed the two individuals were actually men dressed as women (based on their build and body frames) and disappeared before the end of the ceremony.

During the 1989 Unsolved Mysteries broadcast, one of the tips received by the U.S. Marshals was that the escapees were both living on a rural farm in Brazil, but officials later closed out the lead since there was no information provided as to a specific region or location. Three years later, the Anglin

—Staff Photo by Mack Goeth

Smugglers' Plane After It Crashed Into Pine Trees Near North Port

$240,000 In Drugs Is Seized After Shootout With Smugglers

than a quarter million dollars' worth of illegal drugs with each run.

In 1976, while returning from Columbia and weighted down with nearly 700 pounds of marijuana and hashish, Brizzi crashed his aircraft on a makeshift landing strip in North Port, Florida. He suffered minor injuries on impact and left behind a small trail of blood on the cockpit instrument panel which investigators were later able to trace back to Brizzi. His accomplices were waiting in a car when his overweighed plane bounced on landing and then swerved and violently struck several pine trees. Reminiscent of a Hollywood style getaway scene with a violent rain of gunfire, the smugglers fled with a stream of police cars pursuing them at speeds exceeding 100 miles per hour. They evaded capture, but their escape was short-lived. Unknown to Brizzi, he was already the focus of an undercover sting being coordinated by federal customs agents and had been under surveillance for several weeks. After validating that the blood type found on the aircraft instrument panel

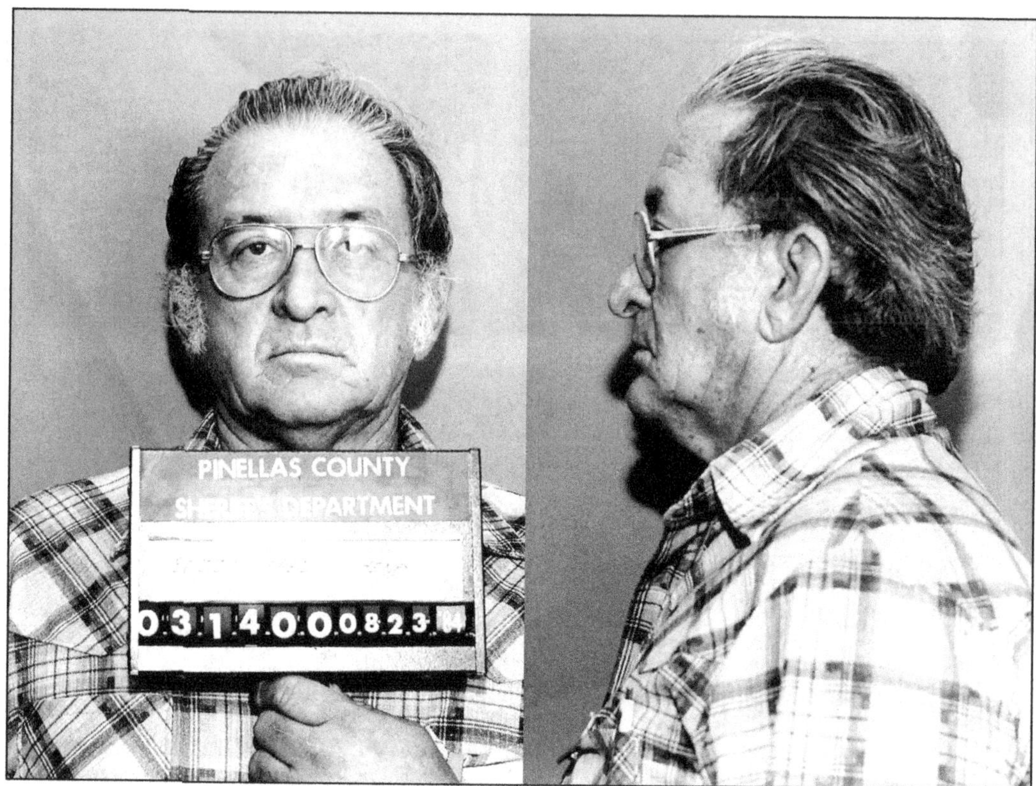

Fred Brizzi

matched Brizzi's, he was arrested and swiftly sentenced to serve fifteen years in a State of Florida prison. Fred's attorney later stated that following his conviction and as part of a plea arrangement, he was recruited as an informant and working with customs agents help put away numerous high profile trafficking figures. In 1984, he was granted an early parole and blended into a quiet neighborhood of Pinellas County, Florida, where he led a simple and unassuming life with his family.

In 1992, as a gesture to allegedly make good on a promise he made to the brothers, he called a meeting with family members. Anglin siblings Robert, Audrey, Mearl, and Marie, along with Alfred's wife Jeanette all met with Fred at Mearl's home outside of Ruskin. As the family convened around the table eager to hear what Brizzi had to reveal, he provided an enthralling and bold claim that he had made contact with John and Clarence nearly twenty years earlier. Marie recorded the conversation on a cassette and Fred described how he made contact with the brothers during a smuggling run in South America and provided photographs to help support his story.

Brizzi claimed that in 1975, while making a drug run in Brazil, he made contact with the brothers in a bar just outside of Rio. He explained that they had cut ties with all former associates and family, and became farmers living quietly in the Brazilian countryside. His voice was clearly captured on the recording stating: "They've gained a little weight since I'd last saw them... They didn't look anything like they had in those pictures where they show what they're supposed to look like now..." Brizzi's photographs allegedly showed their modest hillside home, a river running through their property, and finally, the most significant piece of evidence to surface since the escape, the two brothers standing next to a termite mound. It would be nearly twenty-five years later before the photograph would surface for investigators to analyze.

Brizzi meeting with Anglin family members in 1992.

A year after Brizzi's meeting with the family in November of 1993, ex-convict Thomas Kent provided new information for an episode of America's Most Wanted, a popular television series chasing criminal fugitives. Kent was paroled from prison in 1965 and now claimed that he also had a primary role in the escape, but was forced to back out because he couldn't swim. According to Kent, Clarence had arranged for his girlfriend to meet them on shore and drive them to Mexico. He provided little information to investigators, but the Marshals took the leads seriously and reexamined the evidence. Dave Branham, a United States Marshal spokesman provided a statement commenting: "Although we never found bodies, we presumed they had drowned because a makeshift oar and a life vest turned up on nearby Angel Island... In light of Mr. Kent's account, we think there is a possibility they are alive." Despite this new information from Kent, not everyone, including several fellow convicts, gave him much credibility. James Bulger later recalled:

> I knew Kent real well and you couldn't trust anything coming out of his mouth. He was a bizarre individual. I still laugh at seeing him on television talking about the Alcatraz escape. Most of these were made up stories that he contrived. I've seen Tom Kent's name come up in books and documentaries claiming his expertise on the Alcatraz escape of '62. I saw him many times on TV as the voice of authority. I would always get a good laugh seeing his talking head flash on the screen.

(Above) The photograph that Brizzi provided to the family in 1992 that he alleged he took of John and Clarence Anglin in Brazil in 1975.

(Right) One of the photos used by analysts in the comparison. Most significant were the similarities to John. The comparisons revealed near identical facial features (bone structure) and the watch being worn high on the wrist.

Kent had received $2,000 for his interview, and many felt it was the motivation behind providing what some believed was an exaggerated account and discounted him actually having any role in the plot. While Kent's version was later scrutinized, Fred Brizzi's claim resonated with some investigators and it also tied in a lesser known theory on how they made their escape off the island. His version indicated that the trio didn't paddle or swim to freedom, but instead they were towed by the prison launch. This tied into more than one other inmate account, including an FBI statement made by Woodrow Wilson Gainey where he claimed that during his conversations with John Anglin, he had indicated they were considering leaving from the "docks near

The Alafia River that runs next to Shell Point in Ruskin where the brothers swam throughout their youth. The river runs directly into the Tampa Bay.

where the Alcatraz prison boat docked." Brizzi is heard on the recording telling family members:

> "Nobody, positively, absolutely knows they're alive really but me... And I sat and talked with them. When we were up here with my small boat as kids on the Alafia, these two were like fish. It was in my mind that possibly they had swam, but when I talked with them a little bit, neither of them said anything, then I said I know how you did it now, I remember. Well, down here at the mouth of the Alafia where 41 goes across, we used to go down there and wait for a boat going out. We'd go down there and take a rope and tie it around the rudder post, on the bottom, and we'd wait for the boat to pull on out, and hold on the rope and body surf. I told him I know exactly how you got across there, you tied a line to one of those boats. He said, that's the way we came across."

There is no proof that the trio followed this plan to escape, but it is an important theory to examine. The tow theory posed a greater risk for capture as there were many aspects of this plan that would have placed them in close proximity to the officers working the dock and launch. It was much more complex than simply entering the water and navigating the San Francisco Bay in their homemade raft. Decades later, Darwin Coon stated that John had also mentioned a very similar plan as just one

A photograph looking under the Alcatraz dock structure. One theory suggests they hid in this area of the wharf to attach a cable to the prison launch where they were towed to freedom.

of several options they'd discussed. In this strategy they would enter the water, but circle around the perimeter of the entire island to avoid being seen by the officer working in the dock tower. They would approach the dock from the east side, then come up under the large dock section where they would hide and have easy access to the prison launch docked in the slip.

In 1961, to replace the original Warden Johnston launch that had been constructed by prisoners at the Federal Penitentiary at McNeil Island in 1944, Alcatraz received two larger vessels, decommissioned Army T-Boats that had been constructed for use during the Korean War. These were tug type vessels that later had special hard steel canopy enclosures fabricated for the aft sections to protect passengers from the weather elements. The canopies would have limited visibility for the boat skipper and worked to favor the escapees. T-451, the "Warden Blackwell" was the primary boat and the back-up, T-452, was named the "Warden P.J. Madigan" in honor of the former warden. T-452 was docked at Fort Mason in San Francisco and located in the slip next to the Alcatraz dock tower was T-451, "Warden Blackwell," the active launch ferrying passengers to and from the island.

(Above) A view of the boat slip from the dock tower.

(Right) The Alcatraz dock tower.

The tow concept was to tie a long industrial cord around the cowling assembly that ran near the prop and rudder at the boat's stern. They would slip the cord through a stubbed pipe or weighted ring object, so that that no excess slack would get fouled in the prop as the launch moved astern. This would also help conceal the cable and prevent it from floating on the surface and prevent any detection by the tower officer. Furthermore, the cord was to be strewn around the dock pillars carefully so that they could stay in hiding while the boat moved out of the slip and they would finally push away at

BOAT SCHEDULE

EFFECTIVE OCTOBER 11, 19[illegible]

Leaving Alcatraz

Weekly	Saturday	Sunday	Holiday
A.M.	A.M.	A.M.	A.M.
12:10	12:10	12:10	12:10
6:40	7:05	7:05	7:05
7:20	8:10	8:10	8:10
8:10	9:00	9:00	9:00
10:00	10:00	10:00	10:00
	11:00	11:00	11:00
P.M.	P.M.	P.M.	P.M.
12:45	12:45	12:45	12:45
3:20	3:20	3:20	3:20
3:55	4:55	4:55	4:55
4:40	5:40	5:40	5:40
5:10	7:00	7:00	7:00
5:40	8:45	8:45	8:45
7:00	10:00	10:00	10:00
8:45	11:15	11:15	11:15
10:00			
11:15			

(Reverse Side Leaving Ft. Mason)

USP-AZ—10-8-59—5C—P

The Alcatraz ferry schedule.

the starboard quarter of the vessel and then be towed in darkness far behind as it traveled toward Fort Mason along the San Francisco waterfront. The Sport Illustrated magazine located in Morris's cell included a detailed feature on docking and outboard procedures. While the theory seemed too far-fetched for some investigating the escape, there was at least one potential witness who claimed he had observed something associated with that theory.

The prison launch made up to fifteen scheduled roundtrips daily for both staff and their families. There were also special excursions for incoming inmates and those attending court or being released. There were typically two officers assigned to the vessel, and at night, the dock tower was the only staffed armed post. During the late night hours as the convicts were all locked up in their cells and the prisoner counts properly reckoned, the bright and powerful flood lights that illuminated the dock were dimmed as to not disturb the families sleeping in Building 64, the main apartment complex facing the wharf area. After the final evening count, there were three scheduled departures to Fort Mason; 10:00 P.M., 11:15 P.M. and the last at 12:10 A.M. It was not uncommon for these boats traveling back to the mainland to have few or no passengers. Most officers getting off work in the late shift hours would catch the 12:10 A.M. ferry, and the earlier 11:15 P.M. boat returning to Fort Mason rarely had passengers. Most of the service at later hours was returning staff and residents from the mainland to the island.

On the night of the escape, a highly decorated San Francisco Police Officer named Robert Checchi, witnessed something suspicious that seemed to directly correlate to the tow theory. At about 1:00 A.M., after a tough shift working the Mission District beat, the officer decided to get some air and take a late night stroll near the St. Francis Yacht Harbor, located on the Marina district waterfront. Checci was a trained law enforcement professional and at the time of the escape was assigned to the departments highly specialized "S Squad" and could be considered a

Mystery Boat Clue In Alcatraz Escape

Craft Lurked Off Island, Then Headed Out to Sea

Boat Off Alcatraz On Night of Break

Continued from Page 1

possible route to freedom. Fishing boats don't frequent the Bay at that time of night.

If the convicts are dead, however, their bodies will not be found until at least Thursday, medical experts estimate. The coldness of the Bay water probably would prevent a body from rising until then.

Agents have consulted with tidal and coastal experts in an effort to determine where the bodies would most likely be found. Eastbay law enforcement officials said they had been told an extensive searc... the B... this w...

Whi... searc... confir... facts.

The... the... month... nation...

much trouble and risk without taking into consideration the problem of transportation?

In addition to the ebb tide which could have carried the men to a waiting boat, there was a slack tide for two hours before the escape was discovered. This tide would have given the trio a better than average chance of swimming to freedom.

A fourth convict, who was to have joined the escape but later changed his mind, has told authorities the plan was to leave the island on a raft made from inflated raincoat sleeves. A paddle was found ...it is ...d in ...hop. ...d on ...d. ...only ...very ...alph ...sap- ...They

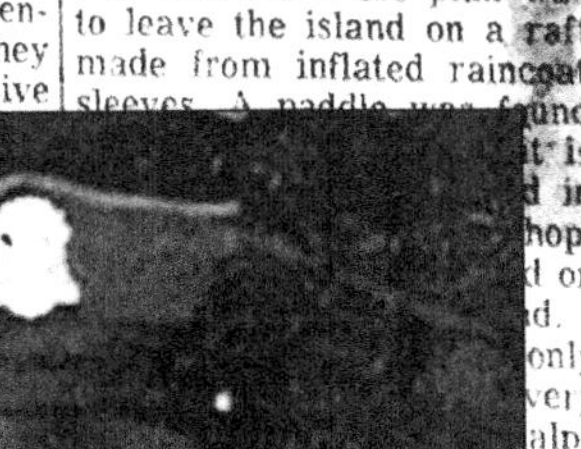

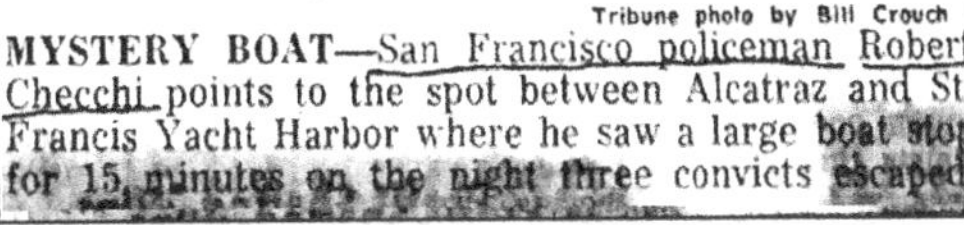

Tribune photo by Bill Crouch

MYSTERY BOAT—San Francisco policeman Robert Checchi points to the spot between Alcatraz and St. Francis Yacht Harbor where he saw a large boat stop for 15 minutes on the night three convicts escaped.

(Above and Left) San Francisco Police Officer Robert Checchi

credible witness. He noticed a 30 foot boat that appeared to have been freshly painted white, he felt something looked suspicious and out of place as it floated just off shore. He remembered in a later interview:

Robert Checchi standing in his kitchen and looking through an old scrapbook featuring the article on the boat sighting. More than fifty years after the escape Checchi remains confident that what he witnessed was on the night of the escape was related to those events.

On June 11th, I had just got off my shift at the Mission Police Station. I went down to the Marina Greens, I went down there to relax after my shift. It was one of my childhood places where we used to swim and surf. I went down there to get some fresh air and clear my head. I happened to see a boat that kind of came in from the east end of the bay, and it came in between Alcatraz and the yacht club. It was very suspicious because at that time of the morning, you wouldn't have any boats out there like that. It was a big white boat... The motor was off... The lights were all off... I didn't see any poles hanging out like someone was actually fishing. It was just sitting there and I started to watch it really closely. Finally, a big floodlight started to flash on and off on the water... The boat was idle for about fifteen minutes before it finally started to cruise out towards the Golden Gate Bridge and then it disappeared from my sight.

I didn't hear about what had happened at Alcatraz until the next morning. Then everything in my mind clicked. I thought, that's how they got away... They got out to that boat and off they went. Right then I notified all the proper authorities.

> The FBI didn't believe me and made me feel like I was making this up. They wanted to know what I was doing out there and who was I with? It got to the point where I took my hands and placed them in front of me and said you can arrest me, but I'm not answering any more questions. I just got up and walked out, and then drove off in my patrol car and did my business. There was a period of time where I was tormented by other officers. They'd cut photos of boats out of magazines and tape them to my locker or on the window of my patrol car. They'd write things like: "Is this the boat, or did it look more like this one?" Most of them thought it was kind of a joke. I believe it was them that night. I know what I saw with my own eyes...

Checci's account would be featured as the front page headline in the Oakland Tribune Sunday Edition on June 17, 1962. The article also pointed out that the boat could have transported the convicts to any number of distant locations. It read in part: "Checci's disclosure also points up a score of possibilities on the whereabouts of the escapees. With a boat of that size, they could still be on the high seas or could have been transported to Mexico, Canada or other ports without being seen." The focus of the investigation during the 1960s was based almost entirely on the assumption that they were attempting to reach Angel Island.

In the 1990's, former Alcatraz Correctional Officer Cliff Fish also challenged some of the official reports of the era. He claimed on the morning of the escape, both him and Olaf Hansen were assigned to help in the manhunt and ventured out in a small vessel to search for any signs of the escapees. They located a raft that he was certain was fabricated by the convicts. When Bill Long was asked if he had ever heard

DEPARTMENT OF JUSTICE
UNITED STATES PENITENTIARY
ALCATRAZ ISLAND, CALIFORNIA

IDENTIFICATION CARD

THIS IS TO CERTIFY THAT
Clifford G Fish
WHOSE SIGNATURE APPEARS ON THE MAR[GIN]
Senior Officer
BADGE NO. 1809 AGE 27 HEIGHT
HAIR light brown EYES [illegible]
DATE OF ISSUE October 16, 1938
WARDEN

Clifford Fish worked on Alcatraz from 1938 until 1962.

of whether a raft was located, he commented: "I personally have no knowledge of the raft being found, but I do remember somebody saying they did find it." Fish remembered in a commentary assembled from two separate interviews:

> When I went to work, there were guys with guns running all around, trying to find out where and how they got out. They knew which way they started, toward Angel Island, but they didn't know where they went from there. They just disappeared... Since I was the best shot on the island, they armed me with a 30-06 rifle and a 45 pistol. They gave me fifty rounds for the 30-06 and 21 for the 45. They told us to go out and see if you can locate anything about this boat the inmates used (referencing the raft used by the escapees). Olaf was an old Swede fisherman. He knew those tides. He was a real boatman...
>
> So Olaf looks at me and says, 'where are we going?' I say, I don't know, we're supposed to look for any sign of the boat. We looked and we looked, and finally Olaf said, you take the helm and head for North Bay. He said you'll have to go into the tide and it's outgoing at the present time. He started to look around and pretty soon he came up with a book and started studying it. He looked at me and said 'What time do you figure those guys got out of there?' I said I don't know but I figure it was around so and so (not remembering the specific time during the interview). He said, 'if that was about the time they got out there was an incoming tide.' I said well, they didn't head out through the Golden Gate, he says 'well they're somewhere in this region.' He put the book back and then he said to me, 'Let me have that wheel.' We went around and headed through what's called Raccoon Straits, which is between Angel Island and Sausalito. He said, 'let's go through Raccoon Straits for fun.'
>
> We were idling through the strait and looking for anything that had been beached. Pretty soon, old Olaf says 'wait a minute... do you see what I see over there on that sandbar?' I said there is something black over there but I can't tell what it is... 'I think it's the raincoats.' Well, before this I had discovered where they had found all the raincoats on top of the cellblock, so I knew they had used a boat made of the rubber jackets that they had glued together. So Olaf said 'let's go over and take a look at that.' Well we went over and there was a great big sandbar. Olaf ran the front of the boat onto it and sure enough it was that boat... So Olaf says 'What do we do now?' and I said, I better go look as that's my job. Olaf said, 'For God's sake be careful because we don't know what they got...' So I said ok, so I got out and very carefully went around and that boat was full of blood, and looked like they had been sticking pigs. The whole bottom of the boat was filled with blood and it wasn't congealed enough to where you could lift the boat and it would run from one end to the other. I looked around and I couldn't see any tracks where

anybody had got out. So I started making circles around the sand to see if I could find anything. There were big trees all the way around there that went back about a quarter mile. I figured I didn't know any way that they could have got around to those trees without leaving tracks. There had to be tracks if they went in that direction. I searched and I search, but finally against my own will and scared to death, I started going through those trees looking for anything that I could find. I didn't know if I would find them or somebody else, or what... I didn't find a confounded thing and pretty soon I gave up and came back to the boat.

Old Olaf had to keep the boat running to keep it up on the sand, and he said, 'Well, what do we do now?' I said we got two choices. We can either leave it here for somebody else to find or we can just take it in... He said, 'If you leave it here the next high tide is going to take it somewhere else. The high tide is what brought the boat in onto the sandbar, but the next high tide will take it out again and wash it off. I suggest we take it in...'

He gave me a rope and we tied it onto the boat and took it back to the island. We called it in on the radio and told them we found a boat and where we found it... We towed it back to the island and they had a big telephone pole that stuck out. It was used to tie the extra boat away from the dock when big storms came in. We tied that boat up to that place. The FBI looked and the Prison Bureau looked, and everybody else looked; there didn't seem to be any big disturbance about it. When I went home that night, the boat was still tied up to that pole. When I came back the next morning, the boat was gone. I've never seen or heard of that boat since... I don't know where it is... I don't know what happened, and I don't know where the blood came from... I don't know if they all got into a fight and killed one another or what? They didn't have anything else that the blood could have come from and I know it was blood... I thought it was the funniest thing because no one ever questioned us about the boat or what was done with it.

In 2002, the United States Marshal Service received what they considered one of their most promising leads in nearly 40 years. Arthur Roderick, a U.S. Marshal assigned to the case back in the early 1990s, came into possession of a deathbed confession that chronicled a conspiracy scheme suggesting the trio had been robbed and murdered following their escape. Roderick continued as one of the prime investigators of the case even beyond his official retirement in 2008. The confession remains unsubstantiated and the principals unidentified by vital records. It has never been determined as more than a popular conspiracy theory by investigators.

In the purported confession dating to 1993, a man allegedly named John Leroy Kelly, who was suffering from a terminal illness and now in a hospice care facility located in the State of Washington, confided to a nurse alleging that he and two other accomplices aided in the escape then murdered all three men. Additionally, he claimed that high ranking guards had a role in the plot and both were paid for their involvement. Kelly had entrusted the nurse who arranged for a priest to counsel him weekly as he lie dying, and his confession was provided to make peace with his past sins and to reveal the truth behind the great mystery. The nurse who allegedly typed the statement claimed Kelly never learned to read or write, and wanted the fate of the escapees to finally be known. The nurse typing the statement indicated Kelly was born near Greenville, Mississippi, in or about September of 1944. He claimed that he grew in a rural and poverty-stricken household and that a birth certificate was never issued and he never learned to write much more than his name and never learned to read. He asked the nurse not to release the confession to anyone until following his death, and she later wrote that she didn't know what to do with the statement or who to give it to...

In the confession, Kelly claimed that his uncle, Donald Leroy Robertson, got him involved to take part in the escape. Now in his late 70s, his uncle had been a driver for well-known bank robbers during the 30s and 40s era and met Frank Lee Morris when they served together at Angola State Prison in Louisiana. In October of 1961, his uncle arranged for him to meet San Francisco Attorney Eugenia MacGowan (the attorney who alleged she had received a call from a man claiming to be John Anglin) at St. Anthony's Catholic Church in San Francisco. She told Kelly that five convicts were going to escape from Alcatraz and that they needed a boat to pick them up and take them to safety. She explained that the convicts had come up with over $60,000 to facilitate the escape. Additionally, Kelly claimed that six guards had knowledge and were receiving payoffs to look the other way and help the convicts get off the island.

MacGowan paid him $5,000 in cash and would provide another $5,000 when she found out the exact night they would escape. In the confession he claimed that she had sealed their fate when his partner, Robert Michael Kyle, learned that the convicts would be traveling with $50,000 in cash. Kyle became obsessed with the idea of robbing them and stealing their money. The confession alleged that Kelly and MacGowan met again in May of 1962 and with her was Alcatraz Captain Thomas Bradley who laid out the plan of the time and rendezvous point of the escapees. Bradley showed them where the convicts would show and provided instructions where to stage their boat. The plan was to have the boat waiting in the St. Francis Yacht Harbor on the night of June 11th, located just beyond Fort Mason.

As everything fell into place, at just before midnight, Kelly and Kyle moved their boat into position and waited in the area just outside the marina. The men were using a commercial fishing boat the "Betty Lou" that had belonged to Kyle's brother-in-law. The "Betty Lou" was named after Kyle's older sister Betty Louise Kyle Davis who had passed away to cancer just a few years earlier. Kelly claimed that at about midnight, he heard splashes in the water, and the convicts were lying across a homemade

(Left to right) Michael Esslinger, David Widner; Kenneth Widner and retired U.S. Marshal Arthur Roderick near the Snowqualmie Pass in Washington State exploring the location of the alleged deathbed confession.

raft. Kyle asked where the other two were, but Morris stated they were the only ones who made it off the island. The boat left the harbor and cruised north to Seattle. When they arrived in Bellingham, they had the convicts get into the rear of their work truck and lie down in the back area, and they hid at his uncles' home for just over a week. They were sure the guards would be arrested and kept listening to the radio for news, but it never happened.

In his confession, Kelly outlined that he'd located a rural spot in the woods and dug a large ditch where they would bury the bodies. He had also concealed shovels and grass seed to use after the murders. They picked up two .38 caliber pistols which were hid under the driver's seat of Kyle's work truck. On June 21st, they started driving towards the Northern Cascade Mountains to Canada, near the Snowqualmie Pass with the convicts in the back. A few minutes after 5:00 P.M., Kyle told the fugitives they were stopping to relieve themselves. They pulled up close to the large trench they'd dug. Kyle drew the pistols from the toolbox under the driver's seat and exited the cab. They opened the tailgate with their handguns pointed at the escapees... In a full throat of anger, Morris screamed, "You sons' of bitches." They opened fire on the three men. Kelly claimed they pulled them by their feet and dragged them into the makeshift grave. John was the last one pulled out and was still alive and begged for his life, but Kyle shot him several more times.

It was claimed that they buried the pistols in with the bodies, along with the bloody canvas they were lying on in the back of the truck. They covered them up and then spread a bag of grass seed. In the 1980s, Kelly claimed he returned to the scene of the crime and nailed horseshoes into the trees around the area. Kelly died on March 17, 1993, and the nurse claimed years later she visited the spot where the murders took place. The confession was typed, then left with a confidential source who allegedly passed a polygraph test later given by authorities. There were several debates as to how the convicts would have acquired $60,000 in cash. One theory was that the money had come from a civil rights coalition that included lawyers who defended prisoners in human rights violations. Their interest in closing Alcatraz was so great that by funding the escape, they knew it would finally result in the closure of the prison. This was another discredited theory by many experts on the escape.

Conspiracy theories always seem more credible in books and movies than in real life. The U.S. Marshal Service and other investigators have never been able to substantiate the claims detailed in the deathbed confession. In several expeditions conducted between 2014 and 2015, investigators failed in locating the supposed location, any actual proof of the murders, buried tools or weapons, or any other attributable evidence. In filing official vital record requests with both county and state agencies, no records of any of the individuals or relational associations were ever located or proven to exist. Lastly, there were no maritime records matching ownership of the sea vessel "Betty Lou." Additionally, the identity of the nurse was never positively verified. It was later implied in the claim that not only did Bradley have a role, but also five other officers (possibly also including Bill Long) who aided the escapees in making their break. This claim was fiercely disputed by former officers and prisoners alike. James Bulger wrote:

> I believe that they acted alone and I'm certain that no guards were involved in the plot. If that were true, they would have been able to move much faster in the escape process. They would have had easier access to equipment and not have to improvise as much. That would have never happened and would have raised suspicions by the other convicts. Why chance involving a guard? What guard would risk everything for money? Plus, guys barely spoke to guards, and never formed a friendship so strong that they would chance this. There was too much mistrust on both sides. Each would think they might be getting set up.
>
> There's no way officers had any role. I knew Bill Long... He was in the clothing room with us for months and I got to know him really well. Of all the guards there, he would have never entered into anything like this. It would have taken nerve and greed to pull something like that

(Above and below) Arthur Roderick made multiple trips to this location as part of the formal investigation conducted by the U.S. Marshal Service. He is seen with the Anglin nephews David and Kenneth Widner looking for any clues related to the confession.

off—Long had neither. You have to consider that he lived on the island with his wife who was also the postal mistress. They had two paychecks for income, cheap rent courtesy of the Bureau of Prisons, and bargains in the commissary for guards and their families, not to mention all the other perks afforded to them. It would have taken a long time to build confidence from the cons. This would have been difficult at best. There was so much hatred and frustration, not to mention that convicts would have caught on and it wouldn't have been kept a secret.

Bill Long was like a big kid. He was very emotional, high strung and he had no criminal tendencies. I have had a lot of experience with corruption—too much—and I have experience paying off law going back into my pre-bank robbing times. I was around it for years. I did it and got real good at it... You have to remember that I was sent to the Rock for allegedly bribing an Atlanta guard to bring in two hacksaw blades. What I was able to acquire was superior to the inventory in the prison industries.

There was an inmate named Darby who told the warden "Give me a parole and I'll tell you who owns the blades that were used to cut through the bars in the hospital." It was an escape attempt gone wrong. I spent a long-long stretch in the hole and back then they raised hell with me to tell them where the blades came from. Warden Wilkerson told me: "You will tell me the name of the guard who brought these blades into the prison... Next thing you know he will be bringing in guns..." I was the only person who knew the name and I NEVER gave him up to anyone. I made a promise, and I've kept it to this day... I'm sure the guard is long gone by now, but it's no one's business. It's still a secret.

I mention this only to point out that it's hard for some people to recognize the potential traits of those more prone to corruption. No convict would have ever trusted someone like Bill Long. Plus, he was not liked and looked at as a bully. I didn't like him and would have never engaged in any small talk with a guy like him. The bottom line here is that I'd bet my life that no officer, especially someone like Bill Long had any role in the escape of Frankie, Johnny and Clarence.

After decades of alleged sightings, false tips and unsubstantiated leads, United States Marshals Arthur Roderick and Michael Dyke breathed new life into the cold case. Roderick later explained that the Marshal Service wasn't involved in the first eighteen years of the case and took over when the FBI officially closed their case on December 31, 1979. "We didn't go back and try to re-create their work... In my opinion the FBI conducted an excellent investigation... They ran the fugitives' fingerprints each year, conducted lengthy surveillances, interviewed family members, and year after year they went back attempting to find anything conclusive... We didn't replicate the original investigation, but when new leads came in, we'd follow the lead out until the end."

Dyke took over the case in 2003 and both men attempted to challenge old theories and reexamine the case files to see if there were any unexplored leads from the original FBI cold case records. Dyke challenged many of the original theories of the FBI. He unearthed several documents that were buried deep in the archives and not exposed during the early phases of the investigation.

Forensic evidence is the bedrock of justice, and Dyke took an aggressive look at the partial skeleton located at Point Reyes in 1963 and with new developments in forensic science, he began collecting DNA samples to conclusively determine the identity. Many investigators believed the bones could hold the golden key to the great mystery. On August 3, 2010, Dyke along with the Marin County Coroner's Office exhumed the bones and took samples for DNA analysis. He was also able to research the lineage of Morris's biological father, Frank Toanker, and secure samples from a confirmed source.

United States Supervisory Marshal Michael Dyke

Five years later, a complex and historic deal was struck between the Anglin family and U.S. Marshal Service that would permit the exhumation of Alfred Anglin. The agreement stipulated that the family would allow investigators to secure pure source DNA samples from his bone marrow, in exchange for approval to conduct an independent autopsy to help rule out theories that Alfred was tortured and then murdered. The exhumation would be filmed and funded by the History Channel and was later showcased in the film documentary Alcatraz: Search for the Truth. The program featured the quest of David & Kenneth Widner (nephews of John, Clarence and Alfred), and examined newly discovered evidence from the family archives in an effort to help prove their two uncles survived.

David and Kenneth grew up with the stories of the escape and it was a center point throughout their lives. As adults, they explored their mother's scrapbooks that included news clippings and family photographs, most of which had been kept under lock and key for more than half a century. Marie and her sister Mearl would also be on-site to watch parts of the exhumation, and for the first time in over fifty years, the painful memories of putting their brother to rest would be

The bones that washed ashore at Point Reyes in 1963 were exhumed in 2010 by Marshal Michael Dyke and the Marin County Coroner's Office.

again unearthed, but all for an important cause. The same documentary crew had met a year earlier in Seattle and traveled to explore the rural mountain region where the alleged deathbed confession murders took place. For David and Kenneth, answers to age old questions within the family could finally be answered.

On June 15, 2015, the United States Marshals, members of the Anglin family, and the documentary film crew converged at the family's burial plot to at last help solve a mystery over a half century old. It showed the extreme measures that the family would take to get answers. In the early morning, Alfred's grave was carefully excavated and after hours of gently being unearthed, the cement vault was craned onto a flatbed truck and then transported with an escort of federal Marshals to the next county where crime scene technicians and forensic experts converged to determine Alfred's true cause of death.

Forensic Pathologist, Dr. Daniel Schultz, and Forensic Anthropologist Maranda Kles would oversee the autopsy and collect tissue and bone samples for DNA analysis. When the vault was finally opened and the coffin unsealed after a half century in wait, Alfred's corpse would again see sunlight and witnesses gasped in astonishment.

A press release photo from the History Channel feature documentary Alcatraz: Search for the Truth. The program explored various escape theories and showcased the exhumation of Alfred Anglin. DNA was compared against the remains that washed ashore at Point Reyes in February of 1963, in addition to performing a full autopsy to verify Alfred's cause of death. It was an important advancement in the cold case as it concluded that the DNA of the bones found at Point Reyes did not match either of the Anglin brothers. (L-R) Arthur Roderick, Kenneth Widner, David Widner and Michael Esslinger.

His remains were compared against the photographs taken before the casket was closed, his eyeglasses were still in place and though partially decomposed from decades underground, Alfred appeared in the same state as when he was buried.t

On the autopsy table, Alfred's corpse proved to be exceptionally well preserved. The cement vault had been sealed by pouring heated tar along the edge before the lid was permanently set. It proved highly effective as the body was mostly free of any extreme decomposition. His fingers had notable ridges that were essential for the crime scene unit who was able to capture a reasonable set of prints. The autopsy lasted approximately six hours, and was comprised of a detailed examination that included the cranial and torso cavities, along with examining all of the extremities. A complete series of head to toe x-rays were taken, 7mm sections of each femur for source DNA, organ and tissue samples, and a full inventory of his clothing was used to assure that Alfred would be returned to his grave with the same dignity and respect his family provided him back in 1964.

The autopsy findings proved significant. The analysis did not present any notable trauma or signs of foul play. The official forensic report included findings

(Below) The sisters of John and Clarence Anglin, Marie & Mearl, both visited Alfred's grave prior to being exhumed. It was an extremely difficult decision by the family to allow authorities to exhume their brother, but they wanted to know the truth as to whether or not he'd been murdered for refusing to provide information to authorities. The sons of Marie, David and Kenneth were present along with U.S. Marshals to oversee the entire process.

dictated by Dr. Schultz affirming in his words:

> No trauma identified... Reportedly this individual succumbed to an electrocution; it should be noted that the lack of thermal-electric styled skin burns may or may not be seen even in freshly electrocuted individuals, depending on degree of skin moisture/degree of electrical amperage received. In the face of severe cutaneous decomposition, the absence of recognizable cutaneous electrical burn manifestations is not surprising, even if truly the case. Thus, death by electrocution is consistent with the findings in this examination. More importantly, other reasonable alternative traumatic or natural causes of death are not identified.

While the autopsy results failed to provide the full spectrum of answers the family originally sought, the report was successful in ruling out age old theories that Alfred was beaten or met an otherwise traumatic cause of death. For the United States Marshals, the findings were more than significant. When the Anglin DNA samples were tested against the skeletal remains recovered from Point Reyes, the results proved negative. The samples tested against

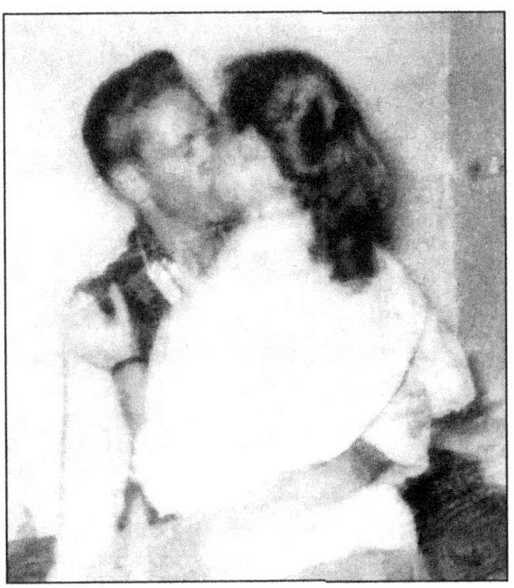

(Above left) Alfred Anglin on the day he was laid to rest in February of 1964. The family placed his glasses back on as he always wore them in his adult life. His casket would be sealed in a cement vault where he would remain until the exhumation fifty one years later.

(Above right) A faded image still discernable of Alfred and Jeanette on the day they announced their marriage located next to his tomb.

Morris's lineage also proved negative. The bones were not related to any of the escaped convicts. The tests proved conclusively that they were not the remains of the escapees. For investigators and for the first time in over half century, a major chapter in the investigation was now closed.

The photographs provided by childhood friend, Fred Brizzi, were also analyzed by two forensic facial imaging experts. The most notable was Michael Streed, an internationally-recognized authority, known for his forensic expertise and working cases for some of the largest and most diverse police agencies in the United States, including the Los Angeles and Baltimore City Police Departments. Streed was hired by the History Channel to examine the photograph of the two brothers allegedly taken in 1975. He studied the photos, carefully examining their anatomical and structural facial features. Both he and the other former FBI investigator rendered their professional opinions that the photograph "was in all probability authentic" and "highly likely that the two individuals in the 1975 photograph are John and Clarence Anglin." It would prove to be one of the most significant leads since the actual escape. The official analysis facilitated by Michael Dyke and the Marshal's unit was not as favorable. In their own analysis, their results were not conclusive and placed doubt as to whether the subjects could be the Anglins. Despite this, Roderick said the combination of the image of the brothers and DNA test results was a 'game changer' in the investigation.

(This page) Photographs from the 2015 exhumation of Alfred Anglin. Unearthing Alfred helped answer age old questions that lingered for both the Anglin family and U.S. Marshal Service more than half a century.

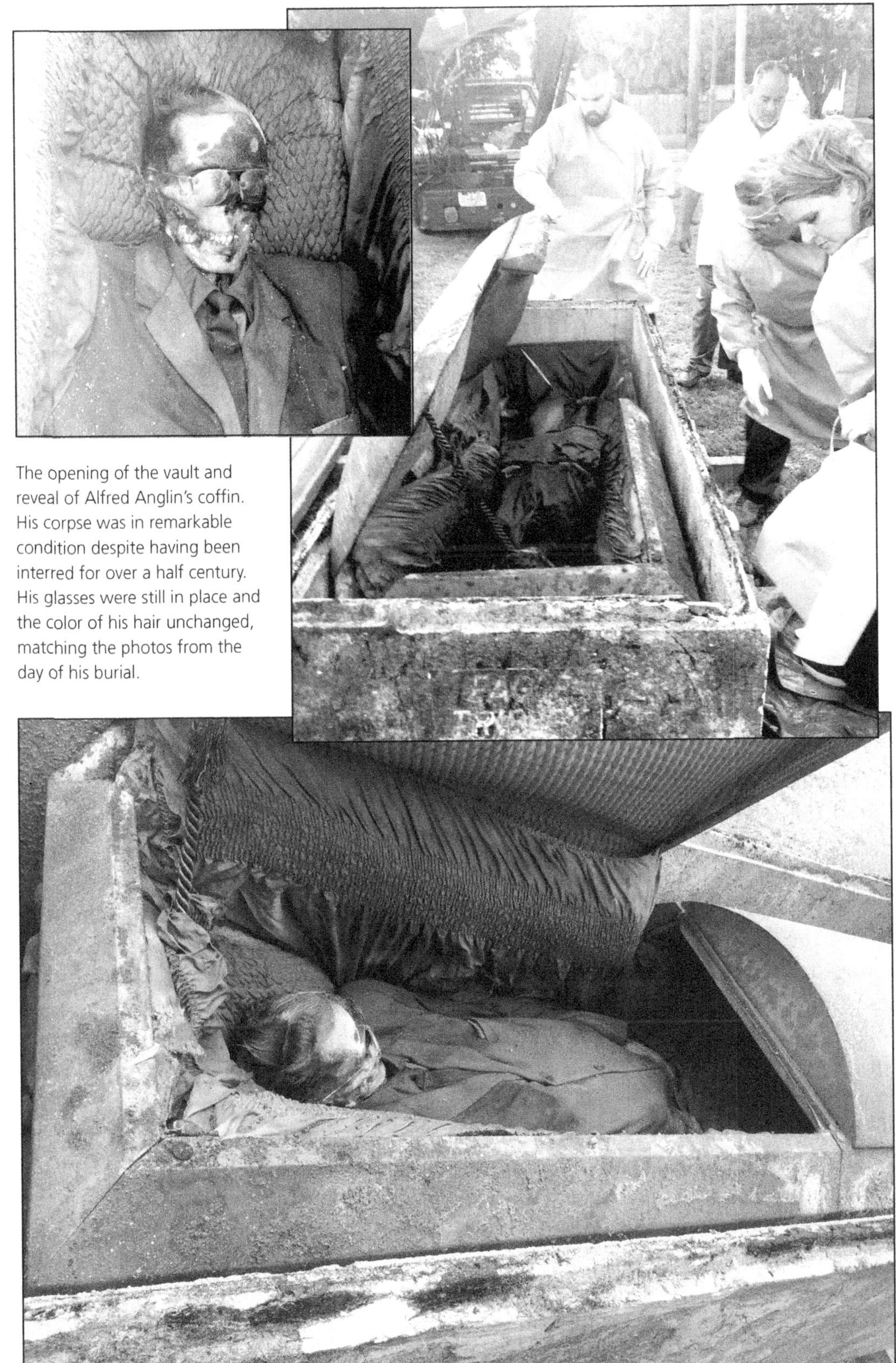

The opening of the vault and reveal of Alfred Anglin's coffin. His corpse was in remarkable condition despite having been interred for over a half century. His glasses were still in place and the color of his hair unchanged, matching the photos from the day of his burial.

Dr. Daniel Schultz explains the autopsy procedure to Roderick and Esslinger who both observed the procedure.

Brizzi's ex-wife Judith also later indicated that she was suspicious and did not place faith in his story, however, she was not able to identify the men or origin of the photographs. She commented about the picture: "He never said anything to me ever about those men escaping from Alcatraz...He showed me the photograph because of the size of the anthill. I've no idea who the men are and Fred never talked about them." Brizzi ultimately left the United States and relocated to Columbia until his death. Experts continue to debate the photograph, and the odds of two subjects being of the same age, during the estimated time period of the photograph, both men having similar builds and features, same region as their suspected destination, and to fall into the hands of a childhood friend seemed to be an extraordinary coincidence. There was no mention about the fate of Frank Morris. Brizzi stated that there was another male with the brothers, but his identity was never revealed to him.

Marshal Dyke had also uncovered two documents that killed the long standing theory that no land based evidence existed relating to the escape. This was a significant discovery in the case. The first was an official FBI telegram dated June 12, 1962, which indicated a raft was discovered on Angel Island. A day later a law enforcement bulletin added more detail indicating: "...footprints were spotted leading away from the raft." A significant lead was that the

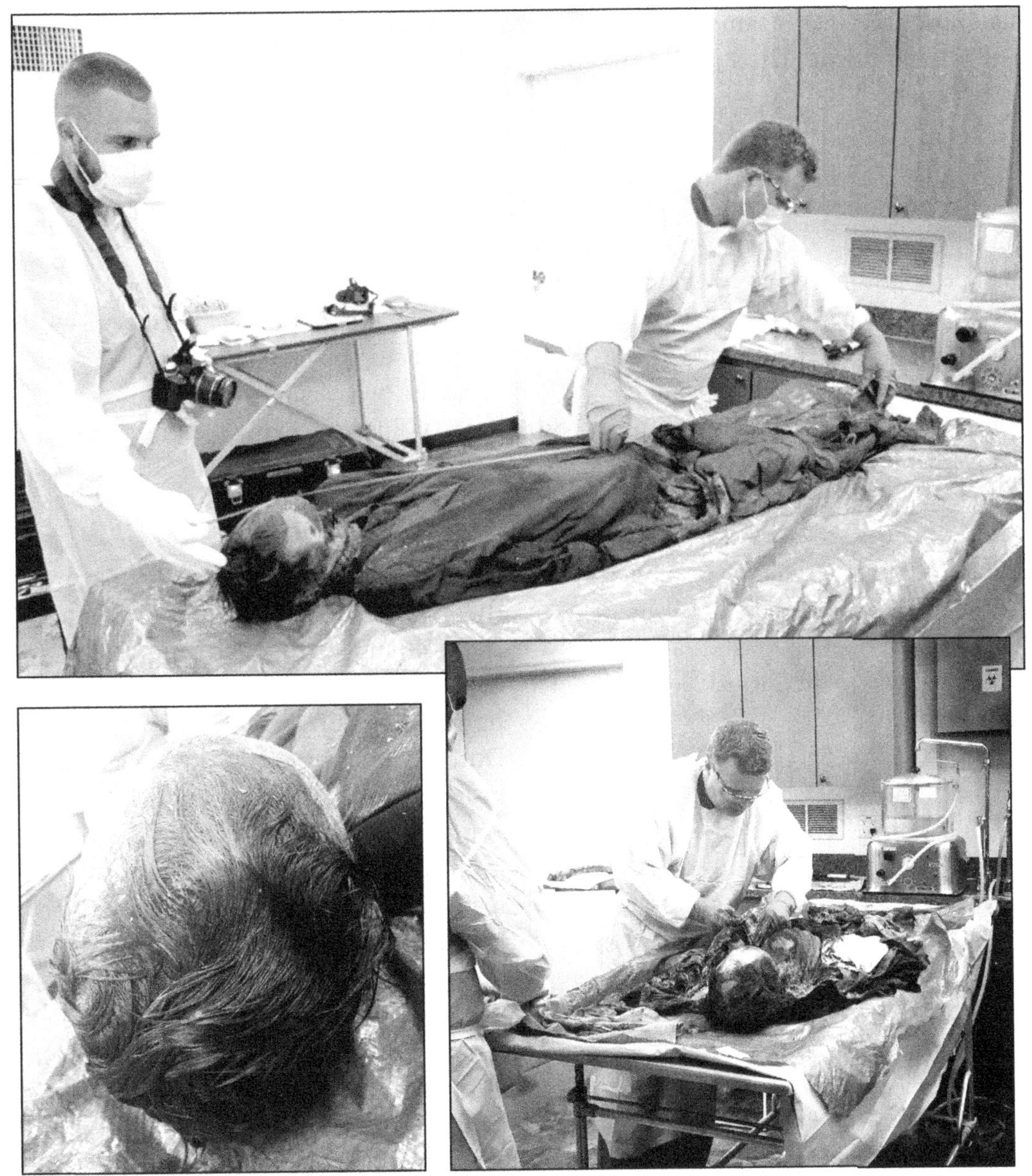

(Above top, left, and right) Alfred's autopsy was performed by Forensic Pathologist, Dr. Daniel Schultz, and Forensic Anthropologist Maranda Kles (not pictured). Both experts handled the exam in an incredibly respectful and detailed manner for the family and observers.

day following the escape, a 1955 Blue Chevrolet was stolen in Marin County. The California license plate number was KPB-076 and at approximately 11:30 A.M., a complainant called CHP to report that he had been forced off the road by three men matching the description of the escapees in a blue Chevrolet in Stockton, California. What is most essential is that this information relating to the stolen vehicle had not been released to the public. The complainant would not have had any knowledge of the stolen car in Marin matching the very same description. The second memo dated June 13, 1962, read in part:

> Since the morning of 6/12/62 his department had been receiving information relating to the possible escape of three prisoners the Federal; Prison, Alcatraz. About noon, or shortly after, they received information that a 1955 Blue Chevrolet, containing three men, had been reported in the Riverbank—Oakdale, California area, and that it might be identical with the 1955 Chevrolet reported stolen in Marin County, California area. Efforts were being made locally to locate such a car. No additional details were known to the Turlock Police Department.
>
> On 6/12/62 Sgt. [OMITTED BY FBI], Desk Sergeant, Stanislaus County Sheriff's Office, Modesto, California, advised that his office had received an All Points Message placed by the California Patrol, Stockton, California, by radio, advising that they should be on the lookout for a 1955 Chevrolet, blue in color, bearing California license KPB-076. According to information received by the Stanislaus County Sherriff's Office, a raft had been found on Angel Island; footprints were found leading from the raft, and it was being assumed that the escapees had come ashore at that point on Angel Island. In addition, the Marin County Sheriff's Office had furnished information that the car, described above, had been stolen in Marin County, date and time of theft unknown to the Stanislaus County Sherriff's Office. At approximately 11:30 A.M., 6/12/62, according to Brooks, an unarmed complainant had called the California Highway Patrol, Stockton, California advising that agency that he had been forced off the road by three men in a blue 1955 Chevrolet. Further descriptive data concerning this latter Chevrolet was not known. On the possibility the two cars might be identical, the California Highway Patrol instituted immediate efforts to locate the vehicle.

Even placing the extreme survival theories aside, the traditional theories still suggest it wasn't impossible to make it land using only paddles and a homemade raft. A study by a group of Dutch scientists using advanced computer generated hydro models of the San Francisco Bay's tides created a multitude of variables including wind resistance and time of departure. They reconstructed the possible routes of the escape and concluded that if the men left Alcatraz before 11:30 P.M., the current would have probably swept them out to sea, but had they left earlier, they could have survived:

> "If the prisoners set off on their raft between 11:30 and midnight, it's likely that they could have landed just north of the Golden Gate Bridge, at Horseshoe Bay... It's really sensitive to timing, which time they entered the water... It's very plausible they made landfall... The models also show that any debris after the landing might have drifted toward Angel Island, north of Alcatraz,

(Above, right, and below) The condition of his corpse was so well preserved, a crime scene unit was able to secure fingerprints of such quality to make a positive identification of the remains.

OPTIONAL FORM NO. 10
5010-104

UNITED STATES GOVERNMENT

Memorandum

TO :SAC, San Francisco (76-2887) DATE: 6/13/62

FROM :SA [redacted]

SUBJECT: JOHN ANGLIN;
CLARENCE ANGLIN;
FRANK LEE MORRIS.
ESCAPED FEDERAL PRISONERS

Re San Francisco telephone calls to Modesto Resident Agency, 6/12and 13/62; and call from SA [redacted] to San Francisco, 6/12/62.

While at the Turlock, California Police Department, conducting other investigation, [redacted] (NA), Chief of Police, Turlock Police Department, advised that they had received information concerning the Alcatraz escapees as follows:

Since the morning of 6/12/62 his department had been receiving information relating to the possible escape of three prisoners from the Federal Prison, Alcatraz. About noon, or shortly after, they received information that a 1955 Blue Chevrolet, containing three men, had been reported observed in the Riverbank - Oakdale, California area, and that it might be identical with the 1955 Chevrolet reported stolen in the Marin County, California area. Efforts were being made locally to locate such a car. No additional details were known to the Turlock Police Department.

A telpphone call was made to Supervisor [redacted] at request of radio dispatcher. The meager information known was discussed with him and he requested that the information be traced to its source in the Stanislaus County area.

On 6/12/62 Sgt. [redacted], Desk Sergeant, Stanislaus County Sheriff's Office, Modesto, California, advised that his office had received an All Points Message placed by the California Highway Patrol, Stockton, California, by radio, advising that they should be on the lookout for a 1955 Chevrolet, blue incolor, bearing California license KPB-076. According to information received by the Stanislaus County Sheriff's Office, a ~~raft~~ (raft) had been found on Angel Island; foot prints were found leading from the raft, and itwas being assumed that the escapees had come ashore at that point on Angel Island. In addition, the Marin County Sheriff's Office had furnished information that the car, described above, had been stolen in Marin County, date and time of theft unknown to the Stanislaus County Sheriff's Office. At approximately 11:30am, 6/12/62, according to BROOKS, an unnamed complainant had called the California Highway Patrol, Stockton, California, advising that agency that he had been forced off the road by three men in a blue 1955 Chevrolet. Further descriptive data concerning this latter vehicle was not known. On the possibility that the two cars might be identical the California Highway Patrol instituted immediate efforts to locate the the vehicle

recorded ... 68

JUN 14 1962

Lc: Riverbank

76-2887-69

(This page and opposite) The two telegrams that were discovered in 2011. One chronicles a recovered raft with footprints leading away from it on Angel Island. The second telegram describes an automobile theft in Marin County which later matched a description of a suspect vehicle with occupants matching the escapees' descriptions in Stanislaus County the same day. These were never substantiated by law enforcement officials.

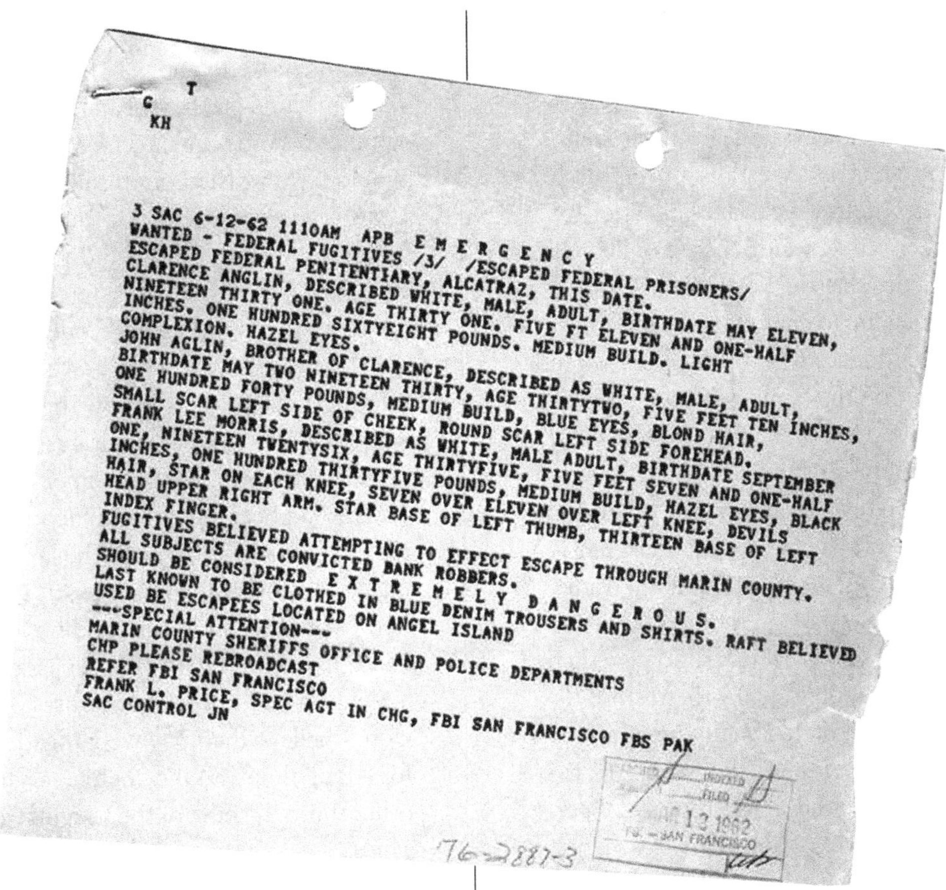

T
G
KH

3 SAC 6-12-62 1110AM APB E M E R G E N C Y
WANTED - FEDERAL FUGITIVES /3/ /ESCAPED FEDERAL PRISONERS/
ESCAPED FEDERAL PENITENTIARY, ALCATRAZ, THIS DATE.
CLARENCE ANGLIN, DESCRIBED WHITE, MALE, ADULT, BIRTHDATE MAY ELEVEN,
NINETEEN THIRTY ONE. AGE THIRTY ONE. FIVE FT ELEVEN AND ONE-HALF
INCHES. ONE HUNDRED SIXTYEIGHT POUNDS. MEDIUM BUILD. LIGHT
COMPLEXION. HAZEL EYES.
JOHN AGLIN, BROTHER OF CLARENCE, DESCRIBED AS WHITE, MALE, ADULT,
BIRTHDATE MAY TWO NINETEEN THIRTY, AGE THIRTYTWO, FIVE FEET TEN INCHES,
ONE HUNDRED FORTY POUNDS, MEDIUM BUILD, BLUE EYES, BLOND HAIR,
SMALL SCAR LEFT SIDE OF CHEEK, ROUND SCAR LEFT SIDE FOREHEAD.
FRANK LEE MORRIS, DESCRIBED AS WHITE, MALE ADULT, BIRTHDATE SEPTEMBER
ONE, NINETEEN TWENTYSIX, AGE THIRTYFIVE, FIVE FEET SEVEN AND ONE-HALF
INCHES, ONE HUNDRED THIRTYFIVE POUNDS, MEDIUM BUILD, HAZEL EYES, BLACK
HAIR, STAR ON EACH KNEE, SEVEN OVER ELEVEN OVER LEFT KNEE, DEVILS
HEAD UPPER RIGHT ARM. STAR BASE OF LEFT THUMB, THIRTEEN BASE OF LEFT
INDEX FINGER.
FUGITIVES BELIEVED ATTEMPTING TO EFFECT ESCAPE THROUGH MARIN COUNTY.
ALL SUBJECTS ARE CONVICTED BANK ROBBERS.
SHOULD BE CONSIDERED E X T R E M E L Y D A N G E R O U S.
LAST KNOWN TO BE CLOTHED IN BLUE DENIM TROUSERS AND SHIRTS. RAFT BELIEVED
USED BE ESCAPEES LOCATED ON ANGEL ISLAND
---SPECIAL ATTENTION---
MARIN COUNTY SHERIFFS OFFICE AND POLICE DEPARTMENTS
CHP PLEASE REBROADCAST
REFER FBI SAN FRANCISCO
FRANK L. PRICE, SPEC AGT IN CHG, FBI SAN FRANCISCO FBS PAK
SAC CONTROL JN

INDEXED
FILED
13 1962
FBI — SAN FRANCISCO

76-2887-3

which is where the FBI found a paddle and some personal items linked to the men."

James Bulger offered some final thoughts on the escape and whether he felt they made it to freedom:

The hope of the warden was "They Drowned!" Convicts, "They Made It!" I think they could have made it fairly easily. They likely stole a car and had many miles behind them before making a move to get money. They were smart and they had different phases and several contingencies in their plan. They put a lot of distance between them and Alcatraz in quick time. They also knew how to avoid suspicion. One guy fronts and the other two stay completely off scene. They stay completely isolated just watching TV and reading. Like President Lyndon Johnson once said about the smart Texas mule: "A big storm comes and the mule hunkers down and lies there still, quietly waiting for it to just blow over." The saying went something like that, but I thought of it often during my own time on the lam.

I believe they all made it to freedom and followed through with their plan to cut all ties. My opinion is that it was a case of strict discipline on their part to completely cut ties with everyone in their past. This is why no one ever heard from them. Not merely to just disappear, but to also protect their families. Prior to the escape, we discussed in detail the tactics that the Feds would employ in trying to capture fugitives. One of their tactics was to use extreme pressure on the families. I know this first hand. One of their most commonly employed tactics was to pressure the family using harassment, monitoring their phones, watching their mail, following them, and making things uncomfortable to the point that the family will grow tired and give them information to make them stop. If they can catch a family member in a lie, then it gives them a means to prosecute them. Essentially, cooperate or go to prison. This is why no one ever heard from them. This is typically how most all fugitives are eventually caught. They trip-up by contacting a family member or close associate, and the Feds intercept their calls and then trace their location. The family's phones are constantly being monitored and their movements traced whenever they travel, etc. The Feds have unlimited resources, money, equipment, man power, etc...

I know it's possible to effectively disappear. I know this first hand. The trio didn't pull off the greatest escape ever in U.S. history and not have a solid plan on how to survive once they were free. I know that as fact...As much thought goes into that as it does the escape. It's a painful dilemma, but for everyone's sake, they had no choice. The Feds place rewards on their heads and the families become the targets. Morris would have insisted on this also. Complete severance of all ties. It was easier for Morris since he didn't have any close family, but it had to be this way for the security of everyone. The love of family is what drove that painful decision. This is how the trio survived. This is what we discussed and debated prior to the escape. Morris had become fluent in Spanish. He could read and write in the language and this was a major asset. His body features (tan, height and build) could have easily helped him pass as a Mexican and not raise any suspicion. I believe that they were together for a long time and they helped each other through some of the tougher times.

I was a fugitive for sixteen years and was hunted aggressively by the FBI. I was on the FBI's Ten Most Wanted List with a two-million dollar reward for my capture, along with a hundred thousand dollar reward for Catherine. I was on countless "Most Wanted" television programs, not to mention the movies and documentaries. The Feds were ruthless in the harassment of my family. They sent my brother Jack to jail for six months and then another term of house arrest—took his pension just as he had retired. Catherine's sisters was subjected a similar punishment. My other brother suffered greatly also...He lost his career in politics, was forced out being the Head of the University of Massachusetts. All this because no one would cooperate, and all this in spite of my not being in contact with any of them. The families become the targets and are subjected to terrible pressure. If they're caught in a lie, then they are prosecuted for perjury for lying to a Federal Officer. Isn't it a bit ironic that they can lie as part of their tactics and it's just part of their job and legal?

In order to survive, I understood the importance of breaking all contact with loved ones and holding to that level of discipline. It was tough to break those ties with those you love, but necessary for my own survival and their protection. We all knew the penalty that would fall on the innocents we cared for. You have to factor that into as to why they were never seen or heard from again. Freedom came at such a big price, but it was still better than the long and lonely years spent in prison.

Whenever I think back to my years on Alcatraz, and that morning of June 12, 1962, it always raises my spirits and I give a silent cheer to Frankie, John and Clarence. God Bless the trio... They helped shut down Alcatraz and made history... I hope they lived a long and happy life after Alcatraz...

—Vaya con Dios Paco!

"No one has ever escaped from Alcatraz...and no one ever will."

CLINT EASTWOOD

ESCAPE FROM ALCATRAZ

The Making of Legends—Escape from Alcatraz

Sometimes I think that's all this place is one... long... count... The prisoners count the hours, the bulls count the prisoners, and the king bulls count the counts.

—ENGLISH (ESCAPE FROM ALCATRAZ)

AFTER MORE THAN A DECADE following the escape, Alcatraz was now merely a skeleton of its former self... Once America's most notorious penitentiary, it had morphed from prison to parkland and the story of the 1962 break had become the touchstone of its sordid past.

Richard Tuggle was a young aspiring writer, and one of those captivated by the famed escape. Despite never having written a book or screenplay, he would pen what was to become a classic motion picture, entertaining generations of movie audiences from around the world, and in turn, transform the escapees from shadowy criminals to American legends. Escape from Alcatraz has sustained for more than a half century, and has brought to life for millions around the world, the epic story of the escape.

Born in Coral Gables, Florida, in 1948, Tuggle was a political science major who migrated to San Francisco in the 1970s. In the mid-1970s, he was offered a position as a feature editor for a healthcare publication, but later fired during a staffing reorganization and found himself broke and out of work. Living on Telegraph Hill, the bright and haunting beacon of Alcatraz permeated Tuggle's apartment at night. He remembered:

> At night the bright beam of the Alcatraz lighthouse would shine into my bedroom. I felt a connection to the place, a sense of wonder, a mystical feeling towards the prison. A friend of mine convinced me to go to Alcatraz for the tour. You walk away with an incredible sense of the history, the escapes, and it's something that stays with you for a long time... The guide had told us of the only unsolved escape attempt and

Richard Tuggle with Clint Eastwood during filming on Alcatraz in 1978.

walked us through the story showing us where Morris and the Anglins dug out of their cells, scaled the walls, and then made it down to the shoreline where they disappeared and were never to be seen again... It seemed impossible as Alcatraz was considered the most secure prison of that era. I was immediately drawn to it. I was consumed by their story...

I went down to Fisherman's Wharf and found a bunch of Alcatraz photo books for tourists, and also located a copy of J. Campbell Bruce's book 'Escape from Alcatraz.' It told the history of all the escapes, and I became inspired to write the story of one escape as a movie. The book bio indicated that Bruce was living in Oakland and after contacting him, he agreed to meet with me. I told him I've never written a screenplay in my life, but I thought I could turn the story of the escape into a good movie. If either of us had known anything about the movie business, we would probably have thought that to be the most ridiculous idea. But instead, he said to me, 'Give it a try.'

Tuggle on Alcatraz in 2012 during an event for the 50th anniversary of the escape.

The next step was contacting Bruce's publisher McGraw-Hill who also held a portion of the screen rights. The book had gone out of print and they had lost interest in it. After months of trying to get the film rights from them, they finally told me they would just give me the rights. I was suspicious and asked them, 'Why would you do that?' They said, 'Because the chance of you getting this movie made is so small it isn't worth our time to deal with the legal issues.' Bruce and I worked out an arrangement and then I took to writing the screenplay.

I ended up going down to a used bookstore in the San Francisco Mission District and found a book on how to write a screenplay for I think around $5.00. From that point, I started doing my own research and began to develop the story around the narrative of Bruce's work. I went both to the FBI and Bureau of Prisons to do research, and later went back to the FBI to fact check what I'd written. A new FBI PR guy, told me forget it, you never should have been allowed access to the case files in the first place. I was able to piece together the true events of the story. The case itself was fascinating... Their tracks stopped dead cold at the shoreline and the case went cold from that point forward.

Campbell's book was a broader history so I interweaved other elements of the prison's past to help frame the prison as a character. I added stories from the entire thirty year history and condensed it into the one year in which the story takes place. As an example, the bit where the inmate chops off his fingers comes from an actual incident that happened in the 30's. I also created new characters to give context to the events and history, as well as create a realistic setting and racial atmosphere. I wanted the film to have a pureness, or maybe better described as an authentic texture to the history spanning the course of the prison's working years.

I started watching as many prison based stories that I could. French Director Robert Bresson's A Man Escaped had a big influence on me as did Siegel's Riot in Cell Block 11. I didn't have an agent, so I went to Los Angeles and started knocking on doors on my

(This page and opposite) Clint Eastwood as Frank Morris in classic motion picture Escape from Alcatraz.

own and decided to seek out Don Siegel straight out of the gate. He had directed Eastwood in Dirty Harry and really captured San Francisco very well I thought. Plus, he had directed Riot in Cell Block 11 which was a really good prison movie and he knew that domain well. So on a whim, I called Don's agent and told him all about the script.

Robert Daley, the Executive Producer and a key partner of Clint Eastwood's Malpaso Company remembered:

Don Siegel had asked Clint to read Tuggle's script Escape from Alcatraz, but since he was off shooting another movie, he asked me to read it for him. I told Clint it was one of the best works I'd ever read; I couldn't put it down. Then Clint read it and agreed with me. Both Clint and I had filmed on Alcatraz a couple of years earlier so we had a good idea what we were up against. We filmed a few scenes from The Enforcer there, and we were familiar with the logistics and visually rich properties of everything it had to offer.

Director and Producer Don Siegel recalled:

About twenty years before, I directed Riot in Cell Block 11, which drew some inspiration from a well-known violent crusade on Alcatraz taking place in the 1940s. That picture was filmed entirely at Folsom Prison. I thought immodestly that picture turned out quite well, and it gave me a good sense of that type of visual territory . . . I was very well familiar with J. Campbell Bruce's book on Alcatraz. In 1966, I turned it into a treatment called 'The Rock,' but the studio wasn't interested at the time and frankly I had forgotten all about it until I was handed Tuggle's script. To my astonishment, I liked it very much, so I bought it . . . It was a terrific story . . . Once everyone decided Escape from Alcatraz was a yarn we wanted to bring to screen, everything moved quickly . . .

Paramount gave the project a go-ahead in May of 1978. By mid-August, our production staff was on Alcatraz restoring several areas of the prison. It was a complicated venture. You have to remember that Alcatraz had been closed since 1963, so erosion had set in along with salt water damage and all of the other natural elements that would hasten the deterioration of the island structures. In addition, there was an Indian occupation that resulted in a lot of damage. About 80% of the film was

shot on the island, and about 20% on a soundstage at Paramount. We wanted the credibility of filming on the island. Many of the scenes were filmed where the actual events took place. It mattered to everyone that we get it right. It needed to be more than believable; it needed to be genuine... It was a formidable task. We had to deal with a lot of obstacles. Alcatraz is a national historic structure and we had to work around all of the restrictions associated with that designation. There was graffiti everywhere and Park Service officials wanted it preserved and refused to let us paint it out. So our production designer covered those areas with removable sections and then painted over those. We also had to work around tourist operations which proved difficult. We had tourist boats landing it seemed every 15 minutes and this forced us into doing most of our location filming after hours. We shot a total of 69 days, and 60 of those were on location at Alcatraz.

Production Designer Al Smith recalled:

Refurbishing Alcatraz was an exciting challenge. You're working with a historic monument known throughout the world. I had shot with Clint there on The Enforcer and had also had the opportunity to examine many of the actual artifacts and FBI files. This was essential in achieving a genuine representation of the island during its working years.

The prison was, of course, in very bad condition. The plumbing was all broken, the electrical lighting facilities had been stripped, and we had to redo each and every cell. Our biggest problem initially was broken windows, with the fog and moisture coming through. We had to seal all of the windows from the outside before we could do any work on

(Right) Director Don Siegel and Tuggle during filming in the Alcatraz recreation yard.

(Below) Siegel and Eastwood discussing a scene in the Alcatraz recreation yard.

(Above) Tuggle and Eastwood discussing the script.

(Above and right) Tuggle with actor Patrick McGoohan who played the Warden, and with Larry Hankin who played the memorable character Charley Butts.

the prison. We also agreed to paint the entire wall if we touch any part of it, and some walls up there are 35 feet high and 150 feet long.

Logistically, it was decided that we couldn't shoot inside a 5 x 9 foot cell, so we determined that we should shoot the mess hall, all of Broadway, the main cellblock, and portions of the kitchen. We also had to rebuild portions of the catwalks, re-recreating the actual escape route, and we refurbished the prison yard bringing it back to the ball-diamond days, and we put in an awful lot of barbed wire. We decided to shoot the workshops back at the studio, as well as the warden's office, shower room, and part of the cell block and interior cell scenes.

The warden portrait painted by the Chester "Doc" Dalton character. The film captured the essence of Alcatraz and painting was an essential pastime and means of escape for many prisoners doing time.

We spent over seven weeks on the island shooting. We had to bring everything over from the mainland, handling every bucket of paint, every piece of plywood, every piece of material, seven times before it reached the cellblock where we could use it. Our biggest barge was 220 feet long by 90 feet wide, loaded with a half million gallons of fresh water. The loading of the barge looked like the invasion of Normandy.

Additionally, we had great cooperation from the wardens at both San Quentin and Folsom. They loaned us 164 beds, mattresses, and sets of sheets and blankets; everything right down to the dinnerware and toothbrushes. Folsom and San Quentin were about the same age and duration as Alcatraz, so it was very helpful.

Finally, the company moved to Los Angeles (GMT Studios in Culver City), where principle photography was completed in the studio. There the cells were re-created and then aged with textures and dust sprays to match the actual cellblock already filmed at Alcatraz. Matching sets and locations is always important, but on Escape from Alcatraz, authenticity was particularly crucial.

Tuggle recounted a lost scene from the script that never made it to film:

> I had done so much research about Alcatraz that the script was too lengthy. Several scenes were never shot... The one lost scene I regret we never got to shoot took place on Christmas. I had learned that during the holiday they played music over the cellblock loudspeakers, and on Christmas, the prisoners received a small bag of candy. The scene was intended to capture the loneliness and painful existence of life there, and featured Morris alone in his cell, just sitting quietly on his bunk. Silent Night echoing through the cement cellblock as a background, and it shows Morris at his lowest – loneliest point. He reaches into his bag of candy and pulls out a gumball. He carefully opens the wrapper, but in one split second, the gumball falls to the floor and then rolls out under the cell bars and out into the prison corridor. He stretches his hand through the bars and tries to reach it but he can't... It's only inches within his reach, but he just can't stretch far enough to grasp it and he finally surrenders. I think I may have considered adding guard walking by and kicking it out of his reach, but regardless, it was a powerful moment that summed up his existence. I wish we wouldn't have lost that scene.
>
> The ending was the most challenging to craft. The biggest puzzle I had to contend with was that we didn't know what happened to these guys... I wanted an interesting ending; not a letdown... I wanted to stay true to the real history without taking any real liberties. I couldn't say they made it to Angel Island, because we didn't have evidence to prove that. I couldn't say they drowned because we didn't know that either, not to mention it would have been such a downer after all the work they did to get off the island. I needed something that was true to the story and mind provoking. Something symbolic... Something they might have left behind that shows that they might have made it. It couldn't be something like the warden's tie clasp because then it would be obvious it was left there just to goad him. So I thought, 'what can I come up with that is symbolic yet doesn't color the facts of the real case?' The answer came unexpectedly from a neighbor of mine in North Beach who mentioned that there are various flowers and botanical varieties that grow on Alcatraz. At first I didn't see how that helped me; how was I going to get a flower into this movie? Then, the Doc character came about as a painter and I had the impulse to use him and put it into his painting as a symbol of freedom. Before he chops his fingers off, he slips the chrysanthemum into Morris's pants. When the warden later sees him with the flower in the mess hall, he confiscates it and crumples it to the floor. This way I was able to make the link so when the warden sees the chrysanthemum on Angel Island he knows Morris left it there. He just won't admit it...
>
> The first cut of the film ended with a still frame of the dummy head,

the image you see in the end credits. That was a decision made I think by Don Siegel and film editor Ferris Webster. It was intended to leave the audience with an upbeat ending. I don't think it resonated with everyone. Clint saw that version and was upset and said he wanted the ending that was in the screenplay... Don and everyone else agreed it was the right decision.

I'm still proud of it after so many decades... I think we captured the real essence of what took place on Alcatraz during those years. More than a half century later, people are still rooting for those men who paddled off under a moon lit sky and into the unknown...

(Above) Capturing the iron fisted rule as part of the Alcatraz life environment was essential in achieving authenticity. The film captured the strict routines and life inside the famous prison.

Escape from Alcatraz opened on June 22, 1979, to 815 screens across the United States and was praised by audiences and critics. Time Magazine applauded the film as being "cool, cinematic grace..." The film continues to enjoy frequent broadcasts on network television, and has earned over a half billion dollars worldwide.

It was nominated by the American Film Institute as one of the top one hundred films of its genre. Most importantly, it has helped bring to life the history of this famed escape and continues to carry forward the mystery and mystique.

After Alcatraz

"Alcatraz was never no good for nobody..."
—FRANK WEATHERMAN, AZ-1576

ON JANUARY 31, 1963, Warden Blackwell received the official order to transfer Allen West to the Federal Penitentiary at McNeil Island located in the State of Washington. On the morning of February 6th, just over one month before the prison's final closing, West boarded the island launch and finally made his way off Alcatraz. After being released from STU #13, one of the six closed front isolation cells located on the flats of D Block a few months prior, he was assigned to D-16, located on the second tier and remained here until the day before his transfer. Ironically, Lieutenant Robert Weir, who had rushed to get off work and failed to report the unusual noises that were heard on the night of the escape, would be in charge of his transfer and escort him to McNeil. It is likely West was able to see Alcatraz as his flight ascended over San Francisco while en route to Washington.

West completed serving his federal sentence in January of 1965, and then was transferred to state prisons in both Georgia and Florida, and ultimately released from prison in 1967. After serving decades in prison, West was unable to acclimate back into free society and less than a year later, he was arrested on robbery and grand larceny charges. He attempted to escape from state custody, and then after receiving harsh sentences, including life in prison, West was sent back to Florida State Prison at Raiford. For West it was a life full circle...On October 30, 1972, West fatally stabbed a fellow inmate and forever sealed his fate. He would never again leave prison. In December of 1978, Allen West died of peritonitis in the Florida State Prison hospital, at only 49 years of age. Looking back, many officers and fellow cons believed West simply lost his nerve on the night of the escape, but at least while at McNeil and Raiford, he held court with all of the other convicts, giving the epic claim that he was behind the

UNITED STATES PENITENTIARY
Alcatraz, California

TREATMENT UNIT LOG

WEST (Last Name) 1335 (Number) (Prev. Cell Loc.) IDLE (Work Assignment)

Committed to Unit ____ Mo. Day Year Time ____ A.M. P.M. By ____ Lieutenant

Released from Unit ____ Mo. Day Year Time ____ A.M. P.M. By ____ Lieutenant

NOTED FEB 5 1963 O. G. BLACKWELL WARDEN

Cell No. 16

Charge ESCAPE ATTEMPT, SUSPICION OF

1963

DATE	COMMENTS	INITIALS
18 JAN	E/W To Bed Early - Very Little Conversation -	MOORE
1-19	M/W. Asleep all of watch.	F.J.R.
1-19	D/W Very quiet	[illegible]
19 JAN	E/W No Change In Conduct - Quiet	MOORE
1-20	D/W Quiet - good conduct	GRONZO
20 JAN	E/W Nothing Unusual - Well Behaved	MOORE
1-21	M/W. Awake and coughing a lot during	—
—	this morning watch. Has a bad cold.	F.J.R.
1-21	D/W Quiet & orderly	[illegible]
21 JAN	E/W Usual Behavior - Nothing To Report	MOORE
1-22	D/W Good conduct.	W.G.
22 JAN	E/W General Conversation - Good Conduct	MOORE
1-23	M/W. Asleep all of morning watch.	F.J.R.
11	D/W Good conduct	W.G.
1-23	E/W Quiet & orderly	[illegible]
1-24	D/W Quiet & orderly	[illegible]
1-24	E/W Quiet	[illegible]

When completed forward to: Captain ____ Assoc. Warden ____ Warden ____ Central File ____

Following the escape, West had been confined to a closed front isolation cell D-13, and was later moved to D-16 located on the second tier of D Block. His casefile reflects that he was watched very closely and monitored for any suspect behaviors.

greatest prison escape in history. On March 7, 1963, only a month after Allen West's release from the Rock, J. Campbell Bruce published his book, Escape from Alcatraz, which later inspired the classic motion picture. Undoubtedly, it likely provided West great notoriety among the convict population.

It was on March 21, 1963, that the last prisoners wearing heavy shackles were paraded down Broadway for the last time. The press captured the historical images of the convicts making their final march through the cellhouse, and leaving behind their legacies.

Warden Blackwell returned to Lewisburg Penitentiary as warden and then in 1965 transferred to USP Atlanta where he worked until he retired in

1970. He died on March 9, 1986, at 71 years of age and was laid to rest at the Hillcrest Cemetery, located in Elbert County, Georgia. In November of 1962, Associate Warden Arthur Dollison was transferred to a minimum security prison located in Seagoville, Texas, and he retired three years later. He passed away in 1983 and both he and Blackwell were never faulted or criticized by prison officials for any aspects of the escape. Thomas Bradley on the other hand was counseled by Wilkinson for his direct responsibility in substandard inspections and security inadequacies by his staff. Nearly all of the officers who worked the night of the escape were haunted by the events for the rest of their lives. Bradley later transferred to Atlanta in 1966 to again work under Blackwell, and in 1968 he was taken hostage during a desperate escape plot, and though unharmed, he was reassigned to work at

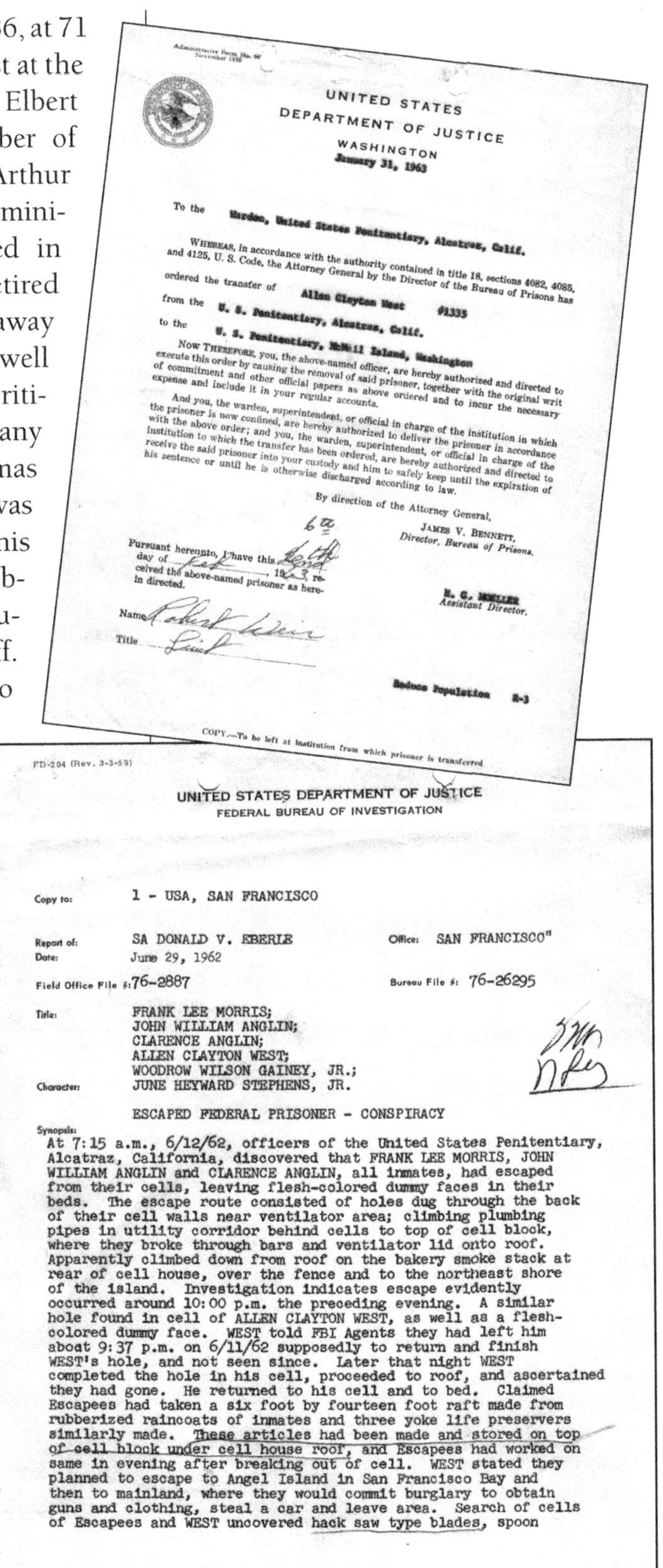

Administrative Form No. 66
November 1938

UNITED STATES
DEPARTMENT OF JUSTICE
WASHINGTON
January 31, 1963

To the Warden, United States Penitentiary, Alcatraz, Calif.

WHEREAS, in accordance with the authority contained in title 18, sections 4082, 4085, and 4125, U. S. Code, the Attorney General by the Director of the Bureau of Prisons has ordered the transfer of Allen Clayton West #1333
from the U. S. Penitentiary, Alcatraz, Calif.
to the U. S. Penitentiary, McNeil Island, Washington

NOW THEREFORE, you, the above-named officer, are hereby authorized and directed to execute this order by causing the removal of said prisoner, together with the original writ of commitment and other official papers as above ordered and to incur the necessary expense and include it in your regular accounts.

And you, the warden, superintendent, or official in charge of the institution in which the prisoner is now confined, are hereby authorized to deliver the prisoner in accordance with the above order; and you, the warden, superintendent, or official in charge of the institution to which the transfer has been ordered, are hereby authorized and directed to receive the said prisoner into your custody and him to safely keep until the expiration of his sentence or until he is otherwise discharged according to law.

By direction of the Attorney General,

JAMES V. BENNETT,
Director, Bureau of Prisons.

Pursuant hereunto, I have this 6th day of Feb, 1963, received the above-named prisoner as herein directed.

Name Robert Weir
Title Lieut

H. G. MOELLER
Assistant Director.

Reduce Population R-3

COPY.—To be left at institution from which prisoner is transferred

FD-204 (Rev. 3-3-59)

UNITED STATES DEPARTMENT OF JUSTICE
FEDERAL BUREAU OF INVESTIGATION

Copy to: 1 - USA, SAN FRANCISCO

Report of: SA DONALD V. EBERLE Office: SAN FRANCISCO"
Date: June 29, 1962

Field Office File #: 76-2887 Bureau File #: 76-26295

Title: FRANK LEE MORRIS;
JOHN WILLIAM ANGLIN;
CLARENCE ANGLIN;
ALLEN CLAYTON WEST;
WOODROW WILSON GAINEY, JR.;
JUNE HEYWARD STEPHENS, JR.

Character: ESCAPED FEDERAL PRISONER - CONSPIRACY

Synopsis:
At 7:15 a.m., 6/12/62, officers of the United States Penitentiary, Alcatraz, California, discovered that FRANK LEE MORRIS, JOHN WILLIAM ANGLIN and CLARENCE ANGLIN, all inmates, had escaped from their cells, leaving flesh-colored dummy faces in their beds. The escape route consisted of holes dug through the back of their cell walls near ventilator area; climbing plumbing pipes in utility corridor behind cells to top of cell block, where they broke through bars and ventilator lid onto roof. Apparently climbed down from roof on the bakery smoke stack at rear of cell house, over the fence and to the northeast shore of the island. Investigation indicates escape evidently occurred around 10:00 p.m. the preceding evening. A similar hole found in cell of ALLEN CLAYTON WEST, as well as a flesh-colored dummy face. WEST told FBI Agents they had left him about 9:37 p.m. on 6/11/62 supposedly to return and finish WEST's hole, and not seen since. Later that night WEST completed the hole in his cell, proceeded to roof, and ascertained they had gone. He returned to his cell and to bed. Claimed Escapees had taken a six foot by fourteen foot raft made from rubberized raincoats of inmates and three yoke life preservers similarly made. These articles had been made and stored on top of cell block under cell house roof, and Escapees had worked on same in evening after breaking out of cell. WEST stated they planned to escape to Angel Island in San Francisco Bay and then to mainland, where they would commit burglary to obtain guns and clothing, steal a car and leave area. Search of cells of Escapees and WEST uncovered hack saw type blades, spoon

(Top right) Allen West's transfer order to leave Alcatraz.

(Below right) The first page of the FBI's final summary report submitted by Special Agent Donald Erbele on June 29, 1962, naming the six convicts as principals. Both the FBI and United States Marshals have never been able to solve the case conclusively. The case will continue to remain open until the convicts reach ninety nine years of age or found. They are still considered fugitives.

(Left and below) George and Rachel Anglin seen holding the photo of Clarence playing the guitar, and a portrait of John taken while at Alcatraz. Both of them perhaps suffered the most as a result from the escape. Contemplating the fate of their children, it weighed heavy on them right up until the day of each of their passings.

189 Below, state briefly what you think you want out of life, think you might get, and how you might get it. Think about this awhile. Then put down honestly and simply what you really want to do with your life from now on. I wonT ~~to~~ get out of prison and have a nice home and a stedy job and live a stright life

Nothing nourished their dreams like the thought of escape.

a minimum security prison in Alabama only a few months later. He retired in 1972 and passed away in 1976 at the age of 65. In his official investigative summary on the '62 escape, Fred T. Wilkinson closed his report stating:

> These men were made desperate by their situation. Serving long terms, faced with years ahead of hopelessly long sentences in southern state prisons, they decided that "nothing can be worth this." West stated that the men cared not what came when they entered the water. They didn't know or care what towers were manned nor which way the tide flowed. A change from endless confinement with suicide by gunfire or the ocean as the alternative was overriding in their every action.

A half century later, etched deep into the cement and steel of Alcatraz cells 138, 150 and 152, are the escape paths that were carefully worked by hand and are all still visible today. The scars in the cement represent both their dreams and desperate desire for freedom at any cost. Despite decades of intensive investigation by authorities, there remains no proof that the escapees either died during their break attempt, or survived to begin new lives in a faraway land.

We may never know their final fate, but in the light of truth, whether it was brief or that of a lifetime, all three men made it to freedom. They didn't die inside the walls of Alcatraz. On June 11, 1962, Frank Lee Morris, John and Clarence Anglin disappeared from their cells and sailed off into history. They are the men who escaped from Alcatraz...

Acknowledgments

While *Escaping Alcatraz* took roughly a half decade to write, the collective research that culminated in this work is a product of more than a half century of interviews and the slow gathering of history. The Anglin-Widner family collected news articles and personal photographs that dated back into John, Clarence and Alfred's youth. Personal letters, court records and news clippings were carefully placed into scrapbooks by their sister Marie in an effort to preserve their family history. This book was only possible because of her. David spent a lifetime studying the escape and his uncles' early criminal past. Michael began conducting interviews with numerous former Alcatraz prisoners and officers dating back more than three decades for previous historical works, several of which ultimately found their way into this book. None of these efforts would hold meaning without the direct support of numerous other individuals who share a common passion for this history. They are the ones truly responsible for helping bring this epic story to life.

First and foremost, our love and deepest appreciation goes to our families who have endured years of muddled desks with piles of FBI file records, historical files, and other cluttering objects to invade our homes and monopolize our time. Their love and understanding was unwavering and a part of them lives in the spirit of these pages. John Reinhardt, the amazing designer and longtime friend always makes the journey meaningful and rewarding. His love for the history always gives every page he touches both life and soul. Jim Zach, the wonderful cover designer is another who creates magic in his art and gives a face to our work. Working together is always a treasured experience. Richard Tuggle, screenwriter of the classic film *Escape from Alcatraz* deserves our heartfelt gratitude. His inspiring work has brought this great story into the homes of millions of people worldwide for several decades. Without him, much of the interest in the escape wouldn't exist.

Regardless of where you stand on the debate of the escapees' ultimate fate, the community of Alcatraz is extraordinary and like an extended family. From National Park Rangers, Parks Conservancy staff and everyone at Alcatraz Cruises, they are a special group of individuals who have dedicated their lives to making this amazing history accessible to the public. Over the years, we've forged close friendships that continue to stand the test of time.

Michael Dyke, who at the time of this writing leads the investigation for the U.S. Marshal's Service deserves a special thanks. Though a tough lawman and a tough critic on many of the theories presented in this book, this never overshadows his obvious affection for the history. His respectful approach and civil treatment of the family has inspired a deep respect. Arthur Roderick, a retired U.S. Marshal who previously led the manhunt for the escapees is another we hold in high regard. Together we've had the privilege to share in this adventure and have traveled across the United States in search of answers. Art made the experience most memorable and we will always be grateful. Discussing the case and exploring various locations that were part of the investigation proved to be an experience we'll never forget.

The History Channel and Texas Crew Productions team deserve a very special thank you for their bold efforts in producing the landmark documentaries *Inside Alcatraz: Legends of the Rock*, and most notably, *Alcatraz: Search for the Truth*. Brad Bernstein, Eric Begley, David Karabinas, Justin Sprague, Steve Ascher, Jonah Hirsch, Patrick Rockecharlie and Terry Stewart gave new life to these stories. Much of the research for this book became in part the basis of both documentaries and together we charted new paths in these age old stories. We are forever grateful…

James Bulger was most gracious in sharing personal memories of the escape and his years spent on Alcatraz. He proved to be one of the most essential sources of this work, as he helped frame the activities during the various stages of the plot, as well as putting into context the complexities and redundancies in planning. We are forever grateful to have his memories included in this body of work.

In line with Bulger, there were many others, both officers and prisoners who were interviewed for previous works and the opportunity to re-explore old interviews helped breathe new life into alternate theories that were originally dismissed or overlooked. Their voices bring to light important elements of not only the '62 events, but also details in other Alcatraz escapes that may have otherwise been lost. Their stories will always have life in these pages and they all deserve special thanks. Most notably, the late Clifford Fish, Philip Bergen, Irving Levinson, Bill Long, A.G. Bloomquist, Dale Stamphill, Darwin Everett Coon, Tom Kent, Jim Quillen, Frank Sprenz, Ben Rayborn, Glenn Nathan Williams, and John Banner. Robert Schibline was generous in sharing his personal memories of the escape plot, while William Baker, Richard Sunday, Robert Luke, George DeVincenzi, Pat Mahoney all helped provide insight into the procedural aspects and everyday life on the Rock.

At Golden Gate National Recreation Area's Park Archives and Records Center, Amanda Williford, Curator and Reference Archivist has always been wonderful and especially supportive in providing materials. Former Archivist Joseph Sanchez and Marisa Louie with the National Archives both helped in casefile research over the course of several projects. Susan McKee with the FBI, and Phillip Edge from Edge West Productions help provide records and photographs related to the escape. Claire Keating and Kelly Rabe are the extraordinary editors of this work and we are forever grateful for the countless hours they spent helping shape the textual elements. Kelly deserves a special thank you for her special care and advice on both the historical presentation and story structure.

Our deep appreciation goes to the rangers and volunteers with National Park Service on Alcatraz. Most notably, John Cantwell, Benny Batom, Lori Brosnan, Steven Cotes, Jayeson Vance, Dan Unger, Al Blank, George Durgerian, Eric Stearns, Steve Cote, Craig Glassner, Melinda Moses, Wendy Solis, Carla Day, Marcus Koenen, Tara Wilson, Steve Johnson, Emelda Zuschlag, Roger Goldberg, Richard Mayer, Anthony Anderson, Donna Spinola, Paul Vivian and Matt Hess.

From the Golden Gate National Parks Conservancy who all do incredible work: Linda Chalmers, Robert Lieber, Nicki Phelps, Sarah Lau, Susan Tasaki, Lala Macapagal, Colin Fairbairn, Jillian Kelling, John Donelan, John Moran, Jim Nelson, Sharlene Baker, Art Owen, Angelita Cecilio, Kelcie Marie, Heather Paris, Jody Hauser, Ameila Letvin, Michael Jacobo, Marilyn Lagandaon, Ethel Jimenez, Marc Wang, Gabriel Pineda, Eric Knackmuhs, Jim Breeden, Wendy Swee, Teresa Williams, Joe Valencia, and all of the dedicated employees from this organization along with the stars at Alcatraz Cruises, Terry MacRae, Denise Rasmussen, Lorelei Octavo and Michael Badolato.

We would also like to extend our sincere appreciation to Jolene Babyak, author of *Breaking the Rock*. While our book took a very different path, we remain respectful towards her extraordinary research and consider her work essential reading for anyone interested in further reading on the escape.

Suzanne Roth, Jamie Clark, Rick Rosen, Emil Nicholas Gallina, Bruce Marshall, Candace Lind Jones, Chuck Stucker, Tim Brazil along with Marie and Kenneth Widner all are deserve our deepest appreciation for their support and encouragement. Finally, Nicholas Widner was unable to see this book in its finished form, but he did get to screen an early working version of *Alcatraz: Search for the Truth*. He loved this chapter in his family's heritage. His spirit will always be a part of this book.

Sources

Bureau of Prisons and National Archive Records

Administrative Files, Records of United States Penitentiary Alcatraz: Extensive research included examination of materials relating to escapes, general prison grounds, buildings, and other facilities; memoranda; blueprints; cell mechanism diagrams; contractor reports; budgetary planning documents; culinary and library reports; administration and correctional staff correspondence. Comprehensive Case Files, Alcatraz Inmates: Extensive research included examination of multiple criminal history files, correspondence, court records, medical records, Warden's Notebook pages (1934–ca. 1963), visitation logs, and conduct reports.

FBI Records

Alcatraz Escape, June 11, 1962. File Numbers: 76-1332, 76-26295, 76-2358, and 76-2887.

Anglin Family Collection

Personal photographs and notes from photo albums, family letters, news clippings, oral histories and court documents from Marie Widner (assembled by David Widner).

Reports, Pamphlets, and Select Papers

Babyak, Jolene, and John Martini. "The Alcatraz Cellhouse Numbering Systems" (Historic Structure Report Addendum). San Francisco, CA: Golden Gate National Recreation Area, 1999.

Bergen, Philip R. Letters and hand-drawn diagrams, special annotations to Alcatraz '46, taped audio commentary discussing same, 1996–1999.

———. Select Memorandums to Correctional Staff, 1952–1953, as Captain of the Guard, Alcatraz (compiled 2001). Washington, D.C.: Bureau of Prisons, 1960.

Bulger, James. Correspondence and interviews assembled for the book *James "Whitey" Bulger, AZ-1428, The Last Interviews* by Michael Esslinger.

Campbell, Eileen, Michael Rigsby, Tacy Dunham. *Discover Alcatraz: A Tour of the Rock*. San Francisco, CA: Golden Gate National Parks Association, 1996.
Dunham, Tacy. *Discover Alcatraz Escapes: A Tour of the Attempts*. San Francisco, CA: Golden Gate National Parks Association, 1997.
Fish, Clifford. Handwritten notes on the 1946 escape attempt, 2001.
Kles, Maranda A. Ph.D. *Report of Osteological Examination of Alfred Anglin*, 2015
Mack, Ellsworth, Lt. *How to Search a Cell*. Sacramento, CA: California State Prison, San Quentin, 1949.
Madigan, Paul J., Warden. *Regulations for Inmates, USP Alcatraz*. San Francisco, CA: US Penitentiary, Alcatraz Island, 1956.
Morrison, Neil W., Lt. "How to Search the Person of an Inmate" (Written for *Wisconsin State Prison Warden's Bulletin*). San Francisco, CA: US Penitentiary, Alcatraz Island, 1949.
Schultz, Daniel L., M.D. *Autopsy Examination of the Remains of Alfred Anglin*. Tampa, Florida, 2015.
Staff. *A Museum of Prison Life (Eastern State Penitentiary)*. Philadelphia, PA: *The Philadelphia Inquirer*, 1999.
Sundstrom, Carl. Handwritten summary of 1946 escape attempt.

Newspapers

Los Angeles Times
News Call Bulletin
Oakland Tribune
San Francisco Call Bulletin
San Francisco Chronicle
San Francisco Examiner

Books

Albright, Jim. *Last Guard Out*. Bloomington, Indiana: AuthorHouse, 2008.
Allsop, Kenneth. *The Bootleggers: The Story of Chicago's Prohibition Era*. New York: Arlington House, 1968.
Audett, Blackie. *Rap Sheet*. New York: Williams Sloan and Co., 1954.
Babyak, Jolene. *Eyewitness on Alcatraz*. Oakland, CA: Ariel Vamp Press, 1988.
———. *Breaking the Rock: The Great Escape from Alcatraz*. Oakland, CA: Ariel Vamp Press, 2001.
Baker, William G. *Alcatraz #1259*. Charleston, SC. CreateSpace Independent Publishing, 2014.
Bates, Sanford. *Prisons and Beyond*. New York: Macmillan, 1938.
Bennett, James V. *I Chose Prison*. New York: Alfred A. Knopf, 1970.
Bruce, J. Campbell. *A Farewell to the Rock: Escape from Alcatraz*. New York: McGraw-Hill, 1963.
Cameron, Robert. *Alcatraz: A Visual Essay*. San Francisco, CA: Cameron & Company, 1974.
Carnes, Clarence. *Interview and Commentary*. Bob Kirby, National Park Service, 1980
Chandler, Roy F., and E. F. Chandler. *Alcatraz: The Hardest Years 1934–1938*. Jacksonville, NC: Iron Brigade Publishing, 1989.
Cohen, Mickey. *In My Own Words, as told to John Peer Nugent*. Englewood Cliffs, NJ: Prentice Hall, 1975.
DeNevi, Don. *Riddle of the Rock: The Only Successful Escape from Alcatraz*. Buffalo, NY: Prometheus Books, 1991.
———. *Alcatraz '46: The Anatomy of a Classic Prison Tragedy*. San Rafael, CA: Leswing Press, 1977.
Esslinger, Michael. *Alcatraz: A History of the Penitentiary Years*. Marina, CA: Ocean View Publishing, 2016.
———. *Letters from Alcatraz*. Marina, CA: Ocean View Publishing, 2016.
Godwin, John. *Alcatraz 1868–1963*. New York: Pocket Books, Inc., 1964.
Golden Gate National Parks Conservancy. *Alcatraz Escape Files: From the Official Records*. San Francisco, CA: GGNPC, 2014.
Gregory, George H. *Alcatraz Screw: My Years as a Guard in America's Most Notorious Prison*. Columbia: University of Missouri Press, 2002.
Howard, Clark. *Six Against the Rock*. New York: The Dial Press, 1977.
Johnston, James A. *Prison Life Is Different*. Boston, MA: Houghton Mifflin Company, 1937.

———. *Alcatraz Prison and the Men Who Live There*. New York: Charles Scribner's Sons, 1949.

Karpis, Alvin. *On the Rock: Twenty-five Years in Alcatraz*. As told to Robert Livesey. New York: Beaufort, 1980.

Lageson, Ernest B. *Battle at Alcatraz: A Desperate Attempt to Escape the Rock*. Omaha, NE: Addicus Books, 1999.

———. *Alcatraz Justice: The Rock's Famous Murder Trial*. Berkeley, CA: Creative Arts Book Company, 2002.

Lieber, Robert. *Alcatraz, The Ultimate Movie Book*. San Francisco, CA: Golden Gate National Parks Conservancy, 2006.

Martini, John A. *Fortress Alcatraz: Guardian of the Golden Gate*. Kailua, HI: Pacific Monograph, 1990.

Odier, Pierre. *The Rock: A History of Alcatraz, The Fort/The Prison*. Eagle Rock, CA: L'Image Odier, 1982.

Quillen, Jim. *Alcatraz from Inside: The Hard Years, 1942–1952*. San Francisco, CA: Golden Gate National Parks Conservancy, 1991.

Swisher, Carl Brent, ed. *Selected Papers of Homer Cummings, Attorney General of the United States, 1933–1939*. New York: Charles Scribner's Sons, 1939.

Thompson, Erwin N. *The Rock: A History of Alcatraz Island, 1847–1972*. Denver, CO: Denver Service Center, Historic Preservation Division, National Park Service, United States Department of the Interior, 1979.

Ward, David A. with Gene G. Kassebaum. *Alcatraz—The Gangster Years* California, University of California Press, 2009

Motion Pictures

Alcatraz: The Whole Shocking Story, NBC-TV (Original Air Date: Nov. 5–6, 1980).

Escape from Alcatraz, Paramount Pictures, 1979.

Riot in Cell Block 11, Allied Artists, 1954.

Six Against the Rock, NBC-TV (Original Air Date: May 18, 1987).

Magazine References

Alcatraz Escape! Secrets of the Island's Most Baffling Mystery, True Detective Mysteries, 1938.

Crushout of Alcatraz, Startling Detective, August 1943

Escape from Alcatraz, An Interview with Director Don Siegel, Film Magazine, July 1979.

Family Outboarding, Shopwalk, Sports Illustrated, May 1962.

Rubber Geese, Popular Mechanics, November 1960.

The Greatest Escape, Bruce Marshall, Cinema Retro, 2009

Why Alcatraz Is a Success, Collier's Magazine, July 1939.

You Can't Beat the Rock: True Detective Mysteries, October 1937.

Your Life Preserver, How will it behave if you need it? Popular Mechanics, March 1962.

Film Documentaries

Alcatraz (The Big House Series). The History Channel/A&E Television Networks, 1998.

Alcatraz Federal Penitentiary 1934–1963. Asteron Productions/ Simitar Entertainment, 1986.

Alcatraz Prison Escape: Deathbed Confession. Green Apple Entertainment, 2015.

Alcatraz: America's Toughest Prison. TMS/ WNT Independent Films, 1977 (MPI Release).

Alcatraz: Escaping America's Toughest Prisons. A&E Television Networks, Hearst, 1993.

Alcatraz: Search for the Truth. History Channel/A&E Television Networks, Texas Crew Productions, 2015.

Alcatraz: The Final Sentence. Huckleberry Films, 1988.

Break Out. Michael Hoff Productions/A La Carte Communications, 1997.

Codes and Conspiracies, Alcatraz. Discovery Channel, New York, 2014

Dungeons of Alcatraz. Michael Hoff Productions/A La Carte Communications, 2002.

Eastern State Penitentiary (The Big House Series). The History Channel/A&E Television Networks, 1997.

Escapes from Alcatraz: The True Stories. Michael Hoff Productions/A La Carte Communications, 2000.

Inside Alcatraz: Legends of the Rock. History Channel/A&E Television Networks, Texas Crew Productions, 2015.

Public Enemies on the Rock. Michael Hoff Productions/A La Carte Communications, 1997.

Real Story: Escape from Alcatraz. Infinity Entertainment/Smithsonian Networks, 2010.

Return to Alcatraz: Secrets of the Rock. Acorn Media Publishing/A La Carte Communications, 1994.

Secrets of Alcatraz. Golden Gate National Park Association/A La Carte Communications, 1992.

Secrets of the Dead: The Alcatraz Escape. Public Broadcasting Service, 2016.

Vanished from Alcatraz. Edge West Productions / National Geographic, 2011.

Interviews

Former Convicts: James "Whitey" Bulger, Dale Stamphill, Elliott Michener, Richard Sunday, Jerie Bremmeyer, Darwin Coon, John Dekker, Herbert "Lucky" Juelich, Tom Kent, Jim Quillen, Willie Radkay, Frank Sprenz, Ben Rayborn, Glenn Nathan Williams, John Banner, Armando Mendoza, Frank Hatfield, Ernest Lopez, William Baker, Robert Schibline and Robert Luke.

Correctional Officers: Philip R. Bergen, Alver G. Bloomquist, Father Bernie Bush, Dale Cox, George DeVincenzi, James Dukes, Clifford Fish, Frank Heaney, John Hernan, Joe Landers, Irving Levinson, Bill Long, Pat Mahoney, Orrin Maybee, John McGoran, Louis Nelson, Larry Quilligan, John Robinson, Sam Hill, Robert E. Sutter, Ned Ubben, Jerry Wheeler and Kingston Witchez.

Former Residents and Correctional Staff/ Convict Relatives: Father Bernie Bush, Betty Horvath, Nancy Bertelsen, Don Bowden, Larry Boyd, John Brunner, Jerry Casey, Harold Clark, Jean Comerford, Nielen Dickens, Herb Faulk, Dick Fisher, Dena Freeman, Bud Hart, Betty Horvath, Renee Keith, Ernest Lageson, Cliff Mickleson, Kathryn O'Brien, Bob Orr, Phyllis Panter, Thomas Reeves, Joyce Ritz, Agnes Roberts, Ray Stewart, Stanley Stewart, Robert Stites, Chuck Stucker, Michael Walter, Ray & Stanley Stewart, Jeannette Williams Anglin, David Widner, Kenneth Widner, Marie Widner and Mearl Taylor.

FBI, U.S. Marshal Service, U.S. Coast Guard and Misc. Law Enforcement: Michael Dyke, Erik Richmond, Arthur Roderick and Robert Checci.

Photograph and Illustration Credits

UNLESS NOTED in the following source index, all prisoner catalog photographs, letters, documents and illustrations are courtesy of the National Archives and Records Administration and/or Bureau of Prisons Archives. If available, specific catalog collection numbers or source information for unique photographs are included in the source index below.

ABBREVIATIONS:

t-top, b-bottom, c-center, l-left, r-right

AAA	Alcatraz Alumni Association, Courtesy Chuck Stucker
AC	Author's Collection (Indicates Personal Collection of/and/or Photographed by Michael Esslinger)
ACME	ACME News Pictures
AP	Associated Press Archives
BOP	Bureau of Prisons Archives
CA	Collier's Archive, William Woodfield
CSA	California State Archives
ELC	Ernest Lageson Collection
ESP	Eastern State Penitentiary Archives
FA	Florida State Archives
FBI	Federal Bureau of Investigation Archives
GGNRA	Golden Gate National Recreation Area, Park Archives
GGNRA-DDN	Don DeNevi Collection, Golden Gate National Recreation Area, Park Archives, Associated Press Photograph, GOGA Catalog Index number provided in description.
GGNRA-PD	Phil Dollison Collection, Golden Gate National Recreation Area, Park Archives, GOGA.
HA	Hulton Archive
INP	International News Photo Service
IVA	Image Vault Archive
LC	Library of Congress Historical Photograph and Document Collection
LCHABS	Library of Congress – Historic American Buildings Survey Photograph Archive
MW	Marie Widner (scanned and assembled by David Widner)

NPS	National Park Service / Golden Gate National Recreation Area Museum Collection
PARC	Park Archives and History Center, National Park Service
PP	Paramount Pictures
RP	Reuters Press Photo
RT	Richard Tuggle
SFC	San Francisco Chronicle
SFCB	San Francisco Call Bulletin
SFE	San Francisco Examiner
SFPL	San Francisco Public Library, History Center Archives
UNR	Universal News Reel Photo
UPI	United Press International
USCG	United States Coast Guard Archives
USMSA	United States Marshal Service Archives
USNCL	Unknown Source – No Credit Listed - Press Photograph
WB	Warner Bros.
WWPS	Wide World Photo Service

Frontis and Foreword: Hulton Archive / Associated Press / Richard Tuggle / Warner Bros.

Custom Illustrations: Phil Hall & Toby Mikle

xv INP; xvi (t) CA, (b); xvii WWPS; xviii AP; xx (t) AP, (tr) SFE, (cl) INP, (b) ACME; 2 (t) AP, (b) UPI; 3 (t) AP, (tc) SFPL, (cl) ACME, (b) AP; 5 (t) UPI, (c) AP; 8 AC; 9 AAA; 10 UNR; 15 ESP; 17 (t) ESP (b) ACME; 18 (t)(c)(b) ESP; 19 (t)(b) RP; 21 (bl) AC, (br) Los Angeles Times; 22 (t) AMCE News Pictures; 23 AC; 26 (tl) AP, (c) AC, (b) AP; 27 (t) SFE, (cr) WWP, (cl)(bl) SFE, Fred Pardini (from original negatives); 30 ACME; 33 (t) WWP, (b) AP; 34 FBI; 55 FBI; 38 FBI; 59 (t); 40 FBI; 42 (t) AMCE News Pictures, (b) SFCB; 43 ACME; 46 (t) SFE, (c) SFC; 47 SFE (from original negatives); 48 (t) SFE (b) AC; 52 (t) AC, (cl) AMCE; 53 (tl) ACME, (tr) SFE; 55 (m) WWP, (b) AAA; 56 USNCL; 57 ACME; 58 (tl) (br) ACME, 66 UPI; 67 NARA; 68 (t) INP, Tribune Telegraph Library, (b) SFE (from original negative); 69 ACME; 92 (t) AP, (bl) AC; 73 AC; 76 ACME; 78 (tl) INP; 100 WB; 84 (t) AP, (cr) Keystone Photos D.H. Library; 85 AP Newswire; 86 (tr)(bl) BOP; 87 FBI; 89 AP; 90 (tl)(b) AC, (tr) CA; 92 (t) ACME News Pictures (bl) INP; 94 (tl) USNCL, (b) ACME; 95 (t) ACME; 95 (t)(bl) Cleveland News Photo (Reference Department); 96 (t)(c) AP, (b) UNR; 98 AC; 99 (t)(b) AP; 100 (t) SF Coroner's Bureau, (c) ACME Telephoto; 101 SFCB; 102 AC; 104-110 MW; 111 FSA: 113-117 MW; 118 FSA; 119 Postcard AC; 120 FSA; 122 MW; 125 State of Alabama, Houston County Evidence Photo; 127 MW; 129 (tl) Chicago Sun Times, (tr) Time Magazine; 131 USMSA; 132-133 Tampa Daily Times; 135 FSA; 138 BOP; 148 AC; 149 (t) LC, (cr) AP; 150 (bl) David Falconer, The Oregonian; 151 BOP; 154 (c) BOP, (b) Reuters/Robert Galbraith; 155 (t) GOGA 17934 – Phil Dollison Collection, (c) CA; 157 AC; 159 (t) BOP, (b) Toby Mikle; 161 iStock; 162 (t)(b) UPI; 163 AC; 165-166 CA; 193 FBI; 174 (bl) USNCL; 175 FBI;

185 PP; 188 AC; 189 (tr) CA, (cl) BOP; 197 AC; 203 (tr) Toby Mikle, (b) USNCL AC;

204 (t) AP, (b) AC; 208 (t) ACME, (cr) (cl) BOP, GOGA 17975 GGNRA-DDN; 217 Popular Mechanics, Hearst; 218-219 Sports Illustrated, Time Warner, Inc.; 220 AP; 221 MW; 222-223 FBI; 224 Music First; 225 AC; 229 SFC; 233 FBI; 234 GGNRA GOGA 356; 235 USMSA; 236 (t) FBI, (cl) AC; 237 (c) GGNRA GOGA 375; 259 AC; 242 BOP; 243 (t) AC, (b) FBI; 244-245 FBI; 246 (t) FBI, (c)(b) AC; 247-249 FBI; 250 AC; 251 (tl) GGNRA GOGA 407, (tr) USMSA, (c) GOGA 404, (b) GOGA 405; 252-255 FBI; 256 (t) Sports Illustrated, (b) FBI; 257 RP; 264 FBI; 265 AP; 267 AP; 268 (t) AC, (b) USMSA; 269 FBI; 270 (t)(b) FBI, (c) AC; 271 AC; 272 (tl) (insert) FBI via Irving Levinson, (b) AC; 274-275 FBI; 277 SFC; 278 (t) UPI, (b) WWPS; 279 (t) UPI, (c) AP, (b) UPI; 282 FBI; 283 BOP; 284 FBI; 286 (t) MW, (b) Pillsbury Madison & Sutro, SF Gate Photo; 287 BOP; 289 (t)(b) USMSA, (cl) GGNRA GOGA 381 (cr) GOGA 362, 363, 364, (bl) GOGA 376; 310 FBI; 292 The Maritime Museum of British Columbia, Vancouver B.C.; 295 GGNRA GOGA 34803; 296 DOT Records, PP; 298 UPI Telephoto; 306 (t) BOP, (b) Tribune, Chris Kjobech; 307 Tribune, Chris Kjobech; 309 BOP; 311 SFE, Fred Pardini; 316 (t)(c)(b) HistoricImages, (bl) David Widner; 317 MW; 318-39 HistoricImages; 320 Center for Health Statistics, Alabama Department of Public Health, Montgomery, Alabama; 322 MW; 322 (t) SFCB, (b) MW; 324 Tony Brizzi; 325 The Tampa Tribune, Staff Photo by Mack Goeth; 326 Florida State Archives; 327 MW; 328 MW; 329 AC; 330 AC; 331 CA; 333 (t) Oakland Tribune, (bl) Robert Checchi; 334 AC; 335 Clifford Fish; 339-43 AC; 344 USMSA; History Channel, A&E Networks, Photo by David S. Holloway; 346 AC; 347 MW; 348-49 AC; 350 AC; 351 (t) History Channel, Texas Crew Productions, (cl)(cr) AC; 353 AC; 354 FBI; 358 PP; 360 PP, Richard Tuggle; 361 AC; 362-63 PP; 364 Allied Artists; 365 PP; 366-69 PP; 370 BOP; 372 (t) Stock Photo, Rolf52; 374 (t) Suncoast Times, Photo by Bill Stewart, (b) BOP

About The Authors

MICHAEL ESSLINGER is a historical researcher and best-selling author; his work has also appeared in film and television documentaries, including segments on the Discovery, National Geographic, Travel and History Channels. His interests include entertainment, science and historical subjects.

From the elusive crew of Apollo 11 to prisoners of Alcatraz, he has interviewed icons and others who have shaped history and continues to write on subjects that explore the entire spectrum of the human experience.

His books *Alcatraz: The History of the Penitentiary Years* and *Letters from Alcatraz* continue as best-selling references chronicling the island's rich historical past. He is the co-author of the movie memoir: *I Want It Now! A Memoir of Life on the Set of Willy Wonka and the Chocolate Factory,* a magical memoir written with Julie Dawn Cole, the original "Veruca Salt" in the classic motion picture starring Gene Wilder.

Current projects include a comprehensive history of the Apollo program, documenting mankind's epic journey to the moon, and based on first person interviews with the Apollo Astronauts, including Neil Armstrong, Buzz Aldrin, Michael Collins, Alan Shepard, James Lovell, Pete Conrad, Dick Gordon, Gene Cernan and many others. Other projects include *Whitey Bulger, 1428-AZ: The Last Interviews*, a book based on interviews between Bulger and Esslinger conducted over a span of seven years.

DAVID WIDNER is the nephew of John & Clarence Anglin. From his earliest years, he was exposed to frequent interrogative visits from the FBI and family stories of their famed prison escapes. For several decades he has worked alongside his mother and brother Kenneth Widner helping preserve their family history. David was instrumental in helping catalog family photographs and early archival records that has resulted in the discovery of materials that lent to new theories in the 1962 Alcatraz escape. Having contributed to several television based documentaries, David is also one of the principal subjects in the History Channel documentary *Alcatraz: Search for the Truth*.

Index

D

E

F

L

M

N

T

U

V

W

XYZ

Made in the USA
Columbia, SC
21 December 2024

50201388R00228